# TSIA2® MASTERY

## ELAR

Teacher Manual

MasteryPrep

Inquiries concerning this publication should be mailed to:

MasteryPrep
7117 Florida Blvd.
Baton Rouge, LA 70806



10 9 8 7 6 5 4 3 2 1

ISBN-13: 978-1-948846-81-3

# Table of Contents

## Essay

## A LETTER TO TEACHERS

To my fellow educators,

In case no one's told you recently, you're doing a great job. Education is perhaps one of the most challenging fields in which to hold a career, and you've chosen to take it on. Dedicating your life to the betterment of future generations is truly a high calling. Here at MasteryPrep, we applaud you.

But we don't just want to stand to the side and watch you do all the hard work. We're here to help in the best way we know how: sharing the good stuff. There's a lot of ambiguity surrounding the content of the TSIA2, and if you've ever taken a look at the standards, you'll know what we're talking about. Those standards tell you everything and nothing. So how can you effectively prepare your students to reach that college-ready score?

We took that question and turned it into a "challenge accepted" moment. We dug into everything that is the TSIA2, ripping open the seams and picking apart every little stitch. Our test prep experts evaluated item after item, poking and prodding, until we knew exactly what they were made of (and what skills students would need to be able to answer them). The result? The book you have here in your hands.

TSIA2 Mastery is a one-of-a-kind curriculum designed specifically to help students earn college-ready scores on the TSIA2. No other test prep company offers a TSIA2 program as thorough or as targeted as ours. We wholeheartedly believe that this program will give you and your students everything you need to prepare for test day.

We wish you the best of luck and hope you enjoy what we've created.

Cheers,

Stephanie Constantino
Director of Curriculum

# A Guide to the Guide: ELAR Edition

## Welcome to TSIA2 Mastery

This curriculum is one of a kind, offering students three paths to boosting their scores:

- Time management
- Test-taking skills
- Content

Traditional test preparation provides a *review* of content. It *discusses* test-taking skills. It *reminds* students about time management. Students who are already strong test-takers, who already perform well academically, will absolutely benefit from those kinds of programs. But for most students, it isn't enough. They forget the content, don't change their test-taking behaviors, and lose focus and momentum due to the untimed nature of the TSIA2.

Our approach is different. We call it the Mastery Pyramid, and it works even for students who need the most help in these areas.

- **Content Mastery:** Engaging, direct instruction based on modern best practices helps students bridge the gap between classroom learning and the TSIA2's assessed standards. By isolating skills, we make each topic easier to learn. We also offer opportunities for students to practice with authentic TSIA2 question emulations for every question type they'll see on test day.
- **Test Mastery:** Test-taking is a skill that can be learned like any other. Our lessons simplify key test-taking strategies, provide many opportunities to practice them, and reinforce the fundamentals again and again until test-taking behavior actually improves.
- **Time Mastery:** The TSIA2 is untimed, so it may seem like learning to move quickly through a question is unnecessary. While time is not limited, mental energy is. Students will learn strategies that can help them stay on-track and focused on the task at hand before their mental energy runs out.

## Three Paths to Boosting Scores:

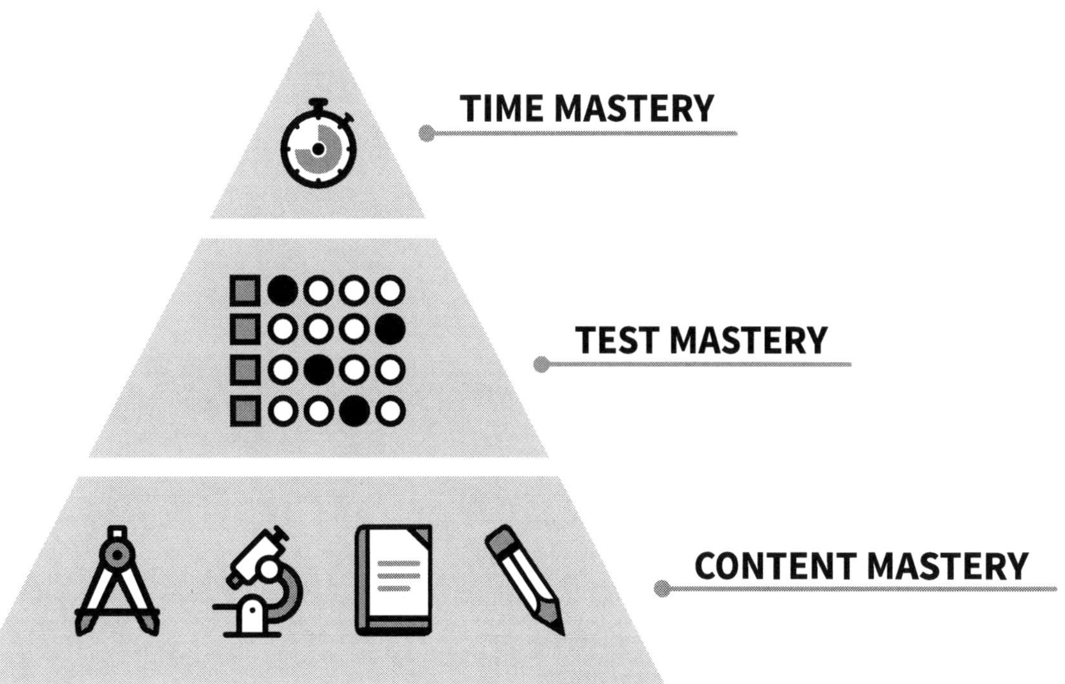

# The TSIA2 Mastery Difference

### Authentic Practice

TSIA2 Mastery features over one hundred TSIA2-aligned ELAR questions that mirror what students will actually face on the test. If they can answer the questions correctly in this book, they'll get them correct on the test. Other test prep programs don't come close to offering the same level of alignment in their test items.

### Isolation

We break the test down one standard at a time. Students are provided with the opportunity to work through authentic TSIA2-aligned questions with the teacher's guidance before flying solo through a practice set. The result is that students better consolidate what they learn and don't get overwhelmed. Traditional test prep programs often fail to provide sufficient practice in isolation.

### Scripted Lessons

TSIA2 Mastery is the only TSIA2 prep program that provides comprehensive, scripted lesson plans. The result is a consistent, score-raising experience for students and minimal planning time for teachers.

### Pre-Built Hooks

Traditional test prep programs are dry and follow the old "drill and kill" philosophy. If this is your first time running a test prep program, it can be challenging to introduce the content while bringing it to life. We've designed the program with hooks and activities built in, making each lesson interesting and engaging.

### Learn by Doing

Unlike traditional test prep programs that resort to "sage on the stage" demonstrations, TSIA2 Mastery students learn from what they do in the lessons, not from what you read them from a slide deck. Every instructional unit is centered around student activity and engagement.

### Scaffolded Instruction

TSIA2 items can be quite rigorous and often demand a demonstration of logic along with the skills of the assessed standards to reach the right answer. Traditional test prep aims directly at rehearsing the items, which can leave many students behind. TSIA2 Mastery is designed to start at a more remedial level and rapidly scaffold students to higher levels of attainment. We don't assume students know the basics, and the result is greater student engagement and achievement.

### Socratic Dialogue

In addition to the hooks and activities, the scripts for each lesson are designed to be highly engaging through the utilization of the Socratic method. There is not a single monotonous lecture in this curriculum, only discussions that push students to engage with the content.

### Detailed Test-Taking Approaches and Strategies

The average test prep program is built for high-performing students who are already solid test-takers. Students who struggle with tests also struggle in those programs. TSIA2 Mastery radically simplifies key strategies and walks students through each concept step-by-step.

### Integrated Time Management Coaching

Though students are not racing a clock, they still need to maintain good momentum in order to utilize their mental energy efficiently. By embedding time management coaching into each subject, TSIA2 Mastery is by far the most reliable program for improving your students' time management skills.

### Slide Decks and Teacher Resources

Unlike traditional test prep designed for tutors to use for weekend programs, we provide everything you need to run a TSIA2 Mastery class during the school day, right out of the box, including lesson plans, slide decks, and entrance and exit tickets.

### Complete

TSIA2 Mastery provides the most comprehensive coverage of TSIA2 standards for students at all score ranges.

When the Texas Success Initiative released the redesigned TSIA2, MasteryPrep began an extensive research project in order to fully understand its design and nuances. We evaluated the offerings of several competitors, along with the actual content of the TSIA2 as a student sees it, and combined these findings with the extensive compilations of classroom best practices and modern findings in cognitive psychology. With our team's test prep expertise, we constructed the MasteryPrep Framework for TSIA2 Prep, a cohesive, data-driven system for improving TSIA2 outcomes that is the foundation for all of our TSIA2 products.

**Why does TSIA2 Mastery work?**

It starts with the research. We've taken enormous care to ensure that each strategy and every topic we cover will have maximum impact for your students.

### Frequency Analysis

MasteryPrep analyzed hundreds of TSIA2 items seen on actual tests to determine the frequency with which each TSIA2 standard is assessed. Thanks to this analysis, our framework predicts not only what content will show up on the TSIA2, but also the nature in which the standard will be assessed. The result? Our programs help you spend time on what matters and avoid wasting time on red herrings.

### Variant Analysis

After we sorted every TSIA2 item we had come across based on their associated standards, we further categorized each standard into variants. In doing so, we were able to answer the question, "How does the TSIA2 test this standard?" This means that our programs can cover every major way in which the TSIA2 asks its questions.

### Item Analysis

Further analysis was conducted at the item level. With each standard, we studied how the TSIA2 constructs its questions. We analyzed the design of the answer choices. We picked apart the related passage's reading level. This research informed our practice test question design. The result is that our practice test questions are closer to the "real thing," providing a genuine TSIA2 experience that is not available with any other program.

### Instructional Design Research

MasteryPrep is committed to incorporating classroom best practices as well as the latest developments in cognitive psychology. We are constantly researching new findings and incorporating them into our framework. The result is that MasteryPrep's programs are truly modern test prep curricula, incorporating new developments such as entrance and exit tickets, spaced practice, and retrieval practice.

### Competitive Analysis

MasteryPrep is committed to leveling the playing field, which is why we conduct an extensive review of competing literature each time we develop a new framework. In doing so, we ensure that our students are not missing out on techniques and strategies typically reserved for the recipients of high-end tutoring.

### Impact Analysis

In the final stage of our framework development, we optimize strategies, techniques, and recommendations for the subject matter. We then conduct an impact analysis of these techniques using all available research to ensure that each component of our program is truly relevant and tightly fits the assessment. Each proposed instructional asset is evaluated in terms of the time and effort it requires to teach compared to the potential benefit in terms of score gains, and the highest-efficiency strategies are prioritized.

# What TSIA2 Mastery Includes

### Student Workbooks (2)

- TSIA2 Mastery ELAR
- TSIA2 Mastery Mathematics

Students work directly in their workbooks. The workbooks allow students to follow along with the classroom activities and include all of the practice materials needed for success on the TSIA2. No printing required!

### Teacher Manuals (2)

- TSIA2 Mastery ELAR
- TSIA2 Mastery Mathematics

Teacher manuals (like the one in your hands here) provide everything you need to facilitate more than 60 TSIA2 Mastery lessons, including answer explanations, scripted lesson plans, and timing suggestions.

### Slide Decks (2 sets)

- TSIA2 Mastery ELAR
- TSIA2 Mastery Mathematics

Every TSIA2 Mastery chapter is accompanied by a slide deck to provide a visual focus for the class. Every exercise and question that appears in the student workbook also appears in the accompanying slide deck, along with its solution.

**Missing a Resource?**

Contact your school support manager directly by emailing support@masteryprep.com

The best way to learn about the TSIA2 and how it's structured is to take an online practice test, read the College Board's website, and, if you're feeling ambitious, study its technical specs.

Of course, we cover what students need to know about the TSIA2 in the instructional content in this book. In case you're new to the TSIA2, there are a few things worth highlighting now, though, so that this guide makes more sense.

1. **The content of the TSIA2 is organized into standards.**

   These standards are a logical grouping of concepts that could be tested on the TSIA2. This is an example of a Reading standard:

   > **Literary Text Analysis**
   > **Explicit information**
   > The student will identify ideas explicitly stated and clearly indicated in literary text.

   To maximize compatibility and help you make the most of your data, we've followed suit and organized our content by the TSIA2's standards.

2. **The TSIA2 is a multiple-choice test with a required essay section.**

   This means that, whether we like it or not, test-taking strategies come into play. Two students who know the same things but have different test-taking habits and guessing strategies will perform at different levels. Better guessers make better scorers. TSIA2 Mastery develops those test-taking skills along with content mastery.

3. **The TSIA2 is adaptive.**

   The TSIA2 adapts to the student as they take the test. As they answer questions correctly, the test offers more challenging questions, and the student's score goes up. On the flip side of things, as students answer incorrectly, they start seeing easier questions, and their score goes down. Because of the TSIA2's adaptive nature, the first few questions of the test will weigh more heavily on student scores, and missing several questions in a row will be more detrimental to their score than missing several questions dispersed evenly throughout the test. This feature also means that no two students will experience the same test questions or assessed standards.

4. **The TSIA2 is an untimed test.**

   Though there are limits to this concept depending on the testing site, students conceptually have as much time as they would like to complete their test. Some testing centers offer the ability to pause the test, as long as the student returns within 14 calendar days to complete the assessment, with the exception that the essay section must be completed within one sitting. This unique feature of the test is meant to ensure that students are given the best opportunity to prove their college readiness. Due to the lack of time constraints, it is very possible for students to lose focus or even avoid completing the test altogether. TSIA2 Mastery works to develop the time management and momentum-building mindset to help students successfully complete their test.

5. **There is a safety net in the form of the Diagnostic.**

   If a student does not achieve a passing score on either the ELAR or Mathematics section of the TSIA2, they are given a second opportunity to prove their skills. This secondary test is called the Diagnostic. Each Diagnostic contains 48 questions. The test will give no indication to the student that they have begun the Diagnostic; it will simply continue from the last question of the main test to the first question of the Diagnostic. If a student fails the main test but earns a passing score on the Diagnostic, they are still considered college ready.

# TSIA2 Mastery Page by Page

When you teach a TSIA2 Mastery lesson, you'll work from the teacher manual. Your students will be looking at their workbooks. On the projector will be the slide deck. There are a lot of moving parts. That's why TSIA2 Mastery uses a system to ensure that you and your class are always, literally, on the same page.

For every page in the student workbook (for example, page 259a below to the left), there are two pages in the teacher manual (for example, page 259b below to the right). This is always an exact match. In the teacher manual, the "a" pages are always on the left, and the "b" pages are always on the right.

The entire student workbook is reprinted in the teacher manual, so you don't need the student workbook open and in front of you to track what your students are seeing.

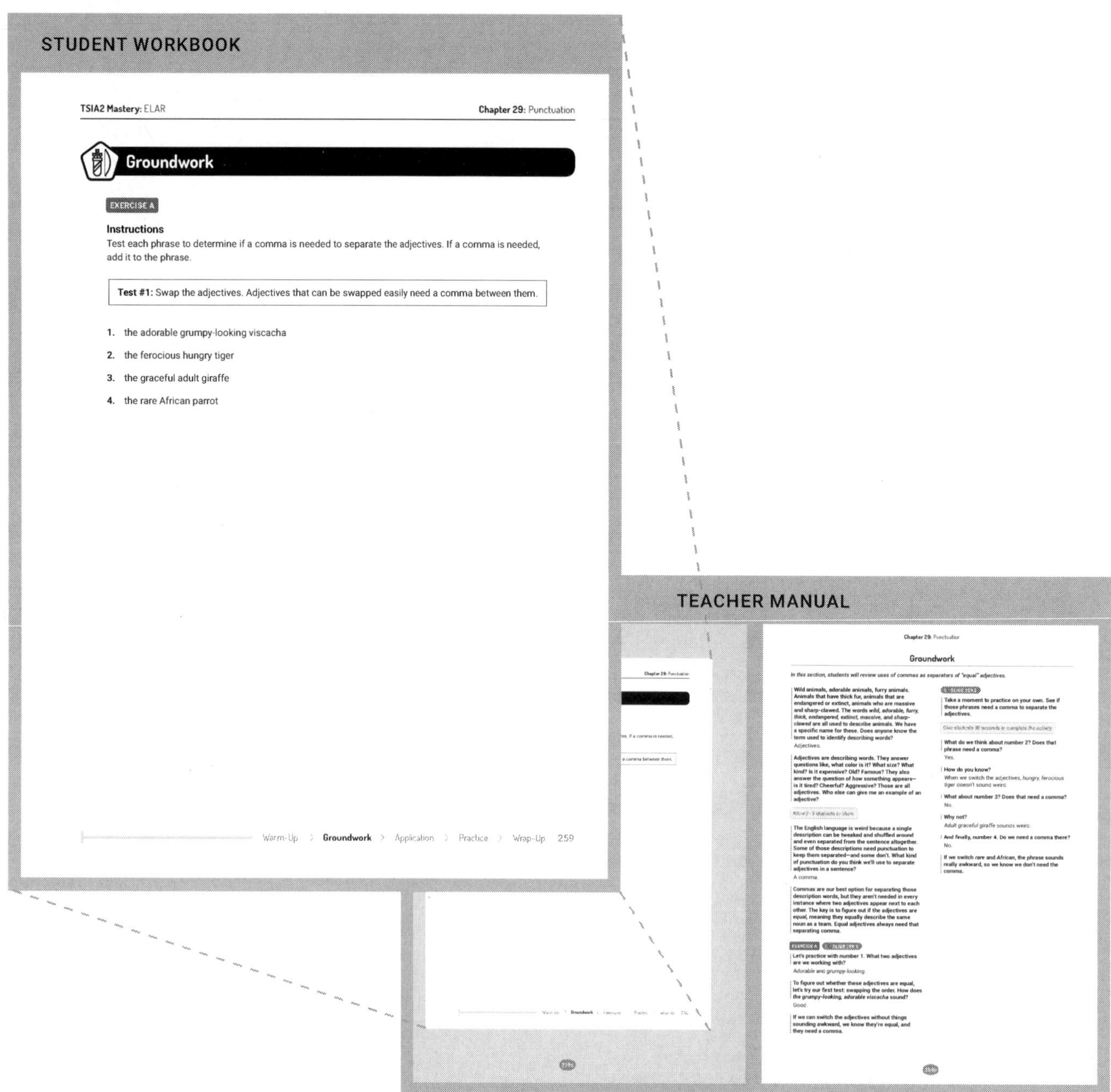

Each page in the student workbook (page 264, for instance) can have one or more slides that go with it. Each slide number starts with the matching page number in the student workbook and teacher manual (for example, slides 264.1, 264.2, 264.3, and 264.4).

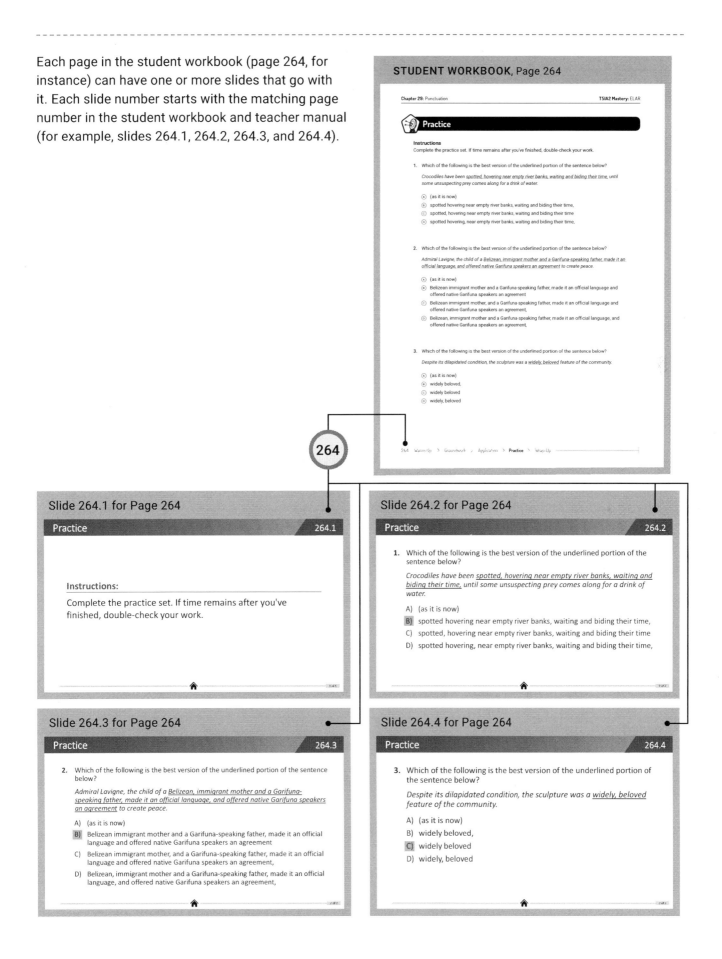

**STUDENT WORKBOOK, Page 264**

Chapter 29: Punctuation — TSIA2 Mastery: ELAR

**Practice**

**Instructions**
Complete the practice set. If time remains after you've finished, double-check your work.

1. Which of the following is the best version of the underlined portion of the sentence below?

   *Crocodiles have been spotted, hovering near empty river banks, waiting and biding their time, until some unsuspecting prey comes along for a drink of water.*

   Ⓐ (as it is now)
   Ⓑ spotted hovering near empty river banks, waiting and biding their time,
   Ⓒ spotted, hovering near empty river banks, waiting and biding their time
   Ⓓ spotted hovering, near empty river banks, waiting and biding their time,

2. Which of the following is the best version of the underlined portion of the sentence below?

   *Admiral Lavigne, the child of a Belizean, immigrant mother and a Garifuna-speaking father, made it an official language, and offered native Garifuna speakers an agreement to create peace.*

   Ⓐ (as it is now)
   Ⓑ Belizean immigrant mother and a Garifuna-speaking father, made it an official language and offered native Garifuna speakers an agreement
   Ⓒ Belizean immigrant mother, and a Garifuna-speaking father, made it an official language and offered native Garifuna speakers an agreement,
   Ⓓ Belizean, immigrant mother and a Garifuna-speaking father, made it an official language, and offered native Garifuna speakers an agreement,

3. Which of the following is the best version of the underlined portion of the sentence below?

   *Despite its dilapidated condition, the sculpture was a widely, beloved feature of the community.*

   Ⓐ (as it is now)
   Ⓑ widely beloved,
   Ⓒ widely beloved
   Ⓓ widely, beloved

264 Warm-Up > Groundwork > Application > **Practice** > Wrap-Up

264

**Slide 264.1 for Page 264**

Practice — 264.1

**Instructions:**

Complete the practice set. If time remains after you've finished, double-check your work.

**Slide 264.2 for Page 264**

Practice — 264.2

1. Which of the following is the best version of the underlined portion of the sentence below?

   *Crocodiles have been spotted, hovering near empty river banks, waiting and biding their time, until some unsuspecting prey comes along for a drink of water.*

   A) (as it is now)
   B) spotted hovering near empty river banks, waiting and biding their time,
   C) spotted, hovering near empty river banks, waiting and biding their time
   D) spotted hovering, near empty river banks, waiting and biding their time,

**Slide 264.3 for Page 264**

Practice — 264.3

2. Which of the following is the best version of the underlined portion of the sentence below?

   *Admiral Lavigne, the child of a Belizean, immigrant mother and a Garifuna-speaking father, made it an official language, and offered native Garifuna speakers an agreement to create peace.*

   A) (as it is now)
   B) Belizean immigrant mother and a Garifuna-speaking father, made it an official language and offered native Garifuna speakers an agreement
   C) Belizean immigrant mother, and a Garifuna-speaking father, made it an official language and offered native Garifuna speakers an agreement,
   D) Belizean, immigrant mother and a Garifuna-speaking father, made it an official language, and offered native Garifuna speakers an agreement,

**Slide 264.4 for Page 264**

Practice — 264.4

3. Which of the following is the best version of the underlined portion of the sentence below?

   *Despite its dilapidated condition, the sculpture was a widely, beloved feature of the community.*

   A) (as it is now)
   B) widely beloved,
   C) widely beloved
   D) widely, beloved

# TSIA2 Mastery Page by Page

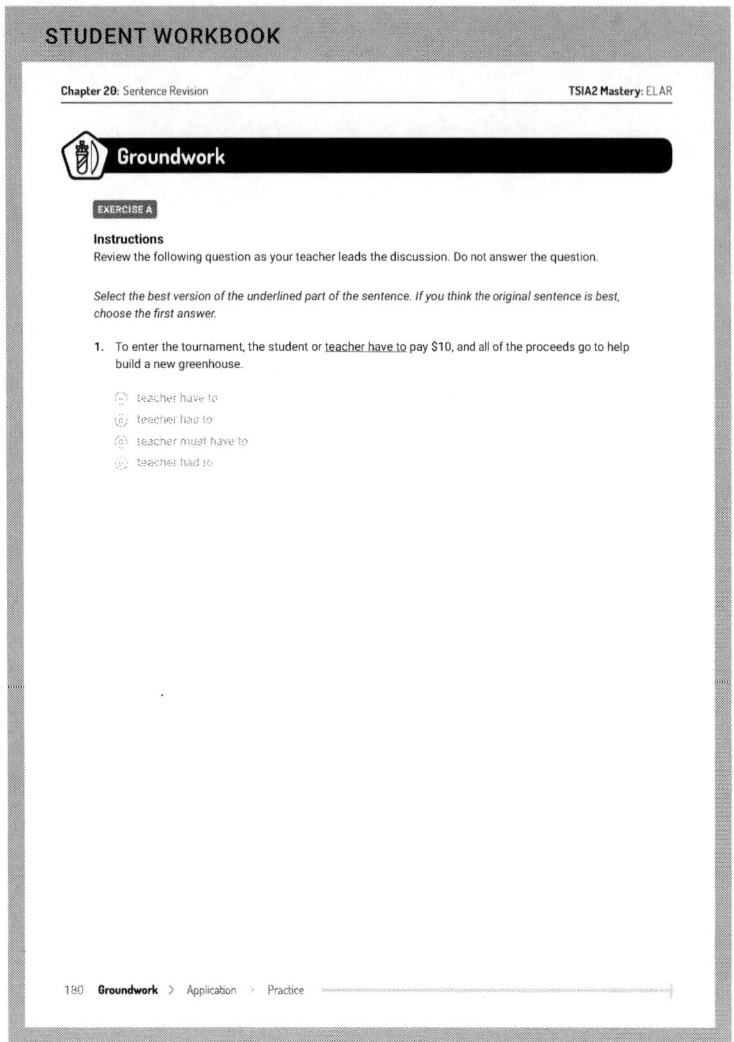

STUDENT WORKBOOK

**Chapter 20:** Sentence Revision    **TSIA2 Mastery:** ELAR

## Groundwork

EXERCISE A

**Instructions**
Review the following question as your teacher leads the discussion. Do not answer the question.

*Select the best version of the underlined part of the sentence. If you think the original sentence is best, choose the first answer.*

1. To enter the tournament, the student or <u>teacher have to</u> pay $10, and all of the proceeds go to help build a new greenhouse.

   (A) teacher have to
   (B) teacher has to
   (C) teacher must have to
   (D) teacher had to

180 **Groundwork** > Application > Practice

If you want to start a lesson on pages 180a and 180b in your teacher manual, have your students turn to page 180 in their workbook and pull up slide 180.1 on the projector.

## TEACHER MANUAL

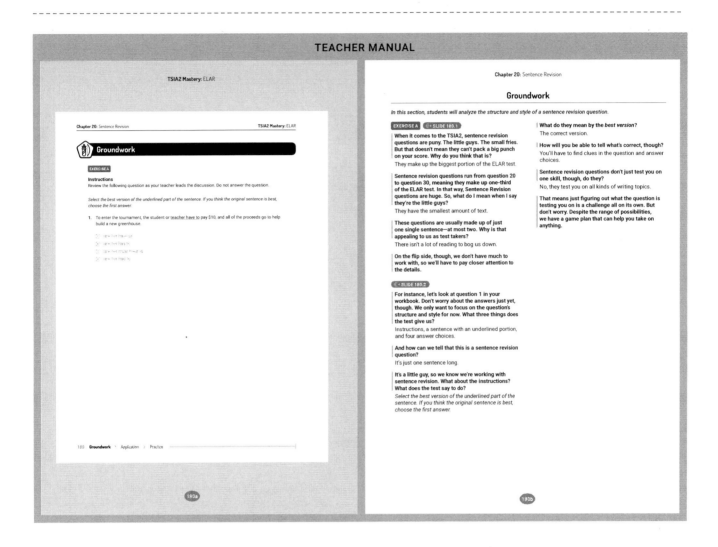

TSIA2 Mastery: ELAR

Chapter 20: Sentence Revision | TSIA2 Mastery: ELAR

### Groundwork

EXERCISE A

**Instructions**
Review the following question as your teacher leads the discussion. Do not answer the question.

*Select the best version of the underlined part of the sentence. If you think the original sentence is best, choose the first answer.*

1. To enter the tournament, the student or <u>teacher have to</u> pay $10, and all of the proceeds go to help build a new greenhouse.

   A) teacher have to
   B) teacher has to
   C) teacher must have to
   D) teacher had to

180 **Groundwork** > Application > Practice

180a

Chapter 20: Sentence Revision

### Groundwork

*In this section, students will analyze the structure and style of a sentence revision question.*

EXERCISE A | SLIDE 180.1

**When it comes to the TSIA2, sentence revision questions are puny. The little guys. The small fries. But that doesn't mean they can't pack a big punch on your score. Why do you think that is?**
They make up the biggest portion of the ELAR test.

**Sentence revision questions run from question 20 to question 30, meaning they make up one-third of the ELAR test. In that way, Sentence Revision questions are huge. So, what do I mean when I say they're the little guys?**
They have the smallest amount of text.

**These questions are usually made up of just one single sentence—at most two. Why is that appealing to us as test takers?**
There isn't a lot of reading to bog us down.

**On the flip side, though, we don't have much to work with, so we'll have to pay closer attention to the details.**

SLIDE 180.2

**For instance, let's look at question 1 in your workbook. Don't worry about the answers just yet, though. We only want to focus on the question's structure and style for now. What three things does the test give us?**
Instructions, a sentence with an underlined portion, and four answer choices.

**And how can we tell that this is a sentence revision question?**
It's just one sentence long.

**It's a little guy, so we know we're working with sentence revision. What about the instructions? What does the test say to do?**
*Select the best version of the underlined part of the sentence. If you think the original sentence is best, choose the first answer.*

**What do they mean by the *best version*?**
The correct version.

**How will you be able to tell what's correct, though?**
You'll have to find clues in the question and answer choices.

**Sentence revision questions don't just test you on one skill, though, do they?**
No, they test you on all kinds of writing topics.

**That means just figuring out what the question is testing you on is a challenge all on its own. But don't worry. Despite the range of possibilities, we have a game plan that can help you take on anything.**

180b

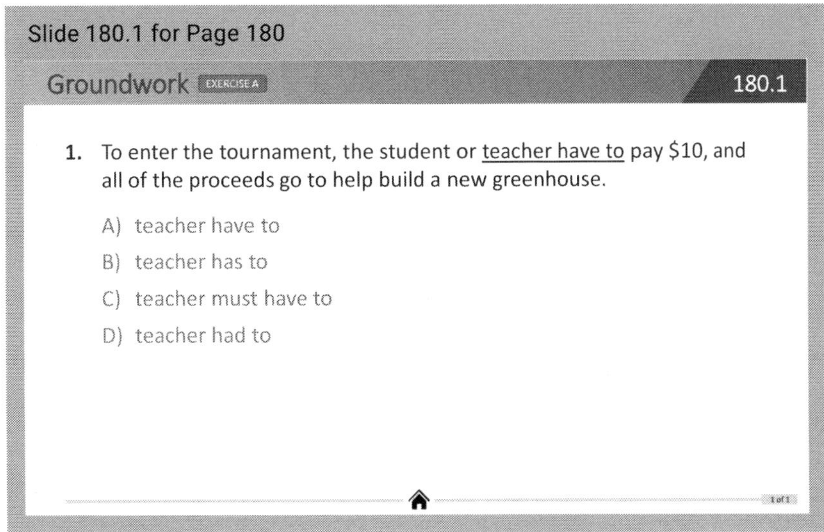

## TSIA2 Mastery Page by Page

As you go through the dialogue on page 233b, helpful slide call-outs tell you when the next slide is relevant (for example, 233.1 and 233.2).

Once you get to the bottom of page 233b, you'll turn to the next pages in your teacher manual, 234a and 234b, while having your students look at page 234 in their workbooks. You'll also click the slide to 234.1.

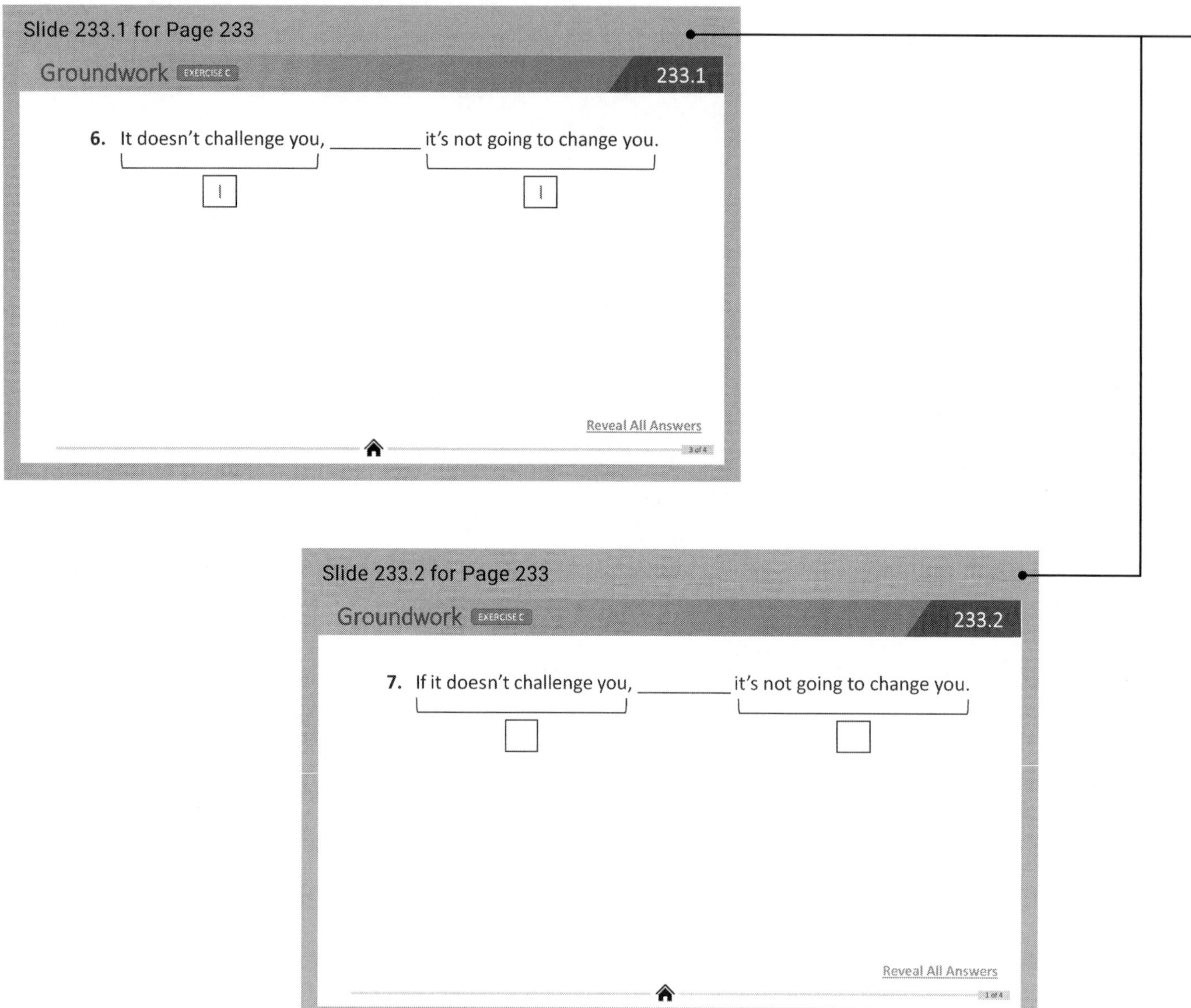

TEACHER MANUAL

**Chapter 26:** Coordinating Conjunctions

Groundwork

*In this section, students will evaluate the characteristics of a compound sentence and a complex sentence and determine which structure requires a coordinating conjunction.*

EXERCISE C SLIDE 233.1

**A dependent clause is a weakling, unable to stand on its own. It needs a big, strong independent clause to make it complete. All we need to connect dependent clauses is something small like a comma, a colon, or maybe even nothing at all. But when two independent clauses get connected, we need a heavy lifter to make that connection. For instance, check out sentence 6. How should we start?**

Figure out if the clauses are independent or dependent.

**Start with the first clause. Is that independent or dependent?**

Independent.

**How can you tell?**

It could stand on its own as a complete sentence.

**What about the second clause? How should we label that one?**

Independent, since it could be its own complete sentence.

**Two independent clauses mean using a stronger connection. What should we add?**

One of the FANBOYS.

**We've got seven options: *for, and, nor, but, or, yet,* or *so*. How do we decide which one will work best?**

Look at the details of the sentence.

**If we can figure out how one clause relates to the other, we'll be able to pick the best coordinating conjunction for the job. What kind of relationship do we see here?**

Cause and effect.

**Which of our FANBOYS would work well in that space?**

*So.*

**Let's read it back to ourselves, just to make sure it works.**

*It doesn't challenge you, so it's not going to change you.*

**Does that sound okay?**

Yes.

SLIDE 233.2

**Using *so* to connect the ideas works well, and we've given our two independent clauses the strong connection they need. Let's look at sentence 7 next. Is the first clause dependent or independent?**

Dependent.

**How do you know?**

It can't be its own complete sentence.

**What about the second clause? Independent or dependent?**

Independent.

**So, we've got a dependent clause connected to an independent clause. Do we need to add a coordinating conjunction?**

No.

**Since the sentence begins with a dependent clause, we don't need anything besides that little comma to make the connection.**

# The Structure of a TSIA2 Mastery Lesson

The TSIA2 Mastery lessons fall into one of two categories: a content chapter or a strategy chapter. A content chapter focuses on a skill or question type seen on the TSIA2 and is based on a specific TSIA2 standard. Strategy chapters dissect the characteristics of specific question type categories or provide students with effective test-taking skills that can be applied to a variety of questions.

The sequence of elements in each chapter type is designed to help students master TSIA2 standards. It also enables them to gradually build test-taking and foundational skills needed to be successful on the test.

At the bottom of each student workbook page is a tracker (as shown below) that lets you know where you are in a chapter.

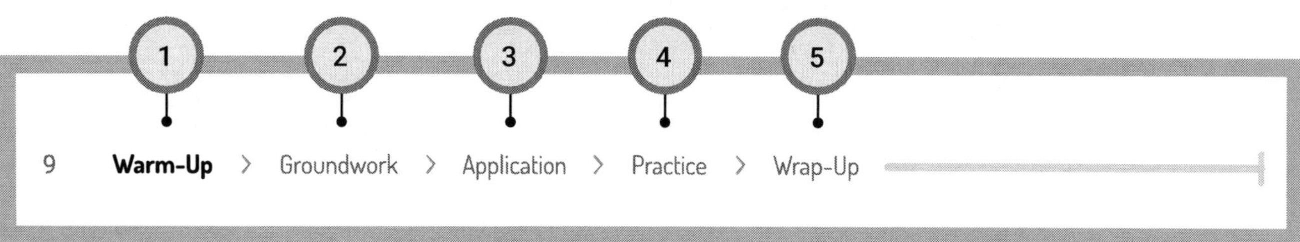


## 1. Warm-Up

A practice question introduces your students to the topic of the chapter and helps you differentiate instruction and monitor growth.

## 2. Groundwork

A scaffolded lesson lets students review the basics of the standard and participate in skill-building activities that improve their grasp on the content.

## 3. Application

Students learn how to identify question types, eliminate incorrect answers using a prescribed set of steps, and double-check their work.

## 4. Practice Set

Three TSIA2-aligned test items provide isolated practice and a way to hone newly acquired skills.

## 5. Wrap-Up

Another practice question, at the same difficulty level as the warm-up item, helps you evaluate students' progress.

Every section of a TSIA2 Mastery lesson is designed to stand on its own. You can use the lessons one after another for a one-semester course, or you can pick and choose resources from lessons and individual sections to suit your students' needs. For example, if you feel your students have mastered the instructional content but need additional practice, you could have them focus only on the warm-up, wrap-up, and practice sets. Teachers may also decide to put more emphasis on content mastery and use only the Groundwork and Application sections.

9 Warm-Up > **Groundwork** > **Application** > Practice > Wrap-Up

Or, if you want to give your students a one-week cram just before test day, you could stick to the warm-up, practice (set), and wrap-up for a lightning-fast review of the types of questions they should expect to see on test day.

9 **Warm-Up** > Groundwork > Application > **Practice** > **Wrap-Up**

For more ideas about how to make the most of TSIA2 Mastery's modular lesson design, see "How to Use TSIA2 Mastery" later in this guide.

# TSIA2 Mastery Features

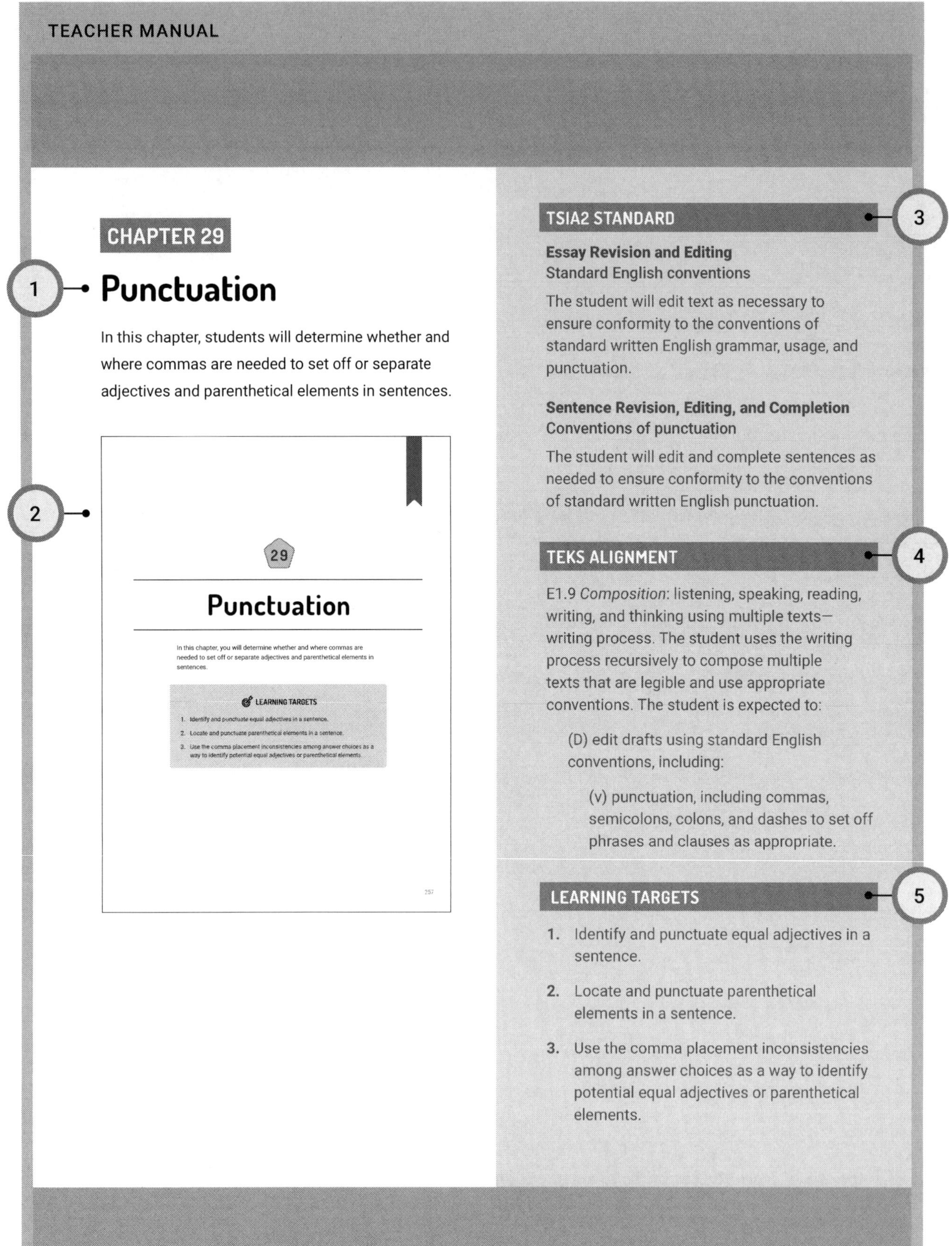

TEACHER MANUAL

CHAPTER 29

1 **Punctuation**

In this chapter, students will determine whether and where commas are needed to set off or separate adjectives and parenthetical elements in sentences.

2

29

Punctuation

In this chapter, you will determine whether and where commas are needed to set off or separate adjectives and parenthetical elements in sentences.

LEARNING TARGETS

1. Identify and punctuate equal adjectives in a sentence.
2. Locate and punctuate parenthetical elements in a sentence.
3. Use the comma placement inconsistencies among answer choices as a way to identify potential equal adjectives or parenthetical elements.

257

TSIA2 STANDARD 3

**Essay Revision and Editing**
Standard English conventions

The student will edit text as necessary to ensure conformity to the conventions of standard written English grammar, usage, and punctuation.

**Sentence Revision, Editing, and Completion**
Conventions of punctuation

The student will edit and complete sentences as needed to ensure conformity to the conventions of standard written English punctuation.

TEKS ALIGNMENT 4

E1.9 *Composition*: listening, speaking, reading, writing, and thinking using multiple texts—writing process. The student uses the writing process recursively to compose multiple texts that are legible and use appropriate conventions. The student is expected to:

(D) edit drafts using standard English conventions, including:

(v) punctuation, including commas, semicolons, colons, and dashes to set off phrases and clauses as appropriate.

LEARNING TARGETS 5

1. Identify and punctuate equal adjectives in a sentence.
2. Locate and punctuate parenthetical elements in a sentence.
3. Use the comma placement inconsistencies among answer choices as a way to identify potential equal adjectives or parenthetical elements.

## Introduction Page

1. **Title**

   We tried to keep the title of each lesson as close to the official TSIA2 standards as possible. Sometimes, we changed it to make it clearer to students, and sometimes we shortened it.

2. **Student Workbook Thumbnail**

   This is the only time the student workbook snapshot isn't full size on the left of the double-page spread. We did this to help you more easily identify when a new chapter is beginning. Don't bust out your magnifying glass, though: everything on this page in the student workbook is also reprinted right here on the teacher manual page in font sizes not designed for ants.

3. **TSIA2 Standards**

   The official TSIA2 standards are included on the cover page of each lesson. Sometimes, there will be a mismatch between the "fancy" language in the standard and what appears in the lesson. When we developed this program, we started with the standard. Then, we found the associated TSIA2 items that matched up with the standard. This gave us the assessed standard. We built the lesson around the assessed standards—what actually shows up on the test. If the TSIA2 doesn't test an aspect of its standard, then we don't teach it. Improvements along the assessed standard are what result in score gains.

4. **TEKS Alignment**

   Each lesson's content has also been carefully aligned to its relevant Texas Essential Knowledge and Skills. This alignment was done by licensed Texas high school teachers to ensure our alignment is accurate and thorough. Many schools require that your learning objectives tie closely with the state standards, so we've done that for you. You're welcome.

5. **Learning Targets**

   Student-friendly learning objectives appear in each lesson. These targets correspond to various elements of the lesson, including the Groundwork exercises, Application processes, and test-taking skills taught within the lesson.

   Some schools require learning targets for every lesson plan, and we love to make things easy on you.

# TSIA2 Mastery Features

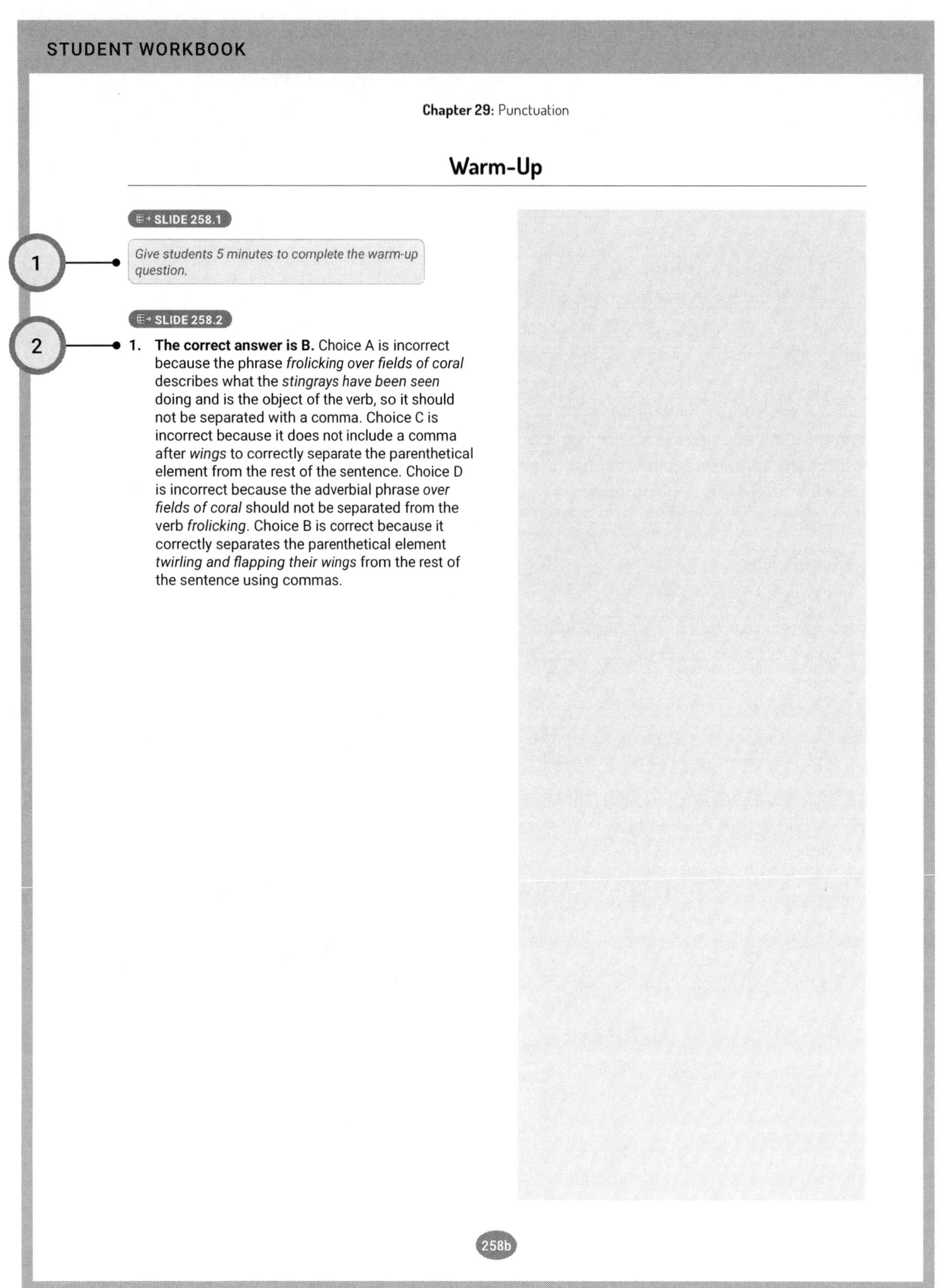
STUDENT WORKBOOK
**Chapter 29:** Punctuation
Warm-Up
SLIDE 258.1
1
Give students 5 minutes to complete the warm-up question.
SLIDE 258.2
2
1. **The correct answer is B.** Choice A is incorrect because the phrase *frolicking over fields of coral* describes what the *stingrays have been seen* doing and is the object of the verb, so it should not be separated with a comma. Choice C is incorrect because it does not include a comma after *wings* to correctly separate the parenthetical element from the rest of the sentence. Choice D is incorrect because the adverbial phrase *over fields of coral* should not be separated from the verb *frolicking*. Choice B is correct because it correctly separates the parenthetical element *twirling and flapping their wings* from the rest of the sentence using commas.
258b

# Warm-Up

The warm-up for each ELAR lesson contains a single question at a middling difficulty level. If it is a Reading chapter, the question will include its associated passage. Writing questions may include either a single sentence or a full essay, depending on the question type.

In a TSIA2 Mastery class, the warm-up can serve as an entrance ticket. Start the timer when the bell rings. When time is up, ensure all students have selected their answer. Then, share the answers and have students score their work.

Note: Strategy chapters do not contain a warm-up or wrap-up question. Essay-writing chapters do not contain warm-ups, wrap-ups, or practice sets.

1. **Time Suggestions**

   Every warm-up has a suggested time limit. Feel free to modify this to your needs, especially if a student is unable to finish in the suggested amount of time. Allowing ample time to answer the question will better mimic the testing experience, since there is no time limit on the TSIA2.

2. **Explanations**

   Explanations are provided, but when you use the warm-up as an entrance ticket, don't review them with the class. The lesson that comes after will likely address your students' questions. Avoid getting sucked into teaching the whole lesson in the warm-up.

### Grading Warm-Ups

Some teachers like to have their students swap books to score the warm-up; some just use the honor system. Either way, entrance tickets should not count as a grade. The score is just to help you quickly survey the class's proficiency level. Once the warm-up is scored, students indicate whether they answered correctly or not. Ask them to show a thumbs up or a thumbs down in front of their bodies, not up in the air, so they can quickly and confidentially share their score.

Alternatively, have your students answer the warm-up question on TSIA2 Mastery Elements, which will give you instant, confidential results.

### Why Warm-Ups?

The quickest way to introduce students to a standard is by giving them real questions.

Some students will start each chapter with the impression they already know everything about a topic. For example, when students see the Verb Tense chapter, some may think, "I've known about that since elementary school!" This creates a barrier to student learning. The warm-up shows students what aspects of verb tense they still need to improve on. When a student misses a warm-up question, it makes them curious about how to get it right.

Pre-testing improves performance. It primes students' brains to listen for instructional content that will help them answer correctly.

How you teach a lesson to students who nailed their warm-up is very different from how you teach the lesson to a class that bombed it. By getting this data early on, you go into the lesson ready to respond to their current skill level.

# TSIA2 Mastery Features

STUDENT WORKBOOK

**Chapter 15:** Combining Sentences

**Groundwork**

1 *In this section, students will review two unconcise sentences and examine a solution that eliminates the problem.*

**Another common obstacle that can send readers stumbling through a sentence is wordiness. What happens when a sentence is too wordy?**

It's hard to figure out what it's saying.

EXERCISE B SLIDE 130.1

**We like our writing like we like our lectures: short and to the point. No one wants to listen to someone ramble, and adding all kinds of extra fluff to a sentence only gets in the way of what we're trying to say. For example, let's look at the first draft in number 4. Who'd like to read that for us?**

2 *"Muckraker" was a term referring to journalists who advocated for reform. "Muckraker" was also a word applied to Upton Sinclair, who was a journalist who investigated the unhygienic practices of meatpacking plants.*

3 **Whoa. That's a lot of information crammed in there, and trying to pull out the details is a little like trying to untangle a ball of old Christmas lights. It's definitely not fun and even a little frustrating. What about the first draft makes it *not* concise?**

It's repetitive. The sentence says *muckraker* and *journalist* more than once.

**All the information is spread out across two sentences in such a way that the writer is getting repetitive when they really don't need to be. How can they fix this?**

They can edit it out of the sentence.

SLIDE 130.2

**Let's see if they managed to do that in number 5. Is that sentence more concise?**

Yes.

**But something went wrong. Why is this first revision not quite right?**

It lost a lot of information.

SLIDE 130.3

**Editing out extra words is only effective if we don't cut out the important stuff. Imagine trying to cut the tag off of a new shirt and ending up with no sleeves and a hole across the shoulders. We need to pull it back and just cut the stuff we don't want. Did the writer get it right in sentence 6?**

Yes, it's concise without losing important information.

**By focusing on just the important details, the writer was able to communicate everything they wanted to without overcomplicating it with extra wordiness. Concision at its best.**

## Groundwork

### How to Work the Groundwork

They call it a standard for a reason. Content mastery is a major driver for score improvements, and if your students master ELAR skills, their scores will improve. They'll reach the standard.

That said, you can't reteach the entire subject of reading comprehension or cover a wide variety of punctuation conventions in a few hours (and that's not required anyway). What is required is that you help students connect what they have mastered—what they do remember—to the TSIA2's assessed standards. That's where the Groundwork section comes in.

We've analyzed what aspect of each standard is most likely to trip students up—what they're most likely to have forgotten or have an issue with—and built focused skill-building exercises to fill the gaps.

In 20 minutes, your students experience a rapid review of content and practice the skills that are most crucial for success.

The goal of the Groundwork section is not to reteach a subject, but to take students who have previously learned a topic and prepare them for the rigor of the TSIA2.

### 1. Summary

At the top of every page of dialogue, there is a summary of what will happen in this part of the lesson.

### 2. Sample Responses and Explanations

After the dialogue asks a question, we provide a sample student response for the answer. Most of our questions are open-ended, so answers can vary. One of the hallmarks of the TSIA2 Mastery program is that every question or exercise that appears in a lesson is accompanied by an explanation or sample response.

### 3. Hooks, Humor, and Hhh-Engagement

We have interspersed our lessons with hooks. These are short attention-getters included at the beginning of lessons and at points where we need students to re-engage. This could be an anecdote, an activity, or an off-the-wall question. When done well, hooks highlight important concepts while breaking up the monotony of practicing TSIA2 questions. Great hooks are highly situational. Their tone and content need to fit your students. Our hooks err on the side of goofy or eye-roll-inducing, but all are tightly focused on the topic at hand, so they do have a point and instructional value in their own right. However, we can't guarantee that they will work with your students every time. Take creative license with them. When you see a hook, take it as a sign that there is a need for a hook there, for something to build or regain interest. If you don't think the given hook or activity will fly with your students, substitute your own. Our hope is that most of our hooks can at least give you a starting point.

Likewise, we've sprinkled some humor throughout the lessons, but great humor is even more situational than hooks. Feel free to modify or drop it. You know your students best.

We thought it better to give you a starting point on hooks and humor rather than give you a completely dry lesson, forcing you to fill it all in.

Note: Side notes always start with "Note:" and address exceptions that you might encounter while teaching the class. We recommend that you not cover this material unless it becomes relevant.

## TSIA2 Mastery Features

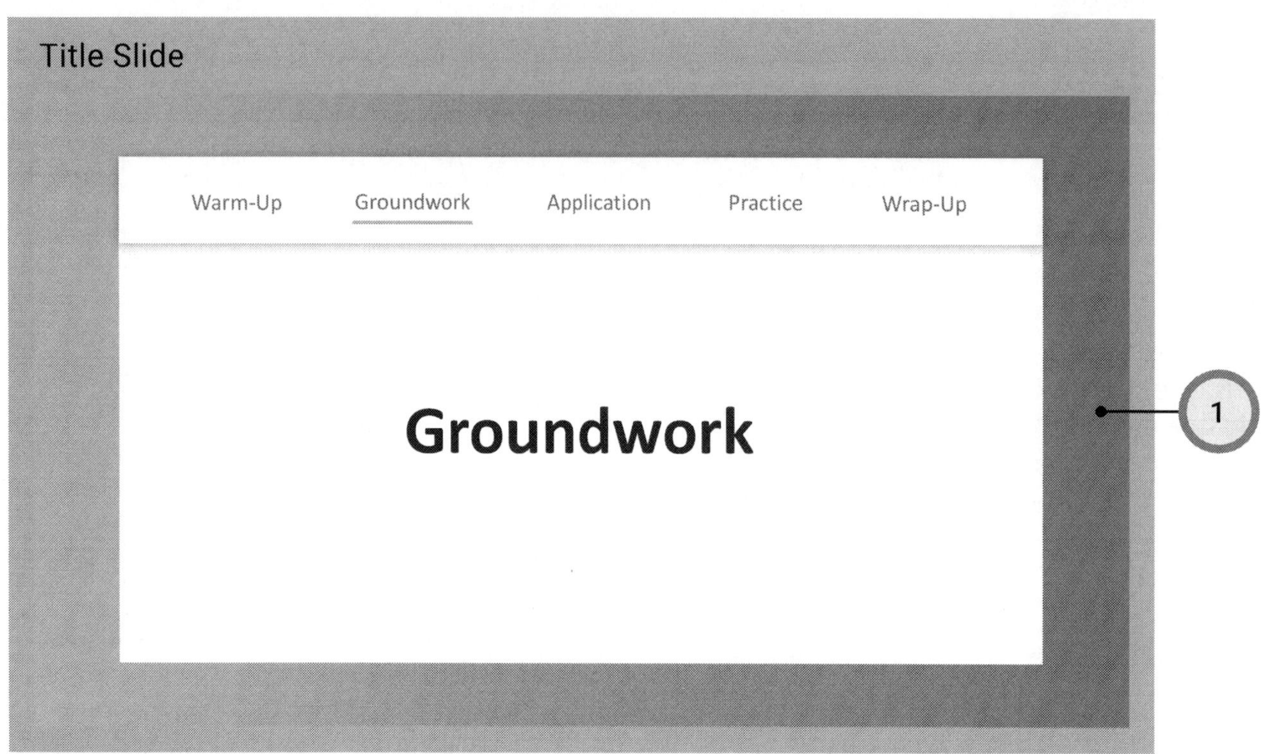


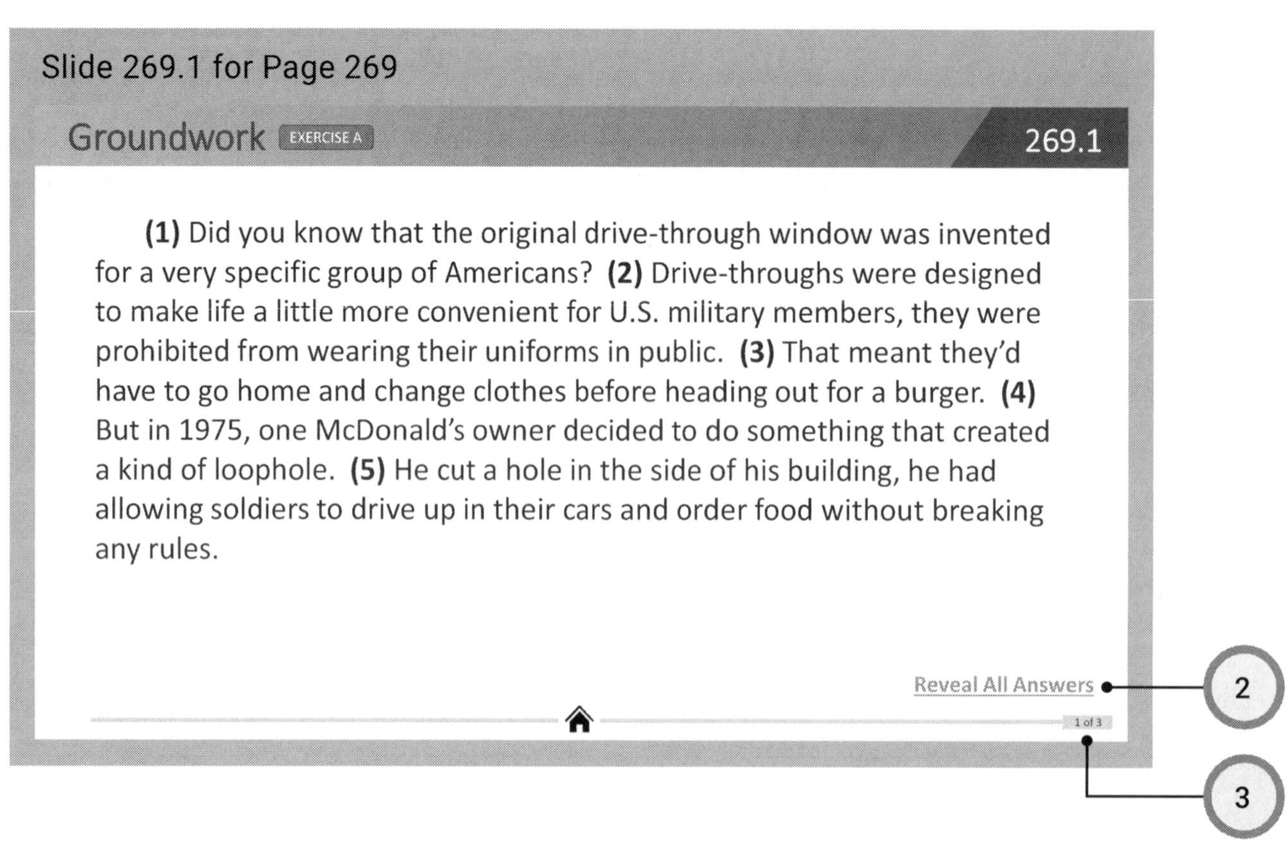

## Groundwork (continued)

### 1. Title Slides

Throughout each slide deck, you will see title slides that indicate the section, such as the Groundwork or Application. These title slides do not have an associated slide number that correlates to a page number. They are included to help you stay oriented as you progress through the lesson.

### 2. Answer Reveals, Reveal Answer

If you wish to reveal the completed answer for a question at once, rather than one at a time, you always have the option to Reveal Answer. By clicking this link, you will progress forward in the slide deck to the final slide of that sequence, where the completed answer will be shown on screen.

> Note: Some slides display multiple questions. In those instances, the button will read "Reveal All Answers," which will populate the Answers for all questions on that slide.

### 3. Answer Reveals, One at a Time

At the bottom right of each slide, there are numbers that correspond to answer reveals and eliminations. The first slide of the sequence (for example: 1 of 3) will never contain answers. To help you see ahead of time how many answers or eliminations will be revealed on that slide, refer to those numbers.

# TSIA2 Mastery Features

STUDENT WORKBOOK

**Chapter 29:** Punctuation

Groundwork

*In this section, students will learn how to identify and punctuate a parenthetical element.*

EXERCISE C SLIDE 261.1

1

**This lesson is all about descriptive phrases and how to punctuate them. Just based on that, what do you think a parenthetical element *is*?**

A description of some kind.

**A parenthetical element is like an adjective on steroids. It's a phrase or a clause that adds more detail or information to a sentence. And it has a unique feature: it's removable. Check it out in sentence 9. Which phrase makes up the parenthetical element here?**

*The world's largest species of bird.*

**That phrase adds a little more info about ostriches. Let's take that phrase out and see what happens. Who'd like to read the sentence without the parenthetical element?**

*The common ostrich can sprint at speeds of over 40 mph.*

**Notice that we still have a grammatically complete sentence, *and* the information still makes sense. How does this sentence punctuate the parenthetical element?**

It has commas around it.

**A parenthetical element will always have some kind of punctuation surrounding it to separate it from the rest of the sentence, and on the TSIA2, you'll be using commas.**

3

SLIDE 261.2

**Next, let's turn our attention to the paragraph, starting with sentence 1. We need to figure out if the sentence contains a parenthetical element and, if so, where to place the commas. Do you see a parenthetical element in sentence 1?**

*A creature containing enough toxin to kill several dozen people at once.*

**How do you know it's a parenthetical element?**

You can take it out of the sentence, and what's left is still grammatically correct and didn't lose any essential information.

**Where should we put the commas?**

Before *a creature* and after *at once*.

SLIDE 261.3

**Take a moment now to review sentences 2 through 4. See if the underlined portion contains a parenthetical element, and if so, where to add commas.**

*Give students 2 minutes to complete this task.*

2

**Let's start with sentence 2. Does the underlined portion contain a parenthetical element?**

Yes.

**What is it?**

*Known in Japanese as fugu.*

**Where should we add our commas?**

Before *known* and after *fugu*.

**What about sentence 3? Who can walk me through that one?**

The parenthetical element is *often with thin slices of meat arranged into the shape of a flower*, but there is already a comma after *flower*, so we just need a comma before *often*.

**And what about sentence 4? Do we need to add commas there?**

There's no parenthetical element, so we don't need to add any commas.

**And just like that, we've got all our commas in place.**

261b

## Groundwork (continued)

1. **Dialogue**

   Bold text with a line along the left side is teacher dialogue. It's what we recommend you say.

   We've written it like a script. That's because it's easier for you to read than us saying, "Point out to your students that the main idea is often found in the first paragraph, and that is it often restated in the conclusion paragraph ...". Even more, the questions are designed to elicit analytical thinking and engagement. The dialogue guides students to make their own conclusions, rather than offering up extensive (and often mind-numbing) lectures.

   Just because we've written it like a script doesn't mean you should read it like a script. The best TSIA2 Mastery classes have their own unique take on the materials. Their teachers adapt and respond to the students' interactions with the chapter.

   The dialogue is a starting point and a reference. Imagine that to the left of every teacher dialogue section is this instruction: "Say something like this ..." And after, there's this disclaimer: "Or, if you'd like, say something else entirely." We don't want anyone to be a TSIA2 Mastery robot.

2. **Directions**

   We italicize directions and wrap them in a rectangle.

3. **Next Slide**

   These labels indicate when it's time to click to the next slide. The number to the left of the dot matches the page number in the student workbook and teacher manual. The number to the right helps you find the specific slide for that segment of the page. For example, Slide 38.2 means that you need the second slide for student workbook page 38.

### Our "script" is intentionally missing a few things. Teachers fill these in on their own.

**Acknowledgements:** We don't include how to respond to your students' answers. Good acknowledgements are often as simple as "Okay" or "That's right." But student responses are so varied that anything we put in there just gets in the way of readability.

**Page Transitions:** When you turn the page in your teacher manual, it's usually a good idea to let your students know to move to the next page in their workbooks.

**Student Selection:** The dialogue asks students a lot of questions. To keep this simple, we phrase questions to the group. Feel free to select individual students to answer. We are big fans of cold calling (see "About Asking Questions" in this section), but sometimes taking volunteers or choral responses is more appropriate.

### About Asking Questions

It's up to you how you engage your students to respond to the dialogue. There are points where a simple call and response to the group makes sense. Questions you gauge as tough may be suited for asking for a volunteer. For most questions, however, we recommend the cold call method.

To cold call, clearly ask the question. Pause. Then, call on a student. Don't ask for volunteers. You choose. The expectation is that the student should be ready to answer when you call on them. More info on cold calling is available at https://bit.ly/3f7ALYo and in *Teach Like a Champion* (Lemov).

This method gives you control over how you spread the work around. It makes it easier to differentiate instruction, since you reserve more straightforward questions for students who are struggling to stay engaged. Cold calls prompt all students to think about the questions you are asking and don't allow anyone to check out. We have designed the questions in our dialogue with the cold call technique in mind.

# TSIA2 Mastery Features

STUDENT WORKBOOK



## Application

1

### THE APPROACH

When you are challenged to correctly punctuate descriptive words and phrases on the test, use the following steps ...

1. Locate equal adjectives or parenthetical elements, if any appear.
2. Eliminate answer choices that contain incorrect comma placement.

2

**10.** Which version of the sentence below is punctuated correctly?

*Cephalopods, a class of animals that includes octopuses and squids possess three separate hearts that pump oxygen-rich, blue-colored blood throughout their bodies.*

Ⓐ (as it is now)

Ⓑ Cephalopods, a class of animals that includes octopuses and squids, possess three separate hearts that pump oxygen-rich, blue-colored blood throughout their bodies.

Ⓒ Cephalopods, a class of animals that includes octopuses and squids possess three separate hearts that pump oxygen-rich blue-colored blood throughout their bodies.

Ⓓ Cephalopods a class of animals that includes octopuses and squids possess three separate hearts that pump oxygen-rich, blue-colored blood throughout their bodies.

# Application

## How the Application Works

This section teaches students how to take the skills they've just reviewed in the Groundwork and apply them to a question very similar to what they will see on the TSIA2.

Every chapter has the same basic structure to the Application. There is an Approach, which is a prescribed set of steps that students will take to answer the question. These steps are designed to offer a straightforward guide to solving most of the items that test the lesson's standard. We've written them to be as simple as possible, serving more as a reminder for students than an exhaustive set of instructions.

The Approach models how strong test-takers attempt standardized tests. It's a decision-making framework that will eventually become second nature for your students. However, your strongest test-takers may have trouble with it because it is akin to making a pro basketball player overanalyze the way they shoot free throws. They are already doing it right, just so quickly and naturally that they don't even notice. For these students, it's okay if they simply use the Approach as a guideline instead of mentally clicking through the steps.

Unless students are having massive difficulties with a standard, they should not be tasked to memorize these steps. Instead, they should use them as guides as they answer the questions in the chapter. That way, students will have the opportunity to internalize the procedure and make it their own.

1. **Elimination-Focused**

   With some exceptions, students should stay elimination-focused on the TSIA2 ELAR test. It is much easier to find the right answer after you have eliminated a choice or two. Usually, it's much clearer when an answer is wrong than when it is right. If students intentionally try to make eliminations whenever the right answer doesn't jump out at them, they will be much less frustrated by the test, and their scores will improve.

2. **Sample Question**

   We always include two practice questions along with the teacher dialogue to illustrate the steps of the Approach to your students. These will appear back-to-back in the Application section.

# TSIA2 Mastery Features

STUDENT WORKBOOK

## Application

### THE APPROACH

When answering a short passage question on the TSIA2, use these steps ...

1 
1. Read the question first.
2. Read the passage.
3. Find your evidence.
4. Use the process of elimination.

**Passage**

In 2012, volunteers for "Let's Do It! World," a worldwide movement to combat the global solid waste problem, planned a six-month series of cleanups around the globe. These "cleanup days" occurred in 96 different countries, including Estonia, Lebanon, Nepal, and the Philippines. Slovenia's cleanup day was the largest that year, with over 289,000 participants. The tradition is gaining momentum, and on February 9, 2014, country cleanup leaders from around the world agreed to the goal of involving 380 million people by 2018.

2 
1. The passage suggests that the main goal of the cleanup days was to encourage people to

Ⓐ spend more time in nature
Ⓑ volunteer for meaningful causes
Ⓒ commit to making a cleaner planet
Ⓓ travel to neighboring countries

## Strategy Chapters

### The Strategy Approach

Just like with a content chapter that focuses on a TSIA2 assessed standard, our strategy chapters also include a prescribed set of steps to help students answer a variety of question types. Some chapters, like the one shown here, focus on a question type unique to the TSIA2. Others offer students test-taking skills that can help them work through questions they may be struggling with.

1. **Strategy Procedure**
   Each strategy begins with an outline of the technique or concept discussed.

2. **Example Question**
   The practice question will align with a content chapter's standard, but the accompanying dialogue will not use a typical approach to the question. Instead, the discussion will revolve around the steps offered in the procedure.

# TSIA2 Mastery Features

STUDENT WORKBOOK

**Chapter 12:** Trap Answers

## Practice

SLIDE 108.1

1 *Give students 10 minutes to complete the practice set.*

SLIDE 108.2

1. **The correct answer is D.** Choice A is incorrect because it is an example of recycled words, using words like *reasonable* and *fair* to make it seem appealing. Choice B is incorrect because it is an outlier; benefits for local governments are not mentioned in either passage. Choice C is incorrect because it is a distractor. Though it seems possible that the author of Passage 2 would not agree with the author of Passage 1, there is no evidence to support the idea that the author of Passage 2 thinks the opposing author is purposely *distorting and exaggerating* their information. Choice D is correct because the author of Passage 2 explains how the equal tolling of drivers would be more challenging for *the lower earner*, who would have a more difficult time budgeting *$50 each month* to account for their driving needs, a fact that is unacknowledged in Passage 1.

SLIDE 108.3

2 

2. **The correct answer is C.** Choice A is incorrect because it is a distractor. The author does not specifically compare toll roads to non-toll roads. Choice B is incorrect because it contains recycled words, such as *small, equal fee* and *budget*. Choice D is incorrect because it is an outlier. The passage does not discuss the happiness of drivers in correlation to shorter commutes. Choice C is correct because the passage explains how *those who drive the most pay the most because they use the road more frequently*, which supports the idea that the cost of repairs is being spread equally among all drivers.

108b

## **Strategy** (continued)

1. **Strategy Practice**

   Strategy chapters contain practice sets, though the questions' assessed standard will vary. This is useful for students because it mirrors the varied nature of questions on the TSIA2. Students will independently apply the strategy learned to three additional practice items.

2. **Strategy Practice Explanations**

   Just as in content chapter explanations, the explanations for strategy practice questions are essential instructional content. They closely follow the procedure or concept of the lesson and help you guide students through the process.

   Some strategies can't get students all the way to the correct answer, and that's okay. The focus should be on making eliminations. That way, if students are unable to isolate a single correct answer, they have given themselves much better odds of getting it right with a guess.

# TSIA2 Mastery Features

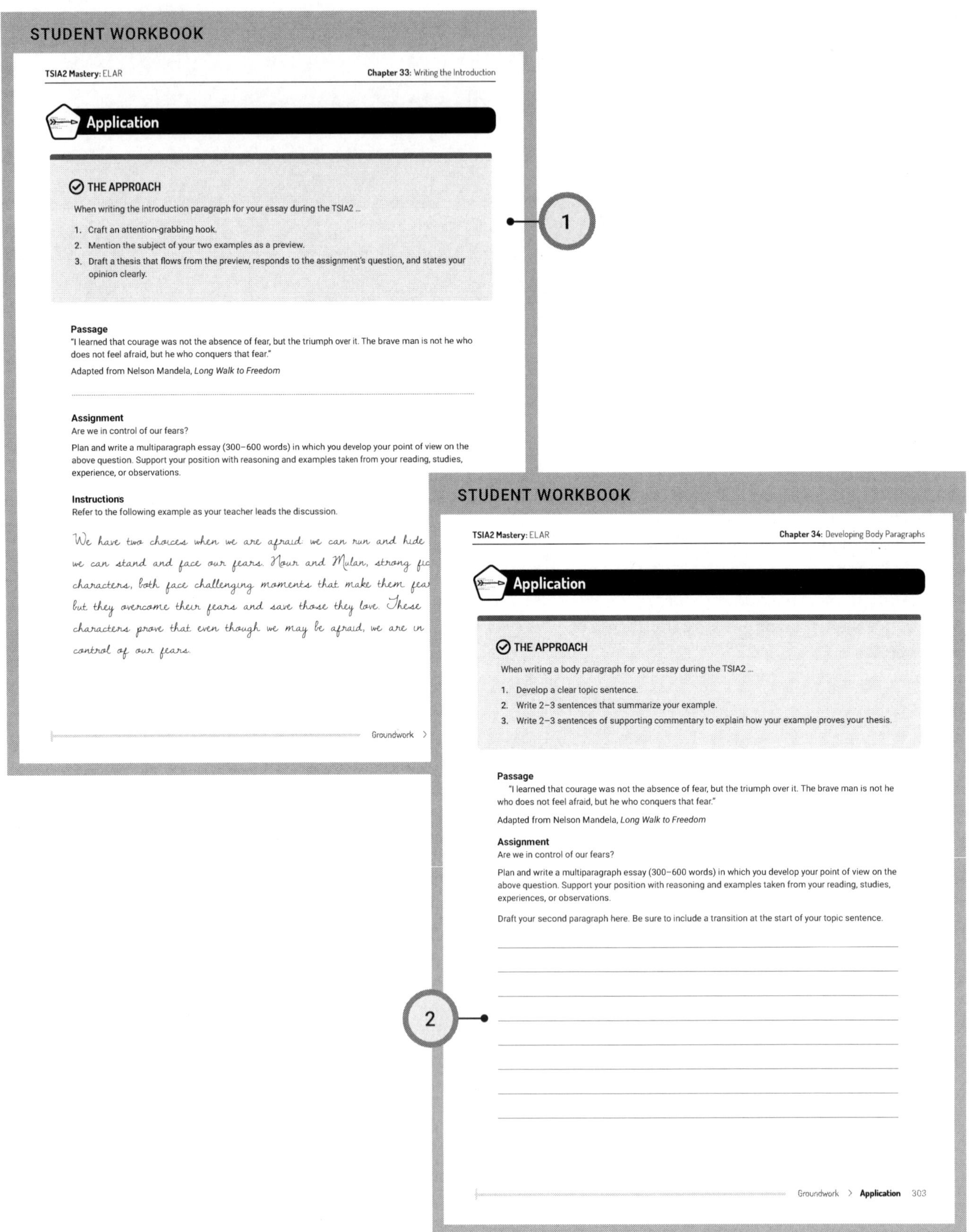
STUDENT WORKBOOK
TSIA2 Mastery: ELAR
Chapter 33: Writing the Introduction
Application
THE APPROACH
When writing the introduction paragraph for your essay during the TSIA2 ...
1. Craft an attention-grabbing hook.
2. Mention the subject of your two examples as a preview.
3. Draft a thesis that flows from the preview, responds to the assignment's question, and states your opinion clearly.
Passage
"I learned that courage was not the absence of fear, but the triumph over it. The brave man is not he who does not feel afraid, but he who conquers that fear."
Adapted from Nelson Mandela, Long Walk to Freedom
Assignment
Are we in control of our fears?
Plan and write a multiparagraph essay (300–600 words) in which you develop your point of view on the above question. Support your position with reasoning and examples taken from your reading, studies, experience, or observations.
Instructions
Refer to the following example as your teacher leads the discussion.
We have two choices when we are afraid: we can run and hide
we can stand and face our fears. Nour and Mulan, strong
characters, both face challenging moments that make them
but they overcome their fears and save those they love. These
characters prove that even though we may be afraid, we are in
control of our fears.
Groundwork
1
STUDENT WORKBOOK
TSIA2 Mastery: ELAR
Chapter 34: Developing Body Paragraphs
Application
THE APPROACH
When writing a body paragraph for your essay during the TSIA2 ...
1. Develop a clear topic sentence.
2. Write 2–3 sentences that summarize your example.
3. Write 2–3 sentences of supporting commentary to explain how your example proves your thesis.
Passage
"I learned that courage was not the absence of fear, but the triumph over it. The brave man is not he who does not feel afraid, but he who conquers that fear."
Adapted from Nelson Mandela, Long Walk to Freedom
Assignment
Are we in control of our fears?
Plan and write a multiparagraph essay (300–600 words) in which you develop your point of view on the above question. Support your position with reasoning and examples taken from your reading, studies, experiences, or observations.
Draft your second paragraph here. Be sure to include a transition at the start of your topic sentence.
2
Groundwork > Application 303

## **Strategy** (continued)

This ELAR book also contains a unique sequence of chapters that provide instruction on how to write an essay for the TSIA2. These chapters contain only a Groundwork and Application section.

### I Do, We Do, You Do

The Essay can be one of the most challenging sections of the TSIA2, especially for reluctant writers. Our chapters focus on building confidence through evaluating example essay elements, developing skills with engaging exercises, and leveraging positive and constructive feedback via peer reviews. Each lesson focuses on a provided example, a guided drafting process, and opportunities for solo writing.

1. **Not Just Writing**
   Students also learn strategies and exercises that help them understand the theory and best practices behind writing and editing a standardized essay for the TSIA2.

2. **Writing Space**
   Because the TSIA2 is a computer-based test, a more authentic practice experience would utilize a word processing program of some kind. However, we know that this is not feasible for every school. We have included space for students to write their essay elements in every chapter, so if computers are unavailable, students still have everything they need to complete their writing directly in their workbooks.

# TSIA2 Mastery Features

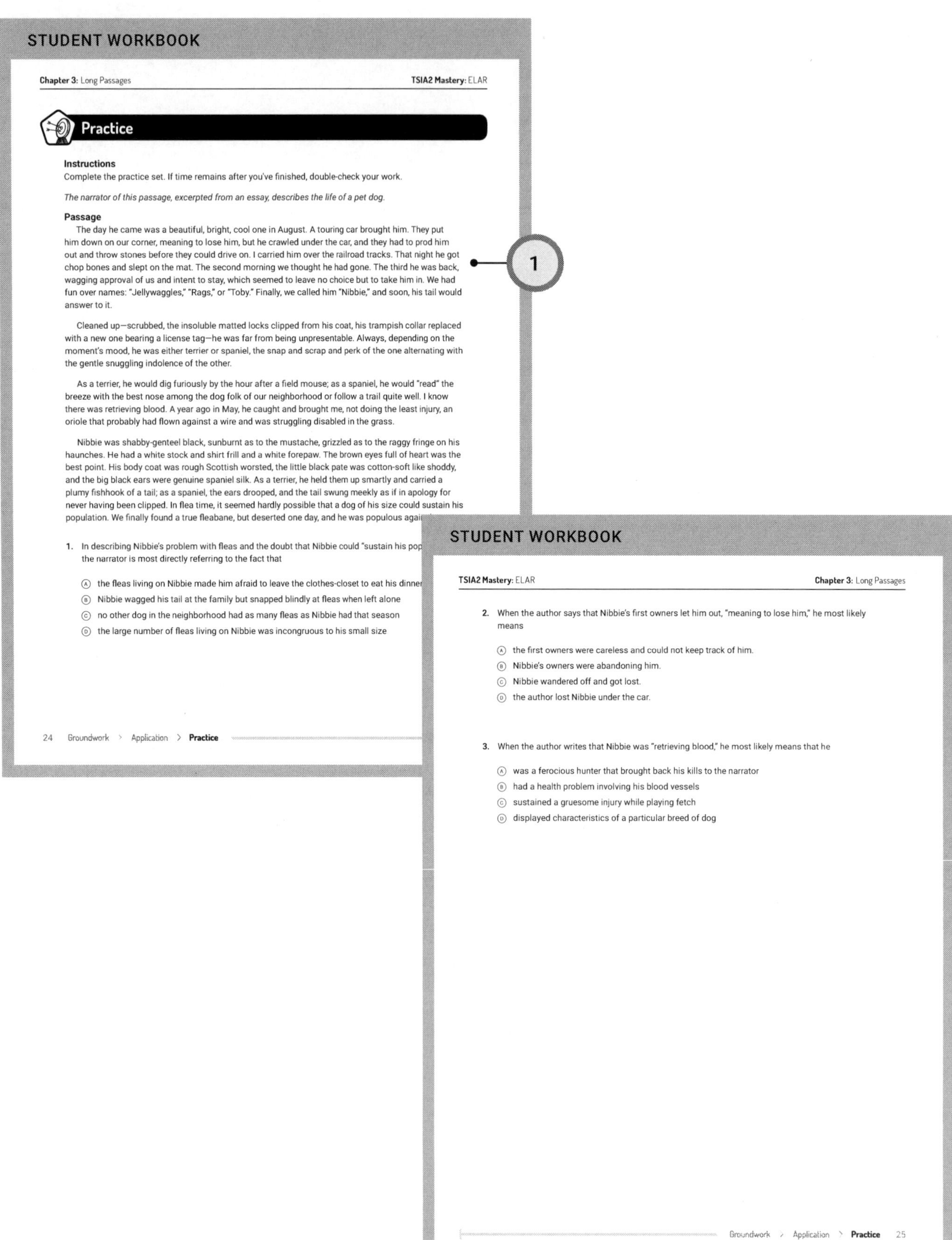

STUDENT WORKBOOK

**Chapter 3:** Long Passages | **TSIA2 Mastery:** ELAR

**Practice**

**Instructions**
Complete the practice set. If time remains after you've finished, double-check your work.

*The narrator of this passage, excerpted from an essay, describes the life of a pet dog.*

**Passage**

The day he came was a beautiful, bright, cool one in August. A touring car brought him. They put him down on our corner, meaning to lose him, but he crawled under the car, and they had to prod him out and throw stones before they could drive on. I carried him over the railroad tracks. That night he got chop bones and slept on the mat. The second morning we thought he had gone. The third he was back, wagging approval of us and intent to stay, which seemed to leave no choice but to take him in. We had fun over names: "Jellywaggles," "Rags," or "Toby." Finally, we called him "Nibbie," and soon, his tail would answer to it.

Cleaned up—scrubbed, the insoluble matted locks clipped from his coat, his trampish collar replaced with a new one bearing a license tag—he was far from being unpresentable. Always, depending on the moment's mood, he was either terrier or spaniel, the snap and scrap and perk of the one alternating with the gentle snuggling indolence of the other.

As a terrier, he would dig furiously by the hour after a field mouse; as a spaniel, he would "read" the breeze with the best nose among the dog folk of our neighborhood or follow a trail quite well. I know there was retrieving blood. A year ago in May, he caught and brought me, not doing the least injury, an oriole that probably had flown against a wire and was struggling disabled in the grass.

Nibbie was shabby-genteel black, sunburnt as to the mustache, grizzled as to the raggy fringe on his haunches. He had a white stock and shirt frill and a white forepaw. The brown eyes full of heart was the best point. His body coat was rough Scottish worsted, the little black pate was cotton-soft like shoddy, and the big black ears were genuine spaniel silk. As a terrier, he held them up smartly and carried a plumy fishhook of a tail; as a spaniel, the ears drooped, and the tail swung meekly as if in apology for never having been clipped. In flea time, it seemed hardly possible that a dog of his size could sustain his population. We finally found a true fleabane, but deserted one day, and he was populous agai…

1. In describing Nibbie's problem with fleas and the doubt that Nibbie could "sustain his pop… the narrator is most directly referring to the fact that

   Ⓐ the fleas living on Nibbie made him afraid to leave the clothes-closet to eat his dinne…
   Ⓑ Nibbie wagged his tail at the family but snapped blindly at fleas when left alone
   Ⓒ no other dog in the neighborhood had as many fleas as Nibbie had that season
   Ⓓ the large number of fleas living on Nibbie was incongruous to his small size

24 Groundwork > Application > **Practice**

1

STUDENT WORKBOOK

**TSIA2 Mastery:** ELAR | **Chapter 3:** Long Passages

2. When the author says that Nibbie's first owners let him out, "meaning to lose him," he most likely means

   Ⓐ the first owners were careless and could not keep track of him.
   Ⓑ Nibbie's owners were abandoning him.
   Ⓒ Nibbie wandered off and got lost.
   Ⓓ the author lost Nibbie under the car.

3. When the author writes that Nibbie was "retrieving blood," he most likely means that he

   Ⓐ was a ferocious hunter that brought back his kills to the narrator
   Ⓑ had a health problem involving his blood vessels
   Ⓒ sustained a gruesome injury while playing fetch
   Ⓓ displayed characteristics of a particular breed of dog

Groundwork > Application > **Practice** 25

## Practice Questions and Exercises

In TSIA2 Mastery, students learn by doing. Not only do students participate by answering questions via dialogue, but nearly every workbook page also requires students to answer questions or complete exercises.

Unlike all of the other practice questions in the chapter, questions in the Groundwork section break the TSIA2 mold. They are often quite similar to TSIA2 questions, but they have been modified to align with the instructional goals of the section.

## Practice Sets

### How Practice Sets Work

After each Application section, we provide a practice set of three emulations of TSIA2 items related to the standards in the chapter. Test-aligned practice is the key to score improvement on the TSIA2.

1. **Passages**

   The TSIA2 utilizes three passage types: long passages, dual passages, and short passages (see the chapters titled as such for more details). The number of passages in a practice set depends on the passage type. Long passages will appear individually, and all three questions of the practice set will relate to that passage. Dual passages and short passages are accompanied by a single question in the same way the TSIA2 presents them. The result is a more authentic practice experience.

   Writing questions are accompanied by either an essay, which mirrors the length of long passages, or a single sentence. We pair the questions of the practice set with a passage length that is most often used with the lesson's standard.

Note: Most passage content is made up. Many of the citations are fictional, and stated facts should not be relied upon.

### Warm-Ups and Wrap-Ups vs. Practice Sets

Practice sets are very similar to the warm-up and wrap-up, though the practice set contains three times as many questions.

There is one other catch. Warm-ups and wrap-ups have been calibrated to match one another. They repeat similar item variants at the same difficulty level (to enable pre- and post-test comparison). Practice sets, however, try to introduce students to all the ways the TSIA2 can test the standard. This means that you cannot directly compare performance on the practice sets to the warm-up and wrap-up scores. It's not apples-to-apples. If a student gets the warm-up question wrong but gets two questions right on the practice set, it doesn't necessarily mean they are doing better.

### Isolation

Unlike the TSIA2, in which a question about main idea, for example, will be interspersed with questions about unrelated topics, our practice sets are isolated to one standard. This helps students develop pattern recognition and zero in on the proper steps for problem solving.

# TSIA2 Mastery Features

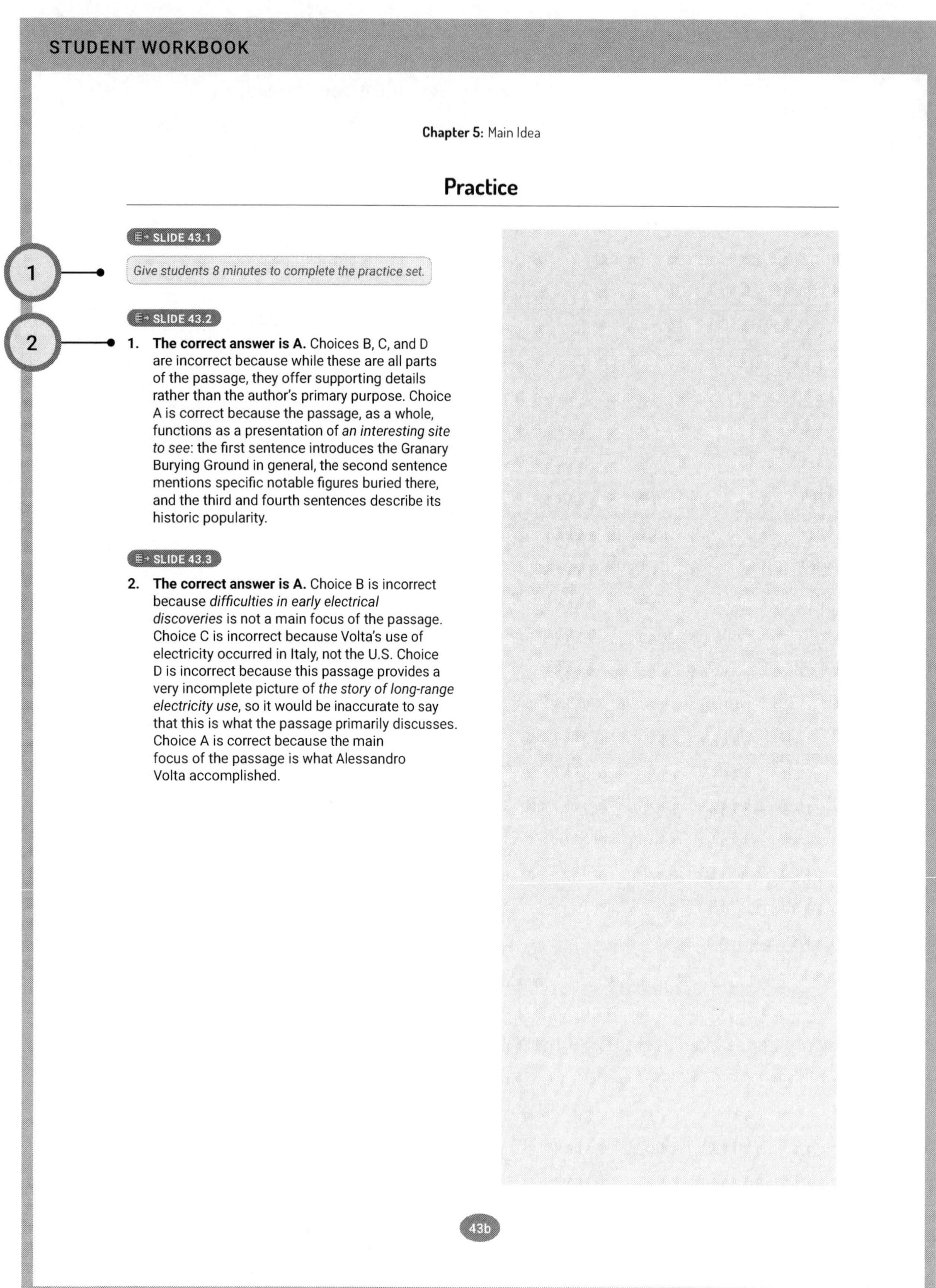

STUDENT WORKBOOK

**Chapter 5:** Main Idea

## Practice

SLIDE 43.1

1 Give students 8 minutes to complete the practice set.

SLIDE 43.2

2 1. **The correct answer is A.** Choices B, C, and D are incorrect because while these are all parts of the passage, they offer supporting details rather than the author's primary purpose. Choice A is correct because the passage, as a whole, functions as a presentation of *an interesting site to see*: the first sentence introduces the Granary Burying Ground in general, the second sentence mentions specific notable figures buried there, and the third and fourth sentences describe its historic popularity.

SLIDE 43.3

2. **The correct answer is A.** Choice B is incorrect because *difficulties in early electrical discoveries* is not a main focus of the passage. Choice C is incorrect because Volta's use of electricity occurred in Italy, not the U.S. Choice D is incorrect because this passage provides a very incomplete picture of *the story of long-range electricity use*, so it would be inaccurate to say that this is what the passage primarily discusses. Choice A is correct because the main focus of the passage is what Alessandro Volta accomplished.

43b

## Practice Sets (continued)

1. **Timing**

   Though the TSIA2 is not timed, we still want students to build an internal motivator when working through questions to avoid stagnation and loss of focus. To encourage this momentum-building skill, we've included recommended time limits for practice sets. Students should aim to answer the questions within that provided time period, but if class time allows, give students the opportunity to work until they have answered everything at their own pace. The goal is to ensure students are actively working on the practice set questions and maintaining their focus and momentum without rushing or picking an answer at random.

2. **Answer Explanations**

   Every question comes with a detailed answer explanation.

   Reviewing the explanations of the answers is an integral part of the program. As you review, consider alternating between showing students the solution paths (I do), asking students to guide you through the solutions (we do), and selecting students to explain their answers (you do).

   Also, as you work through the explanations, look for opportunities to point out trap answers and common errors. Careless errors can destroy otherwise strong scores.

### Gauging Performance

Just like with the warm-up, get a show of fingers at the end of each practice set to see how students are doing. Rather than giving a thumbs up or down, have them hold up 0, 1, 2, or 3 fingers to indicate how many they answered correctly.

### Implementation

To increase engagement, ask if anyone used what they just learned to get a question right. Have students share what they did. Students renew their interest when they see peers earn extra points as a result of the class.

# TSIA2 Mastery Features

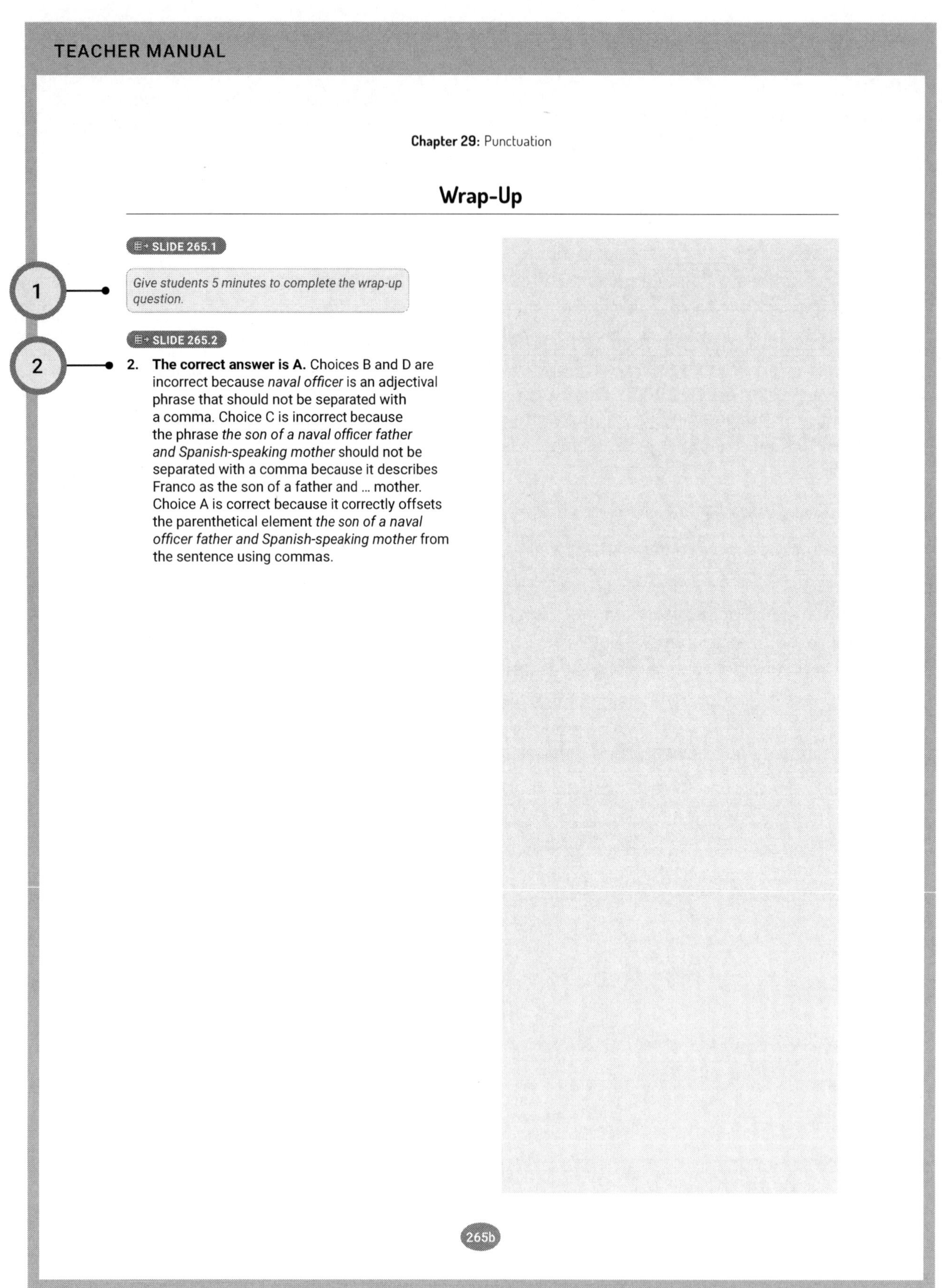
TEACHER MANUAL
**Chapter 29:** Punctuation
Wrap-Up
SLIDE 265.1
1
Give students 5 minutes to complete the wrap-up question.
SLIDE 265.2
2
2. **The correct answer is A.** Choices B and D are incorrect because *naval officer* is an adjectival phrase that should not be separated with a comma. Choice C is incorrect because the phrase *the son of a naval officer father and Spanish-speaking mother* should not be separated with a comma because it describes Franco as the son of a father and ... mother. Choice A is correct because it correctly offsets the parenthetical element *the son of a naval officer father and Spanish-speaking mother* from the sentence using commas.
265b

# Wrap-Up

## How the Wrap-Up Works

The wrap-up parallels the warm-up. Both provide a unique TSIA2 practice question of the same type and difficulty level. This way, you can make an apples-to-apples comparison to gauge the effectiveness of your lesson and determine if you need to provide students with additional support.

### 1. Time Limits

Just like with the warm-up, the time limit is only a suggestion. If class time allows, give students the opportunity to work through the question at their own pace. If time limits are enforced, ensure that you do so with both the warm-up and the wrap-up so the comparison of scores remains valid.

### 2. Explanations

Unlike the warm-up, you should spend some time on the explanations if several of your students struggled to answer the question. This is your last chance to hammer out any confusion before you move on to the next lesson.

## Wrap-Up Data Analysis

There are two ways in which you can use the wrap-up data. First, use it for class-level analysis, day by day.

Compare the total number of students who answered correctly in the warm-up to the total number of students who answered correctly in the wrap-up. This will provide you with a rough estimate of progress.

Alternatively, use it for student-level analysis, week by week.

You can also look at an individual student's data, with this proviso: always compare at least five lessons at a time. Compare their warm-up accuracy to their wrap-up accuracy to get an approximate idea of the student's progress in this subject.

We do not advise that you use a single warm-up/wrap-up pair to measure one student's progress. Guessing effects, mistakes, and slight fluctuations in question difficulty and passage complexity can obfuscate progress. One day of work from one student is too small a sample size to be meaningful.

## Measuring Improvement

We recommend that you set specific performance improvement goals for each lesson as a part of your planning. A good general goal in each chapter is to improve the average number of students answering correctly by 20%. For example, if 40% of the students answer the warm-up question correctly, then the default goal is for 60% of the class to answer the wrap-up question correctly. If you start with 20% of the class answering correctly, then the goal is 40%.

This is, of course, a very broad guideline. Depending on the standard and the class's ability level, a more moderate or more aggressive growth goal may be appropriate.

## Additional Supports

If your class did not make progress, consider revisiting any content skipped in the lesson. If you completed the lesson in its entirety, consider going to our support page (masteryprep.com/support) for TSIA2 Mastery to see if we have any additional resources recommended for this subject or to request them if they aren't available.

# How to Use TSIA2 Mastery

TSIA2 Mastery's modular design means that you can use it in a way that fits your schedule and resources. Here are some common delivery models.

## Half-Credit Course

Deliver TSIA2 Mastery as a half-credit elective. One teacher provides the entire program, or two specialists alternate nine weeks (one specializing in math, the other in ELAR and writing).

To allow for adaptivity, TSIA2 Mastery provides enough content to be selective during a one-semester course. Depending on your pace, you may also need to omit certain lessons in their entirety. On a typical block schedule, a single lesson will likely fill a class period if all elements are implemented. With a standard 55-minute schedule, a single lesson can either be truncated to fit or divided into two separate days of work.

## Core Class Enrichment

Provide TSIA2 Mastery as an enrichment resource in your class. Every chapter, and each section of every chapter, is completely modular. Pick and choose resources as you please.

Select chapters that cover similar content to what you plan on teaching. Use the practice sets to provide additional practice on essential skills.

If you find your students are missing some fundamentals, Groundwork sections can provide a quick review.

Warm-ups and wrap-ups can be repurposed as classroom entrance and exit tickets.

Some teachers like to carve out 30 minutes each week for a TSIA2 Mastery lesson. Doing this, you can get through the entire program (abridged) in a school year.

## Homeroom/Study Hall/Enrichment Period

Use TSIA2 Mastery as the main instructional resource for your homeroom period, study hall, or enrichment time.

Our main advice here is to avoid trying to jam too much into any one period. Select a practice set, or the Application, or even the Groundwork, and focus on just that one element.

Consider teaming up with other teachers and trading classes so that math specialists can focus on their strengths and ELAR teachers can cover their own content areas.

Schools that have adopted our curricula for their flex periods report that the structure helps teachers get a lot more done during that time and reduces the burden of teacher planning. Having a program to progress through helps students avoid feeling like they're doing busy work.

If you provide TSIA2 Mastery during the school day, we recommend that you tie participation to grades if possible.

## Grading One-Semester Classes

Most teachers use a mix of participation, wrap-up, and practice set performance to determine classroom grades.

Performance goals or curves should always be oriented around personal growth. The goal in a TSIA2 Mastery course is not to reach a class-wide cutoff score, but rather to end up with a higher score than where you started. To simplify grading, you may want to group batches of students by their starting TSIA2 scores, as they'll have similar personal growth goals. From a performance growth perspective, an increase of just 1 point should warrant an A grade.

Due to the nature of the TSIA2 and the goals of a prep course, much of the grade is subjective and hinges on the question, "Is this student giving it their best shot?" For more tips on discerning this, visit our support page at masteryprep.com/support.

## Grading Flex Periods

Schools have more success with implementing TSIA2 Mastery in flex periods such as homeroom when they tie participation to grades. This can get very complicated very quickly, since the flex period usually doesn't have its own grade on the report card, and all sorts of work can go into sharing grading information with students' core teachers.

The most elegant solution we've come across for this is to provide the teachers running the flex periods with bonus coupons (assuming your school allows for bonus points). Students who participate get the coupons. They can then use them in their related classes. Those same classes, of course, decrease the amount of bonus work otherwise available so that grade inflation doesn't occur.

Another way to do this, avoiding the bonus point route, is to have the TSIA2 Mathematics work for each semester count as one math test in the students' class that semester, and the same for the TSIA2 ELAR work for the students' English class. In this way, you're only sharing two grades per semester but still accomplishing the grading tie-in.

## Grading Integrated Coursework

Due to the wide variety of ways you can integrate TSIA2 Mastery into your class, it's difficult to make hard and fast recommendations in this scenario. However, you may want to consider counting TSIA2 Mastery as a test grade and deriving that grade from a balance of personal score growth and participation.

## Retesting

The TSIA2 allows students to take and retake the test as often as they would like. They are testing to hit a benchmark, and once they do for a subject, they earn a passing score for the test. Additionally, on subsequent testing periods, they may opt to take only one portion of the test. For example, if a student passes the ELAR section, they can take just the math section the next time they take the TSIA2. Students can test throughout the year and improve their performance grade, and only their best performance should count for their grade, since they only have to meet a minimum benchmark in order to be considered college ready.

If a student chooses to retest, it is highly recommended that they wait at least three days between testing periods. During that time, they should review the standards where they often struggle and reflect on their experiences to determine if there is anything regarding their mental stamina they need to improve.

## CHAPTER 1

# An Introduction to the TSIA2

In this chapter, students will become familiar with the characteristics of the TSIA2 and its rules. Additionally, they will review and evaluate several strategies that can be used to optimize their time and mental energy during their test.

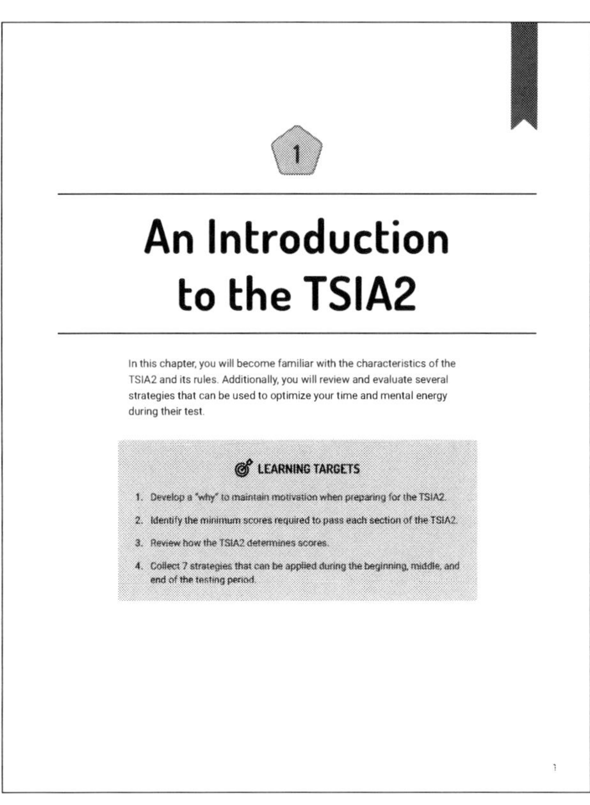

1

An Introduction to the TSIA2

In this chapter, you will become familiar with the characteristics of the TSIA2 and its rules. Additionally, you will review and evaluate several strategies that can be used to optimize your time and mental energy during their test.

LEARNING TARGETS

1. Develop a "why" to maintain motivation when preparing for the TSIA2.
2. Identify the minimum scores required to pass each section of the TSIA2.
3. Review how the TSIA2 determines scores.
4. Collect 7 strategies that can be applied during the beginning, middle, and end of the testing period.

1

## LEARNING TARGETS

1. Develop a "why" to maintain motivation when preparing for the TSIA2.
2. Identify the minimum scores required to pass each section of the TSIA2.
3. Review how the TSIA2 determines scores.
4. Collect 7 strategies that can be applied during the beginning, middle, and end of the testing period.

# Groundwork

EXERCISE A

**Instructions**
Review the following as your teacher leads the discussion. Then, respond to the prompt in the space provided.

Earning a passing score on the TSIA2 means ...

... more money.

... more time.

... being able to support yourself or your family.

... changing your life!

**1.** What is your "why" for doing well on the TSIA2?

______________________________

______________________________

______________________________

______________________________

______________________________

# Groundwork

*In this section, students will review the benefits of doing well on the TSIA2 and develop a personal reason why they want to pass their test.*

EXERCISE A SLIDE 2.1

**Welcome to TSIA2 Mastery. Throughout this course, we'll cover a lot. Lots of topics. Lots of test-taking skills. It's *a lot* to take in. These types of standardized tests are like a rite of passage for high school students, especially as they get ready for college. Show of hands: who thinks standardized tests are one of the best parts of high school?**

*Pause for a show of hands.*

**It's expected that most people will think these tests are pretty awful. And the TSIA2 is no exception. It's two grueling multiple-choice sections plus a full-length essay all in one go. But trust me when I say that this test is *not* the worst part of high school. In fact, it can be one of the best things you do in all four years. Why, you ask? Well, passing the TSIA2 can have positive effects that ripple throughout your lifetime. For instance, who likes money?**

*Pause for a show of hands.*

**The TSIA2 can both save you money and help you earn money. Essentially, if you pass the test, you get to skip the remedial courses at college and dive right into the college-level classes. If you're not paying for those extra remedial courses, you're saving money. How do you think the TSIA2 helps you *earn* money?**

It gets you into college, which can lead to a better paying job.

**Graduating with a college degree means that—in the course of your lifetime—you'll earn an average of 1 million dollars more than your peers who *don't* go to college. What else does the TSIA2 offer more of?**

Time.

**If you're not taking those extra remedial courses, it means more time to focus on the classes that will count toward your degree. That means fewer semesters until you graduate. How do you think that helps you better support yourself or your family?**

Getting through college faster means getting a better-paying job sooner.

**You see, this test is a game changer. Passing the test means starting out strong in your college career. And that degree? It leads to a better quality of life overall. People with college educations tend to have stronger marriages, feel happier and more fulfilled, and even live an average of 6–7 years longer than non-graduates. So, after learning all this, has anyone changed their mind? Who thinks the TSIA2 might not be so bad after all?**

*Pause for a show of hands.*

**Take a moment now to think about your "why." What's your motivation? What's driving you to do well on this exam? Write your answer in your workbook.**

*Give students 2 minutes to complete this task.*

EXERCISE B

**Instructions**
Fill in the blanks below as your teacher leads the discussion.

| Subject | Questions | Score | Passing Score |
|---|---|---|---|
| **English Language Arts and Reading** | | | |
| Multiple Choice | 30 | 910 to 990 | |
| Essay | 1 | 1 to 8 | |
| **Mathematics** | | | |
| Multiple Choice | 20 | 910 to 990 | |

## Groundwork

*In this section, students will review the minimum passing scores for each section of the test.*

EXERCISE B SLIDE 3.1

**The TSIA2 is broken into three sections, each one with its own characteristics and requirements. For instance, how many questions show up on the ELAR multiple-choice section?**

30.

**And how many on the math?**

20.

**Both of those sections have the same score range, between 910 and 990. How many points are *really* in play, though?**

80.

**Though the scores are in the 900s, there's really only a range of 80 points. Why do they do this?**

*Allow 1–2 students to offer suggestions.*

**The real answer? We don't know exactly why they score their test the way they do. Maybe they just enjoy being mysterious. All that matters is that you hit their minimum score for being "college ready." This test is pass or fail, so whether you blow the test out of the water and get a perfect score or barely pass by 1 point, colleges only see that final result: a passing score. Why is that a little bit of a relief for a lot of students?**

There's no pressure to get a perfect score.

**On the ELAR multiple-choice section, the passing score is a 945. And on the math, it's a 950. Write that down in your workbook. What about the essay, though? What's the score range for that section?**

1 to 8.

**Again, we're not sure where the 8 points came from. It's just their way of scoring essays, where a 1 is really low and an 8 is the perfect essay. To pass this section, you need a 5. What happens, though, if you *don't* pass a section? They won't kick you out of the test room if you miss the mark on one section. In fact, they won't even give you a non-passing score. You get a second chance to prove your skills in something called the diagnostic. Here's where things get a little wonky. Let's flip the page to learn more about the sequence of the test sections and when you should expect to see them.**

EXERCISE C

**Instructions**
Refer to the following diagram as your teacher leads the discussion.

### A Map of the TSIA2

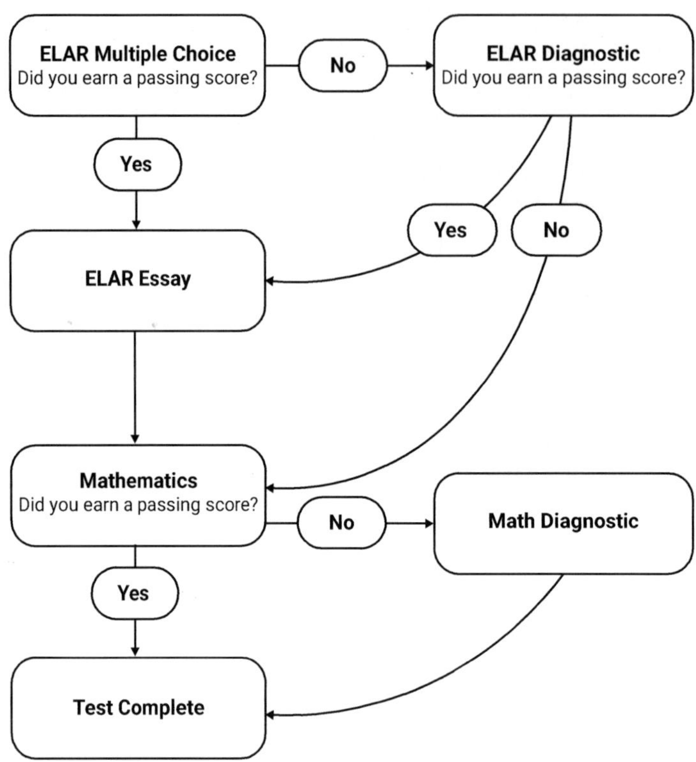

## Groundwork

*In this section, students will review the sequence of tests they may see based on how they perform on each section of the TSIA2.*

EXERCISE C SLIDE 4.1

**In my opinion, "diagnostic" is a misleading title. When would you expect something called *the diagnostic* to show up on the test?**

At the beginning.

**It sounds like it might come first, which is why a lot of people get confused about the sequence of the TSIA2. Think of it more as your second chance. For instance, if you miss the 945 mark on the ELAR test, you'll be given the ELAR diagnostic. No warning. No extra instructions. It just jumps from question 30 of the multiple-choice section to question 1 of the diagnostic. Why might this be discouraging?**

Seeing the ELAR diagnostic means you didn't pass yet.

**The key phrase is "you didn't pass *yet*." You can still earn a passing score on the diagnostic and pass the TSIA2 overall. What happens if you pass the ELAR diagnostic? Where do you go next?**

To the essay.

**The essay follows right on the heels of the ELAR test. When would you *not* get the chance to write the essay?**

If you didn't pass the ELAR diagnostic.

**What would you see instead?**

The Math section.

**The math section is the shortest sprint, with just 20 questions. If you do well and get a 950 on the Math test, where do you go?**

Nowhere, the test ends.

**And if you get below a 950?**

The Math diagnostic.

**The TSIA2 is a unique experience for everyone. Depending on how well you do on each piece, you might see three sections of the test, or you might see as many as five. And the questions that show up will be unique as well. It's not like the SAT, where everyone gets the same question. How can the TSIA2 do that? What about the test format gives them that flexibility?**

The TSIA2 is taken on a computer.

**The TSIA2 is known as an *adaptive* test, meaning that it gives you questions based on how you answered the ones that came before. It tries to understand you, to get to know where your strengths and weaknesses lie. That means you'll likely get a whole different set of questions than your fellow test-takers.**

TSIA2 Mastery: ELAR 

EXERCISE D

**Instructions**

Draw a line to match each situation to the effect it will have on a person's score as they take a computer-adaptive test.

1. If a student answers several questions correctly,
2. If a student answers several questions incorrectly,
3. If a student answers a single question incorrectly,
4. If a student wants to go back and change an answer,

A. their score may dip slightly.

B. the questions will become more difficult.

C. they should click the "back" button.

D. it's too late. The TSIA2 does not allow students to revisit questions they've already answered.

E. their score will go down more dramatically.

## Groundwork

*In this section, students will review the basic characteristics of a computer-adaptive test.*

EXERCISE D SLIDE 5.1

**An adaptive test's one and only goal is to figure out which skills you have and which ones you don't. For instance, perhaps it will offer up a question that asks you to make an inference about a passage. If you answer it correctly, what does that tell the system?**

That you know how to make inferences.

**Yes, and no. An adaptive test is a skeptic. It'll wonder if you *actually* know how to make an inference or if you just guessed right. What do you think it'll do next?**

Give another question about inferences.

**It probably won't give you two questions in a row on the same topic, but it *will* give you opportunities to prove that you have certain skills. What do you think happens to your score as you answer lots of questions correctly?**

Your score will go up.

**And what will happen to the difficulty level of the questions?**

They'll get harder.

**The test wants to push you to your limits to figure out what you know. So if you're getting all the questions right, it's going to give you more challenging stuff. What will happen to your score if you get just one or two questions wrong?**

It'll drop.

**Getting a question wrong isn't a deal breaker. You can get quite a few wrong and still pass the test. However, order matters. If you miss several in a row, what do you think will happen to your score?**

It'll go down a lot.

**Essentially, get questions right to see your score go up and the questions get harder. Missing questions means your score will go down and the questions will get easier. What happens if you change your mind about a question and want to go back to change your answer?**

You can't. The test won't let you.

**Because of the way an adaptive test works, you can't go back and revisit old questions. Once you submit it, that's it. How does this change the way you answer questions on test day?**

We need to be extra sure before we submit our answer.

**The test is untimed, so you can sit and waffle and debate all you want. Don't rush into an answer because you won't be able to come back to it later to check your work. Only click to continue if you're happy with what you've chosen.**

## Application

### THE APPROACH

**At the beginning of the test, you should ...**

1. focus on the early questions.
2. prepare to start with a medium question.

**During the middle of the test, you should not ...**

3. stress if the questions get harder.
4. overthink because you may just be prepared.

**As you get closer to the end of the test, you should ...**

5. finish strong.
6. take more mental breaks to avoid getting tired.

**During the TSIA2, you should never ...**

7. panic!
8. give up if the test gets hard.
9. give up if the questions seem easy.

# Application

*In this section, students will review 6 strategies that can help them be successful as they take the TSIA2.*

SLIDE 6.1

**Don't let the adaptive features of the TSIA2 get you feeling bogged down, though. We may not know *exactly* what you'll see on test day, but we have a pretty good idea, which means we can create a game plan to help guide us. For instance, getting questions right or wrong at the beginning of the test swings your score more than the ones at the end. What does that mean for the beginning of the test?**

We should focus on the early questions.

**It's super important to get those first few questions right. How hard do you think those first questions will be?**

Medium difficulty.

**The test won't bring out the beastly questions until you've gotten a few right, but they won't go too easy on you either. Expect those first questions to be of medium difficulty. As you get to the middle of the test, should you stress if the questions seem really hard?**

No.

**Why not?**

Harder questions mean we've been getting questions right.

**What if they seem really easy? Should you be worried?**

No.

**Why not?**

We might just be prepared.

**A question that seems really easy to you might be really hard for someone else. It doesn't necessarily mean you're getting questions wrong. It might just be that you've prepped really well for test day. What kinds of things should we do as the end of the test approaches?**

Finish strong and take mental breaks.

**Even though those last questions won't have as big of an impact on your score as the first ones, missing two or three in a row could mean missing the passing score by just a few points. Stay focused, and if you feel tired, take a mental break. You have plenty of time to give your brain a little rest so that you can give your best effort on every questions. What are we *not* going to do on test day?**

Panic or give up.

**At the end of the day, this is just a test. In fact, it's a test you can take more than once if you don't pass the first time. It's definitely not make-or-break, so do your best to relax and focus. If you prepare yourself well throughout this course, you'll do just fine.**

**Instructions**

Determine whether each strategy would be helpful during the TSIA2. Put a check mark next to the strategies that you should use.

______ Take mental breaks if I feel tired or bored.

______ Go to sleep in the middle of the test.

______ Reread every question at least 20 times.

______ Change all of my answers after I've picked them.

______ Keep focused and push through to the next question as soon as I'm happy with my answer.

## Application

*In this section, students will evaluate several strategies and determine whether they would be useful during the TSIA2.*

**Remind me: what's the time limit on the TSIA2?**

There is none.

**While your school may not let you camp out for several days to finish the test, you don't have a real time limit. Why is that a good thing?**

We aren't rushed.

**Is there a downside to this, though? What might go wrong if we take that endless time for granted?**

We could lose focus or momentum.

**While you don't want to rush through the test, you also want to avoid falling into the trap of moving so slowly that you come to a grinding halt. Stay active. Actively reading questions. Actively eliminating wrong answers. Actively take mental breaks. Everything you do should help you maximize the opportunity of not having a time limit without drifting into a place of no progress.**

SLIDE 7.1

**For example, do you think it would be a good idea to take a break if you're feeling tired or bored?**

Yes.

**If you're having those kinds of feelings, your brain is begging you to stop taking that test. Why not give in for a bit? Let yourself take a little mental vacation. Or, if you're at one of the testing sites that allows it, get up and go for a walk. Getting your blood flowing is a great way to re-energize. On the other hand, why might going to sleep be a bad strategy?**

It'll make you groggy.

**You might have plenty of time, but you don't have *that much* time. There are only so many hours in a day. And taking a nap will likely leave you less energized than before. What about rereading the question? Is that a good strategy to help us maximize our lack of a time limit?**

Yes.

**Should we do it 20 times?**

Definitely not.

**Rereading questions is great for making sure you understand what's being asked and that you've picked the right answer. But don't go into overdrive. Reading a question 20 times is enough to mentally drain even the strongest of test-takers. What about changing your answer a bunch of times? Is that a good strategy?**

No.

**A lot of times, your first instinct will be the right one. If you feel like you're unsure, don't pick answers at random. Go with your gut. Finally, what do you think about the last strategy? Does that seem like a good plan?**

Yes.

**Why do you think pushing yourself from one question to the next is a good idea?**

It keeps up your momentum.

**Just because we have a lot of time doesn't mean we need to use it all. If you've found your answer and you feel confident, keep pushing forward and stay focused on the task at hand.**

**Instructions**

Identify three things you can change to take ownership of your testing station.

1. ____________________

2. ____________________

3. ____________________

## Application

*In this section, students will review one final strategy that can help boost confidence as they begin the test.*

SLIDE 8.1

**I'm going to leave you with one last strategy for test day. And it has absolutely nothing to do with the actual test. But first, tell me about the way you organize your apps on your phone. Do you group them into folders? Does each screen have a theme or category? Do you just leave your apps in the order you downloaded them? Give me some insight into how you organize your phone.**

*Allow 2–3 students to share.*

**We all have our own preferences, it seems. And it's not just phones. We typically organize and rearrange our world to fit those preferences. Why do you think people like to do that with their stuff?**

It gives them a sense of ownership.

**It's like tailoring it to fit yourself, which makes it feel more comfortable. And we can use this to our advantage on test day. For instance, who says you can't adjust the monitor? Pull it closer so you can see better or push it back so you have more room to write on your scratch paper. What other things can you adjust?**

The seat height, if they're adjustable. Which side of the keyboard the mouse is on. How far away the keyboard is. Etc.

**You can also take in a few items that give you a little control. Maybe you prefer writing with pens or mechanical pencils, or you can bring in your favorite hoodie. Bring water to stay hydrated! Sure, there are some limitations, but in general, you can definitely give yourself a little more comfort and control in your testing environment. This strategy, along with the skills you'll learn in this course, is all you'll need to earn that passing score on the TSIA2.**

CHAPTER 2

# ELAR Orientation

In this chapter, students will learn the ins and outs of the English, Language Arts, and Reading portion of the TSIA2. They will become familiar with the structure and question pattern of the multiple-choice section, as well as gain insight into the rules of the test and minimum scores for passing.

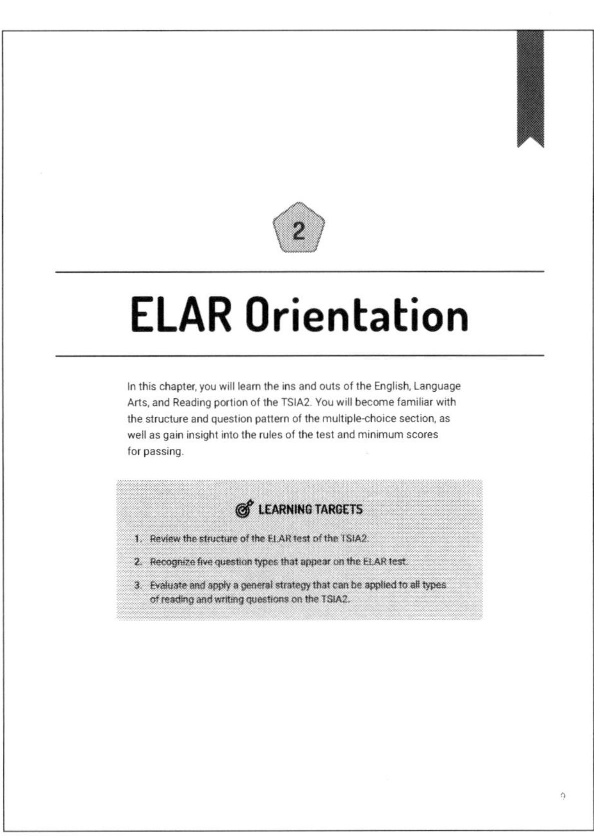

2

ELAR Orientation

In this chapter, you will learn the ins and outs of the English, Language Arts, and Reading portion of the TSIA2. You will become familiar with the structure and question pattern of the multiple-choice section, as well as gain insight into the rules of the test and minimum scores for passing.

LEARNING TARGETS

1. Review the structure of the ELAR test of the TSIA2.
2. Recognize five question types that appear on the ELAR test.
3. Evaluate and apply a general strategy that can be applied to all types of reading and writing questions on the TSIA2.

9

## LEARNING TARGETS

1. Review the structure of the ELAR test of the TSIA2.
2. Recognize the five question types that appear on the ELAR test.
3. Evaluate and apply a general strategy that can be applied to all types of reading and writing questions on the TSIA2.

## Groundwork

EXERCISE A

**Instructions**
Refer to the following chart as your teacher leads the discussion.

The English Language Arts and Reading (ELAR) portion of the test has 30 multiple-choice questions and an essay. The two areas of focus for the multiple-choice section of the ELAR test are:

| Reading Focus | |
|---|---|
| **Literary Text Analysis** | This category includes questions related to the broad concepts of purpose and point of view, as well as specific concepts such as drawing inferences, all in the context of a literary text. |
| **Informational Text Analysis and Synthesis** | This category includes organization, word choice, and other composition issues as it relates to an essay. |

| Writing Focus | |
|---|---|
| **Essay** | This category includes organization, word choice, and other composition issues as it relates to an essay. |
| **Sentence** | This category includes the conventions of standard written English grammar, punctuation, and spelling within the context of a single sentence. |

# Groundwork

*In this section, students will participate in a discussion about the topics covered on the TSIA2 ELAR test.*

**Show of hands: who enjoys learning about random topics, like the chemical structure of rice and corn or the history of cats in Medieval Europe?**

*Pause for a show of hands.*

**As weird as it sounds, the ELAR test of the TSIA2 is a little like getting lost in a Wikipedia rabbit hole, moving from one random topic to the next across several passages. To prep for this, should we study these kinds of random topics?**

No.

**Though these random topics will show up on the test, you don't actually need to know anything about them. You just need the strategies that'll help you tackle the questions.**

EXERCISE A · SLIDE 10.1

**Let's start by looking at what you *will* be tested on. There are two main focuses. What are they?**

Reading and Writing.

**Take a moment now to read through that chart.**

*Allow students 60 seconds to review the information.*

**Questions from the test will fall into one of those two categories, and it's a good idea to be able to tell the difference because we'll need different strategies for each focus type. For instance, if a question asks me about the main idea of a passage, is that a reading or writing focus?**

Reading.

**What about subject-verb agreement? What kind of focus is that?**

Writing.

**You'll also be tested on things like paragraph organization. What focus will that question type have?**

Writing.

**Comma usage?**

Writing.

**Finding a specific detail?**

Reading.

**Writing questions cover a lot of ground. You could be asked about anything from grammar and punctuation to the organization of a paragraph or details that develop a topic. On the other hand, Reading questions all tend to fall into one big category: reading comprehension. That means you don't have to know anything about what's in the passage. The answers are all right there on the screen! You just have to use your reading skills to find the right answer choice.**

EXERCISE B

**Instructions**
Refer to the following figure and fill in the blanks as your teacher leads the discussion.

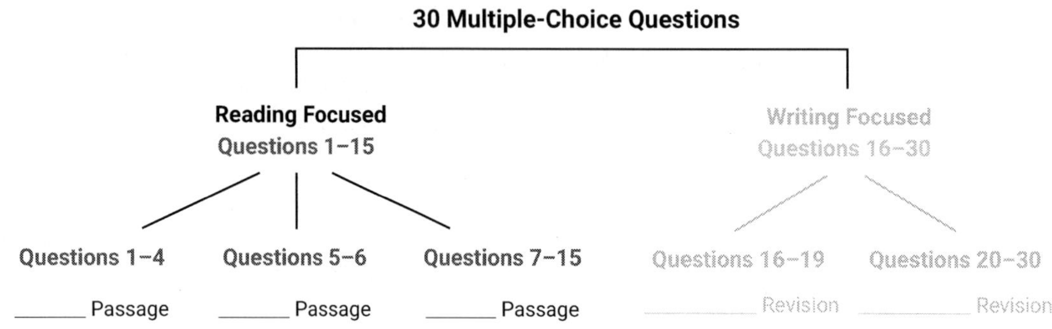

## Groundwork

*In this section, students will learn about the structure of the TSIA2 ELAR test.*

EXERCISE B SLIDE 11.1

**So, studying random topics is a no-go for prepping ourselves for this test. But, that doesn't mean there's *nothing* we can do. For instance, we can get to know the structure of the test. Why might that help us?**

We'll know what to expect on test day.

**If we take the element of surprise out of the test, it definitely gives us a head start. Let's start with the basics. How many multiple-choice questions will be on the ELAR portion of the test?**

30.

**Which focus category will appear first?**

Reading.

**The ELAR test won't just rapid-fire a random mix of Reading and Writing questions, which is good for us. Instead, it follows the same pattern every time, which means you'll always start with Reading questions. There's even a pattern within that focus. Questions 1 through 4 focus on a specific passage type called *long passages*. What do you think a long passage might look like?**

Long?

**The long passage is definitely longer than all the rest, usually about 5 to 8 paragraphs long in fact. And, it's always literary focused. What does that mean?**

It's from a story.

**You'll often see excerpts from classical stories, or it might be from something you've never heard of. Either way, questions 1 to 4 will all be pulled from that same passage. How does that help us?**

We only have to read one passage to get the answers for four questions.

**Always start with a good read-through of the passage. That way, you're prepared to take on the next three questions that go along with the long passage.**

**The next kind of passage we'll see is called a dual passage. Those will always be on questions 5 and 6. What does the word *dual* make you think of?**

Two. Or a fight.

**D-u-a-l means "two," while d-u-e-l means to fight. But, in essence, both of those answers are right. Dual passages will show up in pairs: two paragraphs with opposing ideas. They contrast each other, offering up opposite sides of an argument. What should we look for when we read these kinds of passages?**

Ways they're the same and ways they're different.

**Think of it like a compare-and-contrast assignment. Focus on where the authors agree and where they don't see eye to eye.**

**The last passage type runs from question 7 to question 15. They're known as short passages. Why do you think they're called that?**

They're shorter than the rest.

**These passages are typically made up of just one paragraph, some as short as two sentences! But, don't count them out. They make up the biggest portion of the Reading section, so there are lots of points to be earned.**

EXERCISE C

**Instructions**
Refer to the following figure and fill in the blanks as your teacher leads the discussion.

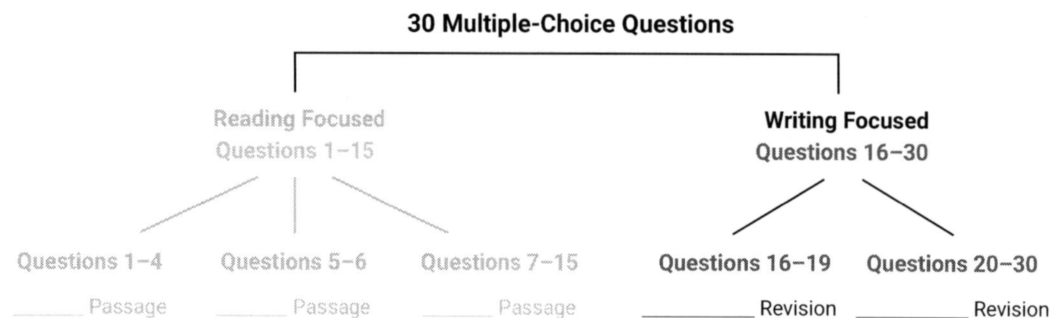

## Groundwork

*In this section, students will continue reviewing the structure of the TSIA2 ELAR test.*

EXERCISE C   SLIDE 12.1

**Reading only covers the R section of ELAR. What about ELA? The test promises to cover those kinds of topics, too. Where should you expect to see questions that test your writing skills?**

On questions 16 through 30.

**Though there are a lot more topics covered in the Writing portion, there are actually fewer types of Writing questions. How many types will you see?**

Two.

**The first type you'll see is called *essay revision*. What kind of passage or text do you think you'll be working with for those questions?**

An essay.

**The essay revision questions work a little like the long passages. There are four questions that go along with a single long passage or essay. Should we read the passage before we dive into the questions?**

No.

**A lot of times, Writing questions will focus on just a sentence or two, possibly even a section as large as a paragraph. Why should we read the question first, instead?**

It can tell us where to look.

**And knowing where to look helps us how?**

We won't waste time reading stuff we don't need.

**By focusing on the question first, we figure out what we need to find and where to find it. No need to waste a bunch of mental energy reading a passage full of information we likely won't even use.**

**The other kind of Writing question is called *sentence revision*. What kind of passage do you think you'll see with those questions?**

Sentences.

**They're small, but they pack a big punch in terms of your score. They make up a *third* of the entire ELAR section, so give them the effort they deserve. The question, now, is how to answer all these different question types.**

## Application

### THE APPROACH

When working on the ELAR portion of the TSIA2, use these steps to answer each question ...

1. Identify the question type.
2. Decode the question.
3. Pick a strategy.
4. Use the process of elimination.

**1.** To enter the tournament, the student or <u>teacher have to</u> pay $10, and all of the proceeds go to help children with cancer.

Ⓐ teacher have to
Ⓑ teacher has to
Ⓒ teacher must have to
Ⓓ teacher had to

# Application

*In this section, students will apply a general strategy to a writing question that mimics the style of the TSIA2.*

**Remind me: how many different question types are on the ELAR test?**

Five.

**With such a wide variety of questions, it might be surprising to know that we can actually use the *same* process to answer all of them. What will always be our first step?**

Identify the question type.

**And what are the five types again?**

Long passage, dual passage, short passage, essay revision, and sentence revision.

SLIDE 13.1

**Let's take a look at question 1. What kind of question do you think it is?**

Sentence revision.

**What gives it away?**

The text is literally just one sentence.

**Once you know what kind of question it is, what's next?**

Decode the question.

**What do you think that means?**

Figure out what the question is asking.

**There are two key pieces of information we want to get from every question: the *what* and the *where*. What the question wants and where to find it. What does this question want?**

A verb to fix this sentence.

**And where does the test want us to look?**

At the underlined section.

**Sentence revision questions will always have this spotlight on the where, which is the underlined section. Essay revision questions are hit-or-miss, though. For instance, it might give you a sentence number or mention a specific paragraph. On the other hand, not every question will tell you where to look, so you may have to hunt the evidence down yourself. What should you do next?**

Pick a strategy.

**We'll learn lots of strategies throughout this course. In fact, we have special strategies for every single question type, along with a few extra tips to help you with some of the more challenging question topics. Let's not get ahead of ourselves, though. What's our last step?**

Use process of elimination.

**Why do you think we eliminate, rather than find the right answer?**

It's easier to pick out wrong answers than to find a right one.

**The odds are right there on the page: 75% of the options are wrong, so they're easier to pick out. In general, take two passes on the answers. For the first one, focus on eliminating answers that are obviously wrong. Why do we do that?**

It narrows down the number of choices quickly.

**The second pass on the answers should be a little more detailed. Why do you think that is?**

It's picking between the answers that aren't so obviously wrong.

**Which pass do you think will take the longest time?**

The second pass.

**Your second pass will be slower and more focused. Take time to compare your remaining answer choices and pick the best option.**

## THE APPROACH

When working on the ELAR portion of the TSIA2, use these steps to answer each question ...

1. Identify the question type.
2. Decode the question.
3. Pick a strategy.
4. Use the process of elimination.

**Passage**

*In this passage from a novel, the writer describes one man's journey to develop a career as a modern-day philosopher.*

Daniel Dennett's eternal search for answers began after his father was killed in an unexplained plane crash. His early life and move from Beirut to Massachusetts was cast in the long shadow of a mythical, unknown father figure. Dennett had come from a family of remarkable brilliance—his father was a counter-intelligence officer in the Office of Strategic Services, a predecessor of the CIA. Dennett attended Harvard University, where he received a doctorate in philosophy. There, he was awarded the prestigious Erasmus prize for his exceptional contribution to society, showcasing how his work was not only important to himself but was also significant within a worldwide community.

During Dennett's first year at Winchester High School, he put all his effort into a term paper on Plato and included a picture of Rodin's *The Thinker* on the cover. He humorously recalled that at the time, he hadn't really understood a word of what he had written. At age seventeen, he had begun pursuing a mathematics degree at Wesleyan University and found himself drowning in his coursework. Studying in the library late one evening, he happened upon the text *From a Logical Point of View*, which had been written at Harvard University by Willard Van Orman Quine. He was utterly transfixed, and by the next morning he had made up his mind to transfer to Harvard.

At the end of his college career, Dennett had begun developing his own thoughts and contradicting the opinions of philosophers who came before him. By 1962, he was twenty and married and could no longer relate to the idyllic days of his youth. He was experiencing for the first time a voracious drive to refute Quine's work. His youthful misguidance had now been given purpose. He chose to follow the path of questioning established truths, and regardless of the daunting complexities involved, he was coming up with His Own Answers. Now there was no turning back; he was the one calling the shots. In his thesis defense, he was so convincing that an established professor defended one of his critiques of Quine against the objectives of another faculty member. This remarkable affirmation inspired in him true self-confidence, and Dennett went on to build an academic career asking poignant questions.

2. The details describing Dennett's father in the first paragraph are most likely included to

   Ⓐ explain that Dennett felt an urge to follow in his father's footsteps
   Ⓑ demonstrate the legacy of intelligence Dennett was born into
   Ⓒ suggest that Dennett's father's military career was similar to that of Dennett's in academia
   Ⓓ show that few philosophers relate to growing up in a military household

## Application

*In this section, students will apply a general strategy to a reading question that mimics the style of the TSIA2.*

SLIDE 14.1

**This passage is a beast, right? It's really... *long*. What kind of question do you think this is?**

Long passage.

**We know it's a literary text because the little blurb at the top tells us. And, since it's really long, we know it's a long passage. What question numbers will have these kinds of questions?**

Numbers 1 through 4.

**Once you know what kind of question you're working with, what comes next?**

Decode the question.

**Which means?**

Finding the what and the where.

**What does question 2 want us to find?**

Why the author included details about this guy's dad.

**And where will we find our answer for this question?**

In the first paragraph.

**With the question decoded, what's our next step?**

Picking a strategy.

**We'll cover these in detail later in the course, but just know that there's a specific strategy we'll use with every long passage question. What's our last step?**

Using process of elimination.

**We'll take those same two passes. What do we eliminate on our first pass?**

The choices that are obviously wrong.

**Our second pass will always be more focused. When you're comparing answer choices for a reading question, what will you use from the passage to help you make eliminations?**

Evidence.

TSIA2 Mastery: ELAR 

### Instructions

Use the provided space to take notes as your teacher leads the discussion.

### Notes

# Conclusion

SLIDE 15.1

**Remember: the TSIA2 has a pattern to its questions. You'll always start with reading for the first half and follow up with writing in the second half. Take the time to figure out what kind of question it is and use the question number to help you. What kind of questions will show up on 1 through 4?**

Long passages.

**And what follows in questions 5 and 6?**

Dual passages.

**When will you switch from reading-focused questions to writing-focused?**

Question 16.

**Once you know what kind of question it is, start decoding. What two things are you looking for?**

The what and the where.

**And then what?**

Pick a strategy.

**And the final step?**

Using process of elimination.

**Why do we eliminate wrong answers instead of picking right answers?**

There are more wrong answers, so they're easier to pick out.

**And how many passes should you take over the choices?**

Two.

**Who can summarize what you look for in each pass?**

The first is looking for obviously wrong answers and the second is more focused on the details.

**And that's it. The ELAR test is just one big countdown. 5 for a passing score, 4 steps to the Approach, 3 reading question types, 2 writing question types, and 1 right answer for every question. You got this.**

This page is intentionally left blank.
Content resumes on the next page.

This page is intentionally left blank.
Teacher content resumes with the next chapter.

CHAPTER 3

# Long Passages

In this chapter, students will evaluate the characteristics of a long passage question from the TSIA2. In addition, they will review and apply a strategy that can be used to answer any TSIA2 question with those characteristics.

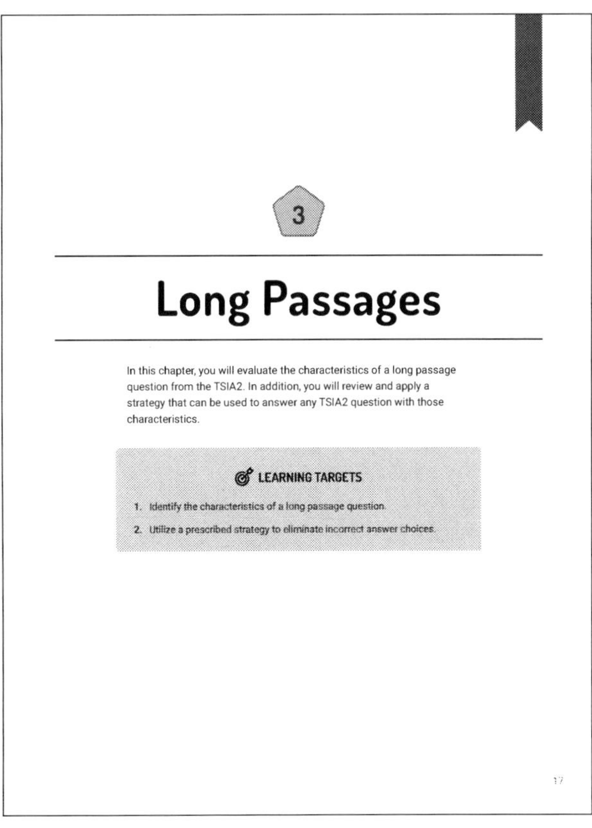
3

Long Passages

In this chapter, you will evaluate the characteristics of a long passage question from the TSIA2. In addition, you will review and apply a strategy that can be used to answer any TSIA2 question with those characteristics.

LEARNING TARGETS

1. Identify the characteristics of a long passage question.
2. Utilize a prescribed strategy to eliminate incorrect answer choices.

17

## TSIA2 STANDARDS

**Literary Text Analysis**

The student will identify and analyze ideas in an elements of literary text.

## LEARNING TARGETS

1. Identify the characteristics of a long passage question.
2. Utilize a prescribed strategy to eliminate incorrect answer choices.

## Groundwork

EXERCISE A

### Instructions

Refer to the following question as your teacher leads the discussion. Do not answer the question.

*In this passage from a novel, the writer describes one man's journey to develop a career as a modern-day philosopher.*

### Passage

Daniel Dennett's eternal search for answers began after his father was killed in an unexplained plane crash. His early life and move from Beirut to Massachusetts were cast in the long shadow of a mythical, unknown father figure. Dennett had come from a family of remarkable brilliance—his father was a counterintelligence officer in the Office of Strategic Services, a predecessor of the CIA. Dennett attended Harvard University, where he received a doctorate in philosophy. There he was awarded the prestigious Erasmus prize for his exceptional contribution to society, showcasing how his work was not only important to himself but was also significant within a worldwide community.

During Dennett's first year at Winchester High School, he put all his effort into a term paper on Plato and included a picture of Rodin's *The Thinker* on the cover. He humorously recalled that at the time, he hadn't really understood a word of what he had written. At age seventeen, he had begun pursuing a mathematics degree at Wesleyan University and found himself drowning in his coursework. Studying in the library late one evening, he chanced upon the text From a Logical Point of View, which had been written at Harvard University by Willard Van Orman Quine. He was utterly transfixed, and by the next morning, he had made up his mind to transfer to Harvard.

At the end of his college career, Dennett had begun developing his own thoughts and contradicting the opinions of philosophers who came before him. By 1962 he was twenty and married and could no longer relate to the idyllic days of his youth. He was experiencing for the first time a voracious drive to refute Quine's work. His youthful misguidance had now been given purpose. The pursuit of a valuable quarry through daunting complexities was the path he had chosen to follow, and regardless of the ambiguity of right and wrong, he was coming up with His Own Answers. Now that there was no turning back, he was the one calling the shots. He defended his thesis well and had so convinced others of his points that an established professor defended a point of contention that Dennett argued against Quine. The remarkable affirmation inspired in him true self-confidence, and Dennett went on to build an academic career asking poignant questions.

1. The main purpose of the passage is to

   (A) propose that by following the steps taken by Dennett, others can become philosophers as well

   (B) persuade the reader that Dennett was only able to ask questions no one could answer

   (C) speculate on how philosophers employ different methods to approach an argument

   (D) describe how Dennett developed from an inexperienced student into an established philosopher

## Groundwork

***In this section, students will evaluate the characteristics of a long passage question.***

EXERCISE A

**They say that first impressions matter. In fact, some scientists say that you start forming an opinion about someone you've just met after seeing their face for less than a tenth of a second. We decide if that person seems trustworthy, attractive, or even competent in those crucial first moments. So, how do you make a good first impression?**

*Allow 2–3 students to share.*

SLIDE 18.1

**The TSIA2 makes a doozy of a first impression. The test starts strong, with questions that look like what you see here in your workbook. Looks pretty impressive, right? What about this question might come across as intimidating?**

The passage is really long.

**The long passage is actually the key characteristic for these types of questions. We even call them *long passage* questions for obvious reasons. But don't let the size scare you. The TSIA2 won't give you a huge passage with every single question. In fact, the first long passage will be the *only* long passage you'll have to read. And, you'll use that same passage for the first four questions of the ELAR multiple-choice section. Why is that a good thing?**

We only have to read one big passage to answer more than one question.

**It's like a two-for-one freebie. Or, a four-for-one—though, that doesn't roll off the tongue quite as nicely. These long passages also have another common feature. Check out the citation at the top of the passage. Is this a fiction or nonfiction text?**

Fiction.

**How can you tell?**

The citation says it's from a novel.

**The long passage will always be a story of some kind, something from literature. The TSIA2 might even pull from stories you know, like *Peter Pan* or other classic stories. How is this information helpful?**

We'll know what to expect.

TSIA2 Mastery: ELAR 

EXERCISE B

**Instructions**

Review the basic steps for answering a long passage question. Put them into the correct sequence by filling in numbers 1–5 in the spaces provided.

_____ Find the big picture.

_____ Read the passage first.

_____ Read the question.

_____ Find your evidence.

_____ Use the process of elimination.

## Groundwork

*In this section, students will sequence the steps for a basic strategy that can be used to answer any long passage questions on the TSIA2.*

EXERCISE B SLIDE 19.1

**Question 1 of the ELAR section will always come with a long passage. Luckily, that long passage will tag along with you as you answer the first four questions of the test. Because we'll use the passage for so many questions in a row, what do you think we should always do first?**

*Read the passage first.*

**We'll have to read it all eventually, so we may as well get familiar with the passage from the start. As you read, take notes. You'll be given some scratch paper or a dry erase board to use during the test, but it's not *just* for math. You can use it as you read these long passages to help keep your thoughts straight. Write down a quick summary of each paragraph from the passage. That will help you when it comes to the next step, which is what?**

*Find the big picture.*

**What do you think I mean by "big picture"?**

The main idea.

**Essentially, you want to take a moment, either while you're reading or after you've summarized each paragraph, to ask yourself, "What is this passage about?" You don't need to write this down if you don't want to, but you should always take a few seconds to identify the main idea. After that, what should you do?**

*Read the question.*

**The key to earning points from a question is actually reading it. Pay close attention to every word, and don't skim. What are you searching the question for?**

What information we'll need to find from the passage.

**The question essentially gives you directions, telling you where to look and what to look for. For instance, if it asks you for the main idea, you'll know to lean heavily on your summaries of the paragraphs. If it asks for a specific detail from the third paragraph, you'll know to narrow your search to just those sentences. This leads us nicely into our fourth step. What is it?**

*Find your evidence.*

**What will we use that evidence for?**

Eliminating wrong answers.

**Essentially, the fourth and fifth steps of our strategy blend together. If we find evidence to support an answer, it's a good choice. What if we find evidence that proves an answer wrong, or if there isn't any evidence at all?**

We should eliminate the answer.

**The best answers will always have clear, strong support from the passage. Okay, so we've spent a bunch of time going over the basic strategy for long passages. Let's see how this will work on test day.**

# Application

## THE APPROACH

When answering a long passage question on the TSIA2, use these steps ...

1. Read the passage first.
2. Read the question.
3. Find the big picture.
4. Find your evidence.
5. Use the process of elimination.

*In this passage from a novel, the writer describes one man's journey to develop a career as a modern-day philosopher.*

### Passage

Daniel Dennett's eternal search for answers began after his father was killed in an unexplained plane crash. His early life and move from Beirut to Massachusetts were cast in the long shadow of a mythical, unknown father figure. Dennett had come from a family of remarkable brilliance—his father was a counterintelligence officer in the Office of Strategic Services, a predecessor of the CIA. Dennett attended Harvard University, where he received a doctorate in philosophy. There he was awarded the prestigious Erasmus prize for his exceptional contribution to society, showcasing how his work was not only important to himself but was also significant within a worldwide community.

During Dennett's first year at Winchester High School, he put all his effort into a term paper on Plato and included a picture of Rodin's *The Thinker* on the cover. He humorously recalled that at the time, he hadn't really understood a word of what he had written. At age seventeen, he had begun pursuing a mathematics degree at Wesleyan University and found himself drowning in his coursework. Studying in the library late one evening, he chanced upon the text From a Logical Point of View, which had been written at Harvard University by Willard Van Orman Quine. He was utterly transfixed, and by the next morning, he had made up his mind to transfer to Harvard.

At the end of his college career, Dennett had begun developing his own thoughts and contradicting the opinions of philosophers who came before him. By 1962 he was twenty and married and could no longer relate to the idyllic days of his youth. He was experiencing for the first time a voracious drive to refute Quine's work. His youthful misguidance had now been given purpose. The pursuit of a valuable quarry through daunting complexities was the path he had chosen to follow, and regardless of the ambiguity of right and wrong, he was coming up with His Own Answers. Now that there was no turning back, he was the one calling the shots. He defended his thesis well and had so convinced others of his points that an established professor defended a point of contention that Dennett argued against Quine. The remarkable affirmation inspired in him true self-confidence, and Dennett went on to build an academic career asking poignant questions.

# Application

***In this section, students will practice applying a basic strategy to a long passage question that asks for the main idea.***

SLIDE 20.1

**The TSIA2 isn't the only one trying to make a good first impression. The first question of the test is your opportunity to shine. These first questions will also weigh more heavily on your overall score, so it's a good idea to take it slow and double-check your answers before submitting. There's no back button on the test, so what you pick is what you're stuck with. What's our first step?**

*Read the passage.*

**Take a moment now to do that, and remember to take notes on the paragraphs. What are we writing down?**

A summary of each paragraph.

*Give students 2 minutes to read the passage.*

**What would you say is the main idea of the first paragraph?**

Dennett came from an intelligent, accomplished family, and he was also very talented.

**And the second paragraph?**

Dennett struggled in school but was inspired to transfer to Harvard.

**What did you write down for the third paragraph?**

Dennett began to think for himself and built a career out of it.

**Time to string it all together into the big picture. What would you say this whole passage is about?**

Dennett was a smart young man who developed into a brilliant thinker after struggling in his early years.

**TSIA2 Mastery:** ELAR 

**1.** The main purpose of the passage is to

Ⓐ propose that by following the steps taken by Dennett, others can become philosophers as well

Ⓑ persuade the reader that Dennett was only able to ask questions no one could answer

Ⓒ speculate on how philosophers employ different methods to approach an argument

Ⓓ describe how Dennett developed from an inexperienced student into an established philosopher

## Application

SLIDE 21.1

**Once you've got a solid understanding of the passage, what's next?**

*Read the question.*

**What's this question asking us for?**

The main purpose.

**Where will we look for our evidence, then?**

In our summary.

**Lucky for us, we took good notes. But let's be real. Sometimes our notes won't always be perfectly reliable. The good news, though, is that the passage always will be. Don't be afraid to do a little rereading. Let's start by eliminating answers that are off-topic. Which answer doesn't cover what this passage is about?**

Choice C, since it doesn't even mention Dennett.

**Dennett is our main character, so not even mentioning him in the answer seems strange. We can eliminate choice C. Let's compare our remaining answers to the summary we came up with. What's the difference between our remaining options?**

Choice A is talking about other people becoming philosophers. Choice B is talking about Dennett answering hard questions. And choice D talks about Dennett's development.

**Only one of those choices really matches our summary, which was all about Dennett developing into a brilliant thinker. Which answer is our *best* option?**

Choice D.

**By reading the passage and taking good notes throughout, you're essentially creating even more evidence that can help you eliminate wrong answers. But what happens when you need to dig into the passage more? What if your summaries don't help? Don't worry. The basic strategy still works!**

## THE APPROACH

When answering a long passage question on the TSIA2, use these steps ...

1. Read the passage first.
2. Read the question.
3. Find the big picture.
4. Find your evidence.
5. Use the process of elimination.

*In this passage from a novel, the writer describes one man's journey to develop a career as a modern-day philosopher.*

### Passage

Daniel Dennett's eternal search for answers began after his father was killed in an unexplained plane crash. His early life and move from Beirut to Massachusetts were cast in the long shadow of a mythical, unknown father figure. Dennett had come from a family of remarkable brilliance—his father was a counterintelligence officer in the Office of Strategic Services, a predecessor of the CIA. Dennett attended Harvard University, where he received a doctorate in philosophy. There he was awarded the prestigious Erasmus prize for his exceptional contribution to society, showcasing how his work was not only important to himself but was also significant within a worldwide community.

During Dennett's first year at Winchester High School, he put all his effort into a term paper on Plato and included a picture of Rodin's *The Thinker* on the cover. He humorously recalled that at the time, he hadn't really understood a word of what he had written. At age seventeen, he had begun pursuing a mathematics degree at Wesleyan University and found himself drowning in his coursework. Studying in the library late one evening, he chanced upon the text From a Logical Point of View, which had been written at Harvard University by Willard Van Orman Quine. He was utterly transfixed, and by the next morning, he had made up his mind to transfer to Harvard.

At the end of his college career, Dennett had begun developing his own thoughts and contradicting the opinions of philosophers who came before him. By 1962 he was twenty and married and could no longer relate to the idyllic days of his youth. He was experiencing for the first time a voracious drive to refute Quine's work. His youthful misguidance had now been given purpose. The pursuit of a valuable quarry through daunting complexities was the path he had chosen to follow, and regardless of the ambiguity of right and wrong, he was coming up with His Own Answers. Now that there was no turning back, he was the one calling the shots. He defended his thesis well and had so convinced others of his points that an established professor defended a point of contention that Dennett argued against Quine. The remarkable affirmation inspired in him true self-confidence, and Dennett went on to build an academic career asking poignant questions.

This page is intentionally left blank.
Teacher content resumes with the next chapter.

TSIA2 Mastery: ELAR 

**2.** The main purpose of the second paragraph is to

Ⓐ describe a specific text written by Dennett's rival, Quine
Ⓑ present the process students undertake to defend their philosophical theses
Ⓒ provide an account of Dennett's transformation from youth to maturity
Ⓓ list several ways Dennett contradicted the teachings of his mentors

## Application

*In this section, students will practice answering a long passage question that focuses on a single element within the passage.*

SLIDE 23.1

**Check out question 2. Notice that we're working with the same passage as before. It will be the same when you actually take the TSIA2. Should we read the passage again?**

No.

**We also don't need to recreate the big picture. It's like we're given a huge head start already. But don't let your guard down. These questions are still really early in the test, which means they'll weigh a little more heavily on your final score. Work slowly and methodically to make sure you pick the right answer—which brings us to the question. What does this question want us to find?**

The purpose of the second paragraph.

**When a question mentions an entire paragraph, what should you do?**

Read that paragraph.

**If the question is going to use the whole paragraph, read the whole paragraph again. What other resource do we have that can give us more information about the second paragraph?**

Our summary we wrote when we read the passage the first time.

**Go over it all. The test is untimed, so you're not racing against a countdown. Use that to your advantage and reread things that will help you with the question. Your summary is a little like the middleman, giving you a big picture view of the whole passage. But when it gets this narrow, you should go back to the original source. Once you have your evidence, what's your next step?**

*Use the process of elimination.*

**Let's start looking at our answers. Can we eliminate choice A?**

Yes.

**Why isn't that a good choice?**

The paragraph is more about how Dennett got inspired by the text, not a description of the text itself.

**Choice A is out. What about choice B? Can we support that one with evidence?**

No, the paragraph doesn't even mention a process used by students.

**Choice B is no good. Can we find evidence that supports choice C?**

Yes, the paragraph starts out talking about his first year in high school and how he ended up going to Harvard.

**That one seems pretty solid, but let's check choice D just in case there's something better in that option. What do you think? Should we keep or eliminate choice D?**

Eliminate it.

**What's wrong with that option?**

The paragraph doesn't talk about him going against the teachings of his mentors.

**That means choice C is definitely our best option. During the real test, you'll also have two more questions that go along with the passage. And once you finish those questions, you'll be free and clear of the long passage. Just remember to focus on the evidence. Use what's in the passage, along with your paragraph summaries, and make sure that the answer you pick is well-supported. The best answers will always have the clearest connection to the passage.**

## Practice

### Instructions

Complete the practice set. If time remains after you've finished, double-check your work.

*The narrator of this passage, excerpted from an essay, describes the life of a pet dog.*

### Passage

The day he came was a beautiful, bright, cool one in August. A touring car brought him. They put him down on our corner, meaning to lose him, but he crawled under the car, and they had to prod him out and throw stones before they could drive on. I carried him over the railroad tracks. That night he got chop bones and slept on the mat. The second morning we thought he had gone. The third he was back, wagging approval of us and intent to stay, which seemed to leave no choice but to take him in. We had fun over names: "Jellywaggles," "Rags," or "Toby." Finally, we called him "Nibbie," and soon, his tail would answer to it.

Cleaned up—scrubbed, the insoluble matted locks clipped from his coat, his trampish collar replaced with a new one bearing a license tag—he was far from being unpresentable. Always, depending on the moment's mood, he was either terrier or spaniel, the snap and scrap and perk of the one alternating with the gentle snuggling indolence of the other.

As a terrier, he would dig furiously by the hour after a field mouse; as a spaniel, he would "read" the breeze with the best nose among the dog folk of our neighborhood or follow a trail quite well. I know there was retrieving blood. A year ago in May, he caught and brought me, not doing the least injury, an oriole that probably had flown against a wire and was struggling disabled in the grass.

Nibbie was shabby-genteel black, sunburnt as to the mustache, grizzled as to the raggy fringe on his haunches. He had a white stock and shirt frill and a white forepaw. The brown eyes full of heart was the best point. His body coat was rough Scottish worsted, the little black pate was cotton-soft like shoddy, and the big black ears were genuine spaniel silk. As a terrier, he held them up smartly and carried a plumy fishhook of a tail; as a spaniel, the ears drooped, and the tail swung meekly as if in apology for never having been clipped. In flea time, it seemed hardly possible that a dog of his size could sustain his population. We finally found a true fleabane, but deserted one day, and he was populous again the next.

**1.** In describing Nibbie's problem with fleas and the doubt that Nibbie could "sustain his population," the narrator is most directly referring to the fact that

Ⓐ the fleas living on Nibbie made him afraid to leave the clothes-closet to eat his dinner

Ⓑ Nibbie wagged his tail at the family but snapped blindly at fleas when left alone

Ⓒ no other dog in the neighborhood had as many fleas as Nibbie had that season

Ⓓ the large number of fleas living on Nibbie was incongruous to his small size

# Practice

SLIDE 24.1

*Give students 10 minutes to complete the practice set.*

SLIDE 24.2

1. **The correct answer is D.** This sentence describes the large infestation of fleas on Nibbie, so the narrator is contrasting Nibbie's size with this volume of fleas. Choices A, B, and C are unsupported by the passage. Only choice D captures the contrast embedded in *sustain his population*, which implies his body was too small to be home to so many fleas.

2. When the author says that Nibbie's first owners let him out, "meaning to lose him," he most likely means

   Ⓐ the first owners were careless and could not keep track of him.
   Ⓑ Nibbie's owners were abandoning him.
   Ⓒ Nibbie wandered off and got lost.
   Ⓓ the author lost Nibbie under the car.

3. When the author writes that Nibbie was "retrieving blood," he most likely means that he

   Ⓐ was a ferocious hunter that brought back his kills to the narrator
   Ⓑ had a health problem involving his blood vessels
   Ⓒ sustained a gruesome injury while playing fetch
   Ⓓ displayed characteristics of a particular breed of dog

## Practice

SLIDE 25.1

2. **The correct answer is B.** The first paragraph describes Nibbie's abandonment by his original owners. Because the owners' actions are deliberate, choices A and C can be eliminated. Choice D is half right: Nibbie crawled under a car, but not because the author lost him. Choice B is correct because *meaning to lose him* conveys that Nibbie's original owners were attempting to abandon him.

SLIDE 25.2

3. **The correct answer is D.** Choice A is too extreme and is contradicted by the fact that Nibbie carried a hurt bird without *doing the least injury* to it. Choices B and C are unsupported by the passage. Right after the phrase *retrieving blood*, the narrator describes how Nibbie brought over an oriole without *doing the least injury* to the bird, suggesting that he may have characteristics of retrieving dogs, similar to his other behaviors related to the potential breeds mentioned earlier in the paragraph. Thus, choice D is the best answer.

This page is intentionally left blank.
Content resumes on the next page.

This page is intentionally left blank.
Teacher content resumes with the next chapter.

CHAPTER 4

# Vocabulary

In this chapter, students will practice a process for evaluating the connotation and denotation of specific vocabulary words in the context of a passage. They will learn a process for identifying context clues and determining the proper definitions through logical reasoning.

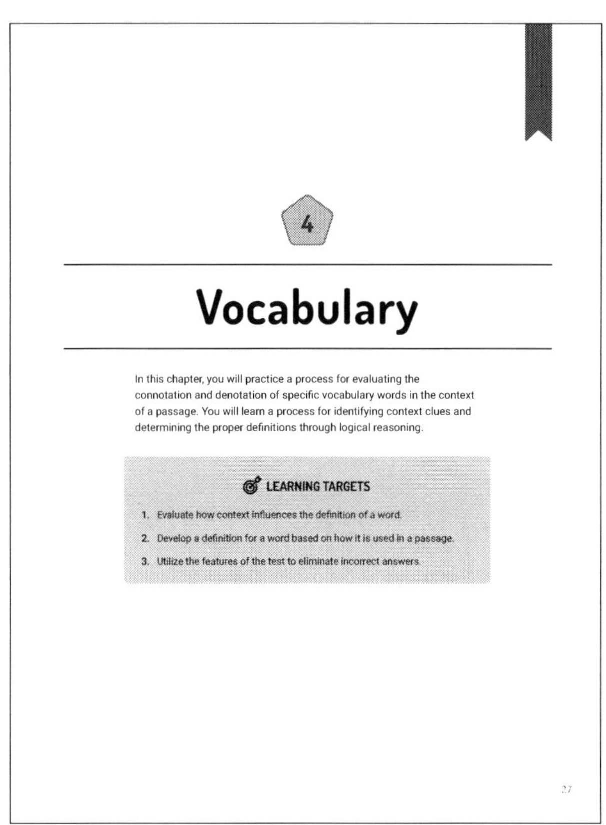

4

Vocabulary

In this chapter, you will practice a process for evaluating the connotation and denotation of specific vocabulary words in the context of a passage. You will learn a process for identifying context clues and determining the proper definitions through logical reasoning.

LEARNING TARGETS

1. Evaluate how context influences the definition of a word.
2. Develop a definition for a word based on how it is used in a passage.
3. Utilize the features of the test to eliminate incorrect answers.

27

## TSIA2 STANDARDS

**Literary Text Analysis**
Vocabulary

The student will determine the meaning of words and phrases in context in literary text.

**Informational Text Analysis and Synthesis**
Vocabulary

The student will determine the meaning of words and phrases in context in informational text and (Diagnostic only) apply decoding skills.

## TEKS ALIGNMENT

E1.2 *Developing and sustaining foundational language skills*: listening, speaking, reading, writing, and thinking—vocabulary. The student uses newly acquired vocabulary expressively. The student is expected to:

(B) analyze context to distinguish between the denotative and connotative meanings of words.

## LEARNING TARGETS

1. Evaluate how context influences the definition of a word.
2. Develop a definition for a word based on how it is used in a passage.
3. Utilize the features of the test to eliminate incorrect answers.

## Warm-Up

**Instructions**

Complete the warm-up question. If time remains after you've finished, double-check your work.

**Passage**

**(1)** Have you ever had the chance to look at the map of a person's heart? **(2)** Science textbooks sometimes include different kinds of diagrams of the heart, and its crisscrossing ventricles can be fascinating, but see them try to draw a map of a child's heart, which is not merely disorganized, but always changing direction. **(3)** Its lines go up and down, just like a heart rhythm on a monitor, and these are likely paths in the forest, for the Evermore is always generally speaking a forest, with dazzling flecks of light here and there, and vines and rusted-over carts in the brush, silent caves, and elves who are usually carpenters, and bridges under which a creek passes, princesses who are the eldest of five sisters, and a shack slowly being lost to ruin, and one large old man with a cleft chin. **(4)** If that were it, it would form a simple map, but there are also first birthday parties, classrooms, mothers, the babbling brook, stitching, thefts, executions, nouns of the third declension, frosted cupcake day, getting a retainer, write four plus three, a nickel for a tooth under your pillow, and so on, and either these are an aspect of the forest or they reveal another map peeking out, and it is all quite disorienting, especially because nothing remains still.

**(5)** Naturally the Evermores differ quite a bit. **(6)** Alex's, for instance, has a bog with bald eagles gliding over it at which Alex was aiming, while Jack, who was still little, had a bald eagle with bogs gliding over it. **(7)** Alex lived in a bus flipped sideways in the undergrowth, Jack in a teepee, Mary in a hut of carefully sculpted clay. **(8)** Alex didn't have friends, Jack had friends only at night, and Mary had a pet snake cast away by its parents, but for the most part the Evermores display a family resemblance, and if they lined up side by side you wouldn't be wrong to say they had each other's eyes, and so on. **(9)** On these enchanted paths kids at play are for ever mounting their buckboards. **(10)** We too have journeyed there; we still can hear the crunching of leaves, though we shall steer its grounds no more.

**(11)** Of all the tantalizing forests the Evermore is the coziest and most compact, not wide and ranging, you see, with tiresome stretches between one adventure and the next, but nicely packed. **(12)** When visiting by day in games with tables and teacups, it isn't alarming in the least, but come the minute before the lights go out, it all becomes quite real. **(13)** That is the reason for bed lamps.

**1.** In sentence 10, "we" most likely refers to

Ⓐ authors
Ⓑ kids
Ⓒ believers
Ⓓ adults

# Warm-Up

SLIDE 28.1

*Give students 2 minutes to complete the warm-up question.*

SLIDE 28.2

1. **The correct answer is D.** When the author says *we too have journeyed there*, the author is addressing the reader and therefore including the reader in a group with themselves. Choices A, B, and C are incorrect because they do not represent groups that both the author and the reader belong to. Choice D is correct because it can be inferred that the author is addressing an intended audience of adults and, as such, uses *we* to mean adults.

## Groundwork

EXERCISE A

**Instructions**
Review the following list of words:

- Pirate
- Ship
- Treasure
- Raid
- Lookout

**1.** What book, movie, or character comes to mind? ________________________________

# Groundwork

*In this section, students will review a list of words without context clues and make a connection to their prior knowledge.*

EXERCISE A | SLIDE 29.1

**When someone says, "A picture is worth 1,000 words," essentially, they're saying that a single image can tell us a whole lot more information than just a few written words. But what about the opposite? Can a few words help us imagine a really detailed picture? It turns out, no. When we're given a single word out of context, we usually come up with really basic images in our minds.**

**Check out this list of words, for example. What do you imagine when you think of a pirate?**

A bad-guy sailor with a peg leg and eye patch who goes around looking for lost treasure.

**Our brains do this automatically, like a visual inference. Say *pirate*, and you're thinking of this bearded guy with a peg leg and a hook instead of a hand. Say *treasure*, and you're imagining said bearded guy opening a huge treasure chest full of gold.**

**Take another pass through this list of words. Would you be surprised if I told you they're all used in the same story?**

Not at all.

**Does a particular story or character come to mind? What does this list remind you of? Take a moment to write down your answer.**

*Give students 30 seconds to write down their answer.*

**Who would like to share what they came up with?**

*Allow 2–3 students to share.*

**The question, now, is whether we're accurate in our assumptions. What if we put these words into context? How could the meaning *possibly* change when this list is so clear-cut? Go ahead and turn the page.**

EXERCISE B

**Instructions**
Refer to the following passage as your teacher leads the discussion.

**Passage**
My brother called to tell me he would **ship** my birthday present so I would be on the **lookout** for it. Although I watched the tracking number online, porch **pirates** **raided** my home before I could get there to pick up my packages. Luckily, my video doorbell caught them. Amazingly, the police retrieved my packages, including my birthday present. I will always **treasure** the handmade scarf my brother sent.

**2.** Was the passage what you expected? Circle your answer.

Yes No

## Groundwork

*In this section, students will discuss how much context can change the definition of a word.*

**Take a moment now to read the passage and see just what the story is about.**

*Give students 1 minute to read the passage.*

**What's the passage about?**

It is about pirates, but the package-stealing kind, not the peg-leg/parrot kind.

**Is this the kind of story you expected? Be honest!**

No.

**But the passage uses all the same words. How did placing the words into a passage change their meaning?**

It gave more information about the words, so we had more clues about their meaning.

**It's funny how the context of a word can change its meaning. Who can tell me what *context* is?**

It's the information that comes before and after.

**For example, let's look at the word *ship*. When we just had that list of words as a reference, what did you think *ship* referred to?**

A big boat.

**But what does it mean here?**

To mail something.

**What about the word *treasure*? What did you originally think it meant?**

Gold or a big chest of jewels.

**And based on how it was used in this passage, how would you define that word?**

To love or keep something because it's special.

**What about that word changed to create such a different definition?**

The word didn't change. Its context did.

**Context is what gives us a better understanding of what something really means. It's like when we're texting with someone and we don't have the context of body language, tone of voice, or facial expressions. It's hard to interpret meaning without context.**

TSIA2 Mastery: ELAR 

EXERCISE C

### Instructions

Read the following passage and use its contents to answer the questions below.

### Passage

The members of the debate team were recruited from the high schools with the highest-ranked programs in the state. At first, the recruits were thrilled to have the opportunity to train with Mr. Sullivan, or "Sully," who was one of the top debate coaches in the country. But they soon realized that working with Sully was no walk in the park. He was meticulous to the point of exacting, and recruits started **dropping**; they were not willing to put up with Sully's criticisms of their efforts. Before long, there were only six of the original fifteen team members remaining. Rather than seeming upset by the diminished size of his team, though, Sully seemed satisfied.

**3.** Underline the nearby words that give you hints about the meaning of the word "dropping."

**4.** Write your own definition for the word "dropping."

______________________________

______________________________

## Groundwork

*In this section, students will practice defining a word based on its context.*

EXERCISE C SLIDE 31.1

**Take a moment now to read this new passage.**

*Give students 1 minute to read the passage.*

**What word are we meant to focus on in this passage?**

*Dropping.*

**Let's re-read the part of the passage where it shows up. Who'd like to read that sentence for us?**

*He was meticulous to the point of exacting, and recruits started dropping; they were not willing to put up with Sully's criticisms of their efforts.*

**This sentence is tricky because there are some pretty high-level vocabulary words in there. Do you see any words or phrases that make you pause?**

*Meticulous* and *to the point of exacting.*

**With all that extra confusion in there, answering the question can be more challenging. We can sidestep it, though, if we're careful. Start by looking at the topic of the sentence, Sully. What do you guys think of Sully? What kind of leader is he?**

One who is demanding and difficult to get along with.

**Do the recruits seem to be happy with his leadership style?**

No.

**How did they respond to him?**

Some of them quit.

**How do you know?**

The passage says so.

**Let's get specific. On the test, the best answer will always have the most direct support from the passage, so it's a good strategy to see if you can point to a specific word, phrase, or sentence that gives you the evidence you need to say, "Aha! I told you!"**

**Take a moment now to look again and underline some key evidence. What words or phrases from the passage tell you they're quitting?**

*... they were not willing to put up with Sully's criticisms of their efforts.*

*... there were only six of the original fifteen team members remaining.*

SLIDE 31.2

***Dropping* could mean a lot of things depending on its context, just like *ship* and *treasure*. But based on what you read here, what would you say the definition of *dropping* is?**

Quitting or leaving the team.

**Think back to the tricky vocabulary words. Did you need to know their definitions to figure out what *dropping* means?**

No.

**What *did* you need?**

Clues from the passage.

**This will be the key on test day, too. We don't need to memorize a bunch of complex vocabulary because the test will have everything we need. We just need to be able to find those context clues that lead us to the right choice.**

## Application

### THE APPROACH

When a question asks you to identify what a word means or refers to, use the following steps ...

1. Read the word in context.
2. Develop your own definition.
3. Select the answer that best matches what you came up with.

**Instructions**

Read the passage below and then choose the best answer to each question. Answer the questions on the basis of what is stated or implied in the passage.

**Passage**

**(1)** It was the very witching time of night that Ichabod, heavy-hearted and crestfallen, pursued his travels homewards, along the sides of the lofty hills which rise above Tarry Town, and which he had traversed so cheerily in the afternoon. **(2)** The hour was as dismal as himself. **(3)** Far below him, the Tappan Zee spread its dusky and indistinct waste of waters, with here and there the tall mast of a sloop, riding quietly at anchor under the land. **(4)** In the dead hush of midnight, he could even hear the barking of the watch-dog from the opposite shore of the Hudson; but it was so vague and faint as only to give an idea of his distance from this faithful companion of man.

From Washington Irving, *The Legend of Sleepy Hollow*.

**5.** In sentence 1, the word "pursued" most nearly means

Ⓐ chased after
Ⓑ proceeded with
Ⓒ strived for
Ⓓ haunted

# Application

*In this section, students will apply the steps of the Approach to a vocabulary question similar to what they will see on the TSIA2.*

SLIDE 32.1

**Check out this new passage. It's actually an excerpt from a real story called *The Legend of Sleepy Hollow*. This part of the story begins when Ichabod, the main character, leaves a party where he's been soundly rejected by a woman he likes.**

**Before you dive into the passage, though, where should you start?**

Reading the question.

**Why should we read the question before the passage?**

Then you can look for the answer while you read.

**And what does this question want?**

The definition of the word *pursued*.

**When you see a vocabulary question like this, what should your first step be?**

*Read the word in context.*

**How much context do you think you'll need?**

A sentence.

**Reading the sentence where the key word appears will often be enough context to help you find the definition. If you need more context, go ahead and keep reading. Just don't go *too* far from the key word. Why should you stick close to where the vocabulary word appears when hunting for context clues?**

The details farther away from the word probably won't be very helpful.

**Let's try it. Who can read sentence 1 for us?**

*(1) It was the very witching time of night that Ichabod, heavy-hearted and crestfallen, pursued his travels homewards, along the sides of the lofty hills which rise above Tarry Town, and which he had traversed so cheerily in the afternoon.*

**What should we do next?**

Come up with our own definition.

**Based on that sentence, can you come up with a definition for *pursued*?**

It means *followed* or *went along*.

**Once you have a general idea of what the word means, what's left to do?**

Compare it to the answer choices to see which one best matches what we came up with.

**And which one matches our definition?**

Choice B.

**Choice A looks pretty tempting, though. Why do you think someone might fall for that trap answer?**

It's the dictionary definition of *pursued*.

**Does it fit the context, though?**

Not really.

**Why not?**

He wasn't really chasing his travels so much as just going along with them or starting them.

**Watch out for these kinds of traps on test day. If you'd only read the question and not the passage, choice A would be *very* tempting. The TSIA2 is untimed, which means you have plenty of time to check the passage and avoid this kind of misstep.**

TSIA2 Mastery: ELAR 

### THE APPROACH

When a question asks you to identify what a word means or refers to, use the following steps ...

1. Read the word in context.
2. Develop your own definition.
3. Select the answer that best matches what you came up with.

**Instructions**

Read the passage below and then choose the best answer to each question. Answer the questions on the basis of what is stated or implied in the passage.

**Passage**

**(1)** All the stories of ghosts and goblins that he had heard in the afternoon now came crowding upon his recollection. **(2)** The night grew darker and darker; the stars seemed to sink deeper in the sky, and driving clouds occasionally hid them from his sight. **(3)** He had never felt so lonely and dismal. **(4)** He was, moreover, approaching the very place where many of the scenes of the ghost stories had been laid. **(5)** In the center of the road stood an enormous tulip-tree, which towered like a giant above all the other trees of the neighborhood, and formed a kind of landmark. . . . **(6)** It was connected with the tragical story of the unfortunate André, who had been taken prisoner hard by; and was universally known by the name of Major André's tree.

**(7)** As he approached the stream, his heart began to thump. . . . **(8)** In the dark shadow of the grove, on the margin of the brook, he beheld something huge, misshapen, black, and towering. **(9)** It stirred not, but seemed gathered up in the gloom, like some gigantic monster ready to spring upon the traveler. . . . **(10)** He appeared to be a horseman of large dimensions, and mounted on a black horse of powerful frame. **(11)** He made no offer of molestation or sociability, but kept aloof on one side of the road, jogging along on the blind side of old Gunpowder. **(12)** Ichabod now quickened his steed, in hopes of leaving him behind. **(13)** The stranger, however, quickened his horse to an equal pace. **(14)** Ichabod pulled up, and fell into a walk, thinking to lag behind—the other did the same.

From Washington Irving, *The Legend of Sleepy Hollow*.

6. In sentence 4, the word "laid" refers to where the ghost stories were

   Ⓐ said to have happened
   Ⓑ buried beneath the ground
   Ⓒ written by the storyteller
   Ⓓ given new life each year

## Application

*In this section, students will practice applying the steps of a vocabulary in context question to a passage.*

SLIDE 33.1

**Give me your first impression of this question: how is it different from the last one?**

The passage is really long.

**Does that change our process in any way?**

No.

**Let's dive in then. What word are we looking for?**

*Laid.*

**And where does it show up?**

In sentence 4.

**Who'd like to read that sentence for us?**

*(4) He was, moreover, approaching the very place where many of the scenes of the ghost stories had been laid.*

**What's our next step?**

Come up with our own definition for it.

**Let's pause for a moment and think. A lot of people get nervous when they take tests, and what happens if someone blanks in that moment? Show of hands: who has ever panicked and completely lost all train of thought?**

*Pause for a show of hands.*

**Blanking on test day happens. But that's why we keep a few strategies in our back pocket to help us get unstuck and moving toward a good answer. Think about it: what is a definition?**

It's the meaning of a word.

**So, if two words mean the same thing, they should be able to be used interchangeably. We can use that to our advantage. If you don't have your own definition, what *do* you have?**

The definitions in the answer choices.

**And how might we use them to get unstuck?**

Swap them into the story in place of the vocabulary word?

**If the definition and the word mean the same thing, we can swap them in to see if they make sense. Let's try it with choice A. Who'd like to read the sentence with that definition plugged in?**

*He was, moreover, approaching the very place where many of the scenes of the ghost stories had been said to have happened.*

**Does the definition make sense in that context?**

Yes.

**Let's hang onto that one and test the others. Does choice B make sense in that sentence?**

Not really.

**Why not?**

Ghost stories can't literally be buried.

**We can eliminate choice B. What about choice C? Can you eliminate that one?**

Yes, because there's no author in the story who sat in that place and wrote ghost stories.

**And what about choice D? Should we eliminate that one?**

Yes, because it's weird to say that the ghost stories were given new life.

**That means choice A is correct.**

**When you run into these kinds of questions on the test, always try to come up with your own answer first and match it to the answer choices. But if you get stuck, use your options to get moving again. Plug each one into the sentence and pick the one that makes the most sense.**

## Practice

### Instructions

Complete the practice set. If time remains after you've finished, double-check your work.

### Passage

If you've ever experienced a slight burning or tingly sensation when eating pineapple, you're not alone. The reason is bromelain, an enzyme found in pineapple that is then easily digested in your stomach. Unfortunately, before reaching your stomach, bromelain breaks down the proteins on your tongue, which the body discerns as an attack. As a result, pineapple can be slightly painful to eat while being perfectly harmless to digestion.

**1.** The word "discerns" in sentence 3 of the passage most nearly means

Ⓐ imagines
Ⓑ produces
Ⓒ anticipates
Ⓓ interprets

### Passage

Incensed by civil and economic injustices in 1786, farmers in rural Massachusetts planned attacks on government forces. This insurrection became known as Shays' Rebellion. In 1787, after militia commander William Shepherd's forces were deemed too small to oppose the growing insurrection, Governor John Bowdoin ordered that a private militia be formed to quash the rebellion. Although only a fraction of the 4,000 rebels were jailed (later to be freed), Shays' Rebellion showed that the new government formed under the Articles of Confederation did not have the resources to suppress violent uprisings against its laws.

**2.** As used in sentence 3, the word "quash" most nearly means

Ⓐ complete
Ⓑ release
Ⓒ protect
Ⓓ suppress

# Practice

SLIDE 34.1

*Give students 10 minutes to complete the practice set.*

SLIDE 34.2

1. **The correct answer is D.** Choice A is incorrect because *imagines* means *creates a mental image of*, and it would not make sense to say *which the body creates a mental image of as an attack*. Choice B is incorrect because this would suggest that the body *produces* bromelain *as an attack*, which is not true; the bromelain comes from pineapple. Choice C is incorrect because *anticipates* means *expects* or *predicts*, which does not match the meaning of *discerns* in context. Choice D is correct because the meaning of *interprets* is close to *recognizes* or *discerns* and fits the context: *which the body interprets as an attack*.

SLIDE 34.3

2. **The correct answer is D.** The passage is about an insurrection (or rebellion). Since William Shepherd's forces were deemed too small to handle the rebellion, Governor John Bowdoin created another small army to *quash the rebellion*, meaning *to crush* or *to end* the rebellion. Choice A is incorrect because John Bowdoin's forces didn't *complete* the rebellion; this would suggest that John Bowdoin was rebelling rather than fighting against the rebellion. Choice B is incorrect because *release* means *let go*, which does not capture the meaning of *quash* in this context. Choice C is incorrect because *protect* means *defend*, which is the opposite of what John Bowdoin's forces did to the rebellion. Choice D is correct because *suppress* means *to put down or end*, which is what John Bowdoin's forces did to the rebellion, so *suppress* captures the meaning of *quash* in this context.

**Passage**

During the process of anaerobic digestion, animal waste produces methane gas. Recently, biochemists sponsored by the Department of Energy discovered a way to make synthetic versions of waste that give off even more methane. You might be asking why the Department of Energy is sponsoring such developments. The reason is that methane produced by such waste could someday generate enough electricity for a whole city.

**3.** As used in sentence 2, the word "synthetic" means

Ⓐ powerful
Ⓑ manufactured
Ⓒ ineffective
Ⓓ safe

## Practice

SLIDE 35.1

3. **The correct answer is B.** The passage discusses a natural way methane gas is produced (*during the process of anaerobic digestion, animal waste produces methane gas*) and then highlights another new way it is being created: human-made production (or synthetic versions). Choices A, C, and D are incorrect because they mean *strong*, *not useful*, and *not risky*, respectively, and none of these meanings adequately describes the versions being created by the Department of Energy. Choice B is correct because *manufactured* can mean *human-made*, which is another way to say *synthetic*.

## Wrap-Up

**Instructions**

Complete the wrap-up question. If time remains after you've finished, double-check your work.

**Passage**

**(1)** Have you ever had the chance to look at the map of a person's heart? **(2)** Science textbooks sometimes include different kinds of diagrams of the heart, and its crisscrossing ventricles can be fascinating, but see them try to draw a map of a child's heart, which is not merely disorganized, but always changing direction. **(3)** Its lines go up and down, just like a heart rhythm on a monitor, and these are likely paths in the forest, for the Evermore is always generally speaking a forest, with dazzling flecks of light here and there, and vines and rusted-over carts in the brush, silent caves, and elves who are usually carpenters, and bridges under which a creek passes, princesses who are the eldest of five sisters, and a shack slowly being lost to ruin, and one large old man with a cleft chin. **(4)** If that were it, it would form a simple map, but there are also first birthday parties, classrooms, mothers, the babbling brook, stitching, thefts, executions, nouns of the third declension, frosted cupcake day, getting a retainer, write four plus three, a nickel for a tooth under your pillow, and so on, and either these are an aspect of the forest or they reveal another map peeking out, and it is all quite disorienting, especially because nothing remains still.

**(5)** Naturally the Evermores differ quite a bit. **(6)** Alex's, for instance, has a bog with bald eagles gliding over it at which Alex was aiming, while Jack, who was still little, had a bald eagle with bogs gliding over it. **(7)** Alex lived in a bus flipped sideways in the undergrowth, Jack in a teepee, Mary in a hut of carefully sculpted clay. **(8)** Alex didn't have friends, Jack had friends only at night, and Mary had a pet snake cast away by its parents, but for the most part the Evermores display a family resemblance, and if they lined up side by side you wouldn't be wrong to say they had each other's eyes, and so on. **(9)** On these enchanted paths kids at play are for ever mounting their buckboards. **(10)** We too have journeyed there; we still can hear the crunching of leaves, though we shall steer its grounds no more.

**(11)** Of all the tantalizing forests the Evermore is the coziest and most compact, not wide and ranging, you see, with tiresome stretches between one adventure and the next, but nicely packed. **(12)** When visiting by day in games with tables and teacups, it isn't alarming in the least, but come the minute before the lights go out, it all becomes quite real. **(13)** That is the reason for bed lamps.

**2.** In sentence 8, the reference to "eyes" most likely represents

- Ⓐ a frequent sight in Evermores
- Ⓑ shared characteristics among siblings
- Ⓒ omens from children's nightmares
- Ⓓ differences among varying Evermores

## Wrap-Up

SLIDE 36.1

*Give students 2 minutes to complete the wrap-up question.*

SLIDE 36.2

2. **The correct answer is B.** Choices A and C are incorrect because there is no strong evidence in the passage to support those interpretations. Choice D is incorrect because the author is using the example of eyes to show similarities, not differences. Choice B is correct because earlier in the sentence, the author mentions that the different Evermores (their personal, imaginary, make-believe places) have a family resemblance, so what the author means by *if they lined up side by side you wouldn't be wrong to say they had each other's eyes* is that there is a family resemblance between their Evermores.

CHAPTER 5

# Main Idea

In this chapter, students will be tasked with reviewing the details of a passage, locating key words and phrases, and identifying the main idea.

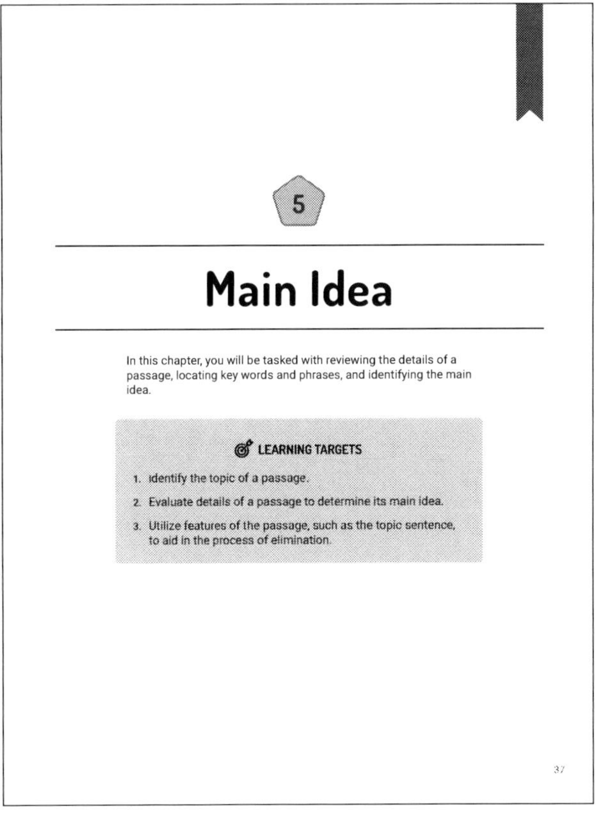

5

Main Idea

In this chapter, you will be tasked with reviewing the details of a passage, locating key words and phrases, and identifying the main idea.

LEARNING TARGETS

1. Identify the topic of a passage.
2. Evaluate details of a passage to determine its main idea.
3. Utilize features of the passage, such as the topic sentence, to aid in the process of elimination.

37

## TSIA2 STANDARD

**Informational Text Analysis and Synthesis**
Main ideas and supporting details

The student will identify main ideas of and comprehend explicitly stated and clearly indicated information and ideas in informational text.

## TEKS ALIGNMENT

E1.4 *Comprehension skills*: listening, speaking, reading, writing, and thinking using multiple texts. The student uses metacognitive skills to both develop and deepen comprehension of increasingly complex texts. The student is expected to:

(G) evaluate details read to determine key ideas.

## LEARNING TARGETS

1. Identify the topic of a passage.
2. Evaluate details of a passage to determine its main idea.
3. Utilize features of the passage, such as the topic sentence, to aid in the process of elimination.

## Warm-Up

### Instructions

Complete the warm-up question. If time remains after you've finished, double-check your work.

### Passage

The Statue of Liberty is one of the most recognizable symbols of American liberty, but on occasion it has come close to losing its signature torch. Shortly after the light first debuted in New York City in 1886, it burned out as it was being tested. The light was repaired; however, it burned out again 12 years later. Finally, as the light shone in 1918 in honor of the end of World War I, it burned out again—damaging the existing torch so much that the whole fixture had to be replaced.

**1.** The passage is mainly concerned with

Ⓐ the creation of the Statue of Liberty

Ⓑ the celebration of the end of World War I

Ⓒ the problems with the Statue of Liberty's torch

Ⓓ important symbols of independence in the United States

# Warm-Up

SLIDE 38.1

*Give students 2 minutes to complete the warm-up question.*

SLIDE 38.2

1. **The correct answer is C.** Choice A is incorrect because the passage does not discuss *the creation of the Statue of Liberty*. Choice B is incorrect because although *the light shone in 1918 in honor of the end of World War I*, this is only a detail in the passage and not the main concern. Choice D is incorrect because the passage doesn't describe *symbols of independence* in general; it only discusses one (the Statue of Liberty). Choice C is correct because the passage details *problems with the Statue of Liberty's torch* over the years.

TSIA2 Mastery: ELAR 

## Groundwork

EXERCISE A

**Instructions**

Read each list of words. Then, create a title for each based on your analysis. Write it in the space provided.

| 1. ____________________ | 2. ____________________ |
|---|---|
| springtime | Spanish |
| holiday | Hmong |
| jokes | Creole |
| pranks | Mandarin |
| the 1st | Arabic |

# Groundwork

*In this section, students will practice identifying a connecting thread among ideas.*

EXERCISE A

**Ideas are powerful. Despite being something that exists only in the imagination, they have the potential to heavily impact our world, especially if you have a really clear vision for it. Think about it: that's how pretty much every successful company got its start. But, what happens when someone has an idea but no vision to back it up?**

Nothing happens, so the idea just falls apart.

**It's kind of like having a bunch of facts and examples without a main idea. It can be challenging to find a main idea from details because you need to find the thread that connects everything.**

SLIDE 39.1

**Before we dive into the concept of a main idea, let's start with something simple: a list. Take a look at the first list of words in your workbook. Who would like to read that list to the class?**

*Springtime*, *holiday*, *jokes*, *pranks*, and *the 1st*.

**A good strategy for identifying the topic is to give the paragraph your own title. Or, in this case, a list of key words. To give our list a good title, though, we need to find a connection. What do these words have in common?**

April Fools' Day.

**If we take a thread and connect all of these words, we know that there's a springtime holiday that falls on the 1st every year, where people play jokes and pranks on one another: April Fools' Day. That's a great title for the first list.**

SLIDE 39.2

**What about the second list? What would you title that one?**

Languages.

**How many of you saw at least one language on that list that you'd never heard of?**

*Pause for a show of hands.*

**Pretty cool, right? Even though we may not have known everything on that list, we were still able to pick up the common thread that links the key words together to create our topic. And finding the topic is our first step when it comes to figuring out the main idea.**

EXERCISE B

**Instructions**

Read the passage and underline the key words. Use those key words to create a title for this passage. Write your answer in the space provided.

**Passage**

3. ______________________________________________

The concept of a "good luck" charm is found in almost every culture on the planet. You're probably familiar with the more common good luck charms, like a four-leaf clover or rabbit's foot. Others are lesser-known. For instance, ancient sailors thought dolphins were lucky because seeing them meant land was likely close by. Vikings were particularly fond of acorns as symbols of good luck. This is linked to their god of thunder, Thor, and how often lightning struck oak trees. Vikings would collect the acorns and keep them in their pocket or windowsill as a way to protect themselves. Yet another example comes from the Navajo tribes. If a dragonfly landed on you, it was considered a lucky omen proving that you would recover from any hardship you'd been suffering through.

## Groundwork

*In this section, students will practice locating key words and using them to identify the topic of the passage.*

EXERCISE B | SLIDE 40.1

**Figuring out the topic of a passage will offer more of a challenge than just a list of words. Why do you think that might be?**

We have to find the key words ourselves.

**Since a passage isn't a neat and tidy list, we'll have to dig for our own key words. Take a minute now to read the paragraph and underline any words you see that you think are important to the topic of the paragraph.**

*Give the students 1 minute to review the paragraph.*

**What are some of the words you came up with?**

*Good luck, good luck charm, lucky, culture, four-leaf clover, rabbit's foot, sailors, dolphins, Vikings, acorns, Thor, lightning, pocket, windowsill, Native Americans, dragonfly.*

**Are there any key words that show up more than once?**

*Good luck, good luck charm, lucky.*

**What connecting topic connects all these key words?**

Good luck charms.

**And that would make a great title for this paragraph. I want to point out two things when it comes to topics of paragraphs. First, check out the opening sentence. Do you notice anything familiar?**

Yes, the first sentence talks about good luck charms, which we named as the topic.

**This happens *so often* on the test. And it makes sense if you think about it: where in a paragraph do you put the topic sentence when it comes to your own writing?**

The first sentence.

**Teachers don't suggest this because they like it that way. That's how real people write paragraphs out in the real world. Another pattern that pops up on the TSIA2 is repetition. You'll see paragraphs specifically mention the topic over and over again. How does that help us?**

If you find a word or phrase that appears in the first sentence, and it gets repeated again later in the paragraph, it's probably the topic.

**Watch for those repetitive words or phrases. If they're not the topic themselves, they're one of the key words that can lead you to the topic.**

**TSIA2 Mastery:** ELAR 

## Application

### THE APPROACH

When you are asked to find the main idea of a paragraph or passage, use these steps ...

1. Locate key words in the passage.
2. Identify the passage's topic.
3. Eliminate answer choices that don't match the passage's topic.

**Passage**

When a person hopes for a good outcome, they often perform a simple gesture: crossing their fingers. But, where does this practice come from? What impact could intertwining one's digits have on an outcome in the real world? The truth of the matter is that no one is exactly sure why we do this. One theory stems from yet another practice: when individuals would make a wish, someone would offer "support" by laying their finger across the other's to help the wish come true. Another possible origin is the Pagan belief that spirits often dwell near crossroads. By crossing fingers, a person could essentially create their own "crossroad," drawing in good luck from the spirits. Despite its unclear origins, the practice of crossing fingers for good luck persists well into today's world.

**4.** This passage is mainly about

Ⓐ how often people cross their fingers
Ⓑ people crossing their fingers in today's world
Ⓒ the reason people cross their fingers
Ⓓ how people wished for good luck in the past

# Application

***In this section, students will practice applying the steps of the Approach to a main idea question.***

**Connecting a thread between key words has been our go-to strategy up to this point, so the first step of the Approach won't be too surprising. What is it?**

Finding key words in the paragraph.

**How will we do that exactly?**

By checking the topic sentence, which is usually the first one, or by noticing words repeated in the paragraph.

SLIDE 41.1

**Go ahead and do that now. Take a pass through this paragraph and underline any key words you see.**

*Give students 90 seconds to complete this task.*

**What did you find?**

*Crossing fingers, luck, origin.*

**What's the connecting idea here? What's the topic of the paragraph?**

The origins of people crossing their fingers for good luck.

**We've got our key words, and we've connected them to identify the paragraph's topic. What should we do next?**

Compare them to the answer choices and eliminate the ones that don't match.

**Let's start with choice A. Does that one fit our topic?**

No.

**Why not?**

The passage doesn't talk about *how often* people cross their fingers.

**That choice was almost perfect. The paragraph *definitely* talks about people crossing their fingers, but that one detail about *how often* they do it ruins the whole thing. Let's eliminate that option. What about choice B? Does it match our topic?**

Yes, since the paragraph is about people crossing their fingers.

**But does that make it the right option? Should we just pick it and move on to another question?**

No, we need to check the other answers just in case.

**Let's hang on to choice B for now. What do you think about choice C?**

It's good, too. The passage talks about how tradition is probably the reason people cross their fingers for good luck.

**We'll hang on to choice C, too. Before we compare it to choice B to see which is better, what do you think about choice D?**

It's wrong.

**Why is that?**

The paragraph does talk about the past, but this choice doesn't mention crossing fingers or the reason people do it.

**Choice D is out, so let's compare what we have left. What's the difference between choice B and choice C?**

Choice B focuses on people in today's world, and choice C is more about the reason people cross their fingers.

**Which choice is better?**

Choice C, because the paragraph isn't just about today's world. It's about the past, too. The passage's main focus is why people cross their fingers.

**Choice B is an example of a pretty common trap answer. It recycles words in hopes that you'll pick it just because it seems familiar. It's always good to keep choices like that on your first pass of elimination, but don't let them fool you: always be sure to pick an answer that's supported by evidence.**

## THE APPROACH

When you are asked to find the main idea of a paragraph or passage, use these steps ...

1. Locate key words in the passage.
2. Identify the passage's topic.
3. Eliminate answer choices that don't match the passage's topic.

**Passage**

In Lopburi, Thailand, the macaques—a unique primate native to the area—have their very own celebration, which is enough to intrigue even the most skeptical of travelers. On the final Sunday of every November, locals put out a massive banquet, comprised of watermelons, durian, pineapple, dragonfruit, and a number of other sweet indulgences for the monkeys. This practice dates back more than 2,000 years and is a celebration of the monkey King Hanuman and the aid he provided the divine prince Rama. Naturally, this spectacle draws tourists every year. However, once the food runs out, the macaques tend to get a bit unruly and often lash out at spectators. For this reason, it's a good idea to leave well before the tables are emptied.

**5.** What is the author's main purpose?

Ⓐ To offer readers an interesting tourist destination
Ⓑ To explain why tourists are often in danger during this event
Ⓒ To point out the location of a unique yearly celebration
Ⓓ To contrast the legends of two cultural deities

## Application

*In this section, students will practice identifying the main idea of a passage.*

SLIDE 42.1

**This question is a little different from the types of questions we've seen so far. What makes it unique?**

It asks for the author's purpose, not the main idea.

**What are some of the most generic reasons why an author writes something?**

To inform, to persuade, to entertain.

**Take a look at the answers in question 5. Do your options include any of those generic purposes?**

Not really.

**These answer choices are actually main ideas in disguise. Notice that each one offers up a potential overarching topic that could describe the main idea of the paragraph. How should we adjust our approach?**

We shouldn't. The process will be the same.

**Where should we start?**

By looking for key words.

**Take a pass through the passage. What key words do you see?**

*Travelers, tourists, macaques, celebration, food.*

**So, what's our connecting thread? What's the topic of this paragraph?**

A celebration for macaques that attracts tourists.

**Let's take a look at our options. Can we eliminate any of them right off the bat?**

Choice D.

**What's wrong with that one?**

The passage only mentions the two deities but doesn't compare them, and they're only mentioned briefly in one of the sentences.

**Let's eliminate choice D. What about choice B? Why might someone pick that one?**

Because the passage does talk about danger when the food runs out.

**But is it the main idea?**

No, it's just a detail from the end of the passage.

**That means choice B is out, and we've got two choices left. If you've narrowed your options this far on test day, you've done a good job. By eliminating incorrect answers, even if you have no idea what the right answer is, you've at least given yourself a 50% chance of getting it right. So, let's compare. What's the difference between choices A and C?**

Choice A is more about a tourist destination as a whole, but choice C is more specific, mentioning the location.

**Which one do you think is better? Which one gives us the main idea?**

Choice A.

**Choice A is definitely the correct choice, since the passage gives us lots of detail about this tourist destination, while the location in choice C is just a detail. Remember: during the test, focus on those key words. They'll help you find the connecting thread that is the main idea.**

## Practice

**Instructions**
Complete the practice set. If time remains after you've finished, double-check your work.

**Passage**
The Granary Burying Ground in Boston, Massachusetts, is where you can find the tombs of thousands of Bostonians, many of whom played major roles in the American Revolution. John Hancock, the statesman and famous signer of the Declaration, was laid to rest there in 1793, and the patriot Paul Revere followed him in 1818. The graveyard quickly became one of the city's most visited tourist attractions. According to historical documents, the two most-frequented sites in the whole state in 1900 were Boston Common and the adjacent Granary Burying Ground.

**1.** What is the author's main purpose?

Ⓐ To present to readers an interesting site to see
Ⓑ To describe why a burial ground gets so many tourists
Ⓒ To point out the final resting place of two significant Bostonians
Ⓓ To contrast two famous sightseeing destinations

**Passage**
American inventor Thomas Edison is thought by most physics historians to have been the first to functionally use the power of electricity, and his 1878 invention of the lightbulb is legendary. Nevertheless, many Italians think of their native son Alessandro Volta, not Edison, as the first to successfully harness electricity. One day in 1800, according to his assistants' accounts, Volta set up an electric circuit, connected his battery, and produced a brief current. Volta could not generate a strong or constant charge, but he achieved something nonetheless.

**2.** What is the passage primarily discussing?

Ⓐ The accomplishment of Alessandro Volta
Ⓑ The difficulties in early electrical discoveries
Ⓒ The first use of electricity in the United States
Ⓓ The story of long-range electricity use

# Practice

SLIDE 43.1

*Give students 8 minutes to complete the practice set.*

SLIDE 43.2

1. **The correct answer is A.** Choices B, C, and D are incorrect because while these are all parts of the passage, they offer supporting details rather than the author's primary purpose. Choice A is correct because the passage, as a whole, functions as a presentation of *an interesting site to see*: the first sentence introduces the Granary Burying Ground in general, the second sentence mentions specific notable figures buried there, and the third and fourth sentences describe its historic popularity.

SLIDE 43.3

2. **The correct answer is A.** Choice B is incorrect because *difficulties in early electrical discoveries* is not a main focus of the passage. Choice C is incorrect because Volta's use of electricity occurred in Italy, not the U.S. Choice D is incorrect because this passage provides a very incomplete picture of *the story of long-range electricity use*, so it would be inaccurate to say that this is what the passage primarily discusses. Choice A is correct because the main focus of the passage is what Alessandro Volta accomplished.

**Passage**

Just downslope from its source in the Rocky Mountains, near the La Poudre Pass Lake, the Colorado River is almost 2 miles above sea level. However, elsewhere there are long stretches of the river, as it nears its mouth (the Gulf of California), where the Colorado is a mere 100 feet above sea level.

**3.** The passage is mainly discussing the Colorado River's

Ⓐ depth
Ⓑ length
Ⓒ elevation
Ⓓ location

## Practice

SLIDE 44.1

3. **The correct answer is C.** Choices A and B are incorrect because the measurements provided in the paragraph are about the Colorado River's elevation *above sea level*, not its *depth* or its *length*. Choice D is incorrect because though the *location* is mentioned as a supporting detail, it is not what the passage is mainly discussing. Choice C is correct because the passage is mostly concerned with *the Colorado River's elevation,* as seen in the quotations *the Colorado River is almost 2 miles above sea level* and *elsewhere ... the Colorado is a mere 100 feet above sea level.*

## Wrap-Up

**Instructions**
Complete the wrap-up question. If time remains after you've finished, double-check your work.

**Passage**
Guam is an island territory of the United States located along the western edge of the Mariana Trench in the Pacific Ocean. Given Guam's history as a colony of Spain and its political situation—it is an unincorporated territory of the United States—one might think that the name "Guam" is of Spanish or English origin. However, "Guam" is actually derived from the Chamorro phrase *Guahan*, meaning "we have," the greeting given to Spanish sailors by fruit sellers from the Chamorro tribe, a group that settled the island almost 4,000 years ago.

**2.** This passage is mainly about

Ⓐ how Guam got its name
Ⓑ where Guam is located
Ⓒ who governs Guam
Ⓓ what happened to Guam in the past

# Wrap-Up

SLIDE 45.1

*Give students 2 minutes to complete the wrap-up question.*

SLIDE 45.2

2. **The correct answer is A.** Choice B is incorrect because although the passage explains where Guam is located, this is not the major discussion point; it is simply an informative detail. Choice C is incorrect because, even though the passage mentions that Guam *is an unincorporated territory of the United States*, the passage does not specifically discuss the government of Guam. Choice D is incorrect because although the passage discusses Guam's history as a Spanish colony and its current political situation, these are presented as facts that lead to a common, mistaken assumption. Choice A is correct because after introducing Guam, the passage primarily talks about the origin of the island's name: *"Guam" is actually derived from the Chamorro phrase* Guahan.

This page is intentionally left blank.
Content resumes on the next page.

This page is intentionally left blank.
Teacher content resumes with the next chapter.

CHAPTER 6

# Author's Craft

In this chapter, students will analyze elements of a text to determine how they contribute to the author's purpose.

6

Author's Craft

In this chapter, you will analyze elements of a text to determine how they contribute to the author's purpose.

LEARNING TARGETS

1. Identify the purpose of a passage.
2. Assess how different types of details work to support a text's purpose.

47

## TSIA2 STANDARDS

**Literary Text Analysis**
Author's craft

The student will analyze an author's word choice rhetorically, analyze text structure, purpose, and audience, and analyze point of view and perspective in literary text.

**Informational Text Analysis and Synthesis**
Author's craft

The student will analyze word choice rhetorically, analyze text structure, purpose, and audience, and analyze point of view and perspective in informational text.

## TEKS ALIGNMENT

E1.8 *Author's purpose and craft*: listening, speaking, reading, writing, and thinking using multiple texts. The student uses critical inquiry to analyze the author's choices and how they influence and communicate meaning within a variety of texts. The student analyzes and applies author's craft purposefully in order to develop his or her own products and performances. The student is expected to:

(B) analyze use of text structure to achieve the author's purpose;

(D) analyze how the author's use of language achieves specific purposes.

## LEARNING TARGETS

1. Identify the purpose of a passage.
2. Assess how different types of details work to support a text's purpose.

## Warm-Up

**Instructions**

Complete the warm-up question. If time remains after you've finished, double-check your work.

**Passage**

Dubai, UAE, is designing the world's first indoor town, a 4,500-square-kilometer development including hotels, shops, entertainment and health centers, and even an indoor ski slope. The Mall of the World, as the project is called, will be eco-friendly. Lush vegetation will be cultivated under a glass dome that encloses the "town," with conifer forests providing natural air filtration. And, a canopy of solar panels will produce electricity, provide shade, and power automobiles for the residents.

**1.** The author refers to vegetation and solar panels in order to

Ⓐ introduce a new topic
Ⓑ counter an argument
Ⓒ criticize a proposal
Ⓓ support a claim

# Warm-Up

SLIDE 48.1

*Give students 2 minutes to complete the warm-up question.*

SLIDE 48.2

1. **The correct answer is D.** Choice A is incorrect because the topic of the paragraph is not *vegetation* or *solar panels*, but instead the *world's first indoor town*. Choices B and C are incorrect because the passage describes the Mall of the World; it does not *counter an argument* about it or *criticize a proposal*. Choice D is correct because the passage states that the project *will be eco-friendly*. In order to support this claim, the author notes the *lush vegetation ... with conifer forests providing natural air filtration* and *a canopy of solar panels*.

## Groundwork

EXERCISE A

**Instructions**
Identify the likely purpose of each of the books described below. Circle your answer.

1. *A Man, a Plan, a Canal, Panama: The Case against Roosevelt*

   Should Roosevelt be seen as the hero of the Panama Canal? This book argues that the commanding engineers on the ground in Panama should get the credit history gives Theodore Roosevelt.

   To Inform     To Entertain     To Persuade

2. *My Quest for Freedom in the Desert*

   A historical fiction novel illustrates the protagonist's thrilling adventures while surviving two years in the Sahara Desert, from fleeing life-or-death danger to discovering hidden miracles.

   To Inform     To Entertain     To Persuade

3. *Silent Islands: The Decline of the Hawaiian Songbird*

   This historical description charts the extinction of many native Hawaiian bird species and explains how the loss of these species can affect ecosystems around the world.

   To Inform     To Entertain     To Persuade

# Groundwork

*In this section, students will assess the description of a text to determine its general purpose.*

**When an author crafts a piece of text, no matter how large or how small, they are sending it on a mission. And to make sure it succeeds in that mission, the author carefully selects every detail that makes up their text, each one with its own role to perform. Discovering the purpose of a text is an important step in analyzing it. For example, would you say a horror novel and your English textbook serve the same purpose?**

No.

**How could we describe the purpose of a horror novel?**

To scare or to entertain.

**Even though textbooks might *seem* scary sometimes, what is more likely their purpose?**

To teach people about something.

**What about a lawyer's closing statement from a trial? What kind of purpose might that serve?**

To argue or persuade.

EXERCISE A SLIDE 49.1

**Let's put our evaluation skills to the test and see if we can figure out the purpose of these books listed here in your workbook. Start with number 1. What's the purpose of that book?**

To persuade.

**How do you know? What evidence do you see?**

The book is trying to convince people that *the commanding engineers on the ground in Panama should get the credit.*

**Sometimes words like *need to, would,* or *should* can clue us in that the author is trying to persuade us, and we're likely to see details that introduce different arguments or provide evidence for or against them.**

SLIDE 49.2

**How about the second book—what's the purpose there?**

To entertain.

**Why is it more likely meant to entertain than inform?**

It's more like a story.

**Fiction passages are usually more focused on getting the reader involved in the story, so dramatic or descriptive details are probably most relevant.**

SLIDE 49.3

**What about number 3? What kind of purpose does that text have?**

To inform.

**Why not entertain or persuade?**

It's not telling a story or trying to convince us that something is true. It's just facts.

**Informative passages have details that introduce topics, support claims made in the text, or provide further information about other details. A passage's purpose can tell us a lot about its details, then. Let's go ahead and take a look at how a passage detail relates to its purpose.**

EXERCISE B

### Instructions

Determine the purpose of the underlined sentence in the passage below.

### Passage

**(1)** The animal overpasses and underpasses on the Trans-Canada Highway have reduced large animal-vehicle deaths by almost 100 percent. **(2)** Unfortunately, animals are not as well protected along Canada's railways. **(3)** <u>Since they have been so successful with the highway programs, wildlife officials should also work with the railways to provide crossings for animals.</u> **(4)** The direct result of wildlife death in a train-animal collision is only part of the problem. **(5)** An animal carcass will attract other animals to the railroad tracks. **(6)** Furthermore, spilled grains and other food products bring animals to the railroad tracks, increasing the likelihood of collisions.

| criticize an idea | provide evidence | support a claim | offer a counterargument |
|---|---|---|---|

**4.** The purpose of sentence **(3)** is to ______________________________.

## Groundwork

*In this section, students will identify the purpose of a specific detail within a passage.*

EXERCISE B 

**Just like a passage has an overall purpose, the details within a passage have individual purposes, as well. And on the TSIA2, this is known as *author's craft*. Essentially, the test asks you to figure out how an author used a specific detail to create their text. For instance, a passage meant to entertain will have details that explain the action or describe a setting. What kinds of purposes do you think details in an argument might have?**

To give evidence, to explain their reasoning, or to give examples.

**The TSIA2 loves to ask you about details of a passage, whether it's the long literary text at the start of the test or in one of the many short passage questions that show up at the end of the reading section. They pick out a sentence, like what you see here with question 4. Which sentence does it want you to analyze?**

Sentence 3.

**And what does sentence 3 say?**

*Since they have been so successful with the highway programs, wildlife officials should also work with the railways to provide crossings for animals.*

**Take a moment to soak in what this sentence is saying. In fact, let's summarize it in a few words. What information shows up in this sentence?**

The highway programs have been successful, so they want to expand to railways.

**Now, take a step back and read the whole passage. What's the overall purpose of this passage?**

To persuade.

**What clues or evidence did you find that make you think this is an argument? Did any key words pop up?**

The third sentence uses the word *should*.

**Based on that, what kind of details might we expect to find in a persuasive passage?**

Arguments and evidence.

**The detail is definitely adding to the argument, but the question is, "how?" What's sentence 3's purpose? Let's take a look at our options. Is anything in our detail arguing against something, or maybe suggesting a different idea instead?**

No.

**Which answers can we rule out?**

*Criticize an idea* and *offer a counterargument*.

**Is sentence 3 giving us any concrete facts or figures to use as evidence?**

No.

**We see a little data in sentence 1 being used as evidence, but that's not what's happening in sentence 3. Think about the overall argument of this passage. What is the author trying to convince readers of?**

That the railroads should put in animal crossings.

**Does sentence 3 support this claim?**

Yes.

**The author starts to build the frame for their argument in sentences 1 and 2 by noting the previous successes of animal crossings and problems that still exist, then sentence 3 leads with a statement that adds to the central argument of the passage. Not a counterclaim. Not specific evidence. Just good, solid support.**

TSIA2 Mastery: ELAR 

EXERCISE C

### Instructions

Match each underlined detail with a purpose suggested in the bank below.

### Passage

**(7)** Due to the high number of animal deaths leading to problems in the genetic pool of wildlife, it would be worth the expense to create bridges and fences to funnel wildlife over railroad tracks in high traffic areas. **(8)** The railroads, however, are privately owned, and therefore do not have to support government projects. **(9)** Railroad company owners note that the high costs of fencing and overpasses would severely deplete their profits. **(10)** But it doesn't have to be this way: to combat the high costs of overpasses, Sweden is experimenting with fencing that guides animals to special crosswalks. **(11)** Before a train approaches, an alarm (like hunting dogs barking) sounds to frighten the animals off the track, and the sound is reinforced by the train speeding by. **(12)** This method is much lower in cost than overpasses since the main expense is installing fencing, around 50,000 euros per 50 kilometers. **(13)** A broader application of these methods would likely prove worthwhile for railroads, their clients, and local wildlife alike.

| criticize an idea | provide evidence | support a claim | offer a counterargument |
|---|---|---|---|

5. The purpose of sentence **(8)** is to ____________________.
6. The purpose of sentence **(10)** is to ____________________.
7. The purpose of sentence **(12)** is to ____________________.

## Groundwork

*In this section, students will evaluate different details within a passage and determine how they contribute to the purpose of the text.*

EXERCISE C SLIDE 51.1

**Not all details in a text will have the same purpose. The best writers know how to mix and match details with varying purposes so that their argument is strong. Let's check out some other potential detail purposes in this next section of the passage. Start with sentence 8. Can someone read that out loud?**

*The railroads, however, are privately owned, and therefore do not have to support government projects.*

**We've already identified this as a persuasive passage, but let's take a look at some surrounding details to put our sentence into context. Is there an argument or idea that leads the passage?**

*It would be worth the expense to create bridges and fences.*

**Is sentence 8 agreeing with, supporting, or explaining this argument?**

No.

**Is there a word cluing us in that sentence 8 might be going down a different track than previous details?**

*However.*

**Which purpose do we think best describes sentence 8, then?**

*Criticize an idea.*

**Why isn't sentence 8 a counterargument, though?**

Because it doesn't offer an alternative solution. It just says why the idea won't work.

SLIDE 51.2

**What about sentence 10? What kind of information does that sentence give us?**

A way to work around the high costs.

**Sounds like an alternative solution. What kind of purpose does sentence 10 have? Is there an answer choice we can match with that purpose for sentence 10?**

It offers a counterargument.

**The best persuasive writers love including this feature. Counterarguments strengthen an argument by pointing out flaws and then responding to them. The author here is using this pattern of details to continue to build their case.**

SLIDE 51.3

**Finally, let's look at sentence 12. What does that one say?**

*The main expense is installing fencing, around 50,000 euros per 50 kilometers.*

**This sentence offers specific data to support their claim. What do we call that when we're writing an argument?**

Evidence.

**So, what's the purpose of this detail?**

To *provide evidence* that other kinds of animal crosswalks might be an affordable option.

**By bringing together all of these different types of details, the author has done their best to persuade the audience that animal crosswalks are a worthwhile part of the railway system. But the test won't always give you persuasive texts, meaning more potential purposes for details are on the menu.**

# Application

## THE APPROACH

When asked to identify the purpose of a detail in a passage, use the following steps ...

1. Locate and review the target detail.
2. Evaluate the surrounding context of the detail.
3. Eliminate answers that do not correctly describe the detail's purpose.

**Passage**

In some locales, wildlife overpasses and underpasses are designed specifically for the kinds of wildlife that need them. In Amherst, Massachusetts, wildlife professionals built tunnels for spotted salamanders to cross under city streets. In Powys, Wales, the city council designed ditches and tunnels to lead toads to their breeding grounds and keep them off the roads. In Kenya, there is even an underpass for elephants. On Christmas Island, in Australia, red crabs migrate to the beach to breed, often crossing highways and roads. To protect this flood of creatures, wildlife biologists and civil engineers have designed crab tunnels and crab bridges to funnel the crabs to the beaches and keep them off the roads.

**8.** The author includes details about red crab breeding grounds in order to

Ⓐ describe an example
Ⓑ criticize an argument
Ⓒ present a solution
Ⓓ introduce a new topic

# Application

*In this section, students will apply the steps of the Approach to an author's craft question.*

SLIDE 52.1

**The TSIA2 offers up author's craft questions in one of two flavors, and the difference is in the answer choices. Take a look at question 8. What about this question tells you that it's asking about author's craft?**

It wants to know why the author used a specific detail, and the answer choices are all possible purposes.

**Now, check out the answer choices. Do they look familiar?**

Yes.

**This first flavor of author's craft gives you generic answer choices. The purposes are really just broad categories of detail types. Does the question give you a specific sentence to look at?**

No.

**What does the question want you to evaluate?**

Why the author included details about *red crab breeding grounds*.

**That means we've got to do a little hunting. What part of the passage talks about *red crab breeding grounds*?**

The last two sentences.

**What does it say? Summarize it in your own words.**

That the crabs have to cross highways and roads to get there, so people made bridges and tunnels to keep them safe.

**What should we do next?**

*Evaluate the surrounding context of the detail.*

**This means reading the passage. When you finish, take a moment to identify the passage's overall purpose. What kind of passage are we looking at?**

Informative.

**Take a quick pass through the answer choices. Are there any that aren't likely to show up in an informative passage?**

Choice B, *criticize an argument*.

**The passage is more interested in straightforward facts here, so let's eliminate choice B. Next, zone in on what comes directly before the detail. What does the passage say?**

*In Kenya, there is even an underpass for elephants.*

**Hm, does that seem directly related to our red crabs here?**

No.

**Let's go back even further and check out the main idea of the passage. What does the topic sentence say?**

*In some locales, wildlife overpasses and underpasses are designed specifically for the kinds of wildlife that need them.*

**Make the connection. How are the elephant underpasses related to the crab bridges and tunnels?**

They're examples of how people keep animals away from dangerous traffic.

**Look through your remaining answers. Which one best fits what we've discovered?**

Choice A, *describe an example*.

**Why isn't this presenting a solution, like in choice C?**

It wasn't responding to a problem in the passage.

**It's the first mention of red crabs in the whole paragraph, though. Couldn't choice D be correct?**

No, because it's not really *a new topic*.

**This whole passage is a long list of different examples illustrating the main idea, and the detail about the red crab bridges just finishes it up. That means it's not really a new topic. Choice A is definitely the best option.**

TSIA2 Mastery: ELAR 

## THE APPROACH

When asked to identify the purpose of a detail in a passage, use the following steps ...

1. Locate and review the target detail.
2. Evaluate the surrounding context of the detail.
3. Eliminate answers that do not correctly describe the detail's purpose.

**Passage**

It is clear that these overpasses and underpasses are amazingly successful. There are approximately one million animal-car collisions each year. These crashes usually kill the animal that is involved, resulting in up to a million large animal deaths due to vehicles per year. A car will kill a small animal with little to no damage to the car. However, a collision with a deer can cause an average of $8,000 of damage to cars, while an impact with a moose or camel is likely to completely destroy a car and possibly kill the driver. However, when a wildlife crossing is constructed, and the animals learn to use it, the rate of animal-vehicle collisions decreases by 85–90%. The increase in safety to motorists and the protection of wildlife would make these crossings a worthy financial investment for any district.

**9.** The author includes $8,000 of damage and 85–90% improvements in order to

Ⓐ underscore the benefits of building wildlife crossings to decrease road hazards

Ⓑ suggest that the cost of animal-vehicle collisions is much less than the cost of the crossings

Ⓒ explain that wildlife crossings are not completely infallible

Ⓓ reiterate that the cost of damage is nothing in comparison to the lost lives of deer

## Application

*In this section, students will evaluate how a detail acts within a text in order to best describe its purpose.*

SLIDE 53.1

**Take a look at question 9. What details are we evaluating?**

$8,000 and 85–90%.

**Numbers? Those are examples of data, which points to what kind of purpose?**

Evidence.

**Without even looking at the passage, we already have our answer! We just have to pick the option that says *provides evidence*. But that's not quite right. What's the issue?**

That's not an option.

**These answer choices are more detailed than the other ones we've seen. This is author's craft flavor #2, where the answers are statements that could either be true or false, depending on the passage. But let's not get ahead of ourselves. First, let's find those details. What does the passage say about those two numbers?**

That damage caused by hitting a deer with a car can cost $8,000, but wildlife crossings decrease the rate of collisions by 85–90%.

**Take a step back and read the whole passage now. What's the main idea?**

That wildlife crossings are worth building.

**How do the details relate to the main idea of the passage?**

They provide evidence that supports the argument.

**These types of author's craft questions want more, though. Notice the verbs at the start of each answer choice. What are they?**

*Underscore, suggest, explain, reiterate.*

**All of these verbs connect to the concept of providing evidence. So, how do we pick which one is right?**

We have to check the details of the answer.

**Let's start with choice A. Would you say these details help show *the benefits of building wildlife crossings to decrease road hazards*?**

Yes.

**Hang on to choice A. What about choice B? Do our details support the idea that the collisions aren't nearly as costly as building the crossings?**

No, they say the opposite.

**The passage tells us how the cost of the crossings is worth it because it reduces those costly collisions with animals. Choice B is out. Check choice C next. What do you think? Is that answer supported by the passage?**

No.

**The animal crossings aren't *infallible*, though. They only reduce the collisions by 85–90%. That's not 100%. Why is choice C unsupported?**

Because the passage isn't talking about how perfect the crossings are, just how they reduce collisions and save money.

**We can eliminate choice C. Last one: is choice D supported by the passage?**

No.

**Why not?**

Because the passage doesn't talk about the *lives of deer* in relation to how much the collisions cost.

**That means choice A is correct. When you run into author's craft questions on the TSIA2—whether it's a literary or an informational text—take a moment to evaluate the question type. Are you looking for a broad purpose or a specific goal the detail accomplishes? In either case, use the details of the passage to help you eliminate wrong answers until you're down to just one correct answer.**

## Practice

### Instructions

Complete the practice set. If time remains after you've finished, double-check your work.

### Passage

*The narrator of this passage from a novel is a teenage girl from the United States who now lives in France. She and her friend Inès are setting out to find a manuscript that may or may not be real.*

**(1)** That name, *Catacombes de Paris*. **(2)** It could mean more than a subterranean network of tunnels. **(3)** It could also refer to the complex interrelationships of the city itself: the crossroads of Paris. **(4)** There's adventure in that name, and mystery. **(5)** It's an intersection, a bridge to the afterlife, a place just underfoot. **(6)** The air felt as heavy with secrecy as it was with the smell of earth, with whispers, with mold.

**(7)** There were other memorable names to be found within the tunnels themselves: the *Sarcophagus of Lacrymatoire*, the *Fountain of the Samaritan*, their titles evocative of antiquity and myth, located in the bowels of the tunnels. **(8)** Looky-loos laden with cameras around their necks and guidebooks in hand hustled through the entrance, eager to make their own finds. **(9)** They talked loudly about the hidden treasures they expected to encounter as if their confidence might actually help locate them. **(10)** The Sepulchral Lamp. **(11)** The Atelier. **(12)** The Crypt of Sacellum.

**(13)** Inès had left to buy tickets. **(14)** I waited patiently by the entrance, scarcely believing that we were really going through with this but not quite nervous. **(15)** If we decided tonight, halfway through our search, to give up, then we could always turn back, and it would be easy to make up a reasonable excuse for why our field trip had ended early.

**(16)** My family had bought the story that we were going on a field trip unquestioningly; all that we had to do was make sure that the school didn't call them when we didn't show up for classes on Friday. **(17)** Inès had faked a doctor's note that Sébastien would turn in, and I had made up a family vacation. **(18)** I seem to remember I said it was for President's Day, although in retrospect, I am shocked anyone would have believed that. **(19)** Whatever excuse I had made up, with little difficulty, we now had the whole day to ourselves. **(20)** We were free to do exactly what we wanted.

**(21)** It wouldn't have been hard for me to borrow a guidebook or city map for the excursion from my parents. **(22)** But obviously, knowing I would give up the whole plot if I asked them for anything like that, I had opted instead to just throw some water and snacks into my regular school satchel. **(23)** Inès, however, had showed up at the school gate that morning with a detailed plan and high-powered flashlights, and I felt like an amateur in contrast. **(24)** Despite all this, there was a *frisson* of excitement in the air as we set off underground—it was an early indication of what has developed into a somewhat reckless impulse in me to leave the map behind and explore freely.

This page is intentionally left blank.
Teacher content resumes on the next page.

**TSIA2 Mastery:** ELAR 

**1.** The imagery of the first paragraph (sentences 1–6) primarily creates a feeling of

Ⓐ mystery and tension
Ⓑ openness and sense of comfort
Ⓒ sadness and a hope for understanding
Ⓓ suspense and fear

**Passage**

To be precise, a moat is a deep, broad ditch dug around the outside of a fortification. It forms a perimeter and is designed as a first line of defense against attackers. The word "moat" came to Middle English from the Old French *motte*, meaning "mound." Originally, the word referred to the central island on which a fortress was built, but it eventually came to refer to the surrounding ring, suggesting a close relation between these two features in construction.

**2.** The author includes and defines the word *"motte"* primarily to

Ⓐ offer a physical description of moats
Ⓑ relate the name and origin of moats
Ⓒ pinpoint the geographical source of moats
Ⓓ indicate the military and protective value of moats

**Passage**

At the onset of World War II, when the company Bausch & Lomb came up with a sunglass design for US Air Force pilots that would reduce glare—the sunglasses "banned" distracting rays to improve visibility—it immediately put all of its manufacturing resources into these Ray-Ban Aviators. Following the war, Americans sought the brand's "heroic" sunglasses, wanting to adopt the look of soldiers and aviators pictured in news photographs.

**3.** Why does the author place quotation marks around the word "heroic" (sentence 2)?

Ⓐ To suggest that Ray-Ban Aviators, though part of a heroic cause, are not literally heroic
Ⓑ To underscore how Ray-Ban Aviators aided US pilots
Ⓒ To indicate that the US pilots used the word "heroic" to describe Ray-Ban Aviators
Ⓓ To point out that the Ray-Ban company changed the sunglasses' name to include the word "heroic"

# Practice

SLIDE 55.1

*Give students 8 minutes to complete the practice set.*

SLIDE 55.2

1. **The correct answer is A.** Choice B is incorrect because the passage describes a busy, underground environment that does not seem very open (*the air felt as heavy with secrecy as it was with the smell of earth, with whispers, with mold*). Choice C is incorrect because there is no mention of sadness in the first paragraph. Choice D is incorrect because the author never explicitly states that she is fearful, so it's a stretch to say the paragraph creates a tone of fear. Choice A is correct because the author says *there's adventure in that name, and mystery*, and the rest of the paragraph establishes a feeling of tension as the girls get ready to embark on their journey.

SLIDE 55.3

2. **The correct answer is B.** Choices A, C, and D are incorrect because even if these are related to the word origin of *moat*, they are not the best characterizations of the reason the author *includes and defines the word* "motte." Choice B is correct because the reason the author mentions the word *motte* is to describe its relationship to the central mounds of fortresses, which explains the origin of moats: *Originally, the word referred to the central island on which a fortress was built, but it eventually came to refer to the surrounding ring.*

SLIDE 55.4

3. **The correct answer is A.** Choice B is incorrect because quotation marks are not used to emphasize how the sunglasses *aided US pilots*. Choice C is incorrect because, in this instance, the quotation marks are not used to indicate actual speech or dialogue. Choice D is incorrect because the author does not indicate that *heroic* was added to the name of the sunglasses. Choice A is correct because the effect of using quotation marks on the word *heroic* indicates that the word is not being used 100% literally or accurately; without the quotation marks, the word *heroic* would be interpreted as completely serious, but with the quotation marks, there is a level of irony added.

## Wrap-Up

### Instructions

Complete the wrap-up question. If time remains after you've finished, double-check your work.

### Passage

Before World War I, the only timepieces created and sold for men were pocket watches—named for the fact that the watches were kept in the pocket—and wristwatches were worn exclusively by women as fashion accessories. During the war, pocket watches proved highly impractical for both soldiers in the trenches and aviators who needed to use both hands at all times, inspiring the development of men's wristwatches for civilian markets.

**2.** The author includes the information about women's fashion accessories primarily to

- Ⓐ offer a physical description of wristwatches
- Ⓑ indicate the convenience and value of wristwatches for soldiers
- Ⓒ pinpoint the time period in which wristwatches were created
- Ⓓ contrast the typical styles of watches worn during that time period

# Wrap-Up

SLIDE 56.1

*Give students 2 minutes to complete the wrap-up question.*

SLIDE 56.2

2. **The correct answer is D.** Choice A is incorrect because the passage does not offer a specific description of the wristwatches. Choice B is incorrect because though the wristwatches were both convenient and useful to the soldiers, this does not relate to the portion of the passage relating to women's fashion accessories. Choice C is incorrect because the passage does not discuss *the time period in which wristwatches were created*. Choice D is correct because the fact that wristwatches were *worn exclusively by women* contrasts the fact that *the only timepieces created and sold for men were pocket watches* prior to World War I.

CHAPTER 7

# Synthesis: Central Arguments

In this chapter, students will evaluate the characteristics of TSIA2 synthesis questions that focus on the central arguments of two passages. In addition, they will review and apply a strategy that can be used to answer any TSIA2 question with those characteristics.

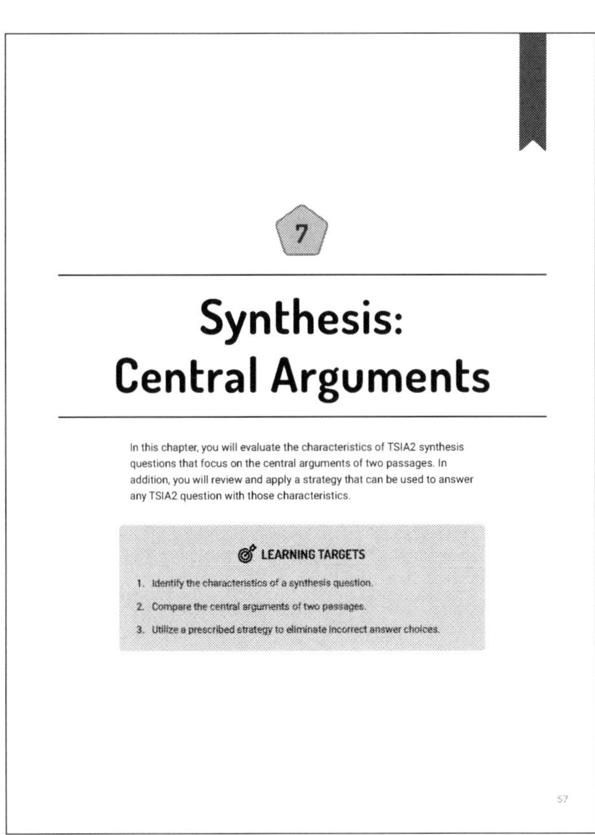

7

Synthesis: Central Arguments

In this chapter, you will evaluate the characteristics of TSIA2 synthesis questions that focus on the central arguments of two passages. In addition, you will review and apply a strategy that can be used to answer any TSIA2 question with those characteristics.

LEARNING TARGETS

1. Identify the characteristics of a synthesis question.
2. Compare the central arguments of two passages.
3. Utilize a prescribed strategy to eliminate incorrect answer choices.

57

## TSIA2 STANDARDS

**Informational Text Analysis and Synthesis**
Synthesis

The student will draw reasonable connections between two related argumentative texts, including determining rhetorical relationships, analyzing commonalities, and analyzing claims and counterclaims.

## TEKS ALIGNMENT

E1.4 *Comprehension skills*: listening, speaking, reading, writing, and thinking using multiple texts. The student uses metacognitive skills to both develop and deepen comprehension of increasingly complex texts. The student is expected to:

(H) synthesize information from two texts to create a new understanding.

E1.5 *Response skills:* listening, speaking, reading, writing, and thinking using multiple texts. The student responds to an increasingly challenging variety of sources that are read, heard, or viewed. The student is expected to:

(B) write responses that demonstrate understanding of texts, including comparing texts within and across genres.

## LEARNING TARGETS

1. Identify the characteristics of a synthesis question.
2. Compare the central arguments of two passages.
3. Utilize a prescribed strategy to eliminate incorrect answer choices.

## Groundwork

EXERCISE A

### Instructions

Refer to the following question as your teacher leads the discussion. Do not answer the question.

### Passage 1

Your learning style is not difficult to adapt to, and the average person can figure theirs out relatively easily. Whether you're a visual, auditory, or tactile learner, most teachers nowadays have the knowledge and resources to meet your needs. To discover your learning style, simply follow these essential steps. First, identify a particular method of learning and what that style entails. Second, list areas where you can put this type of learning into action. Third, commit to sticking to this method as firmly as possible (implementing visual learning might be easier with the help of a teacher). Fourth, and finally—compare with other methods! In a couple of months, you may have the educational breakthrough of a lifetime.

### Passage 2

It's often thought that students learn best through one particular method of learning. That belief seems to have come from a study in the 1990s that found that teachers that reached the widest group of students used several instructional styles. However, approaching subject matter in various ways may be beneficial in and of itself, and the truth is people do not have only one style of learning. Indeed, a study in the *British Journal of Psychology* shows no correlation between reported learning style and memory. Of the 104 students in the experiment, one group reported preferring to remember pictures better than words. But the groups did not ultimately differ when put to the test.

1. The author of Passage 2 most likely would say that the argument expressed in Passage 1 is

   (A) vague and dangerous
   (B) researched and logical
   (C) undeveloped but encouraging
   (D) common but misguided

# Groundwork

***In this section, students will evaluate the characteristics of a synthesis question that focuses on the central arguments of both passages.***

SLIDE 58.1

**Who'd like a little extra cash this week?**

*Pause for a show of hands.*

**Well, the money for this example is fake, but at least the job is too. Today, we're babysitting. And these two kids can't agree on anything. In fact, they're in the middle of an argument right now. Kid 1 says they saw Kid 2 paint the pet cat neon green, and Kid 2 swears he wasn't even in the room when it happened. What should you do?**

Ask more questions to see which story checks out.

**On the TSIA2, you'll be doing something similar, only instead of kids, you'll be working with two passages. We call them dual passages. How do you think these passages will be related to each other?**

They'll give different sides of an argument.

**Dual passages will never agree with each other. Their core opinions, or central arguments, will always be the opposite. And you'll be tasked with evaluating those arguments in a process we call *synthesis*. Does anyone know what *synthesis* means?**

Combining ideas together.

EXERCISE A SLIDE 58.2

**Essentially, you'll have to use the ideas from both passages to come up with one correct answer. But, the TSIA2 is tricky. They have *two* kinds of synthesis questions. The first one focuses on central arguments, which is essentially the big picture of each paragraph. The other challenges you to evaluate a detail from one passage from the perspective of another. Take a look at question 1 in your workbook. What kind do you think this is?**

A central argument question.

**How can you tell?**

It asks about *the argument expressed in Passage 1*.

**If the question asks about an argument as a whole, you can assume that you'll need to get well-acquainted with the central arguments of both passages. What do the answer choices have in common?**

They're just a few words separated by *and*.

**Central argument synthesis questions love to use this formatting. They offer up descriptive words rather than sentences or statements. This feature pushes you to combine everything you learned from the passages into a neat little package in the form of adjectives. Challenging? Yes. Impossible? Definitely not. And we've got a game plan that can help you get what you need from those opposing passages to eliminate wrong answers.**

TSIA2 Mastery: ELAR 

EXERCISE B

**Instructions**

Review the basic steps for answering a short passage question. Put them into the correct sequence by filling in numbers 1–5 in the space provided.

_____ Identify and compare the central argument of each passage.

_____ Read the question first.

_____ Read the passages.

_____ Find your evidence.

_____ Use the process of elimination.

## Groundwork

*In this section, students will sequence the steps for a basic strategy that can be used to answer any synthesis question that compares the passages' central arguments.*

EXERCISE B SLIDE 59.1

**When it comes to synthesis on the TSIA2, are we reading the question or the passages first?**

The question.

**Why do you think that's the best strategy?**

Because then you know what to look for while you read.

**The question could be asking about a specific detail, or it might ask about the central arguments as a whole. It's good to know what you're up against before you dive into reading the passages. Once you've read the passages, what's your next step?**

Identify the central argument of each passage.

**We need to know which side of the debate the authors are taking. It's a good idea to write down what you come up with on your scratch paper, too. How will that help you?**

It will keep everything organized.

**Staying organized is important, especially when it comes to the next step: finding evidence. Can we use our notes as evidence?**

Yes.

**And what should you do once you find the evidence you need?**

Use it to eliminate wrong answers.

**When it comes to synthesis questions that focus on the central arguments of a passage, your notes can be a great resource for getting the process of elimination started, especially if you take really good notes. If you're not as confident with your note-taking skills, though, don't sweat it. You can still use the passage as you normally would for a reading question. Either way you want to go, it's all about the evidence.**

## Application

### THE APPROACH

When a synthesis question asks you about the central arguments of both passages, use these steps ...

1. Read the question.
2. Read the passages.
3. Identify and compare the central claim of each passage.
4. Find your evidence.
5. Use the process of elimination.

**Passage 1**

Your learning style is not difficult to adapt to, and the average person can figure theirs out relatively easily. Whether you're a visual, auditory, or tactile learner, most teachers nowadays have the knowledge and resources to meet your needs. To discover your learning style, simply follow these essential steps. First, identify a particular method of learning and what that style entails. Second, list areas where you can put this type of learning into action. Third, commit to sticking to this method as firmly as possible (implementing visual learning might be easier with the help of a teacher). Fourth, and finally—compare with other methods! In a couple of months, you may have the educational breakthrough of a lifetime.

**Passage 2**

It's often thought that students learn best through one particular method of learning. That belief seems to have come from a study in the 1990s that found that teachers that reached the widest group of students used several instructional styles. However, approaching subject matter in various ways may be beneficial in and of itself, and the truth is people do not have only one style of learning. Indeed, a study in the *British Journal of Psychology* shows no correlation between reported learning style and memory. Of the 104 students in the experiment, one group reported preferring to remember pictures better than words. But the groups did not ultimately differ when put to the test.

1. The author of Passage 2 most likely would say that the argument expressed in Passage 1 is

   Ⓐ vague and dangerous
   Ⓑ researched and logical
   Ⓒ undeveloped but encouraging
   Ⓓ common but misguided

# Application

***In this section, students will practice applying a basic strategy to a synthesis question that focuses on the authors' central arguments.***

SLIDE 60.1

**Let's come back to the question we saw at the start of the lesson. We know it's a synthesis question because it's got those dual passages, and the question doesn't really mention anything specific. It's more about the overall central arguments of these passages. Where do we start?**

With reading the question.

**What does the question want to know?**

How Passage 2's author would describe the argument in Passage 1.

**Do we have to read these passages in order?**

No.

**In fact, it might even be better to read Passage 2 first. Why do you think that would be helpful?**

We would know what Passage 2's author thinks before we even look at Passage 1.

**It might feel like chaos to read all of these elements so out of order, but there's a method to the madness. Knowing what the author of Passage 2 thinks means we'll be able to respond to the argument in Passage 1 in the same way. Think of it like reading Passage 2 to start looking at the topic from their perspective. Step into their shoes. Then dig into the argument of Passage 1 from their perspective. As we're reading, what are we looking for?**

The overall main claim of each passage.

**Remember to take notes on your scratch paper so that you stay organized. Take a moment now to read both of these passages.**

*Give students 90 seconds to read the passages.*

**What would you say is the central argument of Passage 2?**

That there's no benefit or strength in trying to learn using a preferred learning style.

**What about Passage 1? What does that author claim?**

That a person should stick to their preferred learning style.

**Once we've got our central claims, it's time to start pulling evidence to help us eliminate incorrect answers. Let's start with choice A. Is there any evidence to say that the author of Passage 2 thinks Passage 1's argument is vague and dangerous?**

No.

**Passage 1 is anything but vague. It even offers specific steps. And going so far as to say that the argument is *dangerous* is an exaggeration. Choice A can't be right. What about choice B? What evidence can we use to eliminate that one?**

Passage 1 doesn't mention any research.

**Passage 2 definitely talks about a specific study, but Passage 1 doesn't cite any research at all. Choice B is out. Does choice C seem like a potentially good answer?**

Maybe.

**What evidence do we have to support this answer?**

The end of Passage 1 has a very encouraging tone.

**Let's hang onto that one for now and check choice D. Do we have evidence to support choice D?**

The first sentence of Passage 2 supports the idea that the argument is *common*, and the author of Passage 2 says that using learning styles is ineffective, which supports it being *misguided*.

**Compare your options. Between choices C and D, which one has the *best* support?**

Choice D.

**Why that one?**

There's more evidence overall to support choice D, and the evidence we found is more specific.

**When it comes to reading questions, the best answer will always have the strongest evidence. That means choice D is correct.**

## THE APPROACH

When a synthesis question asks you about the central arguments of both passages, use these steps ...

1. Read the question.
2. Read the passages.
3. Identify and compare the central claim of each passage.
4. Find your evidence.
5. Use the process of elimination.

**Passage 1**

The use of online pseudonyms, or fake names, has been a point of controversy since the advent of the Internet. Pseudonyms provide users with privacy and anonymity, but this anonymity can embolden users to act irresponsibly because they know their actions carry no real-world consequences. As a result, pseudonymous users are more likely to harass others and post hateful comments. Additionally, pseudonyms can facilitate dangerous—or even criminal—online activities, such as scams in which a user pretends to be an authority figure and threatens people for money. Given these concerns, some social media platforms like Weibo and Facebook require users to post under their real names. These platforms also make efforts to link people's online and offline social networks to ensure that users are held accountable for their online behavior.

**Passage 2**

Anyone who reads comments on YouTube videos or news articles knows that anonymous users can post some vile stuff, presumably because they know it can't be tracked back to them. However, psychologists who study online anonymity argue that the platform should be held partially responsible for this behavior. In the "deindividuated" model of anonymity, people who feel anonymous start to lose their sense of individual identity. Without a strong personal identity, people rely on group identities and become much more susceptible to group influences. That's why people get caught up in destructive mobs in real life—and why they feel it's appropriate to imitate others who post hurtful comments online. But when a community firmly enforces positivity and prosocial norms, anonymous users are susceptible to those good influences too! Online platforms ought to invest more time into fostering positive communities so they can reap the benefits of anonymity.

2. Both authors would most likely agree with which statement?

Ⓐ Pseudonyms are worth the risk because they provide much-needed privacy to users.

Ⓑ Anonymity is inherently negative in both online and offline contexts.

Ⓒ Online platforms can help to address the problems associated with anonymity.

Ⓓ Using real names online is generally preferable, except in cases where group norms are well-enforced.

## Application

*In this section, students will practice answering a central argument-focused synthesis question that focuses on how the authors agree.*

SLIDE 61.1

**Take a look at question 2. How is this different from the last question we looked at?**

It wants to know how the authors agree.

**The TSIA2 won't always want you to figure out where the two authors disagree. They might also ask you to find places where the authors overlap, or agree with one another. Take a moment now to read the passages, and as you read, try to nail down the central claim of each paragraph.**

*Give students 2 minutes to read the passages.*

**What is the central argument of Passage 1?**

That fake names make people behave badly online, so websites should make people use their real names.

**What about Passage 2? What's that author's main argument?**

That people will follow the group, so websites should push people to be more positive so that everyone follows the example.

**Let's start looking for evidence. Is there anything that helps us eliminate choice A?**

The entire argument of Passage 1 is that fake names shouldn't be allowed, so it's wrong.

**Choice A is out. Can we eliminate any other answer choices just using that detail?**

Choice D, since there isn't anything that says they think there should be exceptions.

**The author of Passage 1 is definitely against fake names, and since they don't talk about *group norms*, we can't say that they'd agree with that idea. Choice D is out. Is there anything to support choice B?**

Passage 1 talks about how anonymity is bad for online contexts, and Passage 2 talks about it being negative both online and offline.

**Passage 1 says *anonymity can embolden users to act irresponsibly because they know* they won't get in trouble, and Passage 2 explains how being anonymous leads to people posting *vile stuff* online and how people can *get caught up in destructive mobs in real life*. With that evidence, choice B seems pretty viable, but let's check choice C just in case. Can we find any evidence to support that one?**

Both passages mention specific ways online platforms can address anonymity.

**Passage 1 talks about how websites could force people to use their real names, and Passage 2 specifically says that online platforms could offer the benefits of being anonymous if they made sure to focus on positive interactions. This is *strong* evidence. But is it stronger than what we have for choice B?**

Yes, since Passage 1 doesn't talk about negative stuff that happens offline, it's not as well-supported.

**When it comes to answering these questions on the TSIA2, you might see questions like this, where there are two choices that *could* be right. But only one will have that strong, clear support like we found here for choice C. Always go for the answer that's *best* supported by the passages.**

## Practice

### Instructions

Complete the practice set. If time remains after you've finished, double-check your work.

### Passage 1

Should time-consuming athletic programs be cut from schools? Ongoing research indicates the opposite. One study looked at various factors indicating the health and social values of both student athletes and their non-sport-playing peers. Researchers found that young people who play competitive sports tend to have a higher GPA and spend more hours studying than students who don't play sports. Additionally, rates of depression and anxiety are lower for student athletes than for their counterparts who don't play sports. Researchers also learned that student athletes are more likely to have an active, healthy lifestyle as they grow older than those who did not participate in sports. Already familiar with exercising, goal setting, and pushing through challenges, teen athletes can carry these habits into adulthood.

### Passage 2

Playing defense on my high school's soccer team, I admit it's hard to focus on whatever is going on in class when it's game day. Practice days can be pretty grueling—we spend hours either in exhausting drills or in mandatory study hall to keep our GPA up. Before I played sports, I got more rest, and I had friends from different organizations around school. I knew other students because we rode the bus together or were in the same group for a science project. Now, I spend most of my time at practice, and since my teammates are my friends, it's natural to spend our free time together, too. Then again, what's free time?

**1.** The authors of both passages would probably characterize student athletes as being generally

Ⓐ overwhelmed
Ⓑ healthy
Ⓒ friendless
Ⓓ satisfied

# Practice

SLIDE 62.1

*Give students 8 minutes to complete the practice set.*

SLIDE 62.2

1. **The correct answer is B.** Passage 1 explains that student athletes have healthy habits in place, and Passage 2 describes grueling and exhausting workouts. This implies that both authors assume athletes are *healthy* as a result of their consistent physical exercise. Choice A is incorrect because only the author of Passage 2 would support *overwhelmed*; Passage 1 does not indicate that student athletes might feel this way. Choice C is incorrect because the author of Passage 2 describes having friends and spending time with them. Choice D is incorrect because neither passage makes this claim. Choice B is correct because there is evidence in both passages to support it.

**Passage 1**

As secondary education options become more diverse, liberal arts colleges are gaining popularity. The size of liberal arts colleges usually allows the students to be well acquainted with one another. Smaller class sizes also mean professors often have more one-on-one time with students. However, the cost of attendance may not be worth it, depending on what kind of lifestyle students expect to have in the future. Another option might be taking liberal arts classes at a state university rather than attending a private liberal arts school. This way, students can still receive a well-rounded education while avoiding many years of paying off student loans.

**Passage 2**

Many students today are choosing to go to a state university because of the greater number of opportunities available. Despite their "small classroom" advantages, private liberal arts schools can miss out on important government funding, so their facilities and resources can be lacking. Students may pay a higher tuition cost, spend more in student fees, and encounter higher prices in the cafeteria or recreation center. Ensuring job security after graduation is also crucial, and students are increasingly opting for majors that are perceived to lead more directly to jobs. A liberal arts college experience can be rewarding, but for many high school graduates, the high cost of tuition is not worth it.

**2.** Both authors would probably agree that for some students, going to a liberal arts college is

Ⓐ essential
Ⓑ unaffordable
Ⓒ practical
Ⓓ unfulfilling

## Practice

SLIDE 63.1

2. **The correct answer is B.** The author of Passage 1 praises liberal arts schools but admits that many students suffer from the cost of attendance, spending *many years ... paying off student loans*. The author of Passage 2 also states that at liberal arts schools, students pay a higher tuition, have more expenses, and might not have high-paying jobs after graduation. Choice A is incorrect because neither author describes attending a liberal arts college as *essential* for students. Choice C is incorrect because both authors cite the financial challenges of attending liberal arts schools, a factor that would not make them *practical*. Choice D is incorrect because both authors acknowledge the positive and fulfilling potential of a liberal arts education, so they would not describe it as *unfulfilling*. Only choice B correctly conveys a detail agreed upon by both authors, so it is the correct answer.

This page is intentionally left blank.
Content resumes on the next page.

This page is intentionally left blank.
Teacher content resumes with the next chapter.

CHAPTER 8

# Synthesis: Evaluating Claims

In this chapter, students will evaluate the characteristics of a TSIA2 synthesis question that focuses on a single claim made within the larger context of the argument. In addition, they will review and apply a strategy that can be used to answer any TSIA2 question with those characteristics.

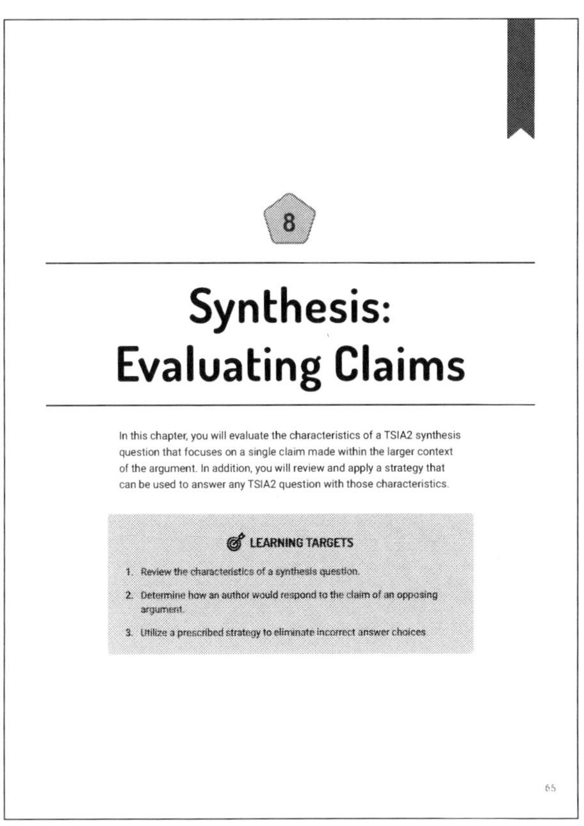

8

Synthesis:
Evaluating Claims

In this chapter, you will evaluate the characteristics of a TSIA2 synthesis question that focuses on a single claim made within the larger context of the argument. In addition, you will review and apply a strategy that can be used to answer any TSIA2 question with those characteristics.

LEARNING TARGETS

1. Review the characteristics of a synthesis question.
2. Determine how an author would respond to the claim of an opposing argument.
3. Utilize a prescribed strategy to eliminate incorrect answer choices

65

## TSIA2 STANDARDS

**Informational Text Analysis and Synthesis**
Synthesis

The student will draw reasonable connections between two related argumentative texts, including determining rhetorical relationships, analyzing commonalities, and analyzing claims and counterclaims.

## TEKS ALIGNMENT

E1.4 *Comprehension skills*: listening, speaking, reading, writing, and thinking using multiple texts. The student uses metacognitive skills to both develop and deepen comprehension of increasingly complex texts. The student is expected to:

(H) synthesize information from two texts to create new understanding.

E1.5 *Response skills*: listening, speaking, reading, writing, and thinking using multiple texts. The student responds to an increasingly challenging variety of sources that are read, heard, or viewed. The student is expected to:

(B) write responses that demonstrate understanding of texts, including comparing texts within and across genres.

## LEARNING TARGETS

1. Review the characteristics of a synthesis question.
2. Determine how an author would respond to the claim of an opposing argument.
3. Utilize a prescribed strategy to eliminate incorrect answer choices.

## Groundwork

EXERCISE A

**Instructions**

Refer to the following question as your teacher leads the discussion. Do not answer the question.

**Passage 1**

A rising number of people are opting to work alone. In the United States, over one-fifth of the workforce describe themselves as "independent workers," and around the world, the number of people who typically work in a solitary setting is increasing as gig work becomes more prevalent. In a recent analysis, many independent workers reported not feeling lonely at work; in fact, the analysis indicates that people who are working alone spend more time making connections and attending networking events. It's possible that these workers appreciate that they can spend time collaborating with others and then return to a private office or turn off emails when they need uninterrupted work time. In more ways than one, it's having your cake and eating it too: coworking when you need it, but flexibility and independence whenever you want.

**Passage 2**

"Coworking" is an arrangement where professionals from different companies share a workspace and split costs such as rent and janitorial services, as well as enjoy office perks such as coffee, office supplies, and camaraderie. There are ever-growing numbers of coworking spaces across the US, such as community-run spaces that are open to the public, private offices that require a monthly or yearly subscription, and industry-specific spaces such as sites that cater to nonprofit sector employees. As the American workforce becomes gig economy-oriented and more people recognize the intrinsic loneliness of independent working, shared workspaces may play a larger role in our careers very soon.

1. The author of Passage 1 would probably respond to the reference in Passage 2 to the "intrinsic loneliness of independent working" by

   (A) pointing to the findings of the analysis described in Passage 1
   (B) casting doubt on the benefits of coworking mentioned in Passage 2
   (C) underscoring the notion that working alongside others makes people happier
   (D) emphasizing the pitfalls of working alone

# Groundwork

*In this section, students will evaluate the characteristics of a synthesis question that asks them to evaluate a claim made in an argumentative text using an opposing author's perspective.*

**EXERCISE A**

**If you could have any wild animal in the world as a pet, what would it be?**

*Allow 2–3 students to share.*

**From your perspective, you'd be doing that animal a favor, right? You'd give it food, shelter, and all the love and attention any good human loves to drown their pets in. But, what about that animal? Do you think the animal would want to live with you?**

Probably not.

**Why not? What's so wrong with living in the human world?**

It wouldn't have the freedom it needs to live a good life.

**Chances are, that wild animal would see your home as a cage, the food as boring and bland, and the adorable knit hat you'd undoubtably force it into as a torture device. In fact, when we look at things from the animal's perspective, we see exactly why keeping that animal is a not-so-great idea. And we'll do this on the TSIA2 as well. What's the most challenging part of looking at things from another person's perspective?**

Not using our own opinions.

**SLIDE 66.1**

**When you take on someone else's point of view, you cast aside your own opinions and experiences, and you look at the issue through their eyes. What about question 1 in your workbook tells you that we're being asked to do this?**

It asks how the author of Passage 1 would respond to something from Passage 2.

**So, whose perspective are we taking on?**

The author of Passage 1.

**And what should we evaluate using that author's perspective?**

The *intrinsic loneliness of independent working* mentioned in Passage 2.

**Do we have a lot of insight into how the author of Passage 1 thinks?**

Not really.

**The test only gives us one paragraph of ideas from that author, meaning we don't have a lot to work with. But don't let that get you down before you even get started. What do we know about the best answer choices to reading questions?**

They are always supported by evidence.

**The test may not give you lots of text to help you figure out how an author thinks, but they won't leave you hanging. There will always be evidence you can use to make eliminations and work toward the correct answer.**

EXERCISE B

**Instructions**

Review the basic steps for answering a synthesis question. Put them into the correct sequence by filling in numbers 1–5 in the space provided.

_____ Read the question first.

_____ Use the process of elimination.

_____ Find your evidence.

_____ Locate and review the details.

_____ Read the opposing author's passage.

## Groundwork

*In this section, students will sequence the steps for a basic strategy that can be used to answer any synthesis question that evaluates a detail from one argument through the perspective of an opposing author.*

EXERCISE B SLIDE 67.1

**Before you take on someone else's point of view, what should you do first when you see this kind of question on the TSIA2?**

*Read the question first.*

**How will that help you?**

It will make your reading more focused.

**It's like reading the instructions before trying to build a piece of IKEA furniture. Trust me. It will make the process a lot less painful. What's our next step after we've read the question?**

*Locate and review the details.*

**The question will always point to a specific detail in one of the passages. Why do you think it's better to focus on that detail, rather than to review the entire paragraph?**

You'll only read the stuff you need, not the other stuff that could distract you.

**Eyes on the prize, right? If you focus on just the stuff the question is asking about, you'll avoid potential trap answers. How much of the detail should you review?**

The whole sentence.

**Sometimes, the question will only ask about a specific phrase, while other times it focuses on a whole sentence. Either way, read the entire sentence to get a good understanding of what the author is saying. If you feel like the sentence doesn't give you everything you need, what should you do?**

Read more.

**There's nothing that says you can only look at the question's detail. Feel free to search a little more if it solidifies your understanding of what the author is saying. Once you feel good about that, what's next?**

*Read the opposing author's passage.*

**And what are you looking for as you read?**

Evidence.

**Since the TSIA2 is on the computer, it can be a challenge to keep track of any evidence you find. On other tests, you get a test booklet you can write on or underline key points. On the TSIA2, though, we do have access to a highlighter tool. Why might it be a good idea to highlight any evidence you find in the passage?**

It makes comparing answer choices to the evidence easier.

**When your evidence is highlighted, the process of elimination becomes a little smoother. You don't have to re-scan the paragraph again and again to make sure you're looking at the right sentence. Use that highlighter to your advantage as you eliminate incorrect answers.**

# Application

## THE APPROACH

When a synthesis question asks you to evaluate a detail in one passage from the opposing author's perspective, use these steps ...

1. Read the question first.
2. Locate and review the details.
3. Read the opposing author's passage.
4. Find your evidence.
5. Use the process of elimination.

**Passage 1**

A rising number of people are opting to work alone. In the United States, over one-fifth of the workforce describe themselves as "independent workers," and around the world, the number of people who typically work in a solitary setting is increasing as gig work becomes more prevalent. In a recent analysis, many independent workers reported not feeling lonely at work; in fact, the analysis indicates that people who are working alone spend more time making connections and attending networking events. It's possible that these workers appreciate that they can spend time collaborating with others and then return to a private office or turn off emails when they need uninterrupted work time. In more ways than one, it's having your cake and eating it too: coworking when you need it, but flexibility and independence whenever you want.

**Passage 2**

"Coworking" is an arrangement where professionals from different companies share a workspace and split costs such as rent and janitorial services, as well as enjoy office perks such as coffee, office supplies, and camaraderie. There are ever-growing numbers of coworking spaces across the US, such as community-run spaces that are open to the public, private offices that require a monthly or yearly subscription, and industry-specific spaces such as sites that cater to nonprofit sector employees. As the American workforce becomes gig economy-oriented and more people recognize the intrinsic loneliness of independent working, shared workspaces may play a larger role in our careers very soon.

1. The author of Passage 1 would probably respond to the reference in Passage 2 to the "intrinsic loneliness of independent working" by

   Ⓐ pointing to the findings of the analysis described in Passage 1
   Ⓑ casting doubt on the benefits of coworking mentioned in Passage 2
   Ⓒ underscoring the notion that working alongside others makes people happier
   Ⓓ emphasizing the pitfalls of working alone

# Application

***In this section, students will practice applying a basic strategy to a synthesis question that focuses on a detail from one of the authors.***

SLIDE 68.1

**Let's practice reviewing the details of one argument through the eyes of the opposite author. Where do we start?**

With the question.

**Take a moment to read the question. What detail are we going to evaluate?**

The *intrinsic loneliness of independent working* in the second passage.

**And whose perspective are we looking through?**

The author of Passage 1.

**Let's consider the passage now. Where does Passage 2 mention our detail?**

In the last sentence.

**In your own words, what is that sentence saying?**

That people are lonely when they do gig jobs, so we're probably going to move back towards shared workspaces.

**Let's make a note of this. You can write things down on the scratch paper you're given during the test, or you can use the highlighting tool on your screen. Note anything you think could be important when it comes time to eliminate wrong answers. What should we do next?**

*Read the opposing author's passage.*

**Take a moment now to do that. As you read, underline any important details you could use as evidence in our next step.**

*Give students 60 seconds to complete this task.*

**What does the author of Passage 1 think about working alone?**

That it's a good thing.

**Passage 1 goes on about how much people thrive when they work independently, so it's easy to say that they are in support of that trend. Before we dig into the choices, though, check out the perspective on the question again. Whose point of view are we looking through?**

The author of Passage 1.

**We want to think about how the author of Passage 1 would respond to Passage 2. What does choice A say about that?**

The author of Passage 1 would point to the findings of the analysis in Passage 1.

**And what is that finding?**

The passage says *the analysis indicates that people who are working alone spend more time making connections and attending networking events.*

**Is that relevant to the stuff the author of Passage 2 said about loneliness?**

Yes, it basically says the opposite of what Passage 2 says.

**That's a pretty good reason to hold onto this choice for now, but let's check the other options. What about choice B? Is there anything in the passage to support that as a possibility?**

No, because there's nothing in Passage 1 to say that the author doesn't support coworking.

**The author of Passage 1 isn't against coworking. They just really like working independently, which means they won't try to respond to Passage 2 this way. Choice B is out. What about choice C? Does that seem like a viable answer?**

No, because Passage 1 says the opposite.

**Passage 1 makes it seem like the independent workers are happier than those coworking, so the author would definitely not try to use that to respond to Passage 2. Choice C is out. What about our last option? Does choice D seem right?**

No.

**Why not?**

The author of Passage 1 doesn't think working alone is a bad thing.

**This answer seems more like something the author of Passage 2 might say, which is a trap answer you'll commonly see on the TSIA2. This is why our setup is so important. We have to make sure we're taking on the correct perspective before we look at our answer choices. That means choice A is the correct answer.**

TSIA2 Mastery: ELAR 

## THE APPROACH

When a synthesis question asks you to evaluate a detail in one passage from the opposing author's perspective, use these steps ...

1. Read the question first.
2. Locate and review the details.
3. Read the opposing author's passage.
4. Find your evidence.
5. Use the process of elimination.

**Passage 1**

I recently met a ninth-grade teacher who told me that over half of her students drank coffee in the mornings. Some of her students said they started drinking coffee as early as sixth grade. Others said they only started in high school—where the gym vending machine sells cold coffee drinks. A handful of the non-coffee drinkers admitted they drink caffeinated soda to wake up every morning. As a matter of fact, about 64% of Americans have a cup of coffee every morning rather than waking up naturally. This is a shame! Now more than ever, people need to return to more natural ways of living—especially young, developing children. Parents, end your children's caffeine consumption and ensure they get enough sleep every night instead!

**Passage 2**

There are almost no conclusive statistics about the number of young people consuming caffeine daily. Fatigued students struggle to focus in class and perform poorly on tests, however, and many other nations with a culture of tea-drinking consistently have higher-scoring students than the United States. It's possible that American students are not as alert and productive as their caffeinated counterparts. Coffee and tea also contain antioxidants and some essential nutrients, so caffeinated drinks can provide a variety of benefits, from improved physical health to mental stimulation and clarity. In addition to encouraging a good night's sleep, it is logical for parents to allow their children to consume caffeine, including coffee, in the morning for their well-being.

2. The author of Passage 2 would probably respond to the last sentence of Passage 1 by

Ⓐ arguing that children should be drinking more coffee in the mornings
Ⓑ pointing out that children consume more caffeine at a young age than their parents did
Ⓒ asserting that children should use more natural methods to wake up
Ⓓ emphasizing that parents should help children balance rest and caffeine consumption

## Application

*In this section, students will practice answering a synthesis question that challenges them to view the opposing argument through an author's perspective.*

SLIDE 69.1

**This question is a little bit different from the last one. How so?**

It focuses on a whole sentence from Passage 1.

**What does that sentence say?**

That parents shouldn't let their kids drink caffeine.

**Take a moment now to read the opposing author's opinion in Passage 2. Underline any relevant evidence you find along the way.**

*Give students 60 seconds to complete this task.*

**What does Passage 2's author think about kids drinking caffeine?**

That it's okay, and it can even be beneficial.

**In the last question, we worked through the answers in order, but you don't always have to do that. Since we know what the author of Passage 2 thinks, how can we use that to eliminate answers?**

By crossing out answers that say the opposite.

**Do any of our choices say the opposite of what we found?**

Yes, choice C.

**The author of Passage 2 doesn't want kids to stop drinking caffeine, so we know they wouldn't respond that way. That answer is out. Any others?**

No.

**Where do we go from here?**

Look at the remaining choices to see if we can eliminate them.

**Does choice A seem like a good option?**

Kind of.

**What makes it a potentially good answer?**

The author of Passage 2 thinks students can benefit from caffeine.

**Let's hang onto that one for now. What about choice B? Is that answer supported by the passage?**

No.

**Neither Passage 1 nor Passage 2 mentions this detail, so choice B isn't supported by evidence. We can cross that one out. Is choice D supported?**

Yes.

**What does Passage 2 say specifically?**

*In addition to encouraging a good night's sleep, it is logical for parents to allow their children to consume caffeine.*

**We have two options that have some potentially solid evidence. But which one is *best* supported, and how can you tell?**

Choice D, since there's a specific sentence that tells us it's the right choice.

**If we want to prove choice A is right, we need to do a little bit of convincing and twisting the passage's meaning to say it's accurate. But with choice D, there's no question. The text explicitly supports that answer, so we know it's the best choice. If you find yourself debating between two options on test day, stick to this strategy. The best answer will be the one that's clearly supported by the passage.**

## Practice

### Instructions

Complete the practice set. If time remains after you've finished, double-check your work.

### Passage 1

Should time-consuming athletic programs be cut from schools? Ongoing research indicates the opposite. One study looked at various factors indicating the health and social values of both student athletes and their non–sport-playing peers. Researchers found that young people who play competitive sports tend to have a higher GPA and spend more hours studying than students who don't play sports. Additionally, rates of depression and anxiety are lower for student athletes than for their counterparts who don't play sports. Researchers also learned that student athletes are more likely to have an active, healthy lifestyle as they grow older than those who did not participate in sports. Already familiar with exercising, goal setting, and pushing through challenges, teen athletes can carry these habits into adulthood.

### Passage 2

Playing defense on my high school's soccer team, I admit it's hard to focus on whatever is going on in class when it's game day. Practice days can be pretty grueling—we spend hours either in exhausting drills or in mandatory study hall to keep our GPA up. Before I played sports, I got more rest, and I had friends from different organizations around school. I knew other students because we rode the bus together or were in the same group for a science project. Now, I spend most of my time at practice, and since my teammates are my friends, it's natural to spend our free time together, too. Then again, what's free time?

1. What would the author of Passage 2 most likely say is the cause of the "more hours" (sentence 4) student athletes spend studying as mentioned in Passage 1?

   Ⓐ the injuries caused by accidents during practice
   Ⓑ the difficulty of completing homework with limited free time
   Ⓒ the interruption to class due to traveling to away games
   Ⓓ the requirement to maintain a high GPA

# Practice

SLIDE 70.1

*Give students 8 minutes to complete the practice set.*

SLIDE 70.2

1. **The correct answer is D.** Choice A is incorrect because the author of Passage 2 does not refer to injuries. Choice B is incorrect because the author does not indicate they are unable to finish their homework in time. Choice C is incorrect because the author does not describe away games or how they disrupt their studies. Choice D is correct because the author describes *mandatory study hall to keep our GPA up*, which indicates they spend many hours studying to maintain a high grade point average.

**Passage 1**

As secondary education options become more diverse, liberal arts colleges are gaining popularity. The size of liberal arts colleges usually allows the students to be well acquainted with one another. Smaller class sizes also mean professors often have more one-on-one time with students. However, the cost of attendance may not be worth it, depending on what kind of lifestyle students expect to have in the future. Another option might be taking liberal arts classes at a state university rather than attending a private liberal arts school. This way, students can still receive a well-rounded education while avoiding many years of paying off student loans.

**Passage 2**

Many students today are choosing to go to a state university because of the greater number of opportunities available. Despite their "small classroom" advantages, private liberal arts schools can miss out on important government funding, so their facilities and resources can be lacking. Students might pay a higher tuition cost, spend more in student fees, and encounter higher prices in the cafeteria or recreation center. Ensuring job security after graduation is also crucial, and studies have shown that students are increasingly avoiding the liberal arts and instead opting for majors that are perceived to lead more directly to jobs. A liberal arts college experience can be rewarding, but for many high school graduates, the high cost of tuition is not worth it.

**2.** The author of Passage 2 would most likely respond to the first sentence of Passage 1 ("As secondary . . . popularity") by

Ⓐ pointing to evidence that liberal arts programs are actually becoming less popular

Ⓑ requesting additional testimonials regarding the popularity of liberal arts programs

Ⓒ explaining that liberal arts programs are not the only ones gaining popularity

Ⓓ maintaining that the popularity of liberal arts programs is indeed increasing

## Practice

SLIDE 71.1

2. **The correct answer is A.** Choice B is incorrect because there is no evidence that indicates that the author of Passage 2 requires additional information to form their opinion. Choice C is incorrect because Passage 2 does not refer to additional programs *gaining popularity*, only that students are *opting for majors that are perceived to lead more directly to jobs*. Choice D is incorrect because Passage 2's central argument is the opposite: the author asserts that *many students today are choosing to go to a state university* over a private liberal arts college. Choice A is correct because the author references research in sentence 4, stating *studies have shown that students are increasingly avoiding the liberal arts*.

This page is intentionally left blank.
Content resumes on the next page.

This page is intentionally left blank.
Teacher content resumes with the next chapter.

CHAPTER 9

# Short Passages

In this chapter, students will evaluate the characteristics of a short passage question from the TSIA2. In addition, they will review and apply a strategy that can be used to answer any TSIA2 question with those characteristics.

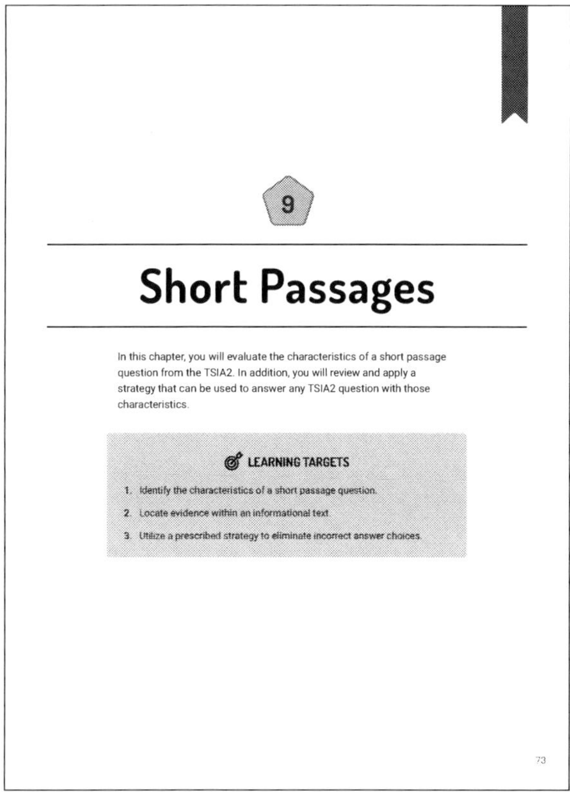
9

Short Passages

In this chapter, you will evaluate the characteristics of a short passage question from the TSIA2. In addition, you will review and apply a strategy that can be used to answer any TSIA2 question with those characteristics.

LEARNING TARGETS

1. Identify the characteristics of a short passage question.
2. Locate evidence within an informational text.
3. Utilize a prescribed strategy to eliminate incorrect answer choices.

73

## TSIA2 STANDARDS

**Informational Text Analysis and Synthesis**

The student will identify and analyze information and ideas in and elements of informational text.

## LEARNING TARGETS

1. Identify the characteristics of a short passage question.
2. Locate evidence within an informational text.
3. Utilize a prescribed strategy to eliminate incorrect answer choices.

## Groundwork

EXERCISE A

### Instructions

Refer to the following question as your teacher leads the discussion. Do not answer the question.

### Passage

In 2012, volunteers for "Let's Do It! World," a worldwide movement to combat the global solid waste problem, planned a six-month series of cleanups around the globe. These "cleanup days" occurred in 96 different countries, including Estonia, Lebanon, Nepal, and the Philippines. Slovenia's cleanup day was the largest that year, with over 289,000 participants. The tradition is gaining momentum, and on February 9, 2014, country cleanup leaders from around the world agreed to the goal of involving 380 million people by 2018.

1. The passage suggests that the main goal of the cleanup days was to encourage people to

Ⓐ spend more time in nature
Ⓑ volunteer for meaningful causes
Ⓒ commit to making a cleaner planet
Ⓓ travel to neighboring countries

# Groundwork

*In this section, students will evaluate the characteristics of a short passage question.*

EXERCISE A SLIDE 74.1

**The short passage questions on the TSIA2 are snack-sized when compared to the Thanksgiving dinner of a passage you'll see with long passages. And since they're so small, they'll only be paired up with one single question. But just because these question types are small, it doesn't mean they don't pack a big punch when it comes to your score. There are more short passages than any other passage type on the test, running from question 7 to question 15. That's more than *half* of the reading section. What would you say is the defining characteristic of this question type?**

The short passage.

**The passages with these questions are small, so you won't have to do a whole lot of reading to find the answer. Some of these are even as short as *two sentences*. How does knowing that help us as we're taking the test?**

There's not a lot of information to look through.

**Even if you need to read the passage three or four times to find the answer, it's okay because it's short. You won't run down your brain trying to sift through a huge piece of text for one little detail. Take a closer look at the passage in your workbook. Would you say its purpose is entertainment, information, or persuasion?**

Information.

**This passage has one purpose: to inform. And that's not a random feature here. In fact, every single one of your short passage questions will be an informational text. That means you already know up front that you won't be reading a short story or some random argument. Nice, right? What kind of advantage does that give you?**

You know what to expect.

**If you know what you're about to come up against, you can better prepare yourself. You know you won't be looking at character relationships or evaluating the plot of a story. What kinds of questions should you expect to see with an informational text?**

Ones that ask about details, the main idea, or making inferences.

**The specifics of the question will vary from question to question, and you'll never see more than one question that goes with a single short passage. But there's one thing we know all short passages have in common: a strategy for answering. Let's take a look on the next page to see what steps we'll use when we're working with short passage questions.**

EXERCISE B

**Instructions**

Review the basic steps for answering a short passage question. Put them into the correct sequence by filling in numbers 1–4 in the space provided.

______ Read the passage.

______ Find your evidence.

______ Use the process of elimination.

______ Read the question first.

## Groundwork

*In this section, students will sequence the steps for a basic strategy that can be used to answer any short passage question on the TSIA2.*

EXERCISE B SLIDE 75.1

**When you're taking a random standardized test and see a passage on top of your screen or page, followed by a question below it, what does your natural instinct tell you to do first?**

Read the passage.

**All our experience with reading has taught us to always begin at the top of a page and to work our way down. But when we take on a short passage during the TSIA2, we want to go against those instincts. What should you read first instead of the passage?**

The question.

**Why do you think that is?**

We'll know what to look for when we read the passage.

**Knowing what to look for makes searching the passage much more manageable. For instance, the question might ask you about a specific person, key word, or detail in the passage. Once you've read the question, what should you do next?**

Read the passage.

**Once you know what the question wants, it's time to read the passage. What should we do when we read?**

Look for information that helps us answer the question.

**That brings us to our third step: finding evidence. The whole point of reading the question first is to get your brain ready to find evidence as you read. It's called "reading with intention." What do you think that means?**

Instead of just reading the words, it's reading with a goal.

**What kinds of evidence do you think you might find?**

Details about the topic, key words, definitions, etc.

**What do you do with that evidence once you've found it?**

Answer the question.

**If an answer choice can't be supported by evidence from the text, you know it's wrong. This leads us to our fourth step. What should we do?**

*Use the process of elimination.*

**In general, we can prove an answer is wrong by either finding evidence in the passage that says the opposite is true, or we can say it's wrong just because there's a lack of strong evidence. If the passage doesn't offer support for an answer, it's not the answer for us. Which step of our strategy do you think will take the longest?**

Finding evidence.

**Finding evidence could be a straightforward process, especially if you find what you need the first time you read the passage. But it could also mean a lot of back and forth, checking answers against the details of the passage. And that's okay. You're allowed and even encouraged to read these passages more than once if you need to. It's more effective to be sure that you've found the support you need before picking an option than to limit yourself to one pass through the text.**

# Application

## THE APPROACH

When answering a short passage question on the TSIA2, use these steps ...

1. Read the question first.
2. Read the passage.
3. Find your evidence.
4. Use the process of elimination.

**Passage**

In 2012, volunteers for "Let's Do It! World," a worldwide movement to combat the global solid waste problem, planned a six-month series of cleanups around the globe. These "cleanup days" occurred in 96 different countries, including Estonia, Lebanon, Nepal, and the Philippines. Slovenia's cleanup day was the largest that year, with over 289,000 participants. The tradition is gaining momentum, and on February 9, 2014, country cleanup leaders from around the world agreed to the goal of involving 380 million people by 2018.

1. The passage suggests that the main goal of the cleanup days was to encourage people to

Ⓐ spend more time in nature
Ⓑ volunteer for meaningful causes
Ⓒ commit to making a cleaner planet
Ⓓ travel to neighboring countries

# Application

***In this section, students will practice applying a basic strategy to a short passage question and eliminating answers not supported by the passage.***

SLIDE 76.1

**Check out question 1 again. We know it's a short passage question because it's just one paragraph. What else do we know about the passage before we even read it?**

It's an informational passage.

**A good strategy is to come at these passages ready to learn something new. Even if it seems really uninteresting, fake it 'til you make it. Pretend like the passage talks about something you're super interested in. But, before we read the passage, what should we do first?**

*Read the question.*

**What does the question want us to find?**

The main goal of the cleanup days.

**We get a little bit of detail from the question. It wants to know what the main goal of the cleanup is, and it goes even further to say that it encourages people to do something. What is that something? Well, we won't know until we read the passage. So, let's do that now! Take a moment to read and soak in this new information.**

*Give students 90 seconds to read the passage.*

**In a few words, who can tell me what the passage was about?**

A cleanup day that went on in a bunch of countries.

**As we read the passage, we're kind of multi-tasking with step 3, right? What are we looking for again?**

Evidence about the main goal of the cleanup days.

**And what does the passage say about it? Is there anything specific that gives us help?**

The first sentence says it was created *to combat the global solid waste problem*.

**Essentially, the whole event was to deal with environmental issues. Makes sense. And now that we've got our evidence, we can use it to start eliminating answers. Remember: the passage is right there, so you can go back to it if you need to. It's a good idea to check back on the evidence with each answer. Let's start with choice A. Do we have any evidence to support that one?**

No.

**What's wrong with it specifically?**

There isn't anything talking about how people spend their time.

**What about choice B? Is there evidence to support that option?**

The passage mentions *volunteers,* and the cleanup day could be considered a *meaningful cause*.

**Let's hang onto that one for the moment. Does choice C have any evidence to support it?**

Yes.

**What does the passage say specifically?**

It says the movement was *a worldwide movement to combat the global solid waste problem*.

**That's some pretty solid evidence, so we can hang onto that one too. Is there evidence to prove that choice D is true?**

No.

**Choice D is out. But we still have two answers to choose from. What makes choices B and C different?**

Choice B is about volunteering for a meaningful cause, and choice C is about cleaning the planet.

**Those choices are really similar, so it might seem like a difficult choice. The trick is to use the evidence, and not our own thoughts and feelings to make the decision. What does the evidence say again?**

That it was created to help clean up the environment.

**That's the beauty of evidence—even though choices B and C both seem pretty solid, we know that only choice C is supported by the passage. And you can use this method again and again to separate even the trickiest of answers. Just stick to what the author says, and you'll be on the right track every time.**

**TSIA2 Mastery:** ELAR 

## THE APPROACH

When answering a short passage question on the TSIA2, use these steps ...

1. Read the question first.
2. Read the passage.
3. Find your evidence.
4. Use the process of elimination.

**Passage**

The red oak, the black oak, and the scarlet oak—all splendid forest trees of the Northeast—are so similar in appearance that they can often only be readily identified by the timber-cruiser, who knows every tree in the forest for its economic value, or by the botanist, with her paperback *Gray's Manual* in hand. I confess to bewilderment in five minutes after the differences have been explained to me, and I enjoyed, not long ago, the confusion of a skillful nurseryman who was endeavoring to show me his young trees of red oak that the label proved to be scarlet!

**2.** Which of the following best describes what "timber-cruiser" means, as it is used in the passage?

Ⓐ a casual lover of nature who uses a guidebook for reference
Ⓑ a botanist or scientist who has extensive knowledge of trees
Ⓒ an individual who assesses the worth of trees for profit
Ⓓ a nurseryman who must assign names to and label young trees

## Application

*In this section, students will practice answering a short passage question that focuses on explicit information from the passage.*

SLIDE 77.1

**Even though your eyes want to read that passage first, where are we starting?**

With the question.

**What does question 2 want us to find?**

The meaning of *timber-cruiser*.

**This question is really specific. It gave us a key word! What should we look for as we read?**

Where the passage talks about *timber-cruisers*.

**Speaking of reading the passage, take a quick look at just the first little phrase that opens this passage. What do you think it's going to be about?**

Trees.

**Who here loves learning about trees?**

*Pause for a show of hands.*

**Yep. Every person here loves learning about trees, right? Go ahead and read this passage like you can't get enough of those things.**

*Give students 90 seconds to read the passage.*

**Let's talk about the evidence. Which sentence talks about *timber-cruisers*?**

The first one.

**What does it say, specifically?**

That the trees can often only be *readily identified by the timber-cruiser, who knows every tree in the forest for its economic value.*

**We can use this evidence to start our process of elimination. Does this evidence say that a *timber-cruiser* is just a regular person using a guidebook?**

No, the passage talks about a *botanist* using the guidebook.

**Choice A is out. What about choice B? Is the *timber-cruiser* a botanist or other scientific expert?**

No.

**The sentence *does* talk about a botanist, but they're separate people. They don't have the same skills. That means we can eliminate choice B. What about choice C? Does that seem like an accurate description?**

Yes.

**What from the passage lines up with choice C?**

The passage mentions how they figure out the *economic value*, which is basically the same as assessing the *worth*.

**That seems like a really good option. Should we stop here and just go with choice C?**

No, we should check choice D just in case.

**Remember: the TSIA2 is untimed, so you aren't working against the clock. Take the time to check each answer choice just in case there's a better option lower on the list. Can we say the evidence supports choice D?**

No, the information about the nurseryman is at the end of the passage.

**So, even though choice D was a bust, it was still good we checked it. And by taking the time to actually read and soak in the passage's information, we're better able to not only find and locate evidence to help us get to a right answer, but we can easily point to evidence that shows another answer is wrong. Spending that little extra time with the passage ultimately worked in our favor, making it easier to use the process of elimination.**

## Practice

**Instructions**
Complete the practice set. If time remains after you've finished, double-check your work.

**Passage**
When we think of blushing, embarrassment, redness, and a rise in temperature come to mind—all noticeable in the face. Most people are surprised to discover the phenomenon of blushing also occurs in the stomach. Because adrenaline causes tiny blood vessels called capillaries to widen and increase blood flow, the tissue around these vessels in the stomach appears as red as a blushing cheek. Though this may seem unnatural to some, the stomach is just another example of how the brain uses chemical processes to prepare the body for fight or flight in often unnoticed ways.

**1.** The main idea of the passage is that

Ⓐ blushing in the face is identical to blushing in the stomach
Ⓑ adrenaline causes blood vessels to widen for increased blood flow
Ⓒ the stomach is the most prepared part of the body for fight or flight
Ⓓ stomach blushing goes unnoticed but is a natural process

**Passage**
A principal reason for the decline of opera singing in modern times is that the tuning of pitch has gradually and considerably risen during the last 150 years. As orchestras increasingly tune at higher frequencies, the vocal apparatus has been unable to bear the strain to which it is now subjected. With regard to tenors, though, the greater evil is that they disregard the falsetto register, singing everything, however high, in chest voice. Certainly they have not been beguiled into this serious mistake by the faint rise of tuning pitch just mentioned. The truth is that they have committed this fatal blunder knowingly and willfully—because they saw that it was more exciting to the public and knew it would draw in larger audiences.

**2.** Based on the passage, the rise of tuning pitch in music occurred

Ⓐ only in modern times
Ⓑ mainly due to the falsetto register
Ⓒ in the past two centuries
Ⓓ with the invention of a new apparatus

# Practice

SLIDE 78.1

*Give students 10 minutes to complete the practice set.*

SLIDE 78.2

1. **The correct answer is D.** The passage explains the surprising fact that the stomach can blush just as much as the face. Choice A is incorrect because this topic is too narrow and only describes one part of the passage. Choice B is incorrect because it is an explanatory detail included in the passage, not the main idea. Choice C is incorrect because it exaggerates the facts stated in the passage. Choice D is correct because it matches the focus of the passage.

SLIDE 78.3

2. **The correct answer is C.** Choice A is incorrect because the passage indicates that the rising in pitch has occurred over the past 150 years, which implies that it began before the modern era. Choice B is incorrect because the passage does not indicate that the falsetto register caused tuning pitch to rise. Choice D is incorrect because the passage does not mention a new invention. Choice C is correct because the passage indicates that the rising in pitch has occurred over the past 150 years.

**Passage**

A narcissist is someone with obsessive admiration for the self and who shows a need for excessive attention or praise. The name comes from a tale in Greek mythology in which Narcissus, a hunter known for his beauty, became so attracted to his reflection in a pool of water that he fell in love. However, when the object of his affection could not love him back, Narcissus became distraught and withered away, leaving behind a narcissus flower.

**3.** What is the overall purpose of the passage?

Ⓐ To recount a tale from Greek mythology
Ⓑ To describe the origin of a word
Ⓒ To stress the need to be cautious in love
Ⓓ To demonstrate the difficulties of finding love

## Practice

SLIDE 79.1

3. **The correct answer is B.** The passage defines a word and gives the history behind its meaning. Choice A is incorrect because it is too broad, leaving out *why* the passage is recounting this story. Choice C is incorrect because the story cautions against self-love, not love in general. Choice D is incorrect because while Narcissus struggles with unrequited love, it is not the main idea of the passage. Choice B correctly identifies the purpose of the passage, which gives the history behind a word.

This page is intentionally left blank.
Content resumes on the next page.

This page is intentionally left blank.
Teacher content resumes with the next chapter.

CHAPTER 10

# Supporting Details

In this chapter, students will analyze a given text and answer questions by picking out details that explicitly support the requested information.

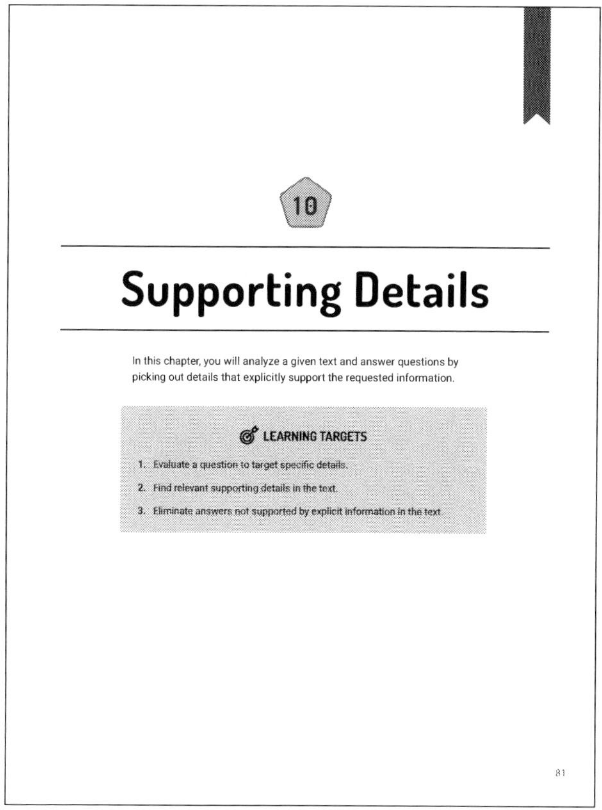

10

Supporting Details

In this chapter, you will analyze a given text and answer questions by picking out details that explicitly support the requested information.

LEARNING TARGETS

1. Evaluate a question to target specific details.
2. Find relevant supporting details in the text.
3. Eliminate answers not supported by explicit information in the text.

81

## TSIA2 STANDARDS

**Literary Text Analysis**
Explicit information

The student will identify ideas explicitly stated and clearly indicated in literary text.

**Informational Text Analysis and Synthesis**
Main ideas and supporting details

The student will identify main ideas of and comprehend explicitly stated and clearly indicated information and ideas in informational text.

## TEKS ALIGNMENT

E1.4 *Comprehension skills*: listening, speaking, reading, writing, and thinking using multiple texts. The student uses metacognitive skills to both develop and deepen comprehension of increasingly complex texts. The student is expected to:

(F) make inferences and use evidence to support understanding.

## LEARNING TARGETS

1. Evaluate a question to target specific details.
2. Find relevant supporting details in the text.
3. Eliminate answers not supported by explicit information in the text.

## Warm-Up

### Instructions

Complete the warm-up question. If time remains after you've finished, double-check your work.

### Passage

**(1)** That name, *Catacombes de Paris*. **(2)** It could mean more than a subterranean network of tunnels. **(3)** It could also refer to the complex interrelationships of the city itself: the crossroads of Paris. **(4)** There's adventure in that name, and mystery. **(5)** It's an intersection, a bridge to the afterlife, a place just underfoot. **(6)** The air felt as heavy with secrecy as it was with the smell of earth, with whispers, with mold.

**(7)** There were other memorable names to be found within the tunnels themselves: the *Sarcophagus of Lacrymatoire*, the *Fountain of the Samaritan*, their titles evocative of antiquity and myth, located in the bowels of the tunnels. **(8)** Looky-loos laden with cameras around their necks and guidebooks in hand hustled through the entrance, eager to make their own finds. **(9)** They talked loudly about the hidden treasures they expected to encounter as if their confidence might actually help locate them. **(10)** *The Sepulchral Lamp*. **(11)** *The Atelier*. **(12)** *The Crypt of Sacellum*.

**(13)** Inès had left to buy tickets. **(14)** I waited patiently by the entrance, scarcely believing that we were really going through with this but not quite nervous. **(15)** If we decided tonight, halfway through our search, to give up, then we could always turn back, and it would be easy to make up a reasonable excuse for why our field trip had ended early.

**(16)** My family had bought the story that we were going on a field trip unquestioningly; all that we had to do was make sure that the school didn't call them when we didn't show up for classes on Friday. **(17)** Inès had faked a doctor's note that Sébastien would turn in, and I had made up a family vacation. **(18)** I seem to remember I said it was for President's Day, although in retrospect I am shocked anyone would have believed that. **(19)** Whatever excuse I had made up, with little difficulty, we now had the whole day to ourselves. **(20)** We were free to do exactly what we wanted.

**(21)** It wouldn't have been hard for me to borrow a guidebook or city map for the excursion from my parents. **(22)** But obviously, knowing I would give up the whole plot if I asked them for anything like that, I had opted instead to just throw some water and snacks into my regular school satchel. **(23)** Inès, however, showed up at the school gate that morning with a detailed plan and high-powered flashlights, and I felt like an amateur in contrast. **(24)** Despite all this, there was a frisson of excitement in the air as we set off underground—it was an early indication of what has developed into a somewhat reckless impulse in me to leave the map behind and explore freely.

1. The primary setting of the passage is

   Ⓐ a school
   Ⓑ a museum
   Ⓒ a temple
   Ⓓ a burial site

# Warm-Up

SLIDE 82.1

*Give students 5 minutes to read the passage and complete the warm-up question.*

SLIDE 82.2

1. **The correct answer is D.** Choice A is incorrect because the passage makes clear that they've skipped school to go to the *Catacombes de Paris*. Choice B is incorrect because, though there are tourists with cameras, the passage does not state that they are in a museum. Choice C is incorrect because although there is a reference to the *afterlife*, there is no evidence they are visiting a *temple*; in fact, the passage states that they are underground *in the bowels of the tunnels*. Choice D is correct because the passage indicates that they are underground (*subterranean* means *underground*), and other clues indicate that it is a vault of sorts (specifically one containing a sarcophagus and a crypt, which are types of burial sites).

## Groundwork

EXERCISE A

**Instructions**
Use the following application to answer the questions below. Write your answers in the spaces provided.

**NEW SERVER APPLICATION**

**Name:** Margot Lowry

**Age:** 19

**Email:** mlowry@applications.com

**Phone:** (209) 555-8392

**Education:**

Thames High School
Class of 2019
Graduated top 10% in class

**Experience:**

Babysitting — The Green Family

- Cared for 3 small children, between the ages of 3 and 7
- Prepared meals
- Planned activities and crafts
- Integrated learning into playtime activities

1. How old is Margot? __________

2. What family did Margot work for? ________________________

3. How did Margot improve playtime? __________________________________

# Groundwork

*In this section, students will practice identifying explicit information from a simplified example passage.*

**Imagine you're at a grocery store, and you're in desperate need of apples. We're talking, it's been days since you've had one, and doctors are banging on your door day and night. You're done dealing with this, so it's apple time. But you've never been to this grocery store. You can't back away from the apple hunt because those doctors are after you. What do you do?**

Go looking for some apples.

**How do you even start looking if you've never been to that grocery store?**

You find the produce section first, then the fruit section.

EXERCISE A SLIDE 83.1

**You look for signs, right? You know what you need to find, and you can use that goal to help narrow down your search until you find those apples. Doctor problem solved. In the same way, when we're asked questions about a passage, we use the goal of the question to help us find our answers. For example, check out question 1. What is it asking for?**

How old Margot is.

**Where do you see that information in the passage?**

Where it says *age*.

**Notice that the wording isn't exact. *Age* and *how old* mean the same thing, so what will our answer be?**

*19*

**What about question 2? What kind of information are we looking for?**

The family she worked for.

**What category will have that information?**

The *Experience* category.

**What did you find? What's our answer?**

*The Green family.*

**Question 3 asks you to find out how she improved playtime. How will you use that question to help you find the answer in the passage?**

We can look for the word *playtime*.

**And what does the passage tell us about how she made playtime better for those kids?**

She *integrated learning into playtime.*

**By finding the key words of the question and using them as signposts in the passage, we're able to pinpoint the information we need.**

EXERCISE B

### Instructions

Use the following passage to answer the questions below. Write your answers in the spaces provided.

### Passage

**(1)** Wilbur and Orville dreamed of flight from the time they received their first toy rubber band helicopter from their father, Milton Wright, and they spent most of their lives building up the skills, funds, and research to make that dream a reality. **(2)** After dropping out of high school, Orville designed and built a printing press with Wilbur's help, and the two brothers opened up a print shop in their home of Dayton, Ohio, in 1889. **(3)** In 1892, the brothers moved into the bicycle business, starting a successful sales and repair shop in Dayton and later manufacturing their own brand of bicycle, also developed by Wright ingenuity.

**4.** Where did the Orville brothers spend their early adulthood?

______________________________________________

**5.** After working in a print shop, the brothers opened what kind of business?

______________________________________________

## Groundwork

*In this section, students will locate explicit information in the passage using key words from the questions.*

EXERCISE B | SLIDE 84.1

**The same concept applies to reading passages. When a question asks for something specific, we can use what shows up in the question to help us search for the answer. For instance, read question 4. What does it want you to find?**

The place where the brothers spent their early adulthood.

**It's a place. A location. It's not going to be a random fact or description. There's no doubt in our minds what the essence of our answer will be. How does that work to our advantage as we skim through the passage hunting for an answer?**

We'll know the answer when we see it.

**Because we know what we're looking for, there's no chance a detail will get lost in translation. The answer will be exactly what the passage says. Should we reread the entire passage to search for the answer?**

No, we should skim it.

**You don't need to read the entire passage all over again. Focus on the goal of the question. We need a location. So, to answer question 4, where did the brothers spend their early adulthood?**

In *Dayton, Ohio*.

**Where did you find that information?**

At the end of sentence 2.

**The key to answering any supporting details question is being able to point to the answer. If you can see it in the passage and actually put your finger on it, you know it's supported. What about question 5? What information does it ask for?**

The kind of business they opened after their print shop.

**Are there any good key words in the question we can scan the passage for?**

*Print shop.*

**And where should our answer be in relation to the keywords *print shop*?**

After it.

**Take a moment to skim the passage. Which sentence talks about the print shop?**

Sentence 2.

**Keep going, since we know the information should follow. What does the passage say about their next business venture?**

That they moved on to bicycles and started *a successful sales and repair shop.*

**By skimming the passage for those key words, we were able to target our search to a specific part of the passage and locate our answer fairly quickly. And even though time isn't an issue on the TSIA2, what are we limited on as we take the test?**

Mental energy.

**Skimming for key words is going to be key in helping us preserve that mental energy, which is especially important since reading questions are the first section of the test.**

TSIA2 Mastery: ELAR 

# Application

## THE APPROACH

When answering a question that requires specific details from a text, use the following steps ...

1. Identify key words in the question.
2. Scan the passage for related key words.
3. Find your evidence near the key words.
4. Eliminate answer choices not directly supported by evidence.

**Passage**

*The narrator of this passage, Nick Carraway, explains a bit about his background and family as he opens the story. Though he is not the main character of* The Great Gatsby, *he provides the perspective through which the story is told.*

**(1)** My family have been prominent, well-to-do people in this Middle Western city for three generations. **(2)** The Carraways are something of a clan, and we have a tradition that we're descended from the Dukes of Buccleuch, but the actual founder of my line was my grandfather's brother, who came here in fifty-one, sent a substitute to the Civil War, and started the wholesale hardware business that my father carries on today.

**(3)** I never saw this great-uncle, but I'm supposed to look like him—with special reference to the rather hard-boiled painting that hangs in father's office. **(4)** I graduated from New Haven in 1915, just a quarter of a century after my father, and a little later I participated in that delayed Teutonic migration known as the Great War. **(5)** I enjoyed the counter-raid so thoroughly that I came back restless. **(6)** Instead of being the warm centre of the world, the Middle West now seemed like the ragged edge of the universe—so I decided to go East and learn the bond business. **(7)** Everybody I knew was in the bond business, so I supposed it could support one more single man. **(8)** All my aunts and uncles talked it over as if they were choosing a prep school for me, and finally said, "Why—ye-es," with very grave, hesitant faces. **(9)** Father agreed to finance me for a year, and after various delays I came East, permanently, I thought, in the spring of twenty-two.

From F. Scott Fitzgerald, *The Great Gatsby*

6. How did the narrator's family make its money?

   (A) in the bond business
   (B) through an inheritance from the Duke of Buccleuch
   (C) in the wholesale hardware business
   (D) by manufacturing and selling ammunition during the Civil War

# Application

*In this section, students will compare answer choices against the passage to find the answer choice supported by the text.*

**During the TSIA2, how will you know if a question is asking you for a supporting detail?**

It will ask a straightforward question about something specifically talked about in the passage.

SLIDE 85.1

**The question will go straight to the nitty gritty and ask for a specific fact or detail from the text. And these show up in both long passages *and* short passages, which means you'll have to find details in both a literary text *and* an informational text. For instance, take a look at the passage that goes with question 6. What kind of passage is that?**

A long passage, so a literary text.

***The Great Gatsby* is a classic piece of literature, so it's definitely a literary text. The author, F. Scott Fitzgerald, can really craft some fine, fancy prose, but we can still nail down our answers if we keep a close eye on the nuts and bolts. This is a long passage, so we should read the passage first. Let's do that now.**

*Give students 2–3 minutes to read through the passage and the question.*

**What was the passage about?**

The narrator was talking about his family's history, his own background, and some of his plans for the future.

**Next, let's turn our attention to the question. What's it asking for?**

How the narrator's family made their money.

**Do you remember any places in the text that talked about making money?**

Yes, in sentences 2 and 7.

**Read and compare those sentences. What details do they offer?**

Sentence 2 talks about a hardware store started during the Civil War, and sentence 7 talks about how the bond business *could support one more single man*.

**Narrow your evidence even further. We're not just talking about making money. We're talking about family money. Which sentence contains that evidence?**

Sentence 2.

**The family gets their money from that hardware business that the father still runs today. That's our evidence. Next, take a pass through the answer choices. Which answers aren't supported by the evidence we found?**

Choices A, B, and D.

**What's wrong with choice A?**

He plans to go into the bond business, so he hasn't made any money doing it yet.

**What about choice B? What's off about that one?**

The passage just says the family is related to Buccleuch, not that they got an inheritance from him.

**Choice D mentions the Civil War. Why isn't that one right?**

Because the passage doesn't say the hardware store made ammunition.

**Which choice is supported by the passage?**

Choice C.

**Remember: these kinds of questions are straight to the point. They don't want you to interpret or infer anything, so if you can't pinpoint any evidence from the passage to support a given answer, you can eliminate it.**

## THE APPROACH

When answering a question that requires specific details from a text, use the following steps ...

1. Identify key words in the question.
2. Scan the passage for related key words.
3. Find your evidence near the key words.
4. Eliminate answer choices not directly supported by evidence.

**Passage**

Many who were alive on November 22, 1963, remember the day that President John F. Kennedy, Jr. was assassinated while participating in a motorcade in Dallas, Texas, sending the world into a state of shock and grief. Incidentally, on the same date, two significant figures of literature, C.S. Lewis and Anthony Burgess, also passed away peacefully in their homes. Their deaths were as not as newsworthy, but they are still remembered for the bodies of work they left behind.

7. According to the passage, why did the deaths of Anthony Burgess and C. S. Lewis receive little news coverage?

    Ⓐ They were not important figures like President Kennedy.
    Ⓑ Because their work was not well-known, few people recognized their names.
    Ⓒ Their deaths coincided with the death of another extremely well-known figure.
    Ⓓ Their deaths were not reported by the local news outlets where they lived.

## Application

*In this section, students will practice eliminating answers due to a lack of evidence in the passage.*

SLIDE 86.1

**Take a look at question 7. Just in appearance, how is it different from question 6?**

The question it asks is bigger.

**This question is meaty. It's got a long question, and all of the answer choices are full sentences. It might seem more intimidating. Should we change how we approach this question?**

No, we should use the same process.

**This *is* a short passage, though, so we'll change things up a bit at the start of our process. Rather than reading the passage first, like how we did with the long passage, what should we read first with a short passage?**

The question.

**By reading the question first, we can make our first read of the passage more pointed. Let's do that now. What does the question ask for?**

The reason the news didn't cover the deaths of Anthony Burgess and C. S. Lewis very well.

**Take a moment now to read the passage.**

*Give students 90 seconds to read the passage.*

**With bigger answer choices like these, it can be easier to compare each answer choice to what you found in the passage, rather than the other way around. Start with choice A. Is there anything in the passage that says that they weren't as important as President Kennedy?**

No, it just says that they were *two significant figures of literature*.

**Choice A is out. What about choice B? Can we find evidence to support that option?**

No.

**The passage even says that *they are still remembered*, so it's hard to say that only a few people would recognize their names. How about choice C? Does that statement seem accurate based on what you read?**

Yes, President Kennedy also died that day.

**It's kind of hard to compete with a presidential assassination in terms of news time, especially since they both died in a not-so-tragic way. It makes sense that the coverage of Kennedy's death was more widespread. Should we pick that choice and move on to the next question?**

No, we should check choice D just in case.

**Does anything in the passage tell us that their deaths weren't reported in their local areas?**

No, that topic isn't even mentioned.

**Choice D isn't supported by evidence, so we can feel confident about picking choice C and moving on. When it comes to questions on supporting details, remember that they're all about points. The question is to-the-*point*. You can *point* to the evidence. And getting the right answers means adding *points* to your final score.**

## Practice

**Instructions**
Complete the practice set. If time remains after you've finished, double-check your work.

**Passage**
*This passage is from a short story in which the narrator describes her time in a Pennsylvania lakeside town.*

**(1)** The time had come to bid fare-well to all my Morris Harbor friends, and my cozy room at the little inn, and return to the city that I worried would no longer be familiar. **(2)** There may be limits to such a winter's enjoyment, but the calm that accompanies a modest way of life is enticing enough to make up for the lack of finer pleasures, and the rewards of contentment are not for the restless.

**(3)** I was to travel the meandering local railway train that departed late in the day, and I sat for some time on the back porch overlooking the frozen blue lake, with loneliness as my companion. **(4)** Mrs. Cole had busied herself all day with tasks that seemingly required all of her attention; it was as if we were strangers passing one another in the street. **(5)** It was difficult to face my going-away with anything resembling a calm demeanor. **(6)** Finally I heard someone coming out onto the porch, and turned to see that Mrs. Cole was standing beside me.

**(7)** "Everything has been seen to," she announced suddenly with an unnaturally formal tone. **(8)** "Your cases must be down at the station by now. **(9)** The station-master he come an' carried 'em over himself, an' he'll make sure they're stowed in the luggage car. **(10)** Yes, I've seen to all your prep'rations," she said in a more familiar voice. **(11)** "The things I've put by the front door you'll want to keep with you; the sandwiches will do for your supper. **(12)** I suppose I shall walk down the Front Road now an' ask how old Mis' Robert Elwood is."

**(13)** I looked at my friend's face, and saw an expression that moved me deeply. **(14)** My emotions at leaving this place had already overwhelmed me.

**(15)** "I suppose you'll understand if I ain't over there to wave from the platform and see you off," she said, with her voice still brusque. **(16)** "Yes, I ought to find out how Mis' Robert Elwood is feelin'; if Mother comes on Tuesday she'll be askin' me how the old aunty is." **(17)** With this explanation, Mrs. Cole abruptly went back inside the inn, as if she had heard someone calling her name, so that I expected her to return, until I heard the front door closing and her footsteps on the path. **(18)** I could not bear such a departure; I hurried around the inn shouting after her, but she looked down and waved without turning around at the sound of my anxious voice, and so I walked away onto the road.

From Alice Mayne Corbett, *The Land of the Silver Maples*. Originally published in 1890.

**1.** Based on the passage, about how long has the narrator been in the town of Morris Harbor?

Ⓐ since childhood
Ⓑ a year
Ⓒ a winter
Ⓓ a week

# Practice

SLIDE 87.1

*Give students 10 minutes to complete the practice set.*

SLIDE 87.2

1. **The correct answer is C.** The narrator refers to the time frame of her stay in Morris Harbor in the opening paragraph: *there may be limits to such a winter's enjoyment*. Choices A and B are incorrect because the passage does not state that the narrator had been in Morris Harbor for longer than the winter. Choice D is incorrect because the passage does not support the narrator being there for only a week. Choice C is correct because the clearest statement of the time frame that the narrator has been in Morris Harbor is *such a winter's enjoyment*.

2. The passage indicates that Mrs. Cole has helped the narrator by

Ⓐ finding her a room at the inn
Ⓑ making arrangements for her departure
Ⓒ inviting her to Mis' Elwood's
Ⓓ providing directions to the train station

**Passage**

The Palace of Westminster in London has stood underneath the tower we know today as "Big Ben" for over 160 years, but "Big Ben" wasn't made the clock tower's official name until 1921. Before then, it was "St. Stephen's Tower." However, in the seventeenth century, more people would have called it "The Clock Tower," "The East Tower," or, in honor of its largest bell, "Big Ben."

3. The official name of the tower above the Palace of Westminster prior to 1921 was

Ⓐ Big Ben
Ⓑ The Clock Tower
Ⓒ St. Stephen's Tower
Ⓓ The East Tower

## Practice

SLIDE 88.1

2. **The correct answer is B.** Choice A is incorrect because the passage doesn't describe in detail how the narrator got the room at the inn. Choice C is incorrect because Mrs. Cole only states that she is going to see Mis' Elwood and she doesn't invite the narrator: *I suppose I shall walk down the Front Road now an' ask how old Mis' Robert Elwood is.* Choice D is incorrect because while the two characters discuss the train on which the narrator will be leaving, Mrs. Cole does not provide the narrator with directions to the station. Choice B is correct because Mrs. Cole says to the narrator, *I've seen to all your prep'rations* for the upcoming trip.

SLIDE 88.2

3. **The correct answer is C.** Choices A, B, and D are incorrect because although the tower has been called *Big Ben*, *The Clock Tower*, and *The East Tower*, none of these was the official name before 1921. Choice C is correct because the second sentence in the passage states that before 1921, *it was "St. Stephen's Tower,"* indicating that this was its official name during that time.

## Wrap-Up

**Instructions**
Complete the wrap-up question. If time remains after you've finished, double-check your work.

**Passage**

**(1)** That name, *Catacombes de Paris*. **(2)** It could mean more than a subterranean network of tunnels. **(3)** It could also refer to the complex interrelationships of the city itself: the crossroads of Paris. **(4)** There's adventure in that name, and mystery. **(5)** It's an intersection, a bridge to the afterlife, a place just underfoot. **(6)** The air felt as heavy with secrecy as it was with the smell of earth, with whispers, with mold.

**(7)** There were other memorable names to be found within the tunnels themselves: the *Sarcophagus of Lacrymatoire*, the *Fountain of the Samaritan*, their titles evocative of antiquity and myth, located in the bowels of the tunnels. **(8)** Looky-loos laden with cameras around their necks and guidebooks in hand hustled through the entrance, eager to make their own finds. **(9)** They talked loudly about the hidden treasures they expected to encounter as if their confidence might actually help locate them. **(10)** *The Sepulchral Lamp*. **(11)** *The Atelier*. **(12)** *The Crypt of Sacellum*.

**(13)** Inès had left to buy tickets. **(14)** I waited patiently by the entrance, scarcely believing that we were really going through with this but not quite nervous. **(15)** If we decided tonight, halfway through our search, to give up, then we could always turn back, and it would be easy to make up a reasonable excuse for why our field trip had ended early.

**(16)** My family had bought the story that we were going on a field trip unquestioningly; all that we had to do was make sure that the school didn't call them when we didn't show up for classes on Friday. **(17)** Inès had faked a doctor's note that Sébastien would turn in, and I had made up a family vacation. **(18)** I seem to remember I said it was for President's Day, although in retrospect I am shocked anyone would have believed that. **(19)** Whatever excuse I had made up, with little difficulty, we now had the whole day to ourselves. **(20)** We were free to do exactly what we wanted.

**(21)** It wouldn't have been hard for me to borrow a guidebook or city map for the excursion from my parents. **(22)** But obviously, knowing I would give up the whole plot if I asked them for anything like that, I had opted instead to just throw some water and snacks into my regular school satchel. **(23)** Inès, however, showed up at the school gate that morning with a detailed plan and high-powered flashlights, and I felt like an amateur in contrast. **(24)** Despite all this, there was a frisson of excitement in the air as we set off underground—it was an early indication of what has developed into a somewhat reckless impulse in me to leave the map behind and explore freely.

2. All of the following are presented to adults as reasons for the girls' absence EXCEPT

Ⓐ a field trip
Ⓑ a family vacation
Ⓒ a visiting relative
Ⓓ an illness

# Wrap-Up

SLIDE 89.1

*Give students 5 minutes to read the passage and complete the wrap-up question.*

SLIDE 89.2

2. **The correct answer is C.** Choice A is incorrect because the narrator says *my family had bought the story that we were going on a field trip unquestioningly*, which indicates that a *field trip* was presented as an excuse for their absence. Choices B and D are incorrect because the narrator states that *Inès had faked a doctor's note that Sébastien would turn in, and I had made up a family vacation*, which indicates that *a family vacation* and *an illness* were used as excuses for their absence. Choice C is correct because the narrator never mentions *a visiting relative* being used as an excuse for their absence.

This page is intentionally left blank.
Content resumes on the next page.

This page is intentionally left blank.
Teacher content resumes with the next chapter.

CHAPTER 11

# Inferences

This chapter will review the steps for drawing inferences from literary and informational texts by combining critical thinking and evidence from the text.

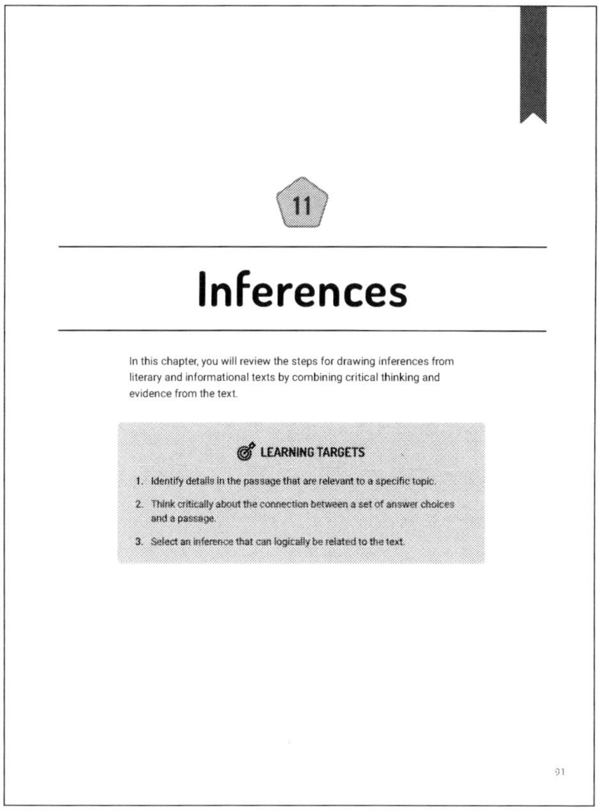

11

Inferences

In this chapter, you will review the steps for drawing inferences from literary and informational texts by combining critical thinking and evidence from the text.

LEARNING TARGETS

1. Identify details in the passage that are relevant to a specific topic.
2. Think critically about the connection between a set of answer choices and a passage.
3. Select an inference that can logically be related to the text.

91

## TSIA2 STANDARDS

**Literary Text Analysis**
Inferences

The student will draw reasonable inferences from literary text.

**Informational Text Analysis and Synthesis**
Inferences (single-passage)

The student will draw reasonable inferences from informational text.

## TEKS ALIGNMENT

E1.4 *Comprehension skills*: listening, speaking, reading, writing and thinking using multiple texts. The student uses metacognitive skills to both develop and deepen comprehension of increasingly complex texts. The student is expected to:

(F) make inferences and use evidence to support understanding.

## LEARNING TARGETS

1. Identify details in the passage that are relevant to a specific topic.
2. Think critically about the connection between a set of answer choices and a passage.
3. Select an inference that can logically be related to the text.

## Warm-Up

### Instructions

Complete the warm-up question. If time remains after you've finished, double-check your work.

### Passage

The Japanese Pagoda—a historic symbol of peace and unity located in Washington, D.C.—was actually created overseas. In 1957, the mayor of Yokohama, Japan, gifted the sculpture to the city of Washington, D.C., as a sign of friendship following World War II. Constructed in Japan, the sculpture was broken down, packed into five crates, and delivered to Washington, D.C., as a puzzle without instructions for reassembly. It then took several weeks for Smithsonian specialists to reconstruct the sculpture.

**1.** Which of the following can be inferred from the passage?

- (A) The United States and Japan continued fighting after World War II.
- (B) The Japanese Pagoda was too big to be shipped to Washington, D.C., in one piece.
- (C) The reconstruction of the Japanese Pagoda took longer than initially thought.
- (D) The Japanese Pagoda is no longer the symbol of friendly diplomatic relations it once was.

# Warm-Up

SLIDE 92.1

*Give students 2 minutes to complete the warm-up question.*

SLIDE 92.2

1. **The correct answer is B.** Choice A is incorrect because the passage states that the sculpture was given to the United States *as a sign of friendship following World War II*, strongly indicating that the United States and Japan did not continue fighting after the war. Choice C is incorrect because there is no mention of how long anyone initially thought it would take to assemble. Choice D is incorrect because the passage states that the Japanese Pagoda is *a historic symbol of peace and unity* and does not indicate that this has changed. Choice B is correct because the passage explains that the sculpture *was broken down, packed into five crates, and delivered to Washington, D.C.*, which reasonably leads to the inference that it could not be shipped in one piece.

**TSIA2 Mastery:** ELAR 

## Groundwork

EXERCISE A

### Instructions

Use the passage and suspects' statements to figure out who filled the stadium with balloons.

### Passage

When the football team at Central High School arrived at the stadium for practice at the end of the first day of school, they found that it had been completely filled with balloons. The coach had been in the stadium right before lunch, so he knew that it was filled between lunch and 3:30. After some investigation, the coach narrowed down the list of potential pranksters to 4 staff members. Each of them provided a statement as to their whereabouts when the prank was committed.

**Suspect #1: The Maintenance Man**

**Statement:** I was working on repairing a faulty air conditioning unit, so there's no way it could've been me.

**Suspect #2: The Cheerleading Coach**

**Statement:** I totally think the balloons were *brilliant,* especially since they were school colors, but it wasn't me. I spent all day decorating the cafeteria for the "Welcome Back!" dance.

**Suspect #3: The Principal's Secretary**

**Statement:** I was grocery shopping trying to make sure the concession stand would be stocked, so I wasn't even on campus at the time.

**Suspect #4: The Math Teacher**

**Statement:** Is it even possible to give a mid-term exam *and* fill the stadium with balloons at the same time? I think not. I was in my classroom the whole time, making sure students were keeping their eyes on their own papers.

# Groundwork

*In this section, students will evaluate evidence to make an inference.*

EXERCISE A

**Show of hands: who knows who Sherlock Holmes is?**

*Pause for a show of hands.*

**What's he famous for, again?**

Solving crimes using tiny clues and logic.

SLIDE 93.1

**Let's channel our inner Sherlock to see if we can solve a mystery of our own. Granted, it's not quite as high-stakes as finding a criminal, but the process is the same: finding evidence and narrowing our options to whoever did it. Take a moment now to read the paragraph at the top of your workbook page.**

*Give students 1 minute to read the passage.*

**We've got our crime: a football stadium filled with balloons. But the question is, who did it? We have four suspects. The first one is the maintenance man. Where does he say he was?**

Fixing the AC.

**Is there anything in the passage that says it was definitely the maintenance guy? Or anything in his statement that seems fishy?**

Not really.

**We can't rule him out, but we definitely can't say he was the one who did it. Let's keep looking through our suspects. Where was the cheerleading coach?**

Decorating the cafeteria for the dance.

**Is there anything that says she might have done it?**

She seems impressed by it and likes the balloon colors.

**We can't say for sure, though. What about the secretary? Is there evidence that says she did it?**

No, she wasn't even on campus.

**Not even being on campus is a good alibi. We can rule out the secretary. What about our last suspect? Where was the math teacher?**

Giving a midterm.

**Is there any evidence that proves the math teacher may have done it?**

Yes, the passage says it was the first day of school, so there's no way he was giving a midterm.

**It's kind of hard to give a midterm exam on the first day of school. Based on that slip-up, we can infer that the math teacher was definitely the prankster. That must have taken him forever to blow those things up. Luckily, answering inference questions on the TSIA2 won't be nearly as difficult as filling an entire stadium with balloons.**

EXERCISE B

### Instructions

Read the passage. Then, determine if each statement is an accurate inference based on the evidence provided. Circle your answer.

### Passage

Sherlock Holmes is best known for his amazing deductive skills. He can take a look at someone's hat and automatically know all kinds of details about that person, like where they've been or what they do for a living. Many of his adventures begin at 221B Baker Street, which is where he lives with his partner Dr. John Watson. Together, they help a variety of clients, including Scotland Yard, solve mysteries. Sir Arthur Conan Doyle may not have been the first author to develop a detective character for his story, but in creating Sherlock Holmes, he created the most celebrated of them all.

**1.** Sherlock Holmes is a fictional character.

Supported    Not Enough Evidence

**2.** Without Sherlock Holmes, Scotland Yard would be unable to solve many cases.

Supported    Not Enough Evidence

**3.** Holmes and Watson spend a lot of time together.

Supported    Not Enough Evidence

## Groundwork

*In this section, students will differentiate between an inference and an assumption.*

EXERCISE B

**Before we start this next exercise, I just wanted to give everyone a heads up: today's going to be my last day. You'll have a new teacher tomorrow. Now, take a moment to read the passage in your workbook.**

*Give students 1 minute to read the passage, and avoid any questions about the statement made in the opening of the lesson.*

**Okay, okay. So, today isn't really my last day. But, I bet your mind came up with all sorts of ideas about why it might be. What were some reasons you thought it could be my last day?**

You were fired. You were quitting. You were moving to another classroom.

**Did you have any evidence to back up your ideas?**

No.

**Even without evidence, we can often cobble together some kind of reason why something happens. But without solid evidence, we're just guessing. We're making an *assumption*. However, if we *do* have evidence, we call it making an *inference*, which has a little more truth to it than a guess. For instance, we just read a passage about a man named Sherlock Holmes. There are three statements following the passage. If the statement is an inference, what will we find in the passage?**

Evidence that supports the statement.

SLIDE 94.1

**Let's look at statement 1. Is there any evidence to prove that Sherlock is a fictional character?**

Yes.

**What does the passage say to help us prove it's true?**

It mentions how he's the main character of a book by Sir Arthur Conan Doyle.

**Being a character in a book definitely means we can make the inference that Sherlock is fictional. What about statement 2? Can we say that Scotland Yard would be hopeless without Sherlock?**

Not really.

**What *does* it say about Scotland Yard?**

That Sherlock and Watson helped them solve some cases.

**There's nothing in the passage that proves Scotland Yard isn't able to solve those crimes without Sherlock, just that he helped them. Without any evidence, we can't really say that sentence 2 is accurate. Let's look at the last statement. Is number 3 supported by evidence?**

Yes.

**What evidence did you use?**

Watson and Sherlock live together, and they solve crimes together.

**If two people live together and work together, it's pretty safe to say that they spend a lot of time with one another. That means sentence 3 is a solid inference. That's the key to finding inferences, though. If you can't prove it based on what's in the passage, it's likely an assumption or even just plain wrong. No evidence means no inference.**

TSIA2 Mastery: ELAR 

EXERCISE C

### Instructions

Read the passage. Then, determine which statements are supported by the passage. Circle any statements that make an accurate inference.

### Passage

Nancy Drew is fashionable, brave, curious, and resourceful. And, she's completely fictional. However, that fact is dismissed when it comes to the millions who see her as an exceptional role model. In fact, her novels have remained in pop culture since 1930, which is more than most protagonists from children's stories can say. Along with her dog, Togo, Nancy spends her time devoted to unearthing the truth behind each and every mystery she encounters. Even more, the stories do not delve into controversial topics, such as religion or politics, providing a safe context for readers to escape from their daily lives and into an adrenaline-inducing adventure.

**4.** Nancy Drew was born in the 1930s.

**5.** Nancy's adventures often involved escaping from kidnappers.

**6.** The *Nancy Drew* series is considered children's fiction.

## Groundwork

*In this chapter, students will analyze typical mistakes made when making an inference on the TSIA2.*

EXERCISE C   SLIDE 95.1

**When trying to figure out if a statement is accurate based on a passage, seeing something we know we saw in the passage tends to create a little spark in our minds, and we're more likely to think it's the right answer. But just because it's familiar, it doesn't necessarily mean it's correct. Let's start by reading this passage.**

*Give students 1 minute to read the passage.*

**When we come across inference questions, we know we're going to need evidence. But where do we look? Is it just a matter of skimming the passage and hoping we'll run into something that fits the bill? Or is there something in the answer we use to help us?**

We use keywords from the answer choice.

**The answer choice is the inference, so if we want to figure out whether it's accurate, we need evidence. And we need to know what the passage says about the topic mentioned in that answer choice. For instance, look at sentence 1. What keywords do you think we could use to help us search for evidence?**

*Born* and *1930*.

**Do we see either of those in the passage?**

*1930* is in the fourth sentence.

**Boom. Evidence found, right? Is sentence 4 an accurate inference?**

No.

**Why not?**

It says that her novels have been popular since then, not that she was born in that year.

**I could easily see someone assuming Nancy Drew was born in the 1930s, especially since that's when the books came out. But that'd be an *assumption*. Can you think of a way she could be popular in the 1930s but not actually born then?**

The book could be about a historical character, or she could've been born in the 1920s and be a teenager when the story takes place.

**Sentence 4 is definitely not supported by the passage. What about sentence 5? What keywords can we use there?**

*Adventures*, *escaping*, or *kidnappers*.

**Do we see those words in the passage?**

Yes, *adventure* and *to escape* show up in the last sentence.

**That's solid evidence, so we should circle statement 5, right?**

No.

**Why not?**

That's not what the passage is saying.

**What's going wrong here? Why isn't finding keywords proof of evidence?**

The words are being used to say different things.

**The TSIA2 loves to offer up this potential misstep. They pull keywords and phrases from the passage, but what the answer choice says doesn't match what the passage says. It's just re-using those words. What about sentence 6? What keywords can we use there?**

*Children's fiction*.

**Can we find those words in the passage?**

It says she's *fictional* in the second sentence and *children's stories* halfway through the passage.

**What is the passage actually saying with those words?**

That she's fictional and that other children's story protagonists don't last as long as she did.

**Using that evidence, can we say that Nancy Drew is a fictional character from a children's series?**

Yes.

**When we take standardized tests like the TSIA2, it can be so tempting to see something familiar and want to jump on it as the right answer. By realizing that the test will try to trick us this way, we're better prepared to avoid these kinds of pitfalls. We know that we need to really dig for our evidence and make sure we've got the support we need.**

# Application

## THE APPROACH

When a question asks you to make an inference based on a passage, use these steps ...

1. Identify the topic of the question.
2. Find evidence in the passage.
3. Eliminate answers that are not supported by the evidence.

**Passage**

On December 9, 2019, about 100 adventure tourists and guides traveled to White Island, an active stratovolcano near New Zealand, for a chance to hike in the caldera, see a bubbling acidic lake, and experience the sensation of walking on another world. About half of the tourists had already departed the island when the volcano erupted, shooting a column of steam and ash a mile into the air, followed by a horizontal blast of super-heated gases and ash that covered the island in an instant. Rescue crews assembled and were ready to fly to the island, but they were sent to a different island due to strict governmental health and safety regulations that prevented them from entering an unsafe area. Initially, a police spokesperson explained that there were no signs of life on the island, but volunteer rescuers later removed 31 people from the island by boat and helicopter, saving the lives of 24 tourists.

7. Which of the following can be inferred from the passage?

Ⓐ The volunteer rescuers are braver than the first responders.

Ⓑ The volcanic gases in the atmosphere make it impossible for helicopters to fly to the island.

Ⓒ Governmental safety policies meant to protect the lives of first responders risked the lives of the victims.

Ⓓ Before the volcano erupted, rescue crews assembled and conducted an on-foot search for signs of life on the island.

# Application

*In this section, students will practice using evidence from a passage to eliminate unsupported inferences.*

SLIDE 96.1

**Inference questions on the TSIA2 are challenging because the answer isn't in the passage, but it's *in* the passage. By that, I mean the text won't specifically say that something is true, but by using evidence, you can prove that it is. But how can you tell if the question is even asking about an inference? What clues do you see in question 7?**

It says *inferred*.

**That keyword is often the biggest clue. The question might also use related words, like *inference, imply,* or even *assumption*. Once we know it's an inference question, what should we do?**

*Identify the topic of the question.*

**What's the topic this time?**

It doesn't really have one.

**This is an example of a general inference. Most of the time, short passage questions will give you general inferences, meaning there really won't be a specific topic. In that case, just go to the next step. Which is what, by the way?**

*Find evidence in the passage.*

**Since we don't have a specific topic we're looking for, we can just read the passage generally. What's it about?**

A volcano that erupts and traps some tourists.

**Well, we found evidence. It's the whole paragraph! There isn't much we can do with that, though, so it's time to dig into the answer choices. What's our goal?**

To eliminate ones that aren't supported by the passage.

**Take the choices one by one, and look for anything that's the opposite of what we read or that only offers up recycled words. Starting with choice A, what does it say about rescuers and first responders?**

That rescuers are braver than first responders.

**Chances are both groups are really brave, so we need some really strong evidence to prove this is true. Does the passage ever directly compare their bravery?**

No.

**We can go ahead and eliminate choice A. What about choice B? What does it say about helicopters?**

That the volcano made it impossible for them to fly to the island.

**Let's go back to the passage. Does it say the volcanic gases made it *impossible* for them to fly there?**

No, it just says the policy kept them from going to the island.

**It sounds to me like it was at least possible, but we can't quite tell if it's what actually happened. This is a good example of an answer choice exaggerating what the passage says. And since we don't have strong evidence, we can cross it off and move to choice C. What does that one say?**

That the government risked the lives of the victims.

**That's a pretty bold statement. Is there any evidence to back it up?**

Yes, the rescuers *were sent to a different island due to strict governmental health and safety regulations that prevented them from entering an unsafe area*, which meant it was unsafe for the tourists too.

**That's pretty reasonable, so let's hang onto it for the time being and check choice D. Is that option a good inference?**

No.

**Why not?**

Because the policies kept the rescue crews from flying there, so there's no way to do an "on-foot" search for survivors.

**Choice D is a good example of recycled words. It uses specific words and phrases from the passages, but the statement made isn't accurate. That makes choice C the right answer. It's the only one that was clearly supported by evidence from the passage, which makes it a good inference.**

## THE APPROACH

When a question asks you to make an inference based on a passage, use these steps ...

1. Identify the topic of the question.
2. Find evidence in the passage.
3. Eliminate answers that are not supported by the evidence.

**Passage**

Adventure tourism isn't just for the most able-bodied and athletic of the human population anymore. These adrenaline-filled vacations are available for anyone, regardless of age, physical abilities, or intellectual limitations. Known as "accessible tourism," these opportunities provide the inclusive benefits that allow anyone who wishes to participate in a variety of thrilling activities. Through the use of newly-designed accessibility features, highly trained staff, and a modern perspective of zero tolerance for limitations, companies are paving the way for equitable access to some of life's greatest thrills.

8. Which of the following can be inferred from the passage?

   Ⓐ Not everyone wants to spend their vacation on thrill-seeking activities.
   Ⓑ Before accessible tourism, not everyone could participate in adventure tourism.
   Ⓒ The adventure tourism industry is the most popular vacation option in the United States.
   Ⓓ The industry's accessibility features are extremely costly.

## Application

*In this section, students will work through the process of eliminating answers with more independence.*

SLIDE 97.1

**Let's take a look at number 8. What's our first step?**

*Identify the topic of the question.*

**Does this question mention a specific topic, or are we just making a general inference?**

A general one.

**That means we can skip forward to the next step: finding evidence. Take a moment now to read the passage.**

*Give students 1 minute to read the passage.*

**Again, we've got a whole paragraph of evidence to work with. Let's start working through our choices. What does choice A claim?**

That not everyone wants to go on these kinds of vacations.

**It seems pretty reasonable when you take it out of context, but remember: no evidence, no inference. Is there evidence from the passage we can use to support this statement?**

No.

**Why not?**

The passage doesn't talk about what kinds of vacations people want to go on, just one option available.

**That means choice A is out. What about choice B? What does it say about accessible tourism?**

Before it was created, not everyone could go on adventure tourism vacations.

**Is there anything in the passage we can use as support?**

The first sentence says it's not just for able-bodied, athletic people *anymore*.

**That little word *anymore* makes it seem very likely that before accessible tourism, adventure tourism wasn't possible for everyone. Let's hang onto that one for now. What about choice C? What does it say about adventure tourism?**

That it's the most popular vacation option in the U.S.

**The *most* popular? That's a strong statement to make, and if it's true, we'll be able to find evidence. Do you see anything in the passage that proves choice C is right?**

No, the passage doesn't even mention the U.S.

**Without any evidence to support it, choice C is out. Choice D is looking pretty good, though. What does that one say?**

That all the accessibility features are expensive.

**What does the passage say about those accessibility features?**

That they're *newly-designed*.

**Does *newly-designed* equal *extremely costly*?**

Not exactly.

**Sometimes the TSIA2 will throw an answer like this your way. It's meant to test your ability to find evidence. Though we could probably argue that choice D is true, it would take a lot of convincing, and we would need more information than just what the passage offers. But, that passage is all you get on test day. And if it's not in the passage, you can't use it to justify your answers. So, which choice is correct?**

Choice B.

**When it comes to making an inference on a standardized test like the TSIA2, be mindful of evidence. The right answer will always have the strongest support from the passage to prove that it's true. No evidence? No inference.**

# Practice

**Instructions**
Complete the practice set. If time remains after you've finished, double-check your work.

**Passage**

While traveling around Seattle, Washington, to discover new bands in the Pacific Northwest, Jonathan Poneman of Sub Pop Records asked the unknown Kurt Cobain about a demo he had allegedly made. He adamantly denied its existence. However, as Poneman was leaving town, Cobain came to his hotel and handed him the demo saying, "Listen before I change my mind." What Poneman heard would launch one of the best-selling bands of all time, the pioneers of a 1990s music revolution: Nirvana.

**1.** The passage implies that Cobain's initial feeling about interest in his demo was

Ⓐ unease
Ⓑ indignation
Ⓒ gratification
Ⓓ enthusiasm

**Passage**

Marquees are often used to lure audiences to cinemas and theaters. The very first marquees were rather small and hardly protruded from the building's façade. In the early 20th century, these would display information to people walking by or entering the theater. It was not until the popularization of the automobile that marquees were made to be larger and to broadcast their messages boldly to attract people to shows.

**2.** We can infer that the reason the marquees were made larger was that

Ⓐ the displays of the early 20th century were considered unsatisfactory
Ⓑ smaller marquees display less information than larger ones
Ⓒ it is hard to read smaller marquees while driving
Ⓓ marquees that were part of building façades were not architecturally sound

# Practice

SLIDE 98.1

*Give students 8 minutes to complete the practice set.*

SLIDE 98.2

1. **The correct answer is A.** Choices B, C, and D are incorrect because Cobain's initial reaction was to conceal the existence of the demo (*he adamantly denied its existence*), which is not consistent with *indignation*, *gratification*, or *enthusiasm*. Choice A is correct because *unease* is an adequate characterization of how Cobain must have felt about the demo to pretend it didn't exist.

SLIDE 98.3

2. **The correct answer is C.** Choices A, B, and D are incorrect because the dissatisfaction with the marquees, amount of information, and architectural soundness are not mentioned in the passage. Choice C is correct because the passage states that the arrival of cars was the reason marquees were made larger: *It was not until the popularization of the automobile that marquees were made to be larger and to broadcast their messages boldly to attract people to shows.*

**Passage**

Most bars are set up to allow patrons to open a "tab" and settle their bill in one transaction when ready to leave. However, many bars used to manage tabs much differently. Certain customers were permitted to settle their tab at the end of the week on their payday, allowing them to leave and never return (of course, this was hardly common because these tabs were only extended to regular customers). These patrons were sometimes called "trust customers" because the bartender trusts that they will pay fairly.

**3.** It can be inferred that bartenders welcomed "trust customers" in part because bar patrons

Ⓐ are generally honorable
Ⓑ hardly ever put purchases on tabs
Ⓒ are wealthier than average
Ⓓ typically are returning customers

## Practice

SLIDE 99.1

3. **The correct answer is D.** Choice A is incorrect because while these customers must behave honorably for the arrangement to work, it is not explicitly stated that bar patrons as a whole are generally honorable. Choice B is incorrect because "trust customers" did exactly that: they put purchases on tabs. Choice C is incorrect because there is no evidence in the passage that trust customers are wealthier than average. Choice D is correct because the passage states that a reason this arrangement worked is that it was usually only extended to returning customers: *Certain customers would be permitted to settle their tab at the end of the week on their payday, allowing them to leave and never return (of course, this was hardly common because these tabs were only extended to regular customers).*

## Wrap-Up

### Instructions

Complete the wrap-up question. If time remains after you've finished, double-check your work.

### Passage

During the process of anaerobic digestion, animal waste produces methane gas. Recently, biochemists sponsored by the Department of Energy discovered a way to make synthetic versions of waste that give off even more methane. You might be asking why the Department of Energy is sponsoring such developments. The reason is that methane produced by such waste could someday generate enough electricity for a whole city.

**2.** What assumption does the author of the passage make?

Ⓐ Gases made from waste will be cheaper to make than other gases.

Ⓑ The Department of Energy has already been using methane-generating waste for electricity.

Ⓒ Synthetic algae will not be able to undergo anaerobic digestion.

Ⓓ Readers would not typically link the Department of Energy with animal waste research.

# Wrap-Up

SLIDE 100.1

*Give students 5 minutes to complete the wrap-up question.*

SLIDE 100.2

2. **The correct answer is D**. Choice A is incorrect because nowhere is the potential cost of this new technology mentioned. Choice B is incorrect because the passage states that this technology is not yet in use: *methane produced by such waste could someday generate enough electricity for a whole city.* Choice C is incorrect because, on the contrary, the passage suggests that they are using synthetic versions of waste to create methane gas through the process of anaerobic digestion. Choice D is correct because the author acknowledges that the reader might be confused as to why the Department of Energy would be linked with animal waste research: *you might be asking why the Department of Energy is sponsoring such developments.* Therefore, it is reasonable to infer that the author assumed that readers would not typically link the Department of Energy with animal waste research.

CHAPTER 12

# Trap Answers

In this chapter, students will learn how to spot and avoid typical trap answers seen in the reading portion of the TSIA2 ELAR multiple-choice section.

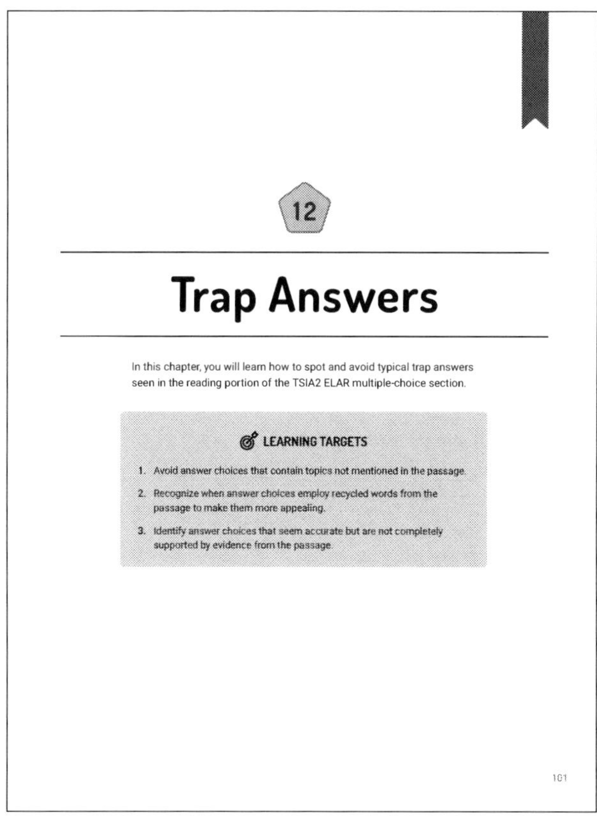
12

Trap Answers

In this chapter, you will learn how to spot and avoid typical trap answers seen in the reading portion of the TSIA2 ELAR multiple-choice section.

LEARNING TARGETS

1. Avoid answer choices that contain topics not mentioned in the passage.
2. Recognize when answer choices employ recycled words from the passage to make them more appealing.
3. Identify answer choices that seem accurate but are not completely supported by evidence from the passage.

101

## TSIA2 STANDARDS

**Literary Text Analysis**

The student will identify and analyze ideas in and elements of literary text.

**Informational Text Analysis and Synthesis**

The student will identify and analyze information and ideas in and elements of informational text.

## LEARNING TARGETS

1. Avoid answer choices that contain topics not mentioned in the passage.
2. Recognize when answer choices employ recycled words from the passage to make them more appealing.
3. Identify answer choices that seem accurate but are not completely supported by evidence from the passage.

## Groundwork

EXERCISE A

### Instructions

Review the instructions for a reading question from the TSIA2. Then, refer to the passage and question as your teacher leads the discussion. Do not answer the question.

*Read the passage below and then choose the best answer to each question. Answer the questions on the basis of what is stated or implied in the passage.*

### Passage

**(1)** Six years have passed since I resolved on my present undertaking. **(2)** I can, even now, remember the hour from which I dedicated myself to this great enterprise. **(3)** I commenced by inuring my body to hardship. **(4)** I accompanied the whale-fishers on several expeditions to the North Sea; I voluntarily endured cold, famine, thirst, and want of sleep; I often worked harder than the common sailors during the day and devoted my nights to the study of mathematics, the theory of medicine, and those branches of physical science from which a naval adventurer might derive the greatest practical advantage. **(5)** Twice I actually hired myself as an under-mate in a Greenland whaler, and acquitted myself to admiration. **(6)** I must own I felt a little proud when my captain offered me the second dignity in the vessel and entreated me to remain with the greatest earnestness, so valuable did he consider my services.

**(7)** And now, dear Margaret, do I not deserve to accomplish some great purpose? **(8)** My life might have been passed in ease and luxury, but I preferred glory to every enticement that wealth placed in my path. **(9)** Oh, that some encouraging voice would answer in the affirmative! **(10)** My courage and my resolution is firm; but my hopes fluctuate, and my spirits are often depressed. **(11)** I am about to proceed on a long and difficult voyage, the emergencies of which will demand all my fortitude: I am required not only to raise the spirits of others, but sometimes to sustain my own, when theirs are failing.

**(12)** This is the most favourable period for travelling in Russia. **(13)** They fly quickly over the snow in their sledges; the motion is pleasant, and, in my opinion, far more agreeable than that of an English stagecoach. **(14)** The cold is not excessive, if you are wrapped in furs—a dress which I have already adopted, for there is a great difference between walking the deck and remaining seated motionless for hours, when no exercise prevents the blood from actually freezing in your veins. **(15)** I have no ambition to lose my life on the post-road between St. Petersburgh and Archangel.

From Mary Wollstonecraft Shelley, *Frankenstein*; or, *The Modern Prometheus*. Originally published in 1818.

This page is intentionally left blank.
Teacher content resumes on the next page.

1. According to the passage, the narrator wanted to experience the hardships mentioned in the first paragraph because

   Ⓐ he had lost his fortune and needed to learn a skill to support himself.
   Ⓑ the captain of a Greenland whaler ship asked him to provide his services.
   Ⓒ he values the opinion of the captain more than anyone else.
   Ⓓ he had spent most of his life living in leisure and privilege.

## Groundwork

*In this section, students will gain insight into the concept of trap answers.*

EXERCISE A

**Trap answers: they're the reason people don't like standardized tests. Well, they're *one* of the reasons why people hate standardized tests. What do you think a trap answer is?**

A wrong answer that's really tempting to pick.

**The test writers of the TSIA2 can't make things too easy on you. They use sneaky strategies for creating those wrong choices to make sure you're reading the passage carefully, and if you're not, you'll fall for one of their traps. But just by knowing what they are and what they look like, you'll have a better chance of spotting and avoiding those bad answers. Before we get too deep, though, let's start with the basics: the instructions.**

SLIDE 103.1

**Check out what it says in your workbook on page 102, just above the passage. What do the instructions tell you?**

To pick an answer based on what's stated or implied *in the passage*.

**Now, put yourself into a test writer's shoes for just a moment. Only one choice is supposedly stated or implied in the passage, right? So how do you make three wrong choices? Can you just put random wrong information?**

No, the wrong answer needs to be close to the right answer, so it's not so obvious.

**There's kind of a science to making wrong answers. You take the right answer and then think of all the ways someone might go a little off-track. For instance, if the right answer was something like *turtles are great pets*, a trap answer might be *turtles are the best pet ever*. What did the test writer do to create that wrong answer?**

They took the fact that the passage says turtles are great and exaggerated it.

**Even if the passage said turtles were great, the passage didn't specifically say they're the best. There might be something that says another pet is even better, such as a cat or a dog. But you can understand why that trap answer might jump out at you since it's close but not quite accurate. Do you think the writers will use this exact strategy for every wrong answer?**

No.

**Why not?**

It would make it too easy.

**If all the traps looked the same, we'd have a much easier time picking them out and eliminating those options. And while they may not use the same trap for every wrong answer, they don't go overboard with their creativity. In fact, most trap answers can be grouped into just a few major categories.**

EXERCISE B

**Instructions**
Write the letter of each definition next to its matching term.

| | |
|---|---|
| ____ Recycled Words | A. Presents information from the passage in an inaccurate way. |
| ____ Distractor | B. Offers details not mentioned in the passage. |
| ____ Outlier | C. Contains words from the passage within an incorrect statement. |

## Groundwork

*In this section, students will review the three types of trap answers commonly seen in reading questions during the TSIA2.*

EXERCISE B SLIDE 104.1

**Test writers have all different kinds of strategies for creating trap answers, but on the TSIA2, there are three that tend to show up a lot. Which one is listed first in your workbook?**

*Recycled words.*

**What comes to mind when you think of *recycled*?**

Using something over again or turning it into something new.

**Test writers aren't trying to make their tests more environmentally friendly. What *are* they trying to do with those recycled words?**

Using words from the passage to make the answer seem like a better option.

**Which definition best matches this concept of reusing words from the passage?**

Choice C.

**Recycled words are effective traps because when you read them, you get this jolt of familiarity. And during the adrenaline rush of an actual test, that emotional response is often enough to get you to fall for a trap. But just because an answer uses some of the same words, it doesn't mean it's supported by evidence. What about outliers? What does an *outlier* make you think of?**

Something that doesn't fit in.

**Which definition goes along with an outlier trap answer?**

Choice B.

**Outliers can be attractive answer choices because they usually make sense based on what you read. But rather than offering up familiar words and phrases, they give you something that's not even talked about in the passage. They send you on a wild goose chase through the passage in hopes of finding evidence. Why is that a waste of time and mental energy, though?**

Because there is no evidence.

**Outliers are almost never totally off the wall or unrelated to the passage topic, so when you read the choice, your brain sort of wants to believe it. In fact, outliers love to offer up things that are totally believable and possibly even completely true. What makes them incorrect, though, is the fact that they're just not supported by evidence anywhere in the passage. What about a distractor? What do you think would make an answer a good distraction?**

It seems like a good choice, even when there's something wrong with it.

**A distractor choice uses ideas supported by the passage but in the wrong context. Either the choice doesn't answer the question directly, it gets one small piece of it wrong, or it mangles something the author said. They're subtle, like a filter over an image that makes everything look a little *too* perfect. Which definition matches this idea?**

Choice A.

**A good way to recognize that you're tempted by a distractor is how much you have to convince yourself. It feels a little like arguing with yourself. Your brain comes up with all kinds of reasons why the answer could be correct. But if an answer needs that much arguing and convincing, it's probably a distractor. The question now is what do these types of trap answers look like in the wild? Let's check out an example to help you get a better grasp on what you'll be up against on test day.**

EXERCISE C

### Instructions

Review the statement made by a defendant in a court trial. Then, review the notes taken by three of the jury members. Determine which type of trap answer appears in each note and circle your answer.

### Defendant's Statement

It had been a long day, and all I wanted was some chicken nuggets. I drove up to the speaker where you order, told them what I wanted, and waited in line. It took *forever* for them to serve the cars in front of me. There were only three of them! By the time I got to the window, I was so hungry I was about to take a bite out of my steering wheel. That's when everything broke down. I realized that I had forgotten my wallet at home, so I had no way to pay. I begged and pleaded for them to please just give me one nugget. One little nugget! They refused, and something in my brain snapped. It was at that point I launched a three-and-a-half-foot alligator through the window and sped away. After refusing my nugget request, I made sure karma would come back around and bite them.

**Juror #1 – Notes**

**The alligator (named Karma) took a bite out of the steering wheel before being launched through the drive-through window.**

**Circle One:** Recycled Words Outlier Distractor

**Juror #2 – Notes**

**The defendant had planned to throw the alligator through the window the whole time.**

**Circle One:** Recycled Words Outlier Distractor

**Juror #3 – Notes**

**The defendant clearly isn't cut out for a job in customer service, but they could be a good candidate for a job at a reptile rehab facility.**

**Circle One:** Recycled Words Outlier Distractor

## Groundwork

*In this section, students will practice identifying types of trap answers using an example passage.*

EXERCISE C | SLIDE 105.1

**Trap answers are a lot like breakdowns in communication. One person says something, and the person listening doesn't interpret their meaning the same way the speaker intended it. For instance, let's take a look at what this defendant had to say about their crimes. Take a moment to read the passage now.**

*Give students 1 minute to read the passage.*

**In a trial like this, all the jurors are listening. They hear the same words and ideas. But somewhere along the way, miscommunication happens, and maybe they don't understand what the defendant actually meant. What did Juror #1 gather from what was said?**

That the alligator was named Karma and that it took a bite out of the steering wheel.

**Based on what you read in the passage, does it seem like Juror #1 really understood what the defendant was saying?**

No.

**Why do you think someone might pick this answer?**

It mentions the alligator, karma, and taking a bite out of the steering wheel.

**It uses plenty of words that show up in the passage, but the statement is inaccurate. What kind of trap answer did Juror #1 create?**

Recycled words.

**Juror #2's note is pretty short and sweet. Who'd like to read that for us?**

*The defendant had planned to throw the alligator through the window the whole time.*

**Why might someone think the defendant had the whole thing planned?**

Because he had the alligator ready.

**Who drives around with an alligator, right? And maybe he didn't actually *forget* his wallet. It's possible he didn't want to pay at all. Or maybe he just had no money and was hoping to get it for free, and the alligator was a backup plan. Could the alligator just be a pet that lives in the car? It seems like there are a lot of possible reasons why someone might think the whole thing was planned. But does any of this reasoning come from the passage?**

No.

**Where did we get these reasons?**

We came up with them.

**To say that Juror #2's note is accurate means we have to spend a lot of time convincing ourselves of something without any specific evidence from the passage. It's a lot of maybes. What kind of trap answer is this?**

A distractor.

**Finally, let's check out Juror #3's notes. What are they focused on?**

The defendant getting a job of some kind.

**What do you think? Would this guy be awful in customer service but great with reptiles?**

Probably.

**But come back to the passage. Does it say anywhere that he's looking for a job?**

No.

**This guy's only mission is to get some chicken nuggets. And if we waste time trying to find evidence to say he's job hunting, we'll come up empty-handed. What kind of trap answer is this?**

An outlier.

**This process of identifying wrong answers and why they're wrong is going to be so helpful during the TSIA2. Ignore the outliers. Avoid recycled words. And fact-check distractors. Everything you need to eliminate these traps will be in the passage.**

# Application

## THE APPROACH

When answering a reading question that requires finding exact information or making an inference based on a passage, use these steps ...

1. Read the question and passage.
2. Find your evidence.
3. Eliminate answer choices that are not supported by the passage.

**Passage**

**(1)** Six years have passed since I resolved on my present undertaking. **(2)** I can, even now, remember the hour from which I dedicated myself to this great enterprise. **(3)** I commenced by inuring my body to hardship. **(4)** I accompanied the whale-fishers on several expeditions to the North Sea; I voluntarily endured cold, famine, thirst, and want of sleep; I often worked harder than the common sailors during the day and devoted my nights to the study of mathematics, the theory of medicine, and those branches of physical science from which a naval adventurer might derive the greatest practical advantage. **(5)** Twice I actually hired myself as an under-mate in a Greenland whaler, and acquitted myself to admiration. **(6)** I must own I felt a little proud when my captain offered me the second dignity in the vessel and entreated me to remain with the greatest earnestness, so valuable did he consider my services.

**(7)** And now, dear Margaret, do I not deserve to accomplish some great purpose? **(8)** My life might have been passed in ease and luxury, but I preferred glory to every enticement that wealth placed in my path. **(9)** Oh, that some encouraging voice would answer in the affirmative! **(10)** My courage and my resolution is firm; but my hopes fluctuate, and my spirits are often depressed. **(11)** I am about to proceed on a long and difficult voyage, the emergencies of which will demand all my fortitude: I am required not only to raise the spirits of others, but sometimes to sustain my own, when theirs are failing.

**(12)** This is the most favourable period for travelling in Russia. **(13)** They fly quickly over the snow in their sledges; the motion is pleasant, and, in my opinion, far more agreeable than that of an English stagecoach. **(14)** The cold is not excessive, if you are wrapped in furs—a dress which I have already adopted, for there is a great difference between walking the deck and remaining seated motionless for hours, when no exercise prevents the blood from actually freezing in your veins. **(15)** I have no ambition to lose my life on the post-road between St. Petersburgh and Archangel.

From Mary Wollstonecraft Shelley, *Frankenstein*; or, *The Modern Prometheus*. Originally published in 1818.

This page is intentionally left blank.
Teacher content resumes on the next page.

**TSIA2 Mastery:** ELAR 

**1.** According to the passage, the narrator wanted to experience the hardships mentioned in the first paragraph because

Ⓐ he had lost his fortune and needed to learn a skill to support himself.

Ⓑ the captain of a Greenland whaler ship asked him to provide his services.

Ⓒ he values the opinion of the captain more than anyone else.

Ⓓ he had spent most of his life living in leisure and privilege.

# Application

*In this section, students will practice eliminating trap answers using the Approach steps for inference questions on the TSIA2 as a guideline. However, the focus of this section remains on identifying and eliminating trap answers.*

SLIDE 107.1

**Which type of trap answer do you think is the most challenging to spot?**

Answers may vary.

**Depending on how well you read the passage and the kind of evidence you find to help you make eliminations, any of the trap answers pose a threat to earning points on the TSIA2. Let's practice spotting those wrong choices using a question similar to what you'll see on test day. Recognize this one from the beginning of our chapter? Take a moment now to read the question and the passage. Read carefully to make sure you understand and take in the passage's details.**

*Give students 3 minutes to read the question and passage.*

**What is this passage about?**

A guy who wants to prep himself for a *great enterprise* by pushing himself physically and mentally.

**This guy is *pumped*. He takes on a grueling job as a sailor and spends his nights studying complex subjects. He's definitely not taking it easy. What does the question want to know about this passage?**

Why the narrator wanted to have those experiences.

**And what will we need in order to eliminate wrong answers?**

Evidence from the passage.

**Is there anything in the passage that tells us he lost his fortune, as mentioned in choice A?**

No, the passage doesn't even mention him losing money.

**What kind of trap is that?**

An outlier.

**If you see an answer choice that offers up a topic that seems unfamiliar or missing from the passage, take a moment to pause and think. Don't just try to convince yourself that it's true. Take time to look for evidence. And if you can't find any compelling support in the passage, eliminate it. What about choice B? Does anything about this choice seem familiar?**

Yes, the passage mentions a Greenland whaler and the captain asking him to provide his services.

**But is that why he became a sailor?**

No.

**The sequence of events seems a little off with choice B because he became a sailor, proved his worth, and then was asked to keep working. He declines it, though, so we know that's not the reason he started that job in the first place. What kind of trap is choice B?**

Recycled words.

**Choice B reuses a lot of words from the passage, but that's not enough evidence to make it correct. The answer should use those words to make an accurate statement based on the passage. Let's check choice C next. Do you think the narrator valued the opinion of the captain?**

Yes, he says he *felt a little proud* when the captain praised him.

**But does that mean the narrator values the captain's opinion more than anyone else's?**

No.

**What kind of trap is this?**

A distractor.

**Even though this choice could be true, we can't really support it with evidence from the passage. And if you really think about it, it doesn't even answer the question. That's a classic distractor move, so we know that one can be eliminated. What about choice D? What evidence helps us support that option as the correct answer?**

He talks about how he *preferred glory to every enticement that wealth placed in [his] path.*

**He'd much rather skip out on the luxury his old life offered and instead take on the challenges that come with being a sailor. Choice D is our best option. This question was definitely a tough one. By playing defense and watching for traps, we're better able to narrow down our options to just one correct answer.**

## Practice

**Instructions**
Complete the practice set. If time remains after you've finished, double-check your work.

**Passage 1**
Life is a highway, or so the song goes. One is free to drive wherever they please, but that doesn't mean that driving is free. Who should pay for roads? How should they be maintained? The most straightforward answer is a simple toll system that requires each person to pay a small fee when they use a road—say one dollar per use. Those who drive the most pay the most because they use the road more frequently, but that is reasonable. And when everyone who uses the road pays a small, equal fee each time, repairs are done faster and driver satisfaction increases.

**Passage 2**
A toll road system, while appealing in its simplicity, has nothing to do with equity. Let's suppose that each person who uses the road daily pays a total of fifty dollars each month. A person making $100,000 a year would spend less than 1% of their monthly income on tolls, while a person making $20,000 would pay 3% of their monthly income. The tolls would be equal for all who use the road, which might seem reasonable. But this "reasonable" idea does not hold when we look at the true impact on real people. It probably wouldn't be difficult for a higher earner to spend $600 a year on tolls, but for the lower earner, having to budget $50 each month would surely affect their finances on a daily basis. Same fee, substantially different burden.

1. The author of Passage 2 would likely find fault with the author of Passage 1 for

   Ⓐ not proving that charging tolls for roads is reasonable and fair
   Ⓑ neglecting to mention how collecting tolls would benefit local governments
   Ⓒ distorting and exaggerating the ease of updating roads to include tolls
   Ⓓ failing to acknowledge the effects of tolls on certain people

2. Passage 1 suggests that

   Ⓐ highways that require tolls are superior to those that don't.
   Ⓑ small, equal fees are easier to budget for than larger, less frequent ones.
   Ⓒ tolls divide the financial burden of road upkeep among drivers fairly.
   Ⓓ drivers are happier when they have shorter commutes.

# Practice

SLIDE 108.1

*Give students 10 minutes to complete the practice set.*

SLIDE 108.2

1. **The correct answer is D.** Choice A is incorrect because it is an example of recycled words, using words like *reasonable* and *fair* to make it seem appealing. Choice B is incorrect because it is an outlier; benefits for local governments are not mentioned in either passage. Choice C is incorrect because it is a distractor. Though it seems possible that the author of Passage 2 would not agree with the author of Passage 1, there is no evidence to support the idea that the author of Passage 2 thinks the opposing author is purposely *distorting and exaggerating* their information. Choice D is correct because the author of Passage 2 explains how the equal tolling of drivers would be more challenging for *the lower earner*, who would have a more difficult time budgeting *$50 each month* to account for their driving needs, a fact that is unacknowledged in Passage 1.

SLIDE 108.3

2. **The correct answer is C.** Choice A is incorrect because it is a distractor. The author does not specifically compare toll roads to non-toll roads. Choice B is incorrect because it contains recycled words, such as *small, equal fee* and *budget*. Choice D is incorrect because it is an outlier. The passage does not discuss the happiness of drivers in correlation to shorter commutes. Choice C is correct because the passage explains how *those who drive the most pay the most because they use the road more frequently*, which supports the idea that the cost of repairs is being spread equally among all drivers.

TSIA2 Mastery: ELAR 

3. Which of the following can be inferred from Passage 2?

Ⓐ Toll roads are easier to plan and build than other kinds of roads.
Ⓑ The practice of charging tolls is more common in some parts of the world.
Ⓒ Roads that charge tolls are preferred by those who drive long distances frequently.
Ⓓ Charging equal road tolls impacts some people more than others.

## Practice

SLIDE 109.1

3. **The correct answer is D.** Choice A is incorrect because it is a distractor. Though the first sentence mentions that a toll road system is *appealing in its simplicity*, this detail refers to the ease of spreading costs "equally" among drivers; it does not imply that the systems are easier to plan and build. Choice B is incorrect because it is an outlier; the passage does not discuss toll roads from other parts of the world. Choice C is incorrect because it is also an outlier since the passage does not talk about the preferences of long-distance drivers. Choice D is correct because it is most directly supported by the passage, which says that though the pay rate is the same, the burden is very different on those with lower incomes.

This page is intentionally left blank.
Content resumes on the next page.

This page is intentionally left blank.
Teacher content resumes with the next chapter.

CHAPTER 13

# Essay Revision

In this chapter, students will evaluate the characteristics of an essay revision question from the TSIA2. In addition, they will review and apply a strategy that can be used to answer any TSIA2 question with those characteristicss.

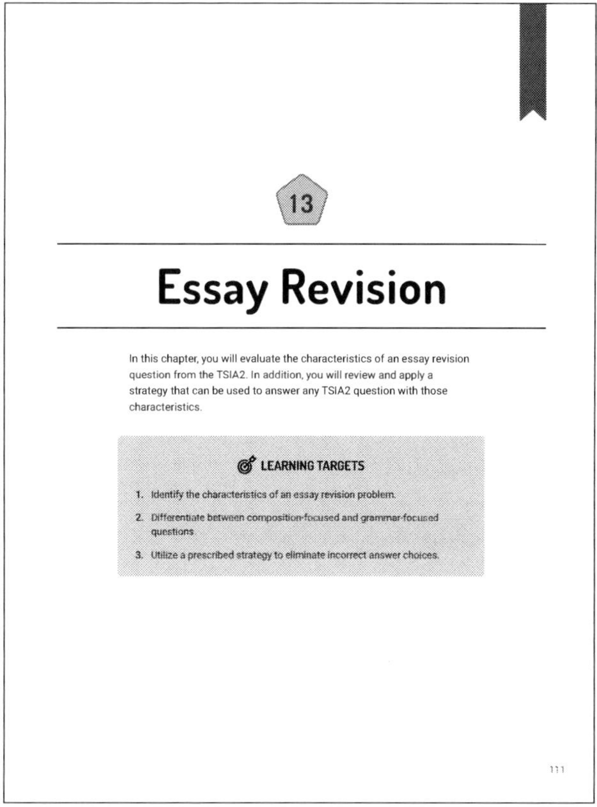

13

Essay Revision

In this chapter, you will evaluate the characteristics of an essay revision question from the TSIA2. In addition, you will review and apply a strategy that can be used to answer any TSIA2 question with those characteristics.

LEARNING TARGETS

1. Identify the characteristics of an essay revision problem.
2. Differentiate between composition-focused and grammar-focused questions.
3. Utilize a prescribed strategy to eliminate incorrect answer choices.

111

## TSIA2 STANDARDS

**Essay Revision and Editing**

The student will revise and edit prose text as needed to improve development, organization, and rhetorical word choice as well as ensure conformity to the conventions of standard written English grammar, usage, and punctuation.

## TEKS ALIGNMENT

E1.9 *Composition*: listening, speaking, reading, writing, and thinking using multiple texts—writing process. The student uses the writing process recursively to compose multiple texts that are legible and uses appropriate conventions. The student is expected to:

(C) revise drafts to improve clarity, development, organization, style, diction, and sentence effectiveness, including use of parallel constructions and placement of phrases and dependent clauses;

(D) edit drafts using standard English conventions.

## LEARNING TARGETS

1. Identify the characteristics of an essay revision problem.
2. Differentiate between composition-focused and grammar-focused questions.
3. Utilize a prescribed strategy to eliminate incorrect answer choices.

## Groundwork

EXERCISE A

### Instructions

Refer to the following question as your teacher leads the discussion. Do not answer the question.

### Passage

**(1)** Technology could one day be driving your car. **(2)** It is more than just the power behind texting or video games. **(3)** According to the latest research, technology may soon replace human drivers in the form of self-driving cars.

**(4)** Up until recently, autopilots were common on planes or in agricultural harvesting, but the development of the self-driving car never saw significant progress. **(5)** One reason why self-driving cars have yet to take off as a modern commuting option is the fact that they must navigate intricate and complex roadways. **(6)** In contrast, the air, sea, and even the surface of Mars are far simpler, with no traffic lights or stray children to run into the path. **(7)** For years, autonomous submarines have roamed wide-open waters, and driverless trains have followed limited, straightforward tracks.

**(8)** A second reason for the delay in the development of self-driving cars is that they require specialized, up-to-date maps. **(9)** Modern technology is teeming with online maps and GPS programs. **(10)** However, for self-driving cars to be successful, GPS isn't sufficient; a reliable backup system is necessary. **(11)** "We are currently developing artificial intelligence that allows an automated car to navigate new roads without [the use of] 3D maps, using a series of sensors that observe road conditions," Leslie Sanchez, chief engineer at Plymouth Labs, said.

**(12)** New car models include features that take over driving if the car swerves out of its lane or if vehicles in front of it stop suddenly. **(13)** These are examples of self-driving technology. **(14)** They say self-driving cars will lower the frequency of accidents on the road and reduce traffic.

1. In context, which of the following sentences would best be inserted between sentences 9 and 10?

   (A) Recent developments indicate that driverless cars may also one day replace ambulance drivers responding to emergencies.

   (B) Developing backup technology will likely take another decade.

   (C) Garmin Ltd., for example, provides GPS and mapping for a variety of users.

   (D) Many think self-driving cars could one day replace taxis and buses.

## Groundwork

*In this section, students will evaluate the characteristics of an essay revision question.*

EXERCISE A SLIDE 112.1

**Remind me: what are the first 15 questions of the ELAR multiple-choice test?**

A long passage, 2 dual passages, and a bunch of short passages.

**Those short passage questions run from questions 7 through 15. With so many of the same question types in a row, it's easy to drop into autopilot. Then, *wham*! Something like what you see in your workbook here overtakes the computer screen. How can we tell that it's an essay revision question?**

The passage is really long.

**It's called *essay* revision for a reason. These questions sync up to a full-length essay, sort of like a long passage on the reading side of the ELAR test. Does anyone remember how many questions will go with this passage?**

Four.

**Questions 16, 17, 18, and 19 are all essay revision questions, and they'll all be taken from the same passage. How does that simplify things for us?**

We don't have to read four big passages, just one.

**Even though it's just one big passage for four questions, we might see something like this and feel a little overwhelmed. Think about it. At this point in the test, you just tackled a bunch of reading questions, and your mind is probably feeling like jelly. Then, this huge passage pops up. How do you think you'll feel?**

Pretty defeated.

**You shouldn't, though! Reaching this big passage on question 16 means you've hit a milestone. What's changed?**

We've switched from reading-focused questions to writing-focused questions.

**If you get to question 16, and this giant passage just feels like too much to take on immediately, give yourself a little mental break. You've got plenty of time, and it might even be a good way to reset your focus for the writing questions that make up the rest of the multiple-choice section.**

**TSIA2 Mastery:** ELAR 

EXERCISE B

**Instructions**

Review the basic steps for answering an essay revision question. Put them into the correct sequence by filling in numbers 1–4 in the space provided.

________ Determine the question type.

________ Read the passage.

________ Use the process of elimination.

________ Use the right strategy.

## Groundwork

*In this section, students will sequence the steps for a basic strategy that can be used to answer any essay revision question on the TSIA2.*

EXERCISE B SLIDE 113.1

**Once we've given ourselves the opportunity to reset a little, we can start working. What do you think we should do first?**

*Read the passage.*

**Why not jump straight to the question?**

Since four questions go with it, we'll have to read the whole thing eventually.

**Essay revision questions don't just have a big passage. They also ask big questions. For instance, they might ask you where a sentence could be added, or they might ask you about the organization of the essay. For that, you'll need to have a good understanding of what's actually in the passage. And, it gives you a little head start, since you'll use the same passage to answer four questions. Once you're done reading, what's next?**

*Determine the question type.*

**There are two types of essay revision questions: composition questions and grammar questions. What do you think composition questions ask about?**

The actual writing or details of the passage.

**And what will grammar questions test you on?**

Grammar and punctuation.

**The type of question you're working with will play a big role in step 3. What do we do next?**

*Use the right strategy.*

**If they're all essay revision questions, why do we need different strategies?**

Composition questions don't test the same kinds of skills as grammar questions.

**The strategy you'll use will depend heavily on what type of question it is, which is why we always take the time to evaluate things before we dive in. Once we know what we're working with and what our strategy will be, what's our last step?**

*Use the process of elimination.*

**Why are we eliminating? What's wrong with just picking out the right choice?**

Finding wrong answers is easier than picking out something that's exactly right.

**The process of elimination also works in our favor because even if we can't narrow things down to just one option, we can at least improve our chances of guessing correctly by eliminating a choice or two.**

# Application

## THE APPROACH

When answering an essay revision question on the TSIA2, use these steps ...

1. Read the passage.
2. Determine the question type.
3. Use the right strategy.
4. Use the process of elimination.

**Passage**

**(1)** Technology could one day be driving your car. **(2)** It is more than just the power behind texting or video games. **(3)** According to the latest research, technology may soon replace human drivers in the form of self-driving cars.

**(4)** Up until recently, autopilots were common on planes or in agricultural harvesting, but the development of the self-driving car never saw significant progress. **(5)** One reason why self-driving cars have yet to take off as a modern commuting option is the fact that they must navigate intricate and complex roadways. **(6)** In contrast, the air, sea, and even the surface of Mars are far simpler, with no traffic lights or stray children to run into the path. **(7)** For years, autonomous submarines have roamed wide-open waters, and driverless trains have followed limited, straightforward tracks.

**(8)** A second reason for the delay in the development of self-driving cars is that they require specialized, up-to-date maps. **(9)** Modern technology is teeming with online maps and GPS programs. **(10)** However, for self-driving cars to be successful, GPS isn't sufficient; a reliable backup system is necessary. **(11)** "We are currently developing artificial intelligence that allows an automated car to navigate new roads without [the use of] 3D maps, using a series of sensors that observe road conditions," Leslie Sanchez, chief engineer at Plymouth Labs, said.

**(12)** New car models include features that take over driving if the car swerves out of its lane or if vehicles in front of it stop suddenly. **(13)** These are examples of self-driving technology. **(14)** They say self-driving cars will lower the frequency of accidents on the road and reduce traffic.

1. In context, which of the following sentences would best be inserted between sentences 9 and 10?

   Ⓐ Recent developments indicate that driverless cars may also one day replace ambulance drivers responding to emergencies.
   
   Ⓑ Developing backup technology will likely take another decade.
   
   Ⓒ Garmin Ltd., for example, provides GPS and mapping for a variety of users.
   
   Ⓓ Many think self-driving cars could one day replace taxis and buses.

# Application

*In this section, students will practice applying a basic strategy to a composition-focused essay revision question.*

SLIDE 114.1

**Before we can dive into eliminating those wrong answers, though, we need to start back at the beginning. When we're working on the essay revision questions, what should we do first?**

*Read the passage.*

**Let's do that now.**

*Give students 1 minute to read the passage.*

**What's this passage about?**

Self-driving cars.

**Each paragraph talks about self-driving cars to some degree, so that's definitely the topic. When you read these passages, it's a good idea to ask yourself basic questions like this just to check that you understood what you read. No sense in reading if you're not going to take in the information. What's next?**

*Determine the question type.*

**What are our options again?**

Composition or grammar.

**Look closely at number 1. What do you think it's testing you on?**

Composition.

**How can you tell?**

It's asking about adding a detail to the essay.

**This question isn't challenging our punctuation skills or asking us to combine sentences. It wants us to make a writing change to the question. That means composition. What should we do next?**

*Use the right strategy.*

**This topic is covered further in the Organization chapter, but I'll give you a quick strategy to use for now. When you're asked to see if a detail fits in a certain spot in an essay, check what comes before and what comes after. In this case, which sentences should we focus on?**

Sentences 9 and 10.

**We want to squeeze an extra detail between sentences 9 and 10, so it needs to go with that information. What does sentence 9 talk about?**

How there are lots of online maps and GPS systems.

**And what does sentence 10 say?**

That those maps aren't always reliable.

**Which answer choices can we eliminate? What's wrong with them?**

Choices A and D bring up a point that doesn't connect with the details of sentence 10, and choice B introduces the idea of a backup plan before it would be mentioned in sentence 10.

**Which answer choice do you think best fits in there?**

Choice C.

**Choice C offers up an example of what was mentioned in sentence 9 and doesn't stray too far from the topic to make sentence 10 seem like it's interrupting a train of thought, so we know it's the right answer.**

## THE APPROACH

When answering an essay revision question on the TSIA2, use these steps ...

1. Read the passage.
2. Determine the question type.
3. Use the right strategy.
4. Use the process of elimination.

**Passage**

**(1)** Technology could one day be driving your car. **(2)** It is more than just the power behind texting or video games. **(3)** According to the latest research, technology may soon replace human drivers in the form of self-driving cars.

**(4)** Up until recently, autopilots were common on planes or in agricultural harvesting, but the development of the self-driving car never saw significant progress. **(5)** One reason why self-driving cars have yet to take off as a modern commuting option is the fact that they must navigate intricate and complex roadways. **(6)** In contrast, the air, sea, and even the surface of Mars are far simpler, with no traffic lights or stray children to run into the path. **(7)** For years, autonomous submarines have roamed wide-open waters, and driverless trains have followed limited, straightforward tracks.

**(8)** A second reason for the delay in the development of self-driving cars is that they require specialized, up-to-date maps. **(9)** Modern technology is teeming with online maps and GPS programs. **(10)** However, for self-driving cars to be successful, GPS isn't sufficient; a reliable backup system is necessary. **(11)** "We are currently developing artificial intelligence that allows an automated car to navigate new roads without [the use of] 3D maps, using a series of sensors that observe road conditions," Leslie Sanchez, chief engineer at Plymouth Labs, said.

**(12)** New car models include features that take over driving if the car swerves out of its lane or if vehicles in front of it stop suddenly. **(13)** These are examples of self-driving technology. **(14)** They say self-driving cars will lower the frequency of accidents on the road and reduce traffic.

2. In context, which is the best revision to sentence 14 (reproduced below)?

   *They say self-driving cars will lower the frequency of accidents on the road and reduce traffic.*

   Ⓐ Replace "They say" with "Developers argue."
   Ⓑ Replace "will lower" with "will reduce."
   Ⓒ Delete "and reduce traffic."
   Ⓓ Insert "their" before "accidents."

## Application

*In this section, students will practice using the steps of the Approach to answer a grammar-focused essay revision question.*

SLIDE 115.1

**Let's take on another question. Do we still need to do step 1?**

No, we already read the passage.

**One of the great things about the test pattern is that the four essay revision questions will always be pulled from the same passage. That's why we read it once, right at the start, so that the following three questions are a little easier to handle. What should we do next?**

Figure out what kind of question it is.

**And what kind of question is it?**

Grammar.

**How do you know?**

It wants us to pick new words for a sentence.

**The question offers up very specific changes to the sentence. What kind of strategy do you think we should use to answer this question?**

Test out each answer choice.

**There's no real pattern in the answer choices. For instance, they're not testing comma placement or verb tense. So, there's not much else to do besides test each one to see which ones break the sentence and which one makes it better. What's our plan?**

To use the process of elimination.

**We're on the hunt for wrong answers. Let's start with choice A. If we swap *they say* with *developers argue*, do we break the sentence?**

No, it seems okay.

**What should we do with choice A?**

Hang onto it.

**Even if you feel like an answer might be correct, try to eliminate all the other ones first anyway. Why is that a good strategy?**

Because there might be a better answer further down the list.

**If multiple-choice questions teach us anything in life, it's to never settle! There could be something better. And if not, we'll still have choice A in our back pocket. Let's test choice B. Does changing *will lower* to *will reduce* break the sentence?**

No.

**Does it add anything of value to the sentence?**

Not really.

**We can still hang onto choice B and keep searching. Does choice C make the sentence better?**

No, it removes good information.

**We want to make a change that will make the sentence better, not shorter or less detailed. Let's eliminate choice C. Check the last option. Does adding *their* before *accidents* improve the sentence?**

No.

**In fact, it makes it worse because we have no idea who "they" are. Choice D is out. Are we done?**

No, we still have to pick between choices A and B.

**Even if you only get down to two choices, consider it a win. That's a 50-50 chance you'll get the question right, which is good odds. But, let's try to get down to just one option anyway. Which one do you think brings the *most* value to this sentence?**

Choice A, because it clarifies who *they* refers to at the beginning of the sentence.

**Choice B just offers up a synonym swap, which doesn't really add much value to the sentence. Clearing up who "they" are adds good detail, though, so we know choice A is correct. Remember: as you take on the essay revision questions on the TSIA2, there is always a light at the end of the tunnel. Read that passage once and use what you learned to get you through all four questions. Once you hit question 20, it'll be much smoother sailing as you take on sentence revision.**

## Practice

### Instructions
Complete the practice set. If time remains after you've finished, double-check your work.

### Passage
**(1)** Why do some people enjoy being scared? **(2)** You might be someone who happily pays money for scary movies, haunted houses, or terrifying thrill rides. **(3)** There's actually a scientific explanation behind this affinity. **(4)** Social psychologist Dr. Clark McCauley of Bryn Mawr College explains it like this: "The fictional nature of horror films affords viewers a sense of control by placing psychological distance between them and the violent acts they have witnessed." **(5)** Dr. McCauley received his Ph.D. from the University of Pennsylvania.

**(6)** Research has shown that stressed or anxious viewers actually feel better after watching horror movies. **(7)** They ultimately help by allowing their brains to artificially focus on survival instead of the issues in their lives that were previously causing worry or fear. **(8)** When you're scared, your prefrontal cortex, responsible for planning and decision making, becomes overshadowed by the limbic system, which controls arousal and stimulation. **(9)** Coming down from this adrenaline rush gives anxious viewers a sense of calm when a movie finishes, so it is not uncommon for sufferers to seek thrills and scares for therapeutic purposes.

1. What is the best way to combine sentences 6 and 7 (reproduced below)?

   *Research has shown that stressed or anxious viewers actually feel better after watching horror movies. They ultimately help by allowing their brains to artificially focus on survival instead of the issues in their lives that were previously causing worry or fear.*

   Ⓐ Research has shown that stressed or anxious viewers actually feel better after watching horror movies, they ultimately help by allowing their brains to artificially focus on survival instead of the issues in their lives that were previously causing worry or fear.

   Ⓑ Research has shown that stressed or anxious viewers actually feel better after watching horror movies ultimately these movies help by allowing their brains to artificially focus on survival instead of the issues in their lives that were previously causing worry or fear.

   Ⓒ Research has shown that stressed or anxious viewers actually feel better after watching horror movies, which ultimately help by allowing their brains to artificially focus on survival instead of the issues in their lives that were previously causing worry or fear.

   Ⓓ Research has shown that stressed or anxious viewers actually feel better after watching horror movies; then, they ultimately help by allowing their brains to artificially focus on survival instead of the issues in their lives that were previously causing worry or fear.

# Practice

SLIDE 116.1

*Give students 8 minutes to complete the practice set.*

SLIDE 116.2

1. **The correct answer is C.** The antecedent of the pronoun *they* in sentence 7 is unclear and needs to be corrected. Choices A and B are incorrect because the changes create run-on sentences. Choice D is incorrect because it does not resolve the pronoun-antecedent ambiguity and introduces an unnecessary transition word. Only choice C removes the ambiguous pronoun and correctly links a dependent clause to the independent clause that precedes it.

2. Which of the following sentences contains irrelevant information that can be deleted from the passage?

   Ⓐ Sentence 1
   Ⓑ Sentence 3
   Ⓒ Sentence 5
   Ⓓ Sentence 8

3. Where in the second paragraph should the following sentence be inserted?

   *These fears are temporarily calmed by the body.*

   Ⓐ After sentence 6
   Ⓑ After sentence 7
   Ⓒ After sentence 8
   Ⓓ After sentence 9

## Practice

SLIDE 117.1

2. **The correct answer is C.** The university where the psychologist obtained his degree is not relevant to the topic of the passage or the paragraph, which focuses on how artificially frightening circumstances can result in calmed anxiety. Choices A, B, and D are incorrect because they all include details that support the passage topic. Therefore, choice C is the best answer.

SLIDE 117.2

3. **The correct answer is B.** *These fears* implies that the fears have already been described, so the new sentence should come only after this description. Choice A is incorrect because fears have not been specifically introduced yet. Choice C is incorrect because it explains how fears are calmed by the body, so it should appear after, not before, the added sentence. Choice D is incorrect because *these fears* should appear closely after the first mention of fears; at the end of the second paragraph is too far removed. This leaves choice B as the clearest, most logical place for the addition.

This page is intentionally left blank.
Content resumes on the next page.

This page is intentionally left blank.
Teacher content resumes with the next chapter.

CHAPTER 14

# Concision

In this chapter, students will review the concepts of redundancy and wordiness. Students will correct concision errors by removing unnecessary words and phrases.

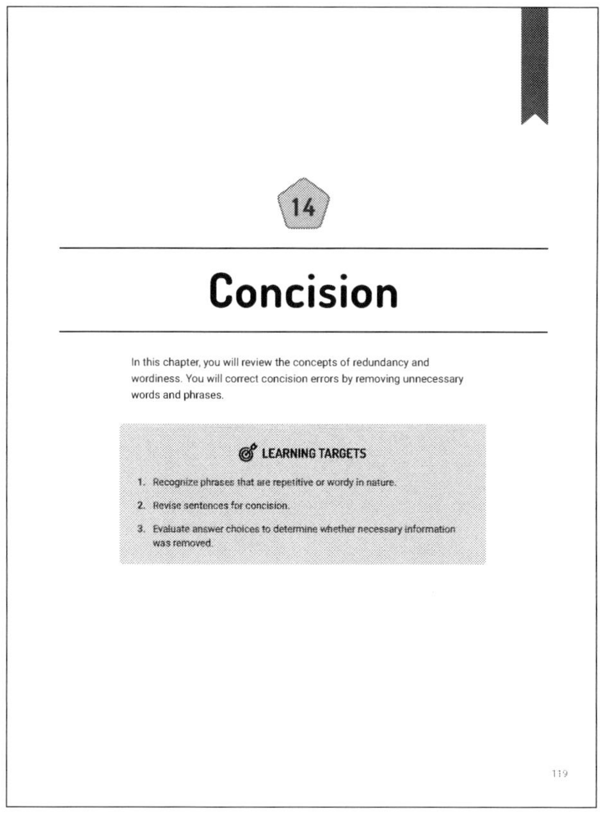

14

Concision

In this chapter, you will review the concepts of redundancy and wordiness. You will correct concision errors by removing unnecessary words and phrases.

LEARNING TARGETS

1. Recognize phrases that are repetitive or wordy in nature.
2. Revise sentences for concision.
3. Evaluate answer choices to determine whether necessary information was removed.

119

## TSIA2 STANDARDS

**Essay Revision and Editing**
Effective language use

The student will revise as necessary to improve the rhetorical use of language.

## TEKS ALIGNMENT

E1.9 *Composition*: Listening, speaking, reading writing, and thinking using multiple texts—writing process. The student uses the writing process recursively to compose multiple texts that are legible and uses appropriate conventions. The student is expected to:

(C) revise drafts to improve clarity, development, organization, style, diction, and sentence effectiveness, including parallel constructions and placement of phrases and dependent clauses.

## LEARNING TARGETS

1. Recognize phrases that are repetitive or wordy in nature
2. Revise sentences for concision.
3. Evaluate answer choices to determine whether necessary information was removed.

## Warm-Up

**Instructions**
Complete the warm-up question. If time remains after you've finished, double-check your work.

**Passage**

**(1)** When schools of fish gather again after time apart, they will swim around each other while waving their fins and performing elaborate dances. **(2)** Stingrays have been seen frolicking over fields of coral, twirling and flapping their wings, even when ample open ocean is readily available. **(3)** Some have argued that these kinds of behaviors show that fish can feel emotions like joy and delight.

**(4)** Even advocates for the argument that fish have feelings acknowledge that scientists can easily misidentify what they are seeing with their eyes. **(5)** The shape of a fish's mouth makes it look like it is surprised; it looks that way even when it is excited or in danger. **(6)** Fish are social, communicating underwater using clicks and bubbles. **(7)** Feelings are challenging to understand even in humans, who have the ability to talk about their emotions.

**(8)** Many oceanographers who devote their time to studying fish behavior have argued that at least some fish, such as triggerfishes and eels, have strong feelings like the ones we experience as humans. **(9)** Other researchers are doubtful. **(10)** They argue that it has not yet been proven that fish feel emotion in any reliable, reproducible scientific experiments.

**(11)** Regardless, scientific consensus on the question of fish emotion is beginning to undergo a shift. **(12)** Many biologists have accepted that fish most likely have "primary" emotions such as fear or anger. **(13)** These responses seem to be found in most fish. **(14)** For instance, a zebrafish will avoid a part of the tank where it was once shocked even if the shock has been removed. **(15)** Additionally, scientists believe that feelings can be inferred from fishes' changes in activity and eye movement, or even from involuntary responses like scale shedding.

1. Which of the following is the best version of the underlined portion of sentence 1 (reproduced below)?

   *When schools of fish gather again after time apart, they will swim around each other while waving their fins and performing elaborate dances.*

   Ⓐ (as it is now)
   Ⓑ after they have had separation between them,
   Ⓒ again after they have not been near each other for a while,
   Ⓓ together after they haven't gotten together for a while,

# Warm-Up

SLIDE 120.1

*Give students 2 minutes to complete the warm-up question.*

SLIDE 120.2

1. **The correct answer is A.** Choice B is incorrect because it is awkward and uses unnecessary language (*separation between them*). Choices C and D are incorrect because they are needlessly wordy and repetitive. Choice A is correct because it concisely conveys that the fish are reuniting after some time has passed.

**TSIA2 Mastery:** ELAR 

## Groundwork

EXERCISE A

### Instructions

Underline the part of the sentence that could be replaced by an abbreviation. Then, select an abbreviation to replace what you underlined.

| ASAP | etc. | vs. |
|---|---|---|

1. The store sells gloves, shoes, belts, and many other similar types of leather-based things.

   Abbreviation: _______

2. Sometimes it feels like me on one side going up against everything else in the world.

   Abbreviation: _______

3. Please return the key as soon as you possibly and reasonably can.

   Abbreviation: _______

# Groundwork

*In this section, students will review the concept of concision and practice identifying wordy phrases.*

EXERCISE A SLIDE 121.1

**Being concise means using as few words as possible to make a point. If we had to say something like, "I am traveling by car to the building in which the medical professional who specializes in teeth operates" every time we went to the dentist, we'd never get through a conversation. Concision problems in the TSIA2 ask us to cut those extra words. The first exercise in your book—what is it asking you to do?**

Pick an abbreviation to fit the sentence.

**How does that relate to the idea of being concise?**

Abbreviations make the sentence shorter.

**Abbreviations like *ASAP*, *etc.*, and *vs.* are one way to cut out unnecessary words. Each of these sentences has a wordy spot that could be replaced by an abbreviation. Can someone read number 1 aloud?**

*The store sells gloves, shoes, belts, and many other similar types of leather-based things.*

**Can you hear a part of the sentence that's way too wordy?**

The end: *and many other similar types of leather-based things.*

**I feel out of breath just hearing it. What abbreviation means something like *many other similar things*?**

Etc.

**We can add *etc.* to the end of a list to mean "and more of the same stuff." If we replace that long phrase with *etc.*, we go from eight words to one. Talk about being concise! Take a second to read sentences 2 and 3, and see what abbreviation could fit.**

*Give students 60 seconds to complete this task.*

**What did you get for number 2? Which abbreviation is relevant here?**

Vs.

**Versus means "against." What wordy phrase could it replace?**

*On one side going up against everything else in.*

**We have more options here than in number 1. We could just say, *me vs. the world*, but we could also say, *me vs. everything else in the world*. The key point is that our edited sentence will be shorter and more concise. What about number 3? What abbreviation can we use?**

ASAP.

**What wordy phrase could it replace?**

*As soon as you possibly and reasonably can.*

***ASAP* literally means "as soon as possible," so we can cut all of those words and pop in our abbreviation. But abbreviations aren't always the best solution to concision issues, especially when it comes to academic writing. For instance, we wouldn't want to use *ASAP* in a college essay or even on the TSIA2. Without an abbreviation to fall back on, how will we fix these concision issues on test day?**

EXERCISE B

**Instructions**
Review the following sentences as your teacher leads the discussion.

4. I couldn't believe what I was hearing with my ears.

5. Sharing her point of view, Doctor Lee gave her perspective on the illness and wrote out a prescription for the patient.

6. The first performance of the recital, Dana's dance was the perfect number to open the beginning of the evening.

   Revised: ____________________

## Groundwork

*In this section, students will review the concept of redundancy.*

EXERCISE B

**We know we should cut down wordy phrases—but to be concise, we also need to remove *redundant* phrases. Redundant phrases repeat information we already know. Redundant phrases are redundant and repetitive. They repeat the same redundant information over and over repeatedly. It's redundant.**

*Pause for effect.*

SLIDE 122.1

**Nobody wants to hear sentences like that—or read them. I mean, who wants to listen to someone rambling on and on? We'd forget the first half of the sentence before we even get to the end of it. So let's practice cutting the unnecessary, starting with number 4. Who'd like to read it aloud?**

*I couldn't believe what I was hearing with my ears.*

**Something in this sentence is redundant: it tells us information we already know. Did anyone catch it?**

*With my ears.*

**Why is that phrase redundant?**

*Hearing* implies that they're already using their ears.

**Hearing can only be done with one body part, so saying that we hear with our ears is redundant. Take a second to read number 5. What phrase do you think we should cut?**

*Sharing her point of view.*

***Sharing her point of view* repeats the same information as a phrase later in the sentence. What's the later phrase?**

*Gave her perspective.*

**Sharing one's point of view and giving one's perspective are the exact same thing. We don't need to say it twice. What about number 6? How does that sentence sound?**

Bad, very repetitive.

**There are problems with concision all over the place. What are some of the redundant words here?**

*First, to open, the beginning.*

**This sentence expresses the idea of starting the recital three times. We only need to say it once. Try revising this sentence on your own by removing the redundant phrases. Write your new sentence on the line below.**

*Give students 60 seconds to complete this task.*

**What did you come up with?**

*Solicit answers from multiple students: e.g., Dana's dance was the perfect number to open the evening's recital.*

**We can revise sentences with concision problems in several ways, depending on how we cut, trim, and rearrange the information. As long as we get rid of wordy and redundant parts, we're on the right track.**

**TSIA2 Mastery:** ELAR 

# Application

## THE APPROACH

When the answer choices offer different phrasings of the same information, use the following steps ...

1. Eliminate answers with redundant information.
2. Eliminate answers with wordy phrases.
3. Select the most concise answer that does not lose any important information.

**7.** Which of the following is the best version of the underlined portion of the sentence below?

*In industrialized countries, air pollution can stem from a number of many various, different, and simultaneous factors.*

Ⓐ (as it is now)

Ⓑ from a number of many and various factors.

Ⓒ from a lot of different factors happening at the same time.

Ⓓ from a number of simultaneous factors.

## Application

*In this section, students will review the process for answering concision questions.*

SLIDE 123.1

**On the TSIA2, of course, there's only one right answer. But we can take the same approach to a test question as we did when revising a sentence on our own. To eliminate answers, what concision issues should we look for first?**

Redundant phrases.

**Remind me what a redundant phrase is?**

Something that's repetitive.

**Let's start with choice A in question 7 and check for redundancy in the original underlined phrase. Does anyone see words that repeat the same meaning?**

*A number of* and *many*; *various* and *different.*

**The original phrase isn't concise, so we can eliminate choice A. What about choice B? Do we see redundancy here?**

Yes.

**What words in B are redundant?**

*A number of* and *many*.

**That's definitely incorrect, so choice B is out. What about choices C and D? Do we see redundancy?**

Not really.

**If there's no repetitive information, what else can we look for?**

Wordiness.

**Let's look at choice C again. Does it seem wordy?**

Yes.

**How so?**

*Happening at the same time* is really long.

***Happening at the same time* is a longer way to say *simultaneous*. We probably don't want choice C. That leaves us with choice D, but let's double-check. Is it wordy?**

No.

**Choice D is nicely concise, so we know it's our best answer for this question. But we should always check that we didn't lose any essential information. Sometimes, when we try to be concise, we end up cutting too many details, which is a whole other problem. Do we see that happening in choice D?**

No.

**Choice D is definitely the way to go.**

## THE APPROACH

When the answer choices offer different phrasings of the same information, use the following steps ...

1. Eliminate answers with redundant information.
2. Eliminate answers with wordy phrases.
3. Select the most concise answer that does not lose any important information.

**8.** Which of the following is the best version of the underlined portion of the sentence below?

*Many of the people who play baseball in the major leagues hail from countries outside the United States, such as the Dominican Republic and Venezuela.*

Ⓐ (as it is now)
Ⓑ Many of the baseball players
Ⓒ Many major league baseball players
Ⓓ Many of the players who participate in the major leagues of baseball

## Application

*In this section, students will practice applying the steps of the process to a concision question.*

SLIDE 124.1

**Let's try it again with question 8. What's the first step in our approach?**

Eliminate redundant and wordy answers.

**How can we check whether choice A should be eliminated?**

Look at the underlined portion of the sentence.

**What do you think? Is there any redundancy or wordiness in the underlined part?**

Yes, it's very wordy, especially *people who play baseball.*

**What's a more concise way to say *people who play baseball?***

Baseball players.

**The original sentence isn't concise, so let's eliminate choice A. Does any other choice look suspiciously wordy?**

Choice D.

***Many of the players who participate in the major leagues of baseball.* What do you think? Is it an improvement over the original sentence?**

No, it's just as bad.

**Choice D and choice A are very similar. Choice D has moved some words around, but it's not concise at all. Let's eliminate it. What about choices B and C? Are they wordy?**

Not really.

**They're both pretty short, right? Neither of them *sound* like bad answers. If you're stuck between two okay-sounding answers, you can use step 3 to choose between them. What's step 3 again?**

Select the most concise answer that does not lose any important information.

**Start with the shortest answer: *many of the baseball players.* Why do you think starting with the shortest option might be a good strategy?**

The shortest answer is probably going to be the most concise.

**Choice B looks nice and concise, but does it contain all the essential information from the original sentence?**

No, it's not clear who the players are.

**The original sentence isn't talking about anybody who plays baseball, but specifically *major league* players from outside the U.S. Although it's concise, choice B loses that essential detail. How about choice C—does it have all the information we need?**

Yes, it does.

**Choice C is concise, *and* it matches the original tone and meaning of the sentence. When you have two nice, short answers, check for missing information. The TSIA2 includes answers like choice B to make sure that you can't automatically pick the shortest answer on all concision questions.**

TSIA2 Mastery: ELAR 

# Practice

**Instructions**
Complete the practice set. If time remains after you've finished, double-check your work.

1. Which of the following is the best version of the underlined portion of the sentence below?

   *Many oceanographers who devote their time to studying fish behavior have argued that at least some fish, such as triggerfishes and eels, have strong feelings like the ones we experience as humans.*

   Ⓐ (as it is now)
   Ⓑ have strong feelings and emotions
   Ⓒ have strong feelings and experience powerful emotions,
   Ⓓ have strong feelings and definitely have emotions,

2. Which of the following is the best version of the underlined portion of this sentence?

   *Regardless, scientific consensus on the question of fish emotion is beginning to undergo a shift.*

   Ⓐ (as it is now)
   Ⓑ is beginning to undergo major shifting.
   Ⓒ is beginning to undergo a number of shifts.
   Ⓓ is beginning to shift.

3. Which of the following is the best version of the underlined portion of this sentence?

   *These responses seem to be found in most fish.*

   Ⓐ (as it is now)
   Ⓑ most fish animals.
   Ⓒ most fish that are animals.
   Ⓓ most.

# Practice

SLIDE 125.1

*Give students 8 minutes to complete the practice set.*

SLIDE 125.2

1. **The correct answer is A.** The phrase *have strong feelings* by itself is enough to communicate to the reader that fish have emotions, since emotions are the same as feelings. Choices B, C, and D are incorrect because the additional statements about the fish having emotions are unnecessary, since it is already stated that they *have strong feelings*. Choice A is correct because *have strong feelings* is the clearest and most concise statement of the author's message.

SLIDE 125.3

2. **The correct answer is D.** Choices A, B, and C are incorrect because the phrase *to undergo* is repetitive; *is beginning* communicates the same idea, so saying *is beginning to undergo* is redundant. Choice D is correct because it communicates the author's message clearly and concisely.

SLIDE 125.4

3. **The correct answer is A.** Choices B and C are incorrect because the word *animals* is unnecessary if we are already using the word *fish*. Choice D is incorrect because if the sentence ends after the word *most* (*these responses seem to be found in most*), it will be unclear what *these responses* are found in. Choice A is correct because the word *fish* clearly indicates where *these responses seem to be found*, and it is the clearest and most concise statement of the author's message.

## Wrap-Up

**Instructions**
Complete the wrap-up question. If time remains after you've finished, double-check your work.

**Passage**

**(1)** When schools of fish gather again after time apart, they will swim around each other while waving their fins and performing elaborate dances. **(2)** Stingrays have been seen frolicking over fields of coral, twirling and flapping their wings, even when ample open ocean is readily available. **(3)** Some have argued that these kinds of behaviors show that fish can feel emotions like joy and delight.

**(4)** Even advocates for the argument that fish have feelings acknowledge that scientists can easily misidentify what they are seeing with their eyes. **(5)** The shape of a fish's mouth makes it look like it is surprised; it looks that way even when it is excited or in danger. **(6)** Fish are social, communicating underwater using clicks and bubbles. **(7)** Feelings are challenging to understand even in humans, who have the ability to talk about their emotions.

**(8)** Many oceanographers who devote their time to studying fish behavior have argued that at least some fish, such as triggerfishes and eels, have strong feelings like the ones we experience as humans. **(9)** Other researchers are doubtful. **(10)** They argue that it has not yet been proven that fish feel emotion in any reliable, reproducible scientific experiments.

**(11)** Regardless, scientific consensus on the question of fish emotion is beginning to undergo a shift. **(12)** Many biologists have accepted that fish most likely have "primary" emotions such as fear or anger. **(13)** These responses seem to be found in most fish. **(14)** For instance, a zebrafish will avoid a part of the tank where it was once shocked even if the shock has been removed. **(15)** Additionally, scientists believe that feelings can be inferred from fishes' changes in activity and eye movement, or even from involuntary responses like scale shedding.

**2.** Which of the following is the best version of the underlined portion of sentence 4 (reproduced below)?

*Even advocates for the argument that fish have feelings acknowledge that scientists can easily misidentify what they are seeing with their eyes.*

Ⓐ (as it is now)
Ⓑ seeing.
Ⓒ seeing with only the help of their eyes.
Ⓓ giving a quick look.

# Wrap-Up

SLIDE 126.1

*Give students 2 minutes to complete the wrap-up question.*

SLIDE 126.2

2. **The correct answer is B.** Choices A and C are incorrect because the phrases *with their eyes* and *with only the help of their eyes* don't add anything to the sentence that isn't already communicated by *seeing*, so they are unnecessary. Choice D is incorrect because the tone of the phrase *giving a quick look* is too informal and imprecise to match the tone of the rest of the passage. Choice B is correct because it effectively conveys the correct meaning and tone while being concise.

CHAPTER 15

# Combining Sentences

In this chapter, students will learn to combine sentences to form a single sentence that is clear, correct, and concise.

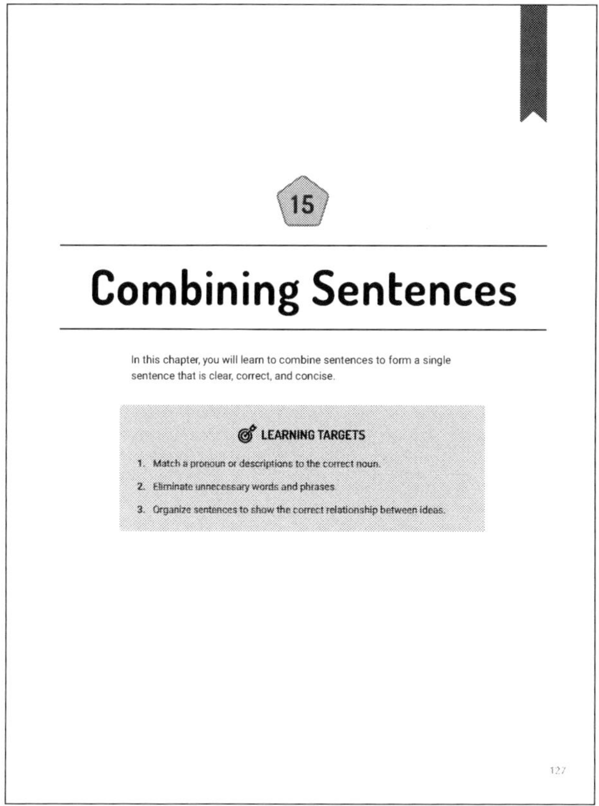
15

Combining Sentences

In this chapter, you will learn to combine sentences to form a single sentence that is clear, correct, and concise.

LEARNING TARGETS

1. Match a pronoun or descriptions to the correct noun.
2. Eliminate unnecessary words and phrases.
3. Organize sentences to show the correct relationship between ideas.

127

## TSIA2 STANDARDS

**Essay Revision and Editing**
Standard English conventions

The student will edit text as necessary to ensure conformity to the conventions of standard written English grammar, usage, and punctuation.

**Sentence Revision, Editing, and Completion**
Sentence combining

The student will combine two sentences into a more effective single sentence.

## TEKS ALIGNMENT

E1.9 *Composition*: listening, speaking, reading, writing, and thinking using multiple texts—writing process. The student uses the writing process recursively to compose multiple texts that are legible and use appropriate conventions. The student is expected to:

(D) edit drafts using standard English conventions, including:

(i) a variety of complete, controlled sentences and avoidance of unintentional splices, run-ons, and fragments.

## LEARNING TARGETS

1. Match a pronoun or descriptions to the correct noun.
2. Eliminate unnecessary words and phrases.
3. Organize sentences to show the correct relationship between ideas.

## Warm-Up

**Instructions**
Complete the warm-up question. If time remains after you've finished, double-check your work.

1. Which of the following is the best way to revise and combine the sentences below?

   *Democratic government was established in the 1970s. Then more actions were taken to preserve Catalan.*

   Ⓐ Democratic government was established in the 1970s, more actions were taken, and Catalan was preserved.

   Ⓑ Democratic government was established in the 1970s, and they took more actions to preserve Catalan.

   Ⓒ In the 1970s, more actions were taken to preserve Catalan because democratic government was established.

   Ⓓ After democratic government was established in the 1970s, more actions were taken to preserve Catalan.

# Warm-Up

SLIDE 128.1

*Give students 2 minutes to complete the warm-up question.*

SLIDE 128.2

1. **The correct answer is D.** Choice A is incorrect because it is needlessly wordy and the sentence lacks a cause-and-effect transition or structure to indicate that the actions were taken in order to preserve Catalan. Choice B is incorrect because it is unclear who the pronoun *they* refers to in this context. Choice C is incorrect because it confuses the sequence of events. Choice D is correct because it correctly and concisely expresses the timing and relationship between *democratic government was established in the 1970s* and *more actions were taken to preserve Catalan* by using the preposition *after*.

TSIA2 Mastery: ELAR 

## Groundwork

EXERCISE A

**Instructions**
Work with your teacher to identify instances of unclear pronouns.

**First Draft:**

1. On the second morning of the battle, the Spartan warriors and the Persian soldiers clashed again. They now outnumbered the enemy by three to one.

**Revision #1:**

2. On the second morning of the battle, the Spartan warriors and the Persian soldiers clashed again and now outnumbered the enemy by three to one.

**Revision #2:**

3. The Spartan warriors and the Persian soldiers, who now outnumbered their enemy by three to one, clashed again on the second morning of the battle.

# Groundwork

***In this section, students will discuss how vague pronouns and misplaced descriptions can reduce the clarity of a text.***

EXERCISE A SLIDE 129.1

**Every piece of writing is a journey, and if the information in a sentence wanders off in the wrong direction, you risk tripping yourself up or losing meaning along the way. For instance, check out the first draft. Who would like to read those sentences aloud for us?**

*On the second morning of the battle, the Spartan warriors and the Persian soldiers clashed again. They now outnumbered the enemy by three to one.*

**Sounds like the Spartan warriors were taking out the Persians left and right. Or wait, were the Persians winning? Who outnumbered their enemy after that battle?**

We can't tell.

**The way it's written leaves readers feeling confused because we can't quite tell who *they* refers to. This is something called a *vague pronoun*. Essentially, it's a pronoun that could refer to more than one noun. Why is this bad?**

Because the sentence is unclear.

**What about Revision #1? The author tried to combine the sentences to avoid the clunky pronoun problem, but something went a little haywire. Let's check it out. First, were they able to get rid of that unclear pronoun?**

Yes.

***They* doesn't show up in the sentence, so there's no vague pronoun. So, who outnumbers whom? Was it the Spartans or the Persians?**

We still can't tell.

**Although the vague pronoun is gone, there's another issue happening. What's our main confusion?**

We don't know who has the most soldiers.

**We have this descriptive phrase that tells us one of the groups outnumbers the other, but since the sentence doesn't organize the information clearly, we're left feeling confused. Let's check out Revision #2. The writer revised again. What changes did they make?**

They put the details about outnumbering the other group next to *the Persian soldiers*.

**Does this fix our issue?**

Yes.

**Combining sentences can help us avoid problems like vague pronouns, but we have to be careful that, when we revise to a single sentence, we keep the information clear and understandable.**

EXERCISE B

### Instructions

Review the following sentences. Determine whether each sentence is too wordy, lacking information, or concise. Circle your answer.

### First Draft:

4. "Muckraker" was a term referring to journalists who advocated for reform. "Muckraker" was also a word applied to Upton Sinclair, who was a journalist who investigated the unhygienic practices of meatpacking plants.

   This sentence is ...

   ... too wordy.

   ... lacking information.

   ... concise.

### Revision #1:

5. "Muckraker" is a term applied to those who advocated for reform, like Upton Sinclair, who was a journalist.

   This sentence is ...

   ... too wordy.

   ... lacking information.

   ... concise.

### Revision #2:

6. "Muckraker" was a term for journalists who advocated for reform, like Upton Sinclair, who investigated the unhygienic practices of meatpacking plants.

   This sentence is ...

   ... too wordy.

   ... lacking information.

   ... concise.

## Groundwork

*In this section, students will review two unconcise sentences and examine a solution that eliminates the problem.*

**Another common obstacle that can send readers stumbling through a sentence is wordiness. What happens when a sentence is too wordy?**

It's hard to figure out what it's saying.

EXERCISE B SLIDE 130.1

**We like our writing like we like our lectures: short and to the point. No one wants to listen to someone ramble, and adding all kinds of extra fluff to a sentence only gets in the way of what we're trying to say. For example, let's look at the first draft in number 4. Who'd like to read that for us?**

*"Muckraker" was a term referring to journalists who advocated for reform. "Muckraker" was also a word applied to Upton Sinclair, who was a journalist who investigated the unhygienic practices of meatpacking plants.*

**Whoa. That's a lot of information crammed in there, and trying to pull out the details is a little like trying to untangle a ball of old Christmas lights. It's definitely not fun and even a little frustrating. What about the first draft makes it *not* concise?**

It's repetitive. The sentence says *muckraker* and *journalist* more than once.

**All the information is spread out across two sentences in such a way that the writer is getting repetitive when they really don't need to be. How can they fix this?**

They can edit it out of the sentence.

SLIDE 130.2

**Let's see if they managed to do that in number 5. Is that sentence more concise?**

Yes.

**But something went wrong. Why is this first revision not quite right?**

It lost a lot of information.

SLIDE 130.3

**Editing out extra words is only effective if we don't cut out the important stuff. Imagine trying to cut the tag off of a new shirt and ending up with no sleeves and a hole across the shoulders. We need to pull it back and just cut the stuff we don't want. Did the writer get it right in sentence 6?**

Yes, it's concise without losing important information.

**By focusing on just the important details, the writer was able to communicate everything they wanted to without overcomplicating it with extra wordiness. Concision at its best.**

EXERCISE C

**Instructions**
Use the word bank below to connect the two parts of each sentence.

**although** **after** **and** **resulting in**

**7.** The lifelong fascination that river travel held for Samuel Clemens inspired his famous pen name, Mark Twain, ____________ helped him paint a vivid setting for *The Adventures of Huckleberry Finn*.

**8.** ____________ ancient Egyptians rarely named their pet cats, they recorded many affectionate names for their dogs, like "Blacky" and "Brave One."

**9.** ____________ Hannibal invaded Rome with war elephants, Romans became terrified of the animals and featured them as monsters in bedtime stories for children.

## Groundwork

*In this section, students will demonstrate the correct relationship between different parts of a sentence by choosing the best word to complete the sentence.*

**Passages won't just be one idea, though. Writing is made up of a bunch of ideas connected to form one overall message. In fact, the TSIA2 asks you to specifically do this with combining sentences questions. How do we link ideas from two sentences to turn them into just one sentence?**

With connecting words.

**Connecting words can be things like transitions or conjunctions. These words are like road signs telling the reader which direction the text is about to go. For instance, we can use them to give the reader a heads up about an addition, a contrast, or a cause-and-effect relationship between ideas. Can anyone think of some examples of a connecting word or phrase?**

But, and, or, so, although, since, however, etc.

EXERCISE C  SLIDE 131.1

**For instance, let's look at sentence 7. What kind of information is the writer giving us?**

How the river inspired Samuel Clemens.

**What kinds of things did it inspire?**

His pen name and one of his stories.

**It sounds like we have one thing plus another thing, both inspired by the same initial source. What connecting word do you think we should use there to link those ideas?**

*And.*

**By adding *and*, we show the reader that one idea adds onto the next. They go together, like a matching set. What about sentence 8? What information does the writer give us?**

The Egyptians named their dogs but not their cats.

**Think about the details of the sentence. What kind of relationship do we see?**

Contrast.

**Which connecting word from our word bank helps us show that contrast?**

*Although.*

***Although* is great for showing that the information is connected by a difference. Finally, let's look at sentence 9. What information are we given?**

That Hannibal invaded Rome with elephants and people became terrified of them.

**What kind of relationship do we see between those details?**

Cause-and-effect.

**Those details help the reader see how one thing led to another. Which connecting word of our choices best shows that relationship?**

*After.*

**Remember: when revising a sentence, pay attention to how the details are related. One wrong connection, and the whole idea is lost.**

## Application

### THE APPROACH

When you are asked to revise and combine two sentences, use the following steps ...

1. Eliminate options with unclear pronouns or misplaced descriptions.
2. Eliminate repetitive terms or unnecessary wordiness.
3. Eliminate answers with illogical connections between ideas.

**10.** Which of the following best combines the two sentences below?

*Japanese artisans don't discard cracked pottery and instead patch the cracks with gold lacquer. The artisans do this to celebrate the object's history and its "scars."*

Ⓐ They patch the cracks with gold lacquer instead of discarding it, which celebrates the object's history and its "scars."

Ⓑ When pottery cracks, Japanese artisans do not discard the cracked pottery, and instead they patch the cracks with gold lacquer, and this is so that the artisans can celebrate the object's history and its "scars"

Ⓒ Instead of discarding cracked pottery, Japanese artisans patch the cracks with gold lacquer in order to celebrate the object's history and its "scars."

Ⓓ Japanese artisans don't discard cracked pottery, patch the cracks with gold lacquer, and celebrate the object's history and its "scars."

# Application

*In this section, students will practice applying the steps of the Approach to eliminate incorrect answer choices and identify the most effective combined sentence.*

SLIDE 132.1

**So far in this lesson, we've mostly spent our time reviewing other people's writing and picking out their flaws. That's exactly what you'll do when you take on combining sentences questions during the TSIA2. You won't be doing the actual revising yourself. You'll just evaluate each answer choice to see which revision did it best. Let's practice using number 10. How can you tell it's a combining sentences question?**

It asks us to combine two sentences.

**While you won't get the chance to write your own version, you *will* get the opportunity to check out a few options for revisions in the form of answer choices. What kinds of errors do you think will show up?**

Vague pronouns, misplaced descriptions, wordiness, and incorrect transitions.

**All the things we just covered, right? And if you find one of those errors in an answer choice, what should you do?**

Eliminate it.

**Let's start with vague pronouns. Do you see any of those among the answer choices?**

Yes, *they* is unclear in choice A.

**An unclear pronoun means you can cross off that choice and move on. What about wordiness? Do any of these answer choices seem wordy or repetitive?**

Choice B.

**Visually, we can see that choice B is longer than the others. Dig in and tell me what's wrong.**

It repeats *artisans* and different versions of *cracked pottery*.

**Let's eliminate choice B. At this point, we're down to two choices. Let's take a moment to compare our options. What's the big difference between choice C and choice D?**

Choice C links the ideas with the connection words *instead* and *in order to*, and choice D lists the three ideas using *and* to connect them.

**What kind of relationship do *instead* and *in order to* create?**

Contrast and cause-and-effect.

**What about *and*? What kind of relationship does that imply?**

Addition.

**Take a look at the ideas in the original sentences. Does celebrating the object's history take place in addition to patching the cracks, despite the patching, or as a result of the patching?**

As a result of patching the cracks.

**Sounds like a cause-and-effect relationship. Which answer has the right transitions to create a cause-and-effect connection?**

Choice C.

**These questions are often some of the most challenging on the writing portion of the TSIA2 because all the options give the same information, just in different ways. Rather than trying to pick out just the right one, focus on errors in clarity and concision. If an answer choice makes a mistake, you know it's wrong, and you can eliminate it.**

## THE APPROACH

When you are asked to revise and combine two sentences, use the following steps ...

1. Eliminate options with unclear pronouns or misplaced descriptions.
2. Eliminate repetitive terms or unnecessary wordiness.
3. Eliminate answers with illogical connections between ideas.

**11.** Which answer choice best combines the two sentences below?

*Although they lived on separate islands, Pacific Islander tribes often sailed across the sea for friendly visits. They exchanged shell necklaces as a show of good faith.*

(A) Even though they lived on separate islands, Pacific Islander tribes often sailed across the sea for friendly visits, but they exchanged shell necklaces as a show of good faith.

(B) Pacific Islander tribes often sailed across the sea for friendly visits, and the tribes of Pacific Islanders that lived on separate islands exchanged shell necklaces as a show of good faith.

(C) Although they lived on separate islands, Pacific Islander tribes often sailed across the sea for friendly visits, exchanged shell necklaces, they showed good faith.

(D) Although they lived on separate islands, Pacific Islander tribes often sailed across the sea for friendly visits and exchanged shell necklaces as a show of good faith.

## Application

*In this section, students will practice applying the Approach to effectively combine sentences and identify whether changing a transition word disrupts the meaning or preserves it.*

SLIDE 133.1

**Let's try it again on question 11. What should we look for first?**

Vague pronouns.

**Take a quick pass through the answer choices. Do you see a pronoun with the potential to go wrong?**

Yes, *they* shows up in almost every answer choice.

**Who does *they* refer to?**

Pacific Islander tribes.

**Is there any place where *they* is unclear?**

The second time *they* is used in choice C.

**The structure of choice C makes it look like the shell necklaces were the ones showing good faith, but we know that's not right. We can eliminate that option and move forward. What should we look for next?**

Wordiness.

**Look at the size of the answer choices. Which one do you think is most likely going to be wordy?**

Choice B.

**Choice B is the longest, so there's a good chance it's not very concise. Read it through just to be sure. Does it get repetitive anywhere?**

Yes, it says *Pacific Islander tribes* more often than it needs to.

**Choice B is out. We're down to two answer choices, so let's compare. How is choice A different from choice D?**

One uses *but* and the other uses *and* to connect the ideas.

**Go back to the original sentences. What kind of relationship do we see between those ideas?**

The second sentence adds detail to the first.

**Does *but* or *and* work better to show that addition?**

*And.*

**That means choice D is the right answer. It's clear and concise, and the ideas are connected using an effective transition. Think of the approach steps like directions, leading you through these kinds of questions. Trace a path from one mistake to the next until you reach your destination: the correct answer.**

## Practice

**Instructions**
Complete the practice set. If time remains after you've finished, double-check your work.

1. Which of the following best combines the sentences below?

   *Each individual fragment is tiny. Picture by picture, enormous databases of street views are transformed into driving directions.*

   Ⓐ Picture by picture, enormous databases of street views are transformed into driving directions, but each individual fragment is tiny.
   Ⓑ Each individual fragment being tiny, enormous databases of street views are transformed into driving directions picture by picture.
   Ⓒ Though each individual fragment is tiny, picture by picture, enormous databases of street views are transformed into driving directions.
   Ⓓ Despite tiny fragments, each individual transforms enormous databases of street views into driving directions.

2. Which of the following best combines the sentences below?

   *Junot Díaz wrote* The Brief Wondrous Life of Oscar Wao. *The 2008 Pulitzer Prize for Fiction was awarded to Díaz for his novel* The Brief Wondrous Life of Oscar Wao.

   Ⓐ *The Brief Wondrous Life of Oscar Wao*, written by Junot Díaz, and awarded the 2008 Pulitzer Prize for Fiction.
   Ⓑ Junot Díaz wrote *The Brief Wondrous Life of Oscar Wao*, he was awarded the 2008 Pulitzer Prize for Fiction for this novel.
   Ⓒ The 2008 Pulitzer Prize for Fiction was awarded to Junot Díaz for his novel *The Brief Wondrous Life of Oscar Wao.*
   Ⓓ Written by Junot Díaz and awarded the 2008 Pulitzer Prize for Fiction, *The Brief Wondrous Life of Oscar Wao.*

3. Which of the following best combines the sentences below?

   *Sonia Sanchez recited her poem "This Is Not a Small Voice." The students were inspired.*

   Ⓐ When Sonia Sanchez recited her poem "This Is Not a Small Voice," the students were inspired.
   Ⓑ The students were inspired, Sonia Sanchez recited her poem "This Is Not a Small Voice."
   Ⓒ The poem "This Is Not a Small Voice" recited by Sonia Sanchez, it was inspiring for the students.
   Ⓓ Inspired by the poem "This Is Not a Small Voice," Sonia Sanchez recited for the students.

# Practice

SLIDE 134.1

*Give students 8 minutes to complete the practice set.*

SLIDE 134.2

1. **The correct answer is C.** Choice A is incorrect because the word *but* doesn't fit before *each individual fragment is tiny* because it would suggest that there is something contradictory about each individual fragment being tiny; this is not contradictory because the enormous databases are created picture by picture. Choice B is incorrect because the introduction leads to an unclear overall sentence. Choice D is incorrect because *despite tiny fragments* doesn't make sense as an introduction and does not properly communicate the author's message. Choice C is correct because it is properly punctuated and communicates the author's message clearly: even though each portion is small, little by little, they turn a huge database of information into driving directions.

SLIDE 134.3

2. **The correct answer is C.** Choice A is incorrect because it lacks a subject-verb pair to make this a complete sentence. Choice B is incorrect because it is a comma splice—two complete sentences that are incorrectly joined by a comma. Choice D is incorrect because it is not a complete sentence. Choice C is correct because it successfully combines the two sentences into one complete sentence.

SLIDE 134.4

3. **The correct answer is A.** Choice B is incorrect because it is a comma splice, with two complete sentences that are incorrectly joined by a comma. Choice C is incorrect because it is not necessary to add the pronoun *it* to refer back to the subject *the poem*, and a comma is needed before the appositive element *recited by Sonia Sanchez*. Choice D is incorrect because it changes the meaning of the original sentences—the students are the ones who were inspired, not Sonia Sanchez. Choice A is correct because it is a complete sentence with the dependent clause correctly joined to the independent clause by a comma, and it has the same meaning as the original sentences.

## Wrap-Up

**Instructions**
Complete the wrap-up question. If time remains after you've finished, double-check your work.

**2.** Which of the following best combines the sentences below?

*Other researchers are doubtful. They argue that it has not yet been proven that fish feel emotion in any reliable, reproducible scientific experiments.*

Ⓐ Although they argue that it has not yet been proven that fish feel emotion in any reliable, reproducible scientific experiments, other researchers are doubtful.

Ⓑ Other researchers are doubtful; furthermore, they argue that it has not yet been proven that fish feel emotion in any reliable, reproducible scientific experiments.

Ⓒ Other researchers are doubtful, arguing that it has not yet been proven that fish feel emotion in any reliable, reproducible scientific experiments.

Ⓓ It has not yet been proven that fish feel emotion in any reliable, reproducible scientific experiments, some researchers argue, although they are, admittedly, doubtful.

# Wrap-Up

SLIDE 135.1

*Give students 2 minutes to complete the wrap-up question.*

SLIDE 135.2

2. **The correct answer is C.** Choice A is incorrect because the conjunction *although* indicates that the other researchers are not doubtful of the argument that fish feel emotion, when in fact they are. Choice B is incorrect because the conjunction *furthermore* suggests that *they argue that it has not yet been proven that fish feel emotion* is a new claim in the argument, when actually it is a supporting detail of *other researchers are doubtful*. Choice D is incorrect because the ordering of the sentence indicates that the researchers mentioned are doubtful about their own arguments, which is not the intended meaning. Choice C is correct because it concisely combines the sentences, making it clear that *arguing that it has not yet been proven that fish feel emotion* is a supporting detail of *other researchers are doubtful*.

This page is intentionally left blank.
Content resumes on the next page.

This page is intentionally left blank.
Teacher content resumes with the next chapter.

CHAPTER 16

# Parallelism

In this chapter, students will be introduced to the concept of parallel structure within sentences and among the elements of lists. In addition, they will practice identifying and correcting errors in parallelism.

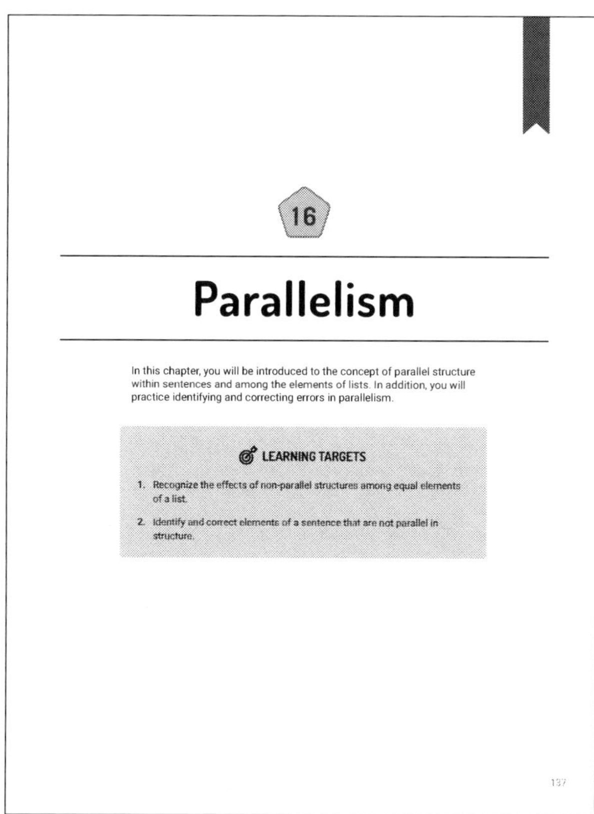

16

Parallelism

In this chapter, you will be introduced to the concept of parallel structure within sentences and among the elements of lists. In addition, you will practice identifying and correcting errors in parallelism.

LEARNING TARGETS

1. Recognize the effects of non-parallel structures among equal elements of a list.
2. Identify and correct elements of a sentence that are not parallel in structure.

137

## TSIA2 STANDARDS

**Essay Revision and Editing**
Standard English Conventions

The student will edit text as necessary to ensure conformity to the conventions of standard written English grammar, usage, and punctuation.

**Sentence Revision, Editing, and Completion**
Conventions of Grammar

The student will edit and complete sentences as needed to ensure conformity to the conventions of standard written English grammar.

## TEKS ALIGNMENT

E1.9 *Composition*: listening, speaking, reading, writing, and thinking using multiple texts—writing process. The student uses the writing process recursively to compose multiple texts that are legible and use appropriate conventions. The student is expected to:

(D) edit drafts using standard English conventions, including:

(i) a variety of complete, controlled sentences and avoidance of unintentional splices, run-ons, and fragments.

## LEARNING TARGETS

1. Recognize the effects of non-parallel structures among equal elements of a list.
2. Identify and correct elements of a sentence that are not parallel in structure.

## Warm-Up

**Instructions**
Complete the warm-up question. If time remains after you've finished, double-check your work.

1. The essence of joy is this: to greet each day as if it were your last, to love, and to be laughing.

    Ⓐ (as it is now)
    Ⓑ for laughing
    Ⓒ to laugh
    Ⓓ laughing

# Warm-Up

SLIDE 138.1

*Give students 2 minutes to complete the warm-up question.*

SLIDE 138.2

1. **The correct answer is C.** Choices A, B, and D are incorrect because *to be laughing*, *for laughing*, and *laughing* do not agree with the form of the two previous items in the series, *to greet* and *to love*, which are infinitives, thus confusing the sentence. Additionally, the verb *to be* is unnecessary, and the preposition *for* illogically suggests that *the essence of joy*, the subject, is intended to be used by *laughing* or belongs to *laughing*. Choice C is correct because the infinitive *to laugh* agrees with the other two infinitives *to greet* and *to love*, completing the 3-item series structure logically.

TSIA2 Mastery: ELAR 

## Groundwork

EXERCISE A

**Instructions**
Revise the following resume skills so that the list maintains parallel structure.

| SKILLS | REVISED SKILLS |
|---|---|
| • Exceptional flexibility | ______________________ |
| • I'm very organized | ______________________ |
| • Responsible | ______________________ |
| • Cooperates with others | ______________________ |

# Groundwork

*In this section, students will review the concept of parallelism through the example of resume skills.*

EXERCISE A · SLIDE 139.1

**Let's say you have a friend who comes to you with a grand plan to buy a motorcycle. Now—ignoring that your friend's parents will immediately veto this, and disregarding the fact that your friend can barely drive a car, never mind a motorcycle—there's one big problem with your friend's plan. Motorcycles cost money. Your friend desperately wants a summer job to save up money, but their resume keeps getting rejected. They've asked you to look it over—specifically, they want you to look at their skills section. Can someone read this section aloud for us?**

*Exceptional flexibility, I'm very organized, Responsible, Cooperates with others.*

**How does the list of skills sound?**

Kind of strange.

**Why's that?**

It's disorganized, doesn't match, doesn't flow.

**Reading this list feels a little like stumbling over your feet because every bullet point has a different structure. For example, *flexibility*—what part of speech is that?**

A noun.

**The next bullet, *I'm very organized*, is more than just a word; it's a full sentence. Then there's *responsible*—what part of speech is that?**

An adjective.

**They're all over the place. To make this list easy-to-read, we need to change them all into the same type of word. What type of word should your friend use to describe themselves on their resume?**

Adjectives.

**We want all of our skills listed as adjectives—describing words. Take a second to write down adjective versions of each bullet point. *Responsible* is already done for you.**

SLIDE 139.2

*Allow students 90 seconds to complete the exercise.*

**What did you write down for the first one?**

*Exceptionally flexible.*

***Flexible* is the adjective form of *flexibility*, so that one works. How about *I'm very organized?***

Organized.

***Organized* is an adjective, so that one's set. What about *responsible*? Do we need to do anything with that one?**

No, it's already an adjective.

**We can write that down as-is and skip to *cooperates with others*. What did you get for that?**

Cooperative.

***Flexible, organized, responsible,* and *cooperative*. How does the list sound now?**

Much better.

**The original list sounded bad because the items were not parallel—meaning they didn't match each other in the way they were structured. Verbs, nouns, and adjectives all mixed together—that's not what we want. To fix errors in parallelism, we need to make sure every item on the list matches the others in the way it's structured.**

EXERCISE B

**Instructions**
In the space provided, identify the type of word each portion of the sentence begins with.

It's important to keep your interview answers

1. ________________________ concise but not so short that you don't get the point across,

2. ________________________ relevant to the question that was asked, *and*

3. ________________________ they should be relatable to the interviewer.

Joe was worried about

4. ________________________ dressing the right way for his interview *and*

5. ________________________ to ask the right questions.

## Groundwork

*In this section, students will practice identifying and correcting parallelism errors in sentences that contain lists.*

EXERCISE B SLIDE 140.1

**The TSIA2 won't ask you to correct your friend's resume, for better or worse. It will, however, challenge you to find parallelism errors within a sentence—but the approach is the same. Take, for instance, the sentences in this exercise. Each sentence has been broken down into a tidy list for you to make checking for parallelism a little easier. Starting with number 1, what kind of word is *concise?***

A descriptive word.

**It's a descriptive word, also known as an adjective, like we saw in the resume. How about *relevant*?**

Another adjective.

**Another adjective. So far, the parallelism hasn't broken. What about *they* in number 3?**

A noun, or pronoun.

**Number 3 definitely breaks our parallel structure. So, how could we fix this?**

Change the phrase so it starts with an adjective.

**Let's check that phrase. Do you see an adjective in there?**

*Relatable.*

**How can we make that the start of number 3?**

Cross off the extra words.

SLIDE 140.2

**When we remove those words, the list sounds much smoother: *keep your interview answers concise, relevant, and relatable.* Let's try the next sentence. What type of word is *dressing* in number 4?**

A verb.

**Dressing is a special kind of word called a verbal, which means it looks like a verb but it doesn't act like a verb. How about *to ask*? What part of speech is that?**

Another kind of verb.

***To ask* is another example of a verbal, but something's off. Does it look the same as *dressing*?**

No.

***Dressing* and *to ask* are both verbals, but not the same *kind* of verbal. They just plain don't match. How could we change *to ask* so that it matches *dressing*?**

*Asking.*

***Joe was worried about dressing and asking.* Sounds much better. Why didn't we change the first word? *To dress and to ask?***

It would sound bad in the sentence.

***Joe was worried about to dress and to ask.* That doesn't sound right. When it comes to parallelism, it's not just a matter of making sure the individual pieces match each other; we need them to fit well within the existing sentence, too.**

TSIA2 Mastery: ELAR 

EXERCISE C

**Instructions**
Underline the two phrases in each sentence that should be parallel. If a parallelism error occurs, rewrite the corrected sentence in the space provided.

**6.** Choosing a career that you love means a person never having to work a day in your life. ________

________________________________________

________________________________________

**7.** An enthusiastic candidate makes a better impression and finishes the interview with a better chance of getting the job. ________________________________________

________________________________________

**8.** An enthusiastic candidate makes a better impression, and more likely to get hired if they make a positive comment about the company.________________________________________

________________________________________

________________________________________

## Groundwork

*In this section, students will resolve parallelism errors that occur in sentences that do not contain lists.*

EXERCISE C SLIDE 141.1

**Let's kick up the challenge level. These sentences aren't split up for you, so you'll have to find the pieces of the sentence that should have parallel structure. Take a moment to hunt through them and underline the phrases that should be parallel.**

*Give students 90 seconds to complete this task.*

**For number 6, what two phrases should be parallel?**

*Choosing a career* and *never having to work*.

**These two phrases are based on *-ing* verbals: *choosing* and *having*. Sounds like they're parallel, right? So is this sentence fine?**

No.

**Something about it sounds weird. What part sounds off to you?**

*A person never having to work.*

**The parallel phrases should be *choosing* and *never having*. But this extra phrase—*a person*—is stuck in there. Who is the sentence discussing in the first part? Who's choosing a career that they love?**

*You.*

**The sentence is about *you*, not a random person. We don't need to introduce a new subject. How can we fix this sentence?**

Remove *a person*.

SLIDE 141.2

**On to number 7. What two phrases should be parallel?**

*Makes a better impression* and *finishes the interview*.

**Both phrases start with matching verbs—*makes* and *finishes*. Is there anything wrong with this list?**

No.

**How do you know?**

The verbs match and there aren't any unneeded subjects inserted between them.

**This sentence is actually fine as is. Remember that sentences on the test can be correct: that's the case here. We're going to compare this one with the next sentence.**

SLIDE 141.3

**Does number 8 have parallel structure?**

No.

**What part of the sentence feels like it's missing something?**

*And more likely.*

**Number 8 is a compound sentence: two independent clauses separated by a comma and conjunction. There should be parallelism at the start of each independent clause. What is the second clause missing?**

A subject.

**What could we add into the sentence to fix it?**

*And the candidate is* or *and they are*.

**Once we add a subject, the two clauses become parallel. Keep an eye out for compound sentences since they do need the subject repeated.**

# Application

## THE APPROACH

When you are asked to correct a parallelism error, use the following steps ...

1. Identify the elements of the sentence that need to be parallel.
2. Eliminate answers that do not create parallel structure.

**9.** Rachel's mother asked her to gather all the leaves in the yard and stuffing them into bags so her father could load them into his truck.

Ⓐ (as it is now)
Ⓑ had stuffed them into bags
Ⓒ could stuff them into bags
Ⓓ to stuff them into bags

# Application

*In this section, students will discuss the process for answering parallelism questions.*

SLIDE 142.1

**Let's apply this to something you'll likely see on the test. Looking at question 9, what do we need to find first?**

The parallel elements.

**Funnily enough, the test questions are actually easier than the ones we've been doing—because one of the parallel elements is usually already underlined for you. What's our underlined element here?**

*Stuffing them into bags.*

**Who's doing this action?**

Rachel.

**What other action is Rachel doing that *stuffing* should be parallel to?**

*To gather all the leaves.*

**Are they parallel?**

No.

**How could we change *stuffing them* to be parallel to *to gather*?**

*To stuff.*

**Is that an available answer choice?**

Yes, choice D.

**Choice D looks good, but let's check the others to be sure. We can eliminate A because we know the underlined section isn't parallel. What about B?**

It's not parallel to the other phrase, and it doesn't fit the sentence.

**Not only is choice B not parallel, but *had stuffed* sounds really strange in the sentence. What about choice C?**

Same thing: it's not parallel and doesn't fit the sentence.

**Why might choice C be a tempting answer, though?**

Because *could stuff them* matches what Rachel's father is doing—*could load them.*

**Choice C looks parallel, so you could easily be drawn to it if you weren't being careful. The TSIA2 is smart, and it knows that you're looking to match the underlined part to something in the sentence. This is why it's so important to identify all the parts of the list before you start trying to make stuff parallel. Have we eliminated every answer other than D?**

Yes.

**That means we can be confident that choice D is the best way to fix the parallelism issue in this sentence.**

**TSIA2 Mastery:** ELAR 

## THE APPROACH

When you are asked to correct a parallelism error, use the following steps ...

1. Identify the elements of the sentence that need to be parallel.
2. Eliminate answers that do not create parallel structure.

**10.** Swimming is an incredible form of exercise that builds muscle and <u>you can minimize joint pain</u>.

Ⓐ (as it is now)
Ⓑ minimizes joint pain
Ⓒ it can minimize joint pain
Ⓓ minimizing joint pain

## Application

*In this section, students will practice applying the steps of the process to a parallelism question.*

SLIDE 143.1

**Let's see if you can guide me through the process this time using question 10. What's our first step?**

Finding the parallel elements.

**What's the underlined element that the test gives us?**

*You can minimize joint pain.*

**What is this describing? What activity minimizes joint pain?**

*Swimming.*

**What else does the sentence claim about swimming?**

It *builds muscle*.

***Builds muscle*** **and** ***you can minimize joint pain*** **are two phrases that describe swimming. They should be parallel. But, are they?**

No.

**What should we do then?**

Eliminate choice A.

**We know choice A is wrong. Are there any other options that look really similar to that choice? It could be a good candidate for another wrong choice.**

Choice C looks like choice A.

**Before you strike it just for looking similar, though, double-check the parallelism. Is it parallel?**

No.

**What's wrong with it?**

It adds an extra subject, just like choice A.

**Choices A and C are similar: both of them add a subject. Do you see any other choices that break the parallelism?**

Choice D uses *minimizing,* which isn't parallel.

**Why isn't it parallel?**

The verb we need to match is *builds,* so we need another verb that matches it.

***Builds muscle*** **and** ***minimizing joint pain*** **don't match in structure, so choice D is also out. What are we left with?**

Choice B.

**Does choice B maintain parallel structure?**

Yes.

**How can you tell?**

*Minimizes* matches *builds*.

**Let's check it just to be sure. A good rule of thumb is that if something** ***sounds*** **wrong, it** ***is*** **wrong. Can someone read the corrected sentence out loud?**

*Swimming is an incredible form of exercise that builds muscle and minimizes joint pain.*

**How does that sound?**

Smooth, normal.

**If you're stuck on a writing question, you can always try reading the sentence aloud—well, reading it under your breath or in your head during the actual test. You may be able to identify errors faster by ear than you can on paper. Use this strategy to eliminate clearly wrong-sounding answers and narrow the choices down to your best guess.**

## Practice

**Instructions**
Complete the practice set. If time remains after you've finished, double-check your work.

1. Doing large puzzles and <u>when she added to her pottery collection are Anastasia's favorite activities</u> to do inside during the winter.

   Ⓐ (as it is now)
   Ⓑ to add to her pottery collection is Anastasia's favorite activity
   Ⓒ adding to her pottery collection is Anastasia's favorite activity
   Ⓓ adding to her pottery collection are Anastasia's favorite activities

2. The astronauts not only had to adjust to working in a weightless environment but also <u>had to sleep</u> while strapped to a wall of the spaceship.

   Ⓐ (as it is now)
   Ⓑ were sleeping
   Ⓒ slept
   Ⓓ had slept

3. Sweeping the floor and <u>when he folded the laundry are Marco's weekly chores</u> to do at home during the school year.

   Ⓐ (as it is now)
   Ⓑ to fold the laundry is Marco's weekly chore
   Ⓒ folding the laundry is Marco's weekly chore
   Ⓓ folding the laundry are Marco's weekly chores

# Practice

SLIDE 144.1

*Give students 8 minutes to complete the practice set.*

SLIDE 144.2

1. **The correct answer is D.** Choices A and B are incorrect because the phrasing of the second activity in those choices is not parallel to the first activity: *when she added to her pottery collection* and *to add to her pottery collection* do not match the construction of *doing large puzzles.* Choice C is incorrect because the singular verb *is* does not match the plural subject, *doing large puzzles and adding to her pottery collection*. Choice D is correct because *adding to her pottery collection* grammatically matches the construction of *doing large puzzles* and uses the plural verb *are,* which agrees with the plural subject of the sentence.

SLIDE 144.3

2. **The correct answer is A.** Choices B, C, and D are incorrect because the verb phrases that follow *not only* and *but also* are not parallel: *were sleeping*, *slept*, and *had slept* do not match *had to adjust*. Choice A is correct because it creates parallel construction with the verb phrases in tense and form: *not only had to adjust ... but also had to sleep*.

SLIDE 144.4

3. **The correct answer is D.** Choices A and B are incorrect because the verb forms *he folded* and *to fold* do not match *sweeping*, so the sentence lacks parallel structure. Choice C is incorrect because the plural subject *sweeping ... and folding* does not agree with the singular verb *is*. Choice D is correct because the plural subject *sweeping ... and folding* is parallel and agrees with the plural verb *are*.

## Wrap-Up

**Instructions**
Complete the wrap-up question. If time remains after you've finished, double-check your work.

**2.** The contestants not only had to blindfold themselves to compete in the race but also had to run while knee-deep in a puddle of mud.

Ⓐ (as it is now)
Ⓑ were running
Ⓒ ran
Ⓓ had ran

# Wrap-Up

SLIDE 145.1

*Give students 2 minutes to complete the wrap-up question.*

SLIDE 145.2

2. **The correct answer is A.** The sentence contains the conjunctions *not only ... but also*, so it requires a parallel structure to follow each in order to be grammatically correct. Choices B, C, and D are incorrect because none of them parallel the structure of the verb phrase *had to blindfold*. Choice A is correct because *had to run* follows the structure of the previous verb phrase *had to blindfold*.

This page is intentionally left blank.
Content resumes on the next page.

This page is intentionally left blank.
Teacher content resumes with the next chapter.

CHAPTER 17

# Misplaced Modifiers

In this chapter, students will correctly identify and place phrases that modify subjects and objects.

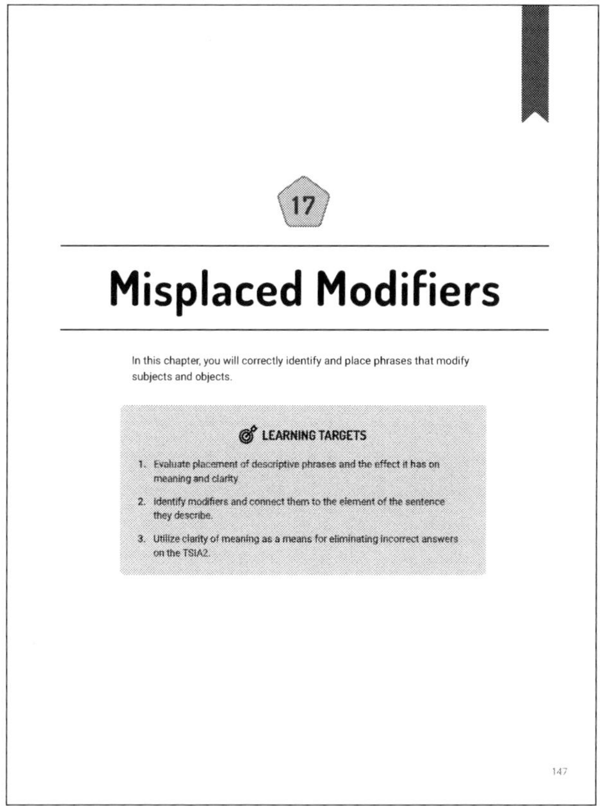

17

Misplaced Modifiers

In this chapter, you will correctly identify and place phrases that modify subjects and objects.

LEARNING TARGETS

1. Evaluate placement of descriptive phrases and the effect it has on meaning and clarity
2. Identify modifiers and connect them to the element of the sentence they describe.
3. Utilize clarity of meaning as a means for eliminating incorrect answers on the TSIA2.

147

## TSIA2 STANDARDS

**Sentence Revision, Editing, and Completion**
Conventions of grammar

The student will edit and complete sentences as necessary to ensure conformity to the conventions of standard English grammar.

## TEKS ALIGNMENT

E1.9 *Composition*: listening, speaking, reading, writing, and thinking—writing process using multiple texts. Student uses the writing process recursively to compose multiple texts that are legible and uses appropriate conventions. The student is expected to:

(D) edit drafts using standard English conventions, including:

(i) a variety of complete, controlled sentences and avoidance of unintentional splices, run-ons, and fragments;

(v) punctuation, including commas, semicolons, colons, and dashes to set off phrases and clauses as appropriate.

## LEARNING TARGETS

1. Evaluate placement of descriptive phrases and the effect it has on meaning and clarity.
2. Identify modifiers and connect them to the element of the sentence they describe.
3. Utilize clarity of meaning as a means for eliminating incorrect answers on the TSIA2.

## Warm-Up

**Instructions**
Complete the warm-up question. If time remains after you've finished, double-check your work.

1. Recognized internationally for her innovative piano compositions, <u>the composer's only musical instruction was her mother</u>, a piano tuner and shop owner.

   Ⓐ the composer's only musical instruction was her mother
   Ⓑ the only instruction the composer received was her mother's
   Ⓒ the composer only received musical instruction that was her mother's
   Ⓓ the composer received her only musical instruction from her mother

# Warm-Up

SLIDE 148.1

*Give students 2 minutes to complete the warm-up question.*

SLIDE 148.2

1. **The correct answer is D.** Choice A is incorrect because *recognized internationally for her innovative piano compositions* is placed so that it modifies *instruction*, when it needs to modify *composer*. Choices B and C are incorrect because the placement of *a piano tuner and shop owner* appears to modify *her mother's* [*instruction*], when it needs to modify *mother*. Choice D is correct because *recognized internationally for her innovative piano compositions* accurately modifies the noun *composer* and *a piano tuner and shop owner* accurately modifies the noun *mother*.

TSIA2 Mastery: ELAR 

## Groundwork

EXERCISE A

**Instructions**
Review the sentence with different placements of the modifier "just" to analyze its effect on the meaning.

1. **(1)** The teacher **(2)** looked at Zach **(3)** as he came in late to class again.

## Groundwork

*In this section, students will review the effects of modifier placement on the meaning of a sentence.*

**In an attempt to make our world a little safer, humans have come up with the concept of a caution sign. Most of the time, they're yellow and diamond-shaped, or they're those little folding stand-ups made of plastic. When you see a caution sign somewhere, what does it tell you?**

To be careful or to watch out for something.

**What if you see a caution sign in the middle of an aisle in a grocery store? What do you think that means?**

That there's probably something broken or spilled there. The floor could be wet.

**What if you see a caution sign on a bridge?**

Maybe the bridge is broken or has a dangerous spot where someone could get hurt.

**It's the same sign, though. How did you get a different meaning in each situation?**

What's happening around the sign affects how we understand what it's saying.

EXERCISE A SLIDE 149.1

**Placement matters. And where you see something affects how you interpret its meaning. We see this in grammar, as well, in the form of modifiers. A modifier is a word or a phrase that adds a little extra description or detail. And depending on where it shows up in a sentence, it can change the meaning completely. Take sentence 1. What modifier are we going to use?**

*Just.*

**Let's put *just* into the first placement. What does the sentence become?**

***Just** the teacher looked at Zach as he came in late to class again.*

**What does that placement of *just* tell us?**

That no one else but the teacher looked at Zach.

**What if we move *just* to placement 2? What will the sentence look like?**

*The teacher **just** looked at Zach as he came in late to class again.*

**What's happening there?**

The teacher didn't do anything else. They just looked at Zach.

**It's almost like it implies a level of disappointment from the teacher. They aren't scolding Zach, deducting points, or doing anything but looking. This is a very different visual than what we got with placement 1. What about placement 3? Who can read the sentence to us with *just* after *Zach*?**

*The teacher looked at Zach **just** as he came in late to class again.*

**What kind of impression are we getting of the situation now?**

It's like Zach was caught coming in late.

**Placement 3 implies that the teacher looked over right at the exact moment Zach was coming into the class. Rather than disappointment, we get this "caught in the act" kind of moment. And all because we moved one little word. When it comes to modifiers, placement matters. A lot.**

EXERCISE B

### Instructions

Determine the best place to add the modifier to the sentence below. Circle your answer.

*Modifier:* that was burnt to an absolute crisp

2. The culinary student **(1)** dumped his poor attempt at a homemade pizza **(2)** into the trash can **(3)**.

## Groundwork

*In this section, students will practice placing a modifying phrase next to the noun it describes.*

EXERCISE B | SLIDE 150.1

**The question becomes "Which spot is the *right* place to put the modifier?" This can be pretty subjective. It's almost like you're trying to read the author's mind to figure out what they meant. The good news is that you can usually figure out where a modifier should go without any psychic abilities. For instance, look at sentence 2. What's the modifier?**

*That was burnt to an absolute crisp.*

**If we put that modifier into the sentence at placement 1, what will the sentence look like?**

*The culinary student* ***that was burnt to an absolute crisp*** *dumped his poor attempt at a homemade pizza into the trash can.*

**When you read the sentence like that, what seems like it was burnt?**

*The culinary student.*

**While it's possible that the culinary student got a bit toasty making his pizza, ask yourself: do you think that's what the author intended?**

No, since it doesn't make sense that a culinary student caught on fire and then took time to throw away a pizza.

**That's the trick to modifier placement. You don't need to know what the author meant to recognize a modifier that breaks the sentence. Let's test the modifier in placement 2. What will the sentence become?**

*The culinary student dumped his poor attempt at a homemade pizza* ***that was burnt to an absolute crisp*** *into the trash can.*

**When we put the modifier there, what does it seem to be describing?**

*The pizza.*

**Does that make sense?**

Yes, since burning it would be a good reason to throw it away.

**Seems like that could be a good place for our modifier, but let's test placement 3 just in case. What will the sentence look like?**

*The culinary student dumped his poor attempt at a homemade pizza into the trash can* ***that was burnt to an absolute crisp****.*

**What seems like it was burnt with this placement?**

*The trash can.*

**Does that seem likely?**

Not really.

**Placement 3 seems a little odd, so placement 2 is our best option. Take a step back and look at the connection between where the modifier is placed and what it appears to describe. Do you see a pattern?**

The modifier describes whatever it's closest to.

**And that's our key takeaway. If a modifier makes the sentence sound nonsensical, it's likely too close to the wrong thing. Instead, it should always be right next to the thing it describes. If it strays too far from what it's trying to describe, things can get pretty confusing for the reader.**

TSIA2 Mastery: ELAR 

EXERCISE C

**Instructions**
Underline the misplaced modifier in each sentence and circle the noun it should describe.

3. He gave cupcakes to his students on napkins.

4. She offered some garlic bread to the man that was dripping with butter.

5. I watched a dog hanging out of his owner's window while driving on the freeway.

## Groundwork

*In this section, students will practice identifying misplaced modifiers and select the nouns they describe.*

**EXERCISE C** SLIDE 151.1

**Take a look at sentence 3. Do you see a modifying phrase there?**

*On napkins.*

**Based on where *on napkins* is placed, what appears to be on those napkins?**

*His students.*

**Does that seem right?**

No.

**What do you think was actually on those napkins?**

The *cupcakes.*

**We need to do a little shuffling to get that modifier in the right place. If we put *on napkins* next to its noun, what will the corrected sentence look like?**

*He gave cupcakes on napkins to his students.*

**What about sentence 4? What went wrong there?**

It seems like *the man* was the thing *dripping with butter.*

**Unless there's a new fashion trend going around, that's really unlikely. What's actually *dripping with butter*?**

The *garlic bread.*

**Fix the sentence by moving that modifier to its noun. What will the corrected sentence become?**

*She offered some garlic bread that was dripping with butter to the man.*

**Sentence 5 has a misplaced modifier, too. What's the modifier?**

*While driving on the freeway.*

**With the modifier sitting there at the end of the sentence, what's happening?**

The dog is the one *driving on the freeway.*

**That's definitely not right. Who is actually driving?**

The narrator, or *I.*

**How should we relocate that phrase to fix the sentence?**

*While driving on the freeway, I watched a dog hanging out of his owner's window.*

**By putting the modifier next to whatever it's describing, we create a sentence that's a whole lot clearer.**

## Application

### THE APPROACH

When a sentence contains modifiers and the answer choices offer a variety of connecting nouns, use these steps ...

1. Locate the modifying phrase(s).
2. Determine what is being modified.
3. Eliminate answer choices that separate the noun from its modifier.
4. Eliminate answer choices that are unclear.

**6.** After losing many belongings during a cross-country move, Alexia treasured her last remaining family heirloom, a vintage tea set from China.

Ⓐ Alexia treasured her last remaining family heirloom
Ⓑ a treasure of Alexia's was the last remaining family heirloom
Ⓒ Alexia's treasured family heirloom was the last one remain
Ⓓ Alexia treasured her family heirloom that was the last one remaining

# Application

*In this section, students will practice applying the steps of the Approach to a misplaced modifier question.*

**The TSIA2 offers up misplaced modifiers in a unique way. It's almost like a jigsaw puzzle. Instead of putting the modifier where you'd expect it—in the underlined section—the modifier usually shows up somewhere else in the sentence. What do you think will be in the underlined portion?**

The stuff the modifier describes.

SLIDE 152.1

**Generally, the underlined section includes the noun or thing being described, and all the answer choices give you options. Your task will be to sift through and find what matches best with the modifying phrase that either comes before or after. Take a look through the answer choices for question 6. What do you notice about the nouns you can choose from?**

They aren't always the same nouns.

**The differences between the answer choices are subtle. For instance, what's the first noun in answer choice A?**

*Alexia*.

**And what's the first noun in answer choice B?**

*A treasure of Alexia's*.

**A person and something owned by that person are two very different nouns. How do we know which is the right one to use in the sentence?**

We can use the closest modifier to see which one makes the most sense.

**What modifying phrase touches that part of the underlined section?**

*After losing many belongings during a cross-country move.*

**Who or what do you think that modifier is meant to describe?**

*Alexia*.

**How do you know?**

Because she is the one who lost belongings during the move, not an object.

**Based on that, can we eliminate any answer choices?**

Choices B and C, since the first nouns in those options are objects.

**Compare the two remaining choices. What's the difference?**

Choice A ends with *family heirloom*, and choice D ends with *the last one remaining*.

**What should we use to help us decide which answer choice is better?**

The modifier at the end of the sentence, *a vintage tea set from China*.

**What is that modifier giving us details about?**

The *family heirloom*.

**So, which choice best connects the noun *family heirloom* to its modifier?**

Choice A.

**It's a little like trying to line up dominos to knock them over. If one domino is out of place, the connection doesn't happen, dominos are left standing, and you end up with a sentence that doesn't work the way it should.**

## THE APPROACH

When a sentence contains modifiers and the answer choices offer a variety of connecting nouns, use these steps ...

1. Locate the modifying phrase(s).
2. Determine what is being modified.
3. Eliminate answer choices that separate the noun from its modifier.
4. Eliminate answer choices that are unclear.

**7.** A work of historical fiction, the story's heavy research was done by its author, who believed accuracy was the key to writing a good book.

Ⓐ the story's heavy research was done by its author
Ⓑ the story had heavy research that was its author's
Ⓒ the story's heavy research was an author
Ⓓ the story was heavily researched by its author

## Application

*In this section, students will evaluate the clarity of meaning in a sentence to improve their eliminations.*

SLIDE 153.1

**What modifying phrases are we working with in question 7?**

*A work of historical fiction* and *who believed accuracy was the key to writing a good book*.

**Which noun do you think *a work of historical fiction* is meant to describe?**

The *story*.

**And what do you think the second modifier describes?**

The *author*.

**Just based on that, can we eliminate any answer choices? Which ones don't line up the modifiers with their nouns?**

Choices A and C, since they don't use *story*, which fits the opening modifying phrase.

**Compare what's left. What's the difference between choice B and choice D?**

Choice B is written in a weird way.

**Choices B and D both connect the modifiers to the nouns they describe, but choice B is wonky. Who'd like to read the whole sentence using choice B for us?**

*A work of historical fiction, <u>the story had heavy research that was its author's</u>, who believed accuracy was the key to writing a good book.*

**Does that sound okay?**

No, it's confusing.

**Sometimes, the TSIA2 will throw in an answer choice that does a good job matching up modifiers with nouns, but when you read it, it's hard to understand. Look back to the instructions for any given writing question. What answer do they tell us to pick?**

They tell us to pick the *best* answer.

**In this case, which option do you think is best?**

Choice D.

**Why choice D?**

Choice B is just a little strange, but choice D sounds natural.

**With every modifier question on the TSIA2, there's always the possibility that you won't be able to eliminate all the answers just based on noun placement, but you should be able to eliminate about half of your options. Take the remaining choices for a test run and see if any of them seem unclear. Pick the option that's the *most* clear.**

## Practice

**Instructions**
Complete the practice set. If time remains after you've finished, double-check your work.

1. Cheered by large crowds of enthusiastic fans, the band owed its popularity to its lead singer, a famous actor known for his role in a recent hit movie.

   Ⓐ the band owed its popularity to its lead singer
   Ⓑ the popularity of the band was its lead singer's
   Ⓒ the band's popularity was its lead singer
   Ⓓ the band owed its popularity that was its lead singer's

2. Nervous before the final round of debate competition, Meena's helpful advice was her speech teacher, an expert in calm breathing techniques.

   Ⓐ Meena's helpful advice was her speech teacher
   Ⓑ the helpful advice Meena got was her speech teacher's
   Ⓒ Meena got helpful advice that was her speech teacher's
   Ⓓ Meena got helpful advice from her speech teacher

3. Buried for thousands of years, the ancient coin's discovery was by a farmer, a local resident who noticed the metal object while working in his field.

   Ⓐ the ancient coin's discovery was by a farmer
   Ⓑ the ancient coin was discovered by a farmer
   Ⓒ the discovery of the ancient coin was a farmer
   Ⓓ the ancient coin had a discovery that was a farmer's

# Practice

SLIDE 154.1

*Give students 8 minutes to complete the practice set.*

SLIDE 154.2

1. **The correct answer is A.** Choices B and C are incorrect because they have misplaced modifiers: these sentences imply that the *popularity*, not *the band*, is *cheered by large crowds of enthusiastic fans*. Choice D is incorrect because the verb *owed* doesn't make sense here without a preposition and an object—this sentence doesn't explain who or what the band's popularity is owed to. Choice A is correct because *cheered by large crowds of enthusiastic fans* correctly modifies *the band* and *a famous actor known for his role in a recent hit movie* correctly modifies *lead singer*.

SLIDE 154.3

2. **The correct answer is D.** Choices A and B are incorrect because they have misplaced modifiers: these sentences imply that the *advice* is *nervous*, but *nervous before the final round of debate competition* should describe *Meena* instead. Choice C is incorrect because it makes *an expert in calm breathing techniques* modify *her speech teacher's* [*advice*], but it needs to modify *her speech teacher*. Choice D is correct because *nervous before the final round of debate competition* correctly modifies the subject *Meena*, and *an expert in calm breathing techniques* clearly modifies *her speech teacher*.

SLIDE 154.4

3. **The correct answer is B.** Choices A and C are incorrect because they have misplaced modifiers: these sentences imply that the *discovery* of *the ancient coin* was *buried for thousands of years*, but actually, *the ancient coin* itself was buried. Choice D is incorrect because it incorrectly uses the modifier *a local resident who noticed the metal object while working in his field* modify the noun *a farmer's* [*discovery*]. Choice B is correct because *buried for thousands of years* correctly modifies *the ancient coin*, and *a local resident who noticed the metal object while working in his field* correctly modifies *a farmer*.

**Instructions**

Complete the wrap-up question. If time remains after you've finished, double-check your work.

2. Praised by the judges for her graceful floor routines, the gymnast's only instruction was her grandmother, a ballroom dancer and choreographer.

   Ⓐ the gymnast's only instruction was her grandmother

   Ⓑ the only instruction the gymnast received was her grandmother's

   Ⓒ the gymnast only received instruction that was her grandmother's

   Ⓓ the gymnast received her only instruction from her grandmother

# Wrap-Up

SLIDE 155.1

*Give students 2 minutes to complete the wrap-up question.*

SLIDE 155.2

2. **The correct answer is D.** Choices A and B are incorrect because they have misplaced modifiers: these sentences imply that *the gymnast's only instruction* is what is *praised by the judges*, which is incorrect—*the gymnast* is *praised by the judges for her graceful floor routines*. Choice C is incorrect because it incorrectly uses the modifier *a ballroom dancer and choreographer* to modify the noun *grandmother's* [*instruction*]. Choice D is correct because *praised by the judges for her graceful floor routines* describes *the gymnast*, and *a ballroom dancer and choreographer* modifies *her grandmother*.

This page is intentionally left blank.
Content resumes on the next page.

This page is intentionally left blank.
Teacher content resumes with the next chapter.

CHAPTER 18

# Development

In this chapter, students will practice identifying and eliminating sentences in passages which are off-topic or distract from the meaning of the passage.

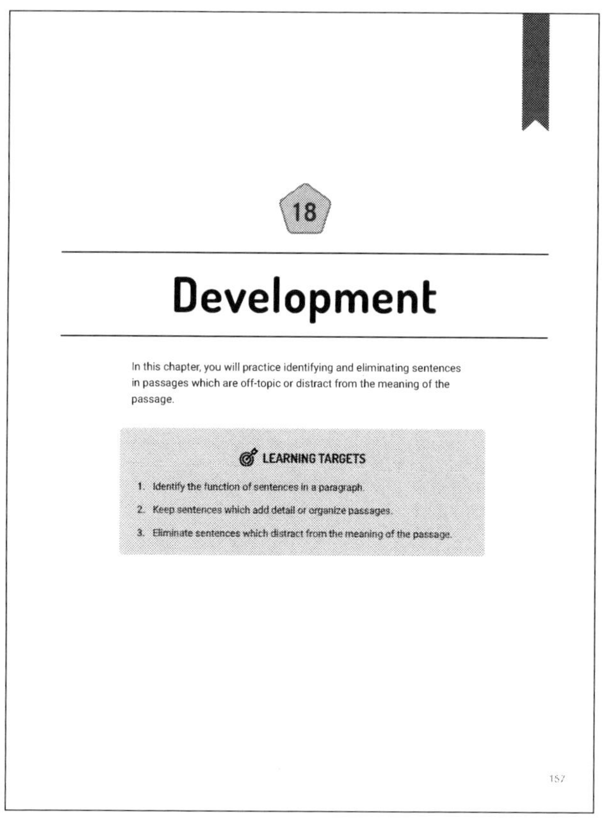

18
Development
In this chapter, you will practice identifying and eliminating sentences in passages which are off-topic or distract from the meaning of the passage.
LEARNING TARGETS
1. Identify the function of sentences in a paragraph.
2. Keep sentences which add detail or organize passages.
3. Eliminate sentences which distract from the meaning of the passage.
157

## TSIA2 STANDARDS

**Essay Revision and Editing**
Development

The student will revise as necessary to improve the development of text.

## TEKS ALIGNMENT

E1.9 *Composition:* listening, speaking, reading, writing, and thinking using multiple texts—writing process. The student uses the writing process recursively to compose multiple texts that are legible and uses appropriate conventions. The student is expected to:

(C) revise drafts to improve clarity, development, organization, style, diction, and sentence effectiveness, including the use of parallel constructions and placement of phrases and dependent clauses.

## LEARNING TARGETS

1. Identify the function of sentences in a paragraph.
2. Keep sentences which add detail or organize passages.
3. Eliminate sentences which distract from the meaning of the passage.

TSIA2 Mastery: ELAR

## Warm-Up

### Instructions

Complete the warm-up question. If time remains after you've finished, double-check your work.

### Passage

**(1)** When schools of fish gather again after time apart, they will swim around each other while waving their fins and performing elaborate dances. **(2)** Stingrays have been seen, frolicking over fields of coral, twirling and flapping their wings, even when ample open ocean is readily available. **(3)** Some have argued that these kinds of behaviors show that fish can feel emotions like joy and delight.

**(4)** Even advocates for the argument that fish have feelings acknowledge that scientists can easily misidentify what they are seeing. **(5)** The shape of a fish's mouth makes it look like it is surprised; it looks that way even when it is excited or in danger. **(6)** Fish are social, communicating underwater using clicks and bubbles. **(7)** Feelings are challenging to understand even in humans, who have the ability to talk about their emotions.

**(8)** Many oceanographers who devote their time to studying fish behavior have argued that at least some fish, such as triggerfishes and eels, have strong feelings like the ones we experience as humans. **(9)** Other researchers are doubtful. **(10)** They argue that it has not yet been proven that fish feel emotion in any reliable, reproducible scientific experiments.

**(11)** Regardless, scientific consensus on the question of fish emotion is beginning to shift. **(12)** Many biologists have accepted that fish most likely have "primary" emotions such as fear or anger. **(13)** These responses seem to be found in most fish. **(14)** For instance, a zebrafish will avoid a part of the tank where it was once shocked even if the shock has been removed. **(15)** Additionally, scientists believe that feelings can be inferred from fishes' changes in activity and eye movement, or even from involuntary responses like scale shedding.

1. Which of the following sentences contains information irrelevant to the passage as a whole and would best be deleted from the passage?

   (A) Sentence 3
   (B) Sentence 6
   (C) Sentence 9
   (D) Sentence 13

# Warm-Up

SLIDE 158.1

*Give students 2 minutes to complete the warm-up question.*

SLIDE 158.2

1. **The correct answer is B**. Choice A is incorrect because *some have argued that these kinds of behaviors show that fish can feel emotions like joy and delight* describes one side of the debate about whether fish have emotions, which is the focus of the passage. Choice C is incorrect because *other researchers are doubtful* describes how some researchers feel about the evidence presented, which directly relates to the debate. Choice D is incorrect because *these responses seem to be found in most fish* describes the strength of the evidence on one side of the debate. Choice B is correct because *fish are social, communicating underwater using clicks and bubbles* is a general fact about fish that does not directly relate to the debate about whether fish have emotions.

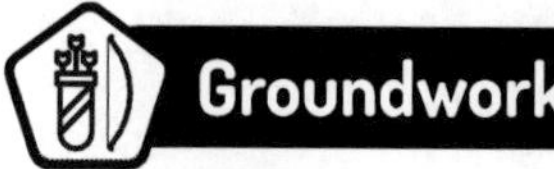

## Groundwork

EXERCISE A

### Instructions

Determine which sentence does not belong in the following passage. Circle your answer.

### Passage

**(1)** The most expensive pizza in the world can be found in a town called Salerno, Italy. **(2)** A restaurant called Luis XIII offers its customers the opportunity to indulge in a pizza made from a handcrafted, aged pizza dough, which is carefully rolled out and coated in sauce. **(3)** Toppings range from three different types of expensive caviar to rare grains of pink sea salt from Australia and lobster imported from Norway. **(4)** What's more is that this pizza is *for delivery*. **(5)** That's right. **(6)** A chef will appear at your home, where they will construct and serve this show stopper of a pizza. **(7)** Strangely enough, famous actor Bill Murray worked as a pizza delivery person before his big break into show business. **(8)** In total, this pizza will cost someone just over $12,000 to enjoy.

1. Sergio is considering cutting a sentence from his essay, but he can't decide. Should he remove sentence 3 or sentence 7?

   **Sentence 3** **Sentence 7**

# Groundwork

***In this section, students will identify a sentence that does not fit the context of a passage.***

**For some reason, pizza toppings are a hot topic in today's society. I mean, one person just *mentions* pineapples, and everyone goes nuts. What else *doesn't* belong on pizza?**

*Allow 2–3 students to share.*

**If we put something not-so-great on our pizza, it ruins the whole thing. Even if the sauce is amazing, the cheese is all gooey and melty, and the crust is just the way we like it, adding something strange like canned tuna on top can make it all taste bad. In the same way, if there's a sentence in a paragraph that just doesn't belong, it can throw the reader off, and they get lost in what we're really trying to say.**

EXERCISE A SLIDE 159.1

**For instance, check out the passage in your workbook. The writer is thinking about cutting one sentence, either sentence 3 or sentence 7. Why do you think someone would want to pull a sentence out of their writing altogether?**

It doesn't fit with the topic.

**What is sentence 3 about?**

Different expensive pizza toppings.

**What about sentence 7? What does that one talk about?**

How Bill Murray delivered pizzas before becoming an actor.

**Both seem like pretty interesting ideas. What should we use to help us decide which one has to go?**

The other sentences in the paragraph.

**Take a moment now to read this paragraph. What's the main idea of Sergio's essay?**

A $12,000 pizza you can get delivered from a restaurant in Italy.

**Which sentence do you think *best* fits with the main idea of the paragraph?**

Sentence 3.

**Sentence 3 offers up the specific toppings that appear on that expensive pizza, so it's a good idea to keep it. Take a closer look at sentence 7, though. Why shouldn't we keep that one?**

Because it talks about something random.

**That sentence goes way outside the box to talk about a random actor and his early job experiences. In fact, if a reader didn't realize that the sentence didn't belong, they might even think Bill Murray was one of the guys delivering those fancy pizzas. Why might someone think sentence 7 has keeper-potential?**

The paragraph talks about pizza delivery in sentence 4, and *show stopper* from sentence 6 seems like it might connect to *show business* in sentence 7.

**The TSIA2 won't always make it glaringly clear which sentence needs to be taken out of a passage, and they'll often include little details like what we saw in sentence 7 to make you at least *consider* keeping an out-of-place sentence. This is why we dig into the details to make sure we're making the right cut.**

EXERCISE B

### Instructions

Review the following reasons why a sentence might need to be deleted as your teacher leads the discussion. Then, match each reason to the underlined sentence from the passage that makes that mistake.

| Delete the sentence when | ... it blurs the focus of the passage. |
|---|---|
| | ... it contradicts the information in the passage. |

### Passage

**(1)** One of the reasons why pizza is such a popular meal is its customizability. **(2)** Countries, cultures, and even individuals take the essence of what a pizza is and add in their personal tastes to make it into exactly what they crave. **(3)** For instance, Americans can't stand anchovies and it's the least requested topping in the country. **(4)** The most popular pizza topping across the U.S. is pepperoni. **(5)** In Japan, they often top their pizza with mayonnaise, though it is a sweeter variant than what is commonly seen in America. **(6)** South Africa opened its first Pizza Hut in 2008 thinking that most individuals would eat in the restaurant, but delivery became a much more popular option. **(7)** Regardless of toppings, pizza remains one of the most universal foods in the world.

**2.** Sentence _______ blurs the focus of the paragraph.

**3.** Sentence _______ contradicts information in the paragraph.

## Groundwork

***In this section, students will identify sentences that blur focus or contradict the information in the passage.***

EXERCISE B SLIDE 160.1

**When you take the TSIA2, there are generally two reasons why you might decide to delete something from a passage. When should you cut a sentence?**

If it blurs the focus of the passage or if it contradicts the information in the passage.

**What do you think it means when we say that something *blurs the focus*?**

It goes off-topic, so the reader isn't sure what the main idea is.

**We saw that in the last example, where the sentence gave a random detail about an actor, even though the passage was about a specific pizza. What about a contradiction? What might that look like?**

It would argue against the main idea of the passage.

**Contradictions can be a bit more subtle because they won't always outright argue with the passage. Instead, they offer up details that are on-topic but not what the author wants to say. Let's see how these two kinds of sentences show up in the passage in your workbook.**

SLIDE 160.2

**Take a moment to read the passage. What's the main idea?**

Pizza toppings that people from different countries like.

**Do any of the sentences offer something that's *not* about topping preferences from different countries?**

Sentence 6.

**What does that sentence talk about?**

South Africa got a Pizza Hut in 2008.

**Why might someone think that sentence *could* fit in the passage?**

Because it mentions a different country and a pizza company.

**So, why do we want to cut it?**

It doesn't mention the toppings they prefer in South Africa.

**Sentence 6 blurs the focus, so it should be cut. Do you see a sentence that goes against the main idea of the passage?**

Sentence 3.

**What does that one say?**

That Americans don't like anchovies.

**How does that contradict the passage?**

The passage is about toppings countries *do* like, not the ones they *don't* like.

**Notice how it's still on-topic. It specifically mentions a country and a topping, but it doesn't quite align with the main idea of the passage. That one should get cut from the passage as well. During the TSIA2, we'll have a little more direction than just searching a passage for an out-of-place sentence. You'll only have to test four sentences from the answer choices to see which one needs to go.**

# Application

## THE APPROACH

When a question asks you which sentence from the passage should be deleted or removed, use these steps ...

1. Determine the main idea of the paragraph or passage.
2. Review each answer choice.
3. Eliminate the sentence that blurs focus or contradicts the passage.

**Passage**

**(1)** There is growing concern that public golf courses are a drain on resources and are environmentally unsustainable, especially as the sport has become less popular. **(2)** According to the National Golf Foundation, only 1.5 million people took up golf in 2011, down from 2.4 million in 2000. **(3)** Golf can provide a good, low intensity workout in which players burn up to 400 calories an hour. **(4)** At the same time, golf courses require massive amounts of water and fertilizer to maintain the grass. **(5)** Due to the decreasing number of golfers, some people feel that having public golf courses is no longer necessary and that the land could be put to better use.

**4.** Which sentence contains information irrelevant to the passage as a whole and should be deleted?

Ⓐ Sentence 1
Ⓑ Sentence 2
Ⓒ Sentence 3
Ⓓ Sentence 4

## Application

*In this section, students will apply the steps of the Approach to a development question.*

SLIDE 161.1

**Development questions stick out like a sore thumb. For instance, check out question 4. What makes these kinds of questions so easy to spot?**

They ask which sentence should be deleted.

**If you know you'll need to delete one sentence from the passage, where should you start?**

By finding the main idea of the passage.

**You can't pick the odd-one-out if you don't know what the sentences need to fit into. Take time to read the passage carefully and to figure out the main idea. You should write the main idea on your scratch paper or board, too. Why might that be helpful?**

We can quickly look back to it as we go through all the answers.

**There's no quick way to eliminate answers on these types of questions. You have to give them their due diligence and check each answer choice carefully. By having the main idea written down, it's one less thing you have to keep in your brain as you work. Let's do that now. Take a moment to read the passage.**

*Give students 1 minute to complete this task.*

**What did you write down for the main idea?**

That golf is unpopular and golf courses are a waste of resources.

**While some people love the sport, it's clear that this author doesn't really dig it. Where do we go from here?**

We check the answer choices.

**Once you have a solid grasp on the main idea of the passage, it's time to dig into our options. Let's start with choice A. What does sentence 1 talk about?**

How golf courses are a drain on resources and golf is unpopular.

**Does that fit with our main idea?**

Yes.

**That sentence gives us the main idea almost word-for-word, which makes sense based on where it's at in the paragraph. The main idea will almost always show up in the first sentence. What do we do with choice A?**

Eliminate it since we're looking for a sentence to *delete*.

**That can feel pretty awkward if you think about it, but keep your focus on the goal of the question. The worst sentence is the best answer. What about choice B? What does sentence 2 say?**

That fewer people are taking up golf each year.

**Sentence 2 lays down some cold, hard facts that prove golf is getting more and more unpopular. Does that fit with our main idea?**

Yes.

**Let's eliminate choice B and keep going. Choice C says we should cut sentence 3. What does that sentence talk about?**

How golf can be a good workout.

**Does that fit with the main idea of the paragraph?**

No.

**Why not?**

It contradicts the passage.

**The passage is all about how golf is an awful sport, so a detail talking about why golf could be a good thing works against the main idea. Sentence 3 seems like a good contender to cut, but let's check our last option just in case. Does sentence 4 align with our main idea?**

Yes, since it talks about how golf courses need lots of water and fertilizer.

**So, which sentence are we cutting?**

Choice C, sentence 3.

**It's a little like those one-of-these-is-not-like-the-other kind of puzzles. If three of our options fit the main idea of the passage, we want to keep them. And the one that doesn't gets the boot.**

## THE APPROACH

When a question asks you which sentence from the passage should be deleted or removed, use these steps ...

1. Determine the main idea of the paragraph or passage.
2. Review each answer choice.
3. Eliminate the sentence that blurs focus or contradicts the passage.

**Passage**

**(1)** Today, the 19th-century American author Kate Chopin is well known for her controversial novel *The Awakening* and her colorful short stories about life in New Orleans. **(2)** Her contemporary, George Washington Cable, is also known for his stories set in New Orleans. **(3)** After falling into obscurity, Chopin's work was rediscovered in the 1960s by Norwegian academic Per Seyersted. **(4)** Chopin's stories are especially notable for their presentation of issues facing women of the day, such as a lack of independence.

5. Which sentence contains information irrelevant to the passage as a whole and should be deleted?

   Ⓐ Sentence 1
   Ⓑ Sentence 2
   Ⓒ Sentence 3
   Ⓓ Sentence 4

## Application

*In this section, students will eliminate a sentence that blurs the focus of the passage.*

SLIDE 162.1

**Let's try it again with this new passage and question 5. Where do we start?**

By finding the main idea of the passage.

**Take a moment now to read.**

*Give students 1 minute to complete this task.*

**What would you say is the main idea of this passage?**

An author named Kate Chopin.

**This passage reads like an informational text, giving us lots of information about this author. Let's see which sentence doesn't belong. Start with choice A. What does sentence 1 talk about?**

The stories that Kate Chopin is famous for.

**Does that relate to our main idea?**

Yes.

**The first sentence of a paragraph is usually the topic sentence, meaning its main job is to introduce the topic. And in this case, sentence 1 does a great job of that. Let's eliminate choice A and keep moving. What does sentence 2 say?**

That another author was also popular for stories about New Orleans.

**Does that relate to Kate Chopin?**

No.

**What error does this sentence make?**

It blurs the focus.

**This paragraph is all about Kate Chopin, so bringing up another author could confuse the reader. Sentence 2 seems pretty cuttable. Should we stop here with choice B, though?**

No, we should check the others just in case.

**Let's do it. Choice C says we should cut sentence 3. Do you agree?**

No, because it talks about Chopin's work being *rediscovered*, so it relates to the main idea.

**What about sentence 4? Does that sentence fit in the paragraph?**

Yes, because it talks about why her stories are so *notable*.

**It looks like our first instinct was right: choice B is the best choice. When you tackle these kinds of questions on the TSIA2, it can feel overwhelming to look at the whole passage while trying to pick out one little sentence to cut. Stay focused on those answer choices. You can even use the highlighting tool that shows up in the top right corner of your screen to help you isolate those sentences. Compare them to the main idea of the passage or paragraph to see which one doesn't fit.**

TSIA2 Mastery: ELAR 

## Practice

**Instructions**
Complete the practice set. If time remains after you've finished, double-check your work.

**Passage**

**(1)** Before logging into or buying an item from some websites, you may have been asked to identify everyday objects in a series of images. **(2)** Most internet users have encountered this online security measure, but not many are aware that this widget is essential for training artificial intelligence programs for self-driving vehicles.

**(3)** These Turing tests—programs designed to distinguish between humans and computers—work because some images are more easily identified by humans than by computers. **(4)** Alan Turing was an English mathematician and an influential thinker in the field of computer science's early days. **(5)** The primary online Turing test, CAPTCHA, is used to block malware, or "bots," from accessing sensitive parts of websites. **(6)** Initially, CAPTCHAs were made up of smudged text the user had to decipher—a difficult task for a robot. **(7)** But by 2014, a team of computer programmers at Waymo, a self-driving car company owned by Google, created a new version of the CAPTCHA that put all these identifications to better use.

**(8)** In the new version, users are shown a grid of nine images to identify, instead of a snippet of smudged text. **(9)** Some of the images are known by the program and used for comparison. **(10)** But the other images are fragments of street views that computer vision techniques have been unable to recognize. **(11)** The same image fragment is shown to a number of users, and their identifications are compared by the software. **(12)** Once a consensus is found, the software goes on to the next block of unidentified images. **(13)** Image identification technology has applications in diverse fields, ranging from surveillance to cryptography, and even social media.

**(14)** Globally, 200 million image CAPTCHAs are solved daily. **(15)** Each individual fragment is tiny. **(16)** Picture by picture, enormous databases of street views are transformed into driving directions. **(17)** For example, CAPTCHAs have been used to develop algorithms for the first self-driving taxi service and for the Paris Metro's automated trains, which have been in service since 2019. **(18)** Their construction began in 2012. **(19)** So if you find yourself frustrated with a CAPTCHA, try to remember that you are contributing to the technology that may one day change the way we navigate the modern world.

1. Which of the following sentences contains information irrelevant to the passage as a whole and would best be deleted from the passage?

   Ⓐ Sentence 2
   Ⓑ Sentence 4
   Ⓒ Sentence 5
   Ⓓ Sentence 6

# Practice

SLIDE 163.1

*Give students 8 minutes to complete the practice set.*

SLIDE 163.2

1. **The correct answer is B.** The main focus of the paragraph is to explain in more detail the origins of CAPTCHAs and how they work. Choices A, C, and D are incorrect because they contribute to the discussion of CAPTCHAs and, therefore, should not be deleted. Choice B is correct because sentence 4, *Alan Turing was an English mathematician and an influential thinker in the field of computer science's early days*, provides biographical information about Alan Turing, which shifts the focus of the paragraph in a distracting way.

**Instructions**

Complete the practice set. If time remains after you've finished, double-check your work.

**Passage**

**(1)** Before logging into or buying an item from some websites, you may have been asked to identify everyday objects in a series of images. **(2)** Most internet users have encountered this online security measure, but not many are aware that this widget is essential for training artificial intelligence programs for self-driving vehicles.

**(3)** These Turing tests—programs designed to distinguish between humans and computers—work because some images are more easily identified by humans than by computers. **(4)** Alan Turing was an English mathematician and an influential thinker in the field of computer science's early days. **(5)** The primary online Turing test, CAPTCHA, is used to block malware, or "bots," from accessing sensitive parts of websites. **(6)** Initially, CAPTCHAs were made up of smudged text the user had to decipher—a difficult task for a robot. **(7)** But by 2014, a team of computer programmers at Waymo, a self-driving car company owned by Google, created a new version of the CAPTCHA that put all these identifications to better use.

**(8)** In the new version, users are shown a grid of nine images to identify, instead of a snippet of smudged text. **(9)** Some of the images are known by the program and used for comparison. **(10)** But the other images are fragments of street views that computer vision techniques have been unable to recognize. **(11)** The same image fragment is shown to a number of users, and their identifications are compared by the software. **(12)** Once a consensus is found, the software goes on to the next block of unidentified images. **(13)** Image identification technology has applications in diverse fields, ranging from surveillance to cryptography, and even social media.

**(14)** Globally, 200 million image CAPTCHAs are solved daily. **(15)** Each individual fragment is tiny. **(16)** Picture by picture, enormous databases of street views are transformed into driving directions. **(17)** For example, CAPTCHAs have been used to develop algorithms for the first self-driving taxi service and for the Paris Metro's automated trains, which have been in service since 2019. **(18)** Their construction began in 2012. **(19)** So if you find yourself frustrated with a CAPTCHA, try to remember that you are contributing to the technology that may one day change the way we navigate the modern world.

2. Which of the following sentences contains information irrelevant to the passage as a whole and would best be deleted from the passage?

   Ⓐ Sentence 8
   Ⓑ Sentence 10
   Ⓒ Sentence 12
   Ⓓ Sentence 13

## Practice

SLIDE 164.1

2. **The correct answer is D.** The main focus of the paragraph is explaining in detail how *the new version* of CAPTCHAs works. Choices A, B, and C are incorrect because they help explain the step-by-step procedure of a CAPTCHA, so they should not be deleted. Choice D is correct because sentence 13, *image identification technology has applications in diverse fields, ranging from surveillance to cryptography, and even social media*, shifts the focus toward where image identification technology can be useful, so the sentence does not fit in this paragraph and should be deleted.

**Instructions**
Complete the practice set. If time remains after you've finished, double-check your work.

**Passage**

**(1)** Before logging into or buying an item from some websites, you may have been asked to identify everyday objects in a series of images. **(2)** Most internet users have encountered this online security measure, but not many are aware that this widget is essential for training artificial intelligence programs for self-driving vehicles.

**(3)** These Turing tests—programs designed to distinguish between humans and computers—work because some images are more easily identified by humans than by computers. **(4)** Alan Turing was an English mathematician and an influential thinker in the field of computer science's early days. **(5)** The primary online Turing test, CAPTCHA, is used to block malware, or "bots," from accessing sensitive parts of websites. **(6)** Initially, CAPTCHAs were made up of smudged text the user had to decipher—a difficult task for a robot. **(7)** But by 2014, a team of computer programmers at Waymo, a self-driving car company owned by Google, created a new version of the CAPTCHA that put all these identifications to better use.

**(8)** In the new version, users are shown a grid of nine images to identify, instead of a snippet of smudged text. **(9)** Some of the images are known by the program and used for comparison. **(10)** But the other images are fragments of street views that computer vision techniques have been unable to recognize. **(11)** The same image fragment is shown to a number of users, and their identifications are compared by the software. **(12)** Once a consensus is found, the software goes on to the next block of unidentified images. **(13)** Image identification technology has applications in diverse fields, ranging from surveillance to cryptography, and even social media.

**(14)** Globally, 200 million image CAPTCHAs are solved daily. **(15)** Each individual fragment is tiny. **(16)** Picture by picture, enormous databases of street views are transformed into driving directions. **(17)** For example, CAPTCHAs have been used to develop algorithms for the first self-driving taxi service and for the Paris Metro's automated trains, which have been in service since 2019. **(18)** Their construction began in 2012. **(19)** So if you find yourself frustrated with a CAPTCHA, try to remember that you are contributing to the technology that may one day change the way we navigate the modern world.

3. Which of the following sentences contains information irrelevant to the passage as a whole and would best be deleted from the passage?

   Ⓐ Sentence 15
   Ⓑ Sentence 16
   Ⓒ Sentence 17
   Ⓓ Sentence 18

## Practice

SLIDE 165.1

3. **The correct answer is D.** The main focus of the paragraph is putting the size of the CAPTCHA project into perspective and concluding the passage. Choices A, B, and C are incorrect because they offer details that put the CAPTCHA project into context. Choice D is correct because sentence 18, *their construction began in 2012*, shifts the focus of the paragraph toward the construction of Paris's new Metro trains in a distracting way, so the sentence should be deleted from the paragraph.

## Wrap-Up

**Instructions**

Complete the wrap-up question. If time remains after you've finished, double-check your work.

**Passage**

**(1)** When schools of fish gather again after time apart, they will swim around each other while waving their fins and performing elaborate dances. **(2)** Stingrays have been seen frolicking over fields of coral, twirling and flapping their wings, even when ample open ocean is readily available. **(3)** Some have argued that these kinds of behaviors show that fish can feel emotions like joy and delight. **(4)** The study of fish is known as "Ichthyology."

**(5)** Even advocates for the argument that fish have feelings acknowledge that scientists can easily misidentify what they are seeing with their eyes. **(6)** The shape of a fish's mouth makes it look like it is surprised; it looks that way even when it is excited or in danger. **(7)** Fish are social, communicating underwater using clicks and bubbles. **(8)** Feelings are challenging to understand even in humans, who have the ability to talk about their emotions.

**(9)** Many oceanographers who devote their time to studying fish behavior have argued that at least some fish, such as triggerfish and eels, have strong feelings like the ones we experience as humans. **(10)** Other researchers are doubtful. **(11)** They argue that it has not yet been proven that fish feel emotion in any reliable, reproducible scientific experiments.

**(12)** Regardless, scientific consensus on the question of fish emotion is beginning to shift. **(13)** Many biologists have accepted that fish most likely have "primary" emotions such as fear or anger. **(14)** These responses seem to be found in most fish. **(15)** For instance, a zebrafish will avoid a part of the tank where it was once shocked even if the shock has been removed. **(16)** Additionally, scientists believe that feelings can be inferred from fishes' changes in activity and eye movement, or even from involuntary responses like scale shedding.

**2.** Which of the following sentences contains information irrelevant to the passage as a whole and would best be deleted from the passage?

- Ⓐ Sentence 1
- Ⓑ Sentence 2
- Ⓒ Sentence 3
- Ⓓ Sentence 4

# Wrap-Up

SLIDE 166.1

*Give students 2 minutes to complete the wrap-up question.*

SLIDE 166.2

2. **The correct answer is D**. Choice A is incorrect because this description of fish behavior is a good introduction to the topic of the passage (considering whether analyzing fish behaviors can shed light on the question of what kinds of emotions they feel). Choice B is incorrect because it provides another description of fish behavior, which develops the author's introduction to the topic of the passage. Choice C is incorrect because this sentence connects the descriptions of fish behavior (sentences 1 and 2) to the question of whether these behaviors indicate that fish feel emotions, which is the topic of the passage. Choice D is correct because the sentence *the study of fish is known as "Ichthyology"* is not directly relevant to the way the paragraph introduces the topic of fish emotion, and so it would be best to remove sentence 4.

CHAPTER 19

# Organization

In this chapter, students will evaluate the placement of a sentence within the context of a passage to determine its relevance to the surrounding ideas.

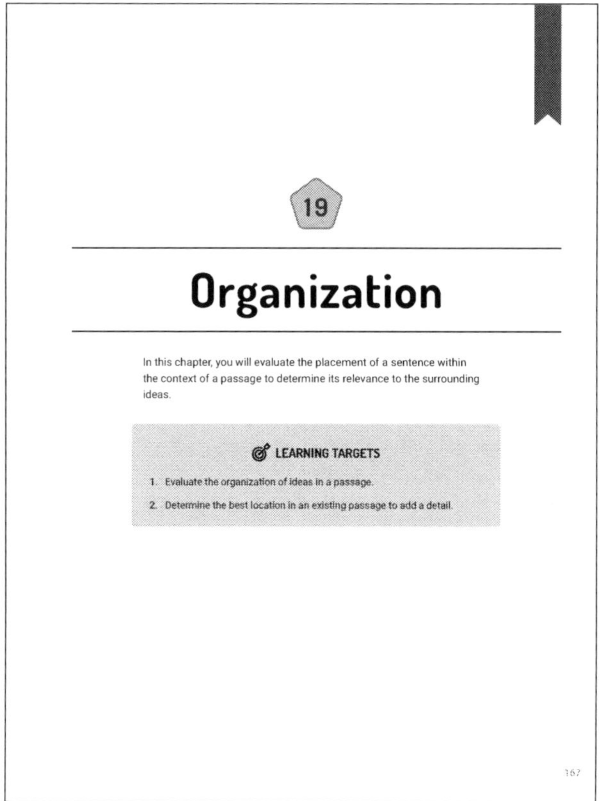
19

Organization

In this chapter, you will evaluate the placement of a sentence within the context of a passage to determine its relevance to the surrounding ideas.

LEARNING TARGETS

1. Evaluate the organization of ideas in a passage.
2. Determine the best location in an existing passage to add a detail.

## TSIA2 STANDARDS

**Essay Revision and Editing**
Organization

The student will revise as necessary to improve the organization of text.

## TEKS ALIGNMENT

E1.9 *Composition*: listening, speaking, reading, writing, and thinking using multiple texts—writing process. The student uses the writing process recursively to compose multiple texts that are legible and uses appropriate conventions. The student is expected to:

(C) revise drafts to improve clarity, development, organization, style, diction, and sentence effectiveness, including parallel constructions and placement of phrases and dependent clauses.

## LEARNING TARGETS

1. Evaluate the organization of ideas in a passage.
2. Determine the best location in an existing passage to add a detail.

## Warm-Up

**Instructions**
Complete the warm-up question. If time remains after you've finished, double-check your work.

**Passage**

**(1)** Before logging into or buying an item from some websites, you may have been asked to identify everyday objects in a series of images. **(2)** Most internet users have encountered this online security measure, but not many are aware that this widget is essential for training artificial intelligence programs for self-driving vehicles.

**(3)** These Turing tests—programs designed to distinguish between humans and computers—work because some images are more easily identified by humans than by computers. **(4)** The primary online Turing test, CAPTCHA, is used to block malware, or "bots," from accessing sensitive parts of websites. **(5)** Initially, CAPTCHAs were made up of smudged text the user had to decipher—a difficult task for a robot.

**(6)** In the new version, users are shown a grid of nine images to identify, instead of a snippet of smudged text. **(7)** Some of the images are known by the program and used for comparison. **(8)** The same image fragment is shown to a number of users, and their identifications are compared by the software. **(9)** Once a consensus is found, the software goes on to the next block of unidentified images.

**(10)** Globally, 200 million image CAPTCHAs are solved daily. **(11)** Each individual fragment is tiny. **(12)** Picture by picture, enormous databases of street views are transformed into driving directions. **(13)** For example, CAPTCHAs have been used to develop algorithms for the first self-driving taxi service and for the Paris Metro's automated trains, which have been in service since 2019. **(14)** So if you find yourself frustrated with a CAPTCHA, try to remember that you are contributing to the technology that may one day change the way we navigate the modern world.

1. In context, where would the following sentence best be placed?

   *But the other images are fragments of street views that computer vision techniques have been unable to recognize.*

   Ⓐ After sentence 7
   Ⓑ After sentence 10
   Ⓒ After sentence 13
   Ⓓ After sentence 14

# Warm-Up

SLIDE 168.1

*Give students 2 minutes to complete the warm-up question.*

SLIDE 168.2

1. **The correct answer is A.** The sentence needs to be placed right after a sentence that talks about a group of images because it begins with the phrase *but the other images*. Choices B, C, and D are incorrect because the phrase *but the other images* doesn't make sense when placed right after these sentences, none of which properly sets up a reference to *the other images*. Choice A is correct because *some of the images are known by the program* leads into *but the other images are fragments of street views* in a logical way: a sentence beginning with *but the other images* makes sense after a sentence describing *some of the images*.

TSIA2 Mastery: ELAR 

## Groundwork

EXERCISE A

**Instructions**
Rewrite each detail beneath its relevant topic.

**Details**

St. Petersburg Beans Lens Zoom Miami

Portrait Shanghai Roasted Aroma

| Cities |
|---|
| |
| |
| |

| Coffee |
|---|
| |
| |
| |

| Photography |
|---|
| |
| |
| |

# Groundwork

*In this section, students will practice matching details to a topic.*

**One of the most basic skills we literally have from the time we're born is the ability to group relevant things into categories. We start out with categories like *food* and *not-food*, and things only get more complicated from there: shapes, colors, things that definitely shouldn't go up your nose. Where else in your world do you see categories?**

*Allow 2–3 students to share.*

**Our brain is already pretty familiar with these topics, so we can pick out related details based on our experience. The TSIA2 will ask you to do something similar on the test, though instead of grouping ideas together, your challenge will be to find the place in a passage where a detail fits best.**

EXERCISE A  SLIDE 169.1

**We are constantly making decisions about whether something is relevant to a concept or situation. We do it so naturally that sometimes we don't even realize it. For instance, imagine you read a paragraph about a bunch of different *cities*. Which of the details at the top of your workbook would you expect to see there?**

*St. Petersburg*, *Miami*, and *Shanghai*.

SLIDE 169.2

**Those are all cities, so it makes sense that they would be relevant to that paragraph. What about *coffee*? That's more of a broad topic, and none of the details we have name specific coffee types. Which details go with that topic?**

*Beans*, *roasted*, *aroma*.

**How did you pick those?**

They are words that show up with *coffee* all the time.

SLIDE 169.3

**Even though the words aren't specific types of coffee, they give us details we often associate with coffee. What about *photography*? What details would fit with that?**

*Lens*, *zoom*, *portrait*.

**Again, these aren't specific camera types. How do we know they go into the category?**

They are details that relate to the category of *photography*.

EXERCISE B

### Instructions

Determine which sentences are irrelevant or out of sequence in the passage. Draw a line through your answers.

### Passage

**(1)** Ferdinand Magellan is most famously credited for being the first person to circumnavigate the world. **(2)** This expedition—spanning from 1519 to 1522—was not only the first of its kind, but it also provided humans with solid evidence showing that the Earth is not, in fact, flat. **(3)** Christopher Columbus attempted to sail around the world during his own explorations, but he was unsuccessful. **(4)** Magellan gained his sailing experience participating in expeditions to Southeast Asia between 1505 and 1512, bringing trade goods back to Portugal. **(5)** After Magellan returned with evidence of a round Earth, people of that time still did not want to accept that there was no possibility of "sailing off the edge of the world," and it would be more than 100 years until science would provide a more convincing argument.

## Groundwork

*In this section, students will practice identifying sentences that are not relevant or that break the sequence of events.*

EXERCISE B

**People love a good adventure story. It's why we enjoy movies that take us to places we've never been and stories about pirates or space explorers. There's a bit of an adrenaline rush that comes along with diving headfirst into the unknown—from the relative safety of our couches, that is. But imagine that you're watching a movie about diving to the bottom of the ocean, and the director decides to include a random scene focusing on desert camels. What might you be thinking as you watch?**

This is random, or it doesn't belong in the movie.

**It's a little like getting interrupted mid-conversation. It's not relevant to what's happening. What if the director decides to show the characters successfully arriving home right at the beginning of the movie and then goes back and shows what happened before? Would that work?**

No, because it gives away the ending and ruins the movie.

SLIDE 170.1

**Good stories also follow the right sequence of events. If they hop around in the timeline, it gets confusing for us as viewers. We need them to keep things in order. You'll need to find these same kinds of errors on the TSIA2, where placing a sentence in the passage will either interrupt the conversation or break the sequence of events. Let's practice finding those awkward placements. Take a moment to read the passage in your workbook.**

*Give students 1 minute to read the passage.*

**What would you say is the main idea of this paragraph?**

Magellan sailing around the world and proving the Earth is round.

**Did you notice any sentences that didn't feel like they belonged in that paragraph?**

Sentence 3.

**Why is that one out of place?**

It talks about Columbus.

**Does that seem like an interruption or a sequence error?**

An interruption.

**Sentence 3 offers up details related to the idea of sailing around the world, but the paragraph focuses on Magellan. We don't need Columbus to put in his two cents on this topic, so we can cross off that sentence. Take another pass now that we've cut one sentence. Do you see any sentences that seem out of order?**

Sentence 4.

**Why does that one break the sequence?**

Because it talks about Magellan's experience in 1505 to 1512, but sentence 2 mentions 1519 to 1522.

**The order of events got a little mixed up. Sentence 4 doesn't belong there. During the TSIA2, you'll have the same opportunity to evaluate the placement of details in a passage. The challenge, though, will be plugging those details into the passage in your head. The sentence you'll need to add will be shown in the question, not in the actual passage.**

TSIA2 Mastery: ELAR 

EXERCISE C

### Instructions

Determine the best location in the following passage to place the provided detail sentence.

### Detail:

*For example, many of the most popular locations have heavy, rounded arches or thick pillars spanning the front of the home, both characteristics that provide stability to the structures.*

### Passage

**(1)** Urban explorers are known for seeking out abandoned buildings and other locales, photographing them, and sharing the stories of those lonely places on social media. **(2)** Many of these individuals feel that urban exploration allows them to connect with the history of a place in a way that they never could in a book or even at a museum.

**(3)** If you ignore the wear and tear, these old, now-abandoned buildings can be seen as works of art with outstanding examples of craftsmanship and creativity in architecture. **(4)** When these buildings were originally constructed, the architects and designers expected them to be permanent, not lost to ruin. **(5)** Unfortunately, our culture has come to discard old or worn-out places and build new ones, rather than preserving the efforts of the past.

## Groundwork

*In this section, students will practice finding the best place to insert a detail into a passage.*

EXERCISE C   SLIDE 171.1

**It's a little like lining up dominos. One sentence will have a topic that leads into the next sentence's topic, and you have to figure out where the domino sentence from the question fits into the lineup of the passage. If your domino isn't in the right place, it might mean that not all the dominos fall when they need to. What happens if you put a sentence in the wrong place?**

The ideas won't flow together, or they might not make sense.

**Let's practice with the detail and passage here in your workbook. We've been given a detail, so let's start there. What does the detail talk about?**

Characteristics that made the buildings stronger.

**Let's dig through the paragraph and try to find a relevant spot for our detail. Think of it as the reverse process of what we saw on the last page. Rather than picking things out, we need to put something in. Start with the first paragraph. What's the main idea, or topic, of that paragraph?**

Urban explorers.

**What about the second paragraph? What's the topic of that one?**

The different buildings that urban explorers visit.

**Which paragraph do you think the detail belongs in?**

The second one.

**Let's test it with a little trial and error, then. Plug the detail into the paragraph after sentence 3. Do the ideas flow there?**

Kind of, yes.

**What makes that placement seem good?**

Because sentence 3 talks about how the buildings were made with craftsmanship and creativity, and the detail we're adding is all about the characteristics of the buildings.

**Perhaps that creativity leads into the idea of those buildings being strong, but let's check the other placements just in case. Let's drop our detail into the passage after sentence 4. Do the ideas from sentence 4 flow into what's said in our detail?**

Yes, because the sentence talks about how the architects wanted the buildings to last a long time, and then the detail gives examples about the things that made the buildings strong.

**Wanting the buildings to last a long time definitely connects to the idea of using features to make the buildings stronger. What about sentence 5? Could our detail go after that one?**

No.

**Why not?**

Because it talks about society wanting to throw old things away.

**Our detail really doesn't fit in with the ideas of sentence 5, so we know that's not right. So, what do you think? Check out that transition at the start of our detail: *for example*. That phrase tells us that our detail needs to be an example of whatever comes before. Does the detail flow better coming after sentence 3 or after sentence 4?**

After sentence 4.

**What makes that the better placement?**

Because examples of making the building stronger go better with the architects wanting the buildings to last a long time, rather than just the buildings being good examples of craftsmanship and creativity.

**Even though there were a couple of places this sentence could have gone, following sentence 4 is definitely the best position for it. Think of each sentence like a topic. If the detail we need to add isn't related to that topic, you know you're looking at the wrong spot.**

## Application

### THE APPROACH

When a question asks where you should add a sentence, use these steps ...

1. Review the detail to be added.
2. Test each answer choice placement.
3. Eliminate answer choices that create a disconnect between ideas.

**Passage**

**(1)** Today's explorers are professionals with degrees in archaeology and anthropology, high-tech equipment, excellent communication solutions, and teams of people standing by to organize rescue operations. **(2)** Unlike today's explorers, those who set out 100 years ago had few supplies and little support, and they were primarily amateurs and enthusiasts. **(3)** Percy Fawcett was an explorer who disappeared into the Amazonian rainforests in 1925. **(4)** When Fawcett joined the British Royal Geographical Society (RGS), they offered one year of training courses in surveying, observing, and taking notes on the natural world, botany, geology, meteorology, and leadership. **(5)** Fawcett took this one-year course and aced the final with flying colors.

**(6)** Fawcett's first assignment with the RGS sent him to the Amazonian rainforests. **(7)** Bolivia and Brazil were in conflict about the border between their two nations. **(8)** They appealed to the RGS to send a neutral third party to map the region and determine the border. **(9)** The RGS chose Percy Fawcett for this 600-mile trek, and in doing so propelled Fawcett toward his legacy.

**(10)** Percy Fawcett's first expedition to the Amazon was a resounding success. **(11)** He traveled over 600 miles through the jungle, mapped rivers and national borders, and completed his assignment in half of the time. **(12)** During this mission, Fawcett heard tales of a city lost in the jungle—a marvelous city full of gold and treasure. **(13)** Fawcett became obsessed with finding this city, which he called "Z" in his notes. **(14)** He returned to the region in 1908 and 1909 to measure the Rio Verde on the border between Bolivia and Brazil. **(15)** In 1910 and 1911, Fawcett was specifically requested by Peru and Bolivia to survey and map the border between those countries. **(16)** With their help, Fawcett got the chance to lead a non-government expedition to find a lost Inca city in the Andes from 1913 to 1914. **(17)** Although he didn't find the city, he felt successful in leading the expedition. **(18)** After World War I, Fawcett got the chance to search for his lost city, Z, in the jungles of Brazil. **(19)** Finally, in April 1925, Fawcett, his son Jack, and Jack's friend Raleigh set out to search once again for Z. **(20)** After a telegram in May 1925, the three were ever heard from again.

This page is intentionally left blank.
Teacher content resumes on the next page.

**TSIA2 Mastery:** ELAR 

1. In context, where would the following sentence best be placed?

   *Due to the urgency created by this conflict, the Society needed to move swiftly and to select an individual who would no doubt do a thorough job.*

   Ⓐ After sentence 4
   Ⓑ After sentence 8
   Ⓒ After sentence 11
   Ⓓ After sentence 14

# Application

*In this section, students will practice applying the steps of the Approach to an organization question.*

SLIDE 173.1

**Organization questions look pretty similar, and they only show up as essay revision questions. They also have a pretty unique feature. What is it?**

They give you a sentence and ask you where to add it to the essay.

**If you're given a sentence and all the answers give you placements, like before or after a sentence number, you know you're dealing with an organization question. Luckily, they limit your options, which makes things a little easier. Look at question 1. How many placements will we have to test?**

Four.

**We know that the added detail can only go into the essay in one of four places. Where do we start?**

By reviewing the detail we need to add.

**Take a moment to look over that sentence. Don't just skim. Get familiar with its details. One little phrase could be the key to finding the exact right placement. What's our added detail about?**

Some sort of *urgency* to find someone for a job.

**Just based on that, what should you look for when evaluating a possible placement?**

Some event that creates that sense of *urgency*.

**What's our next step?**

Test each answer choice placement.

**Our first option says sentence 4. Do we need to count the sentences?**

No, the sentences are numbered for us.

**The TSIA2 doesn't want any issues cropping up with students checking the wrong sentence, so it numbers all the sentences in the essays. Let's test it. Who'd like to read sentence 4, along with our added detail right after?**

*When Fawcett joined the British Royal Geographical Society (RGS), they offered one year of training courses in surveying, observing, and taking notes on the natural world, botany, geology, meteorology, and leadership. Due to the urgency created by this conflict, the Society needed to move swiftly and to select an individual who would no doubt do a thorough job.*

**Do those ideas flow together?**

Not really.

**What's missing?**

The event that creates the *urgency*.

**That means we can eliminate choice A and move on to the next option. Choice B says to put the sentence after sentence 8. Does that placement work?**

A little bit.

**Let's back up even more. If a placement seems good, we can make extra-sure that it works by reading even more of what comes before. When we add in sentence 7 and read through sentence 8, does the placement still work?**

Yes, it works even better now because the conflict between the countries created the *urgency*.

**Choice B seems *really* promising, but let's check the others just in case. Does the added detail work when we put it right after sentence 11?**

No, because it's talking about the time after Fawcett was already chosen for the job.

**When you're trying to find a good place for these sentences, be on the lookout for sequence problems. If Percy Fawcett already had the job, talking about the urgency to give him a job seems weird and out of order. That means choice C is out. What about choice D? Does the detail work after sentence 14?**

No, since it's still talking about the time after he got the job mapping the border.

**Usually, if you find a sequence problem in one placement, any placements that follow are going to have the same issue. That's the thing about sequence—it goes in order! And since sentence 14 comes after sentence 11, it's pretty safe to say that choice D is out and choice B is our best answer.**

## THE APPROACH

When a question asks where you should add a sentence, use these steps ...

1. Review the detail to be added.
2. Test each answer choice placement.
3. Eliminate answer choices that create a disconnect between ideas.

**Passage**

**(1)** Today's explorers are professionals with degrees in archaeology and anthropology, high-tech equipment, excellent communication solutions, and teams of people standing by to organize rescue operations. **(2)** Unlike today's explorers, those who set out 100 years ago had few supplies and little support, and they were primarily amateurs and enthusiasts. **(3)** Percy Fawcett was an explorer who disappeared into the Amazonian rainforests in 1925. **(4)** When Fawcett joined the British Royal Geographical Society (RGS), they offered one year of training courses in surveying, observing, and taking notes on the natural world, botany, geology, meteorology, and leadership. **(5)** Fawcett took this one-year course and aced the final with flying colors.

**(6)** Fawcett's first assignment with the RGS sent him to the Amazonian rainforests. **(7)** Bolivia and Brazil were in conflict about the border between their two nations. **(8)** They appealed to the RGS to send a neutral third party to map the region and determine the border. **(9)** The RGS chose Percy Fawcett for this 600-mile trek, and in doing so propelled Fawcett toward his legacy.

**(10)** Percy Fawcett's first expedition to the Amazon was a resounding success. **(11)** He traveled over 600 miles through the jungle, mapped rivers and national borders, and completed his assignment in half of the time. **(12)** During this mission, Fawcett heard tales of a city lost in the jungle—a marvelous city full of gold and treasure. **(13)** Fawcett became obsessed with finding this city, which he called "Z" in his notes. **(14)** He returned to the region in 1908 and 1909 to measure the Rio Verde on the border between Bolivia and Brazil. **(15)** In 1910 and 1911, Fawcett was specifically requested by Peru and Bolivia to survey and map the border between those countries. **(16)** With their help, Fawcett got the chance to lead a non-government expedition to find a lost Inca city in the Andes from 1913 to 1914. **(17)** Although he didn't find the city, he felt successful in leading the expedition. **(18)** After World War I, Fawcett got the chance to search for his lost city, Z, in the jungles of Brazil. **(19)** Finally, in April 1925, Fawcett, his son Jack, and Jack's friend Raleigh set out to search once again for Z. **(20)** After a telegram in May 1925, the three were ever heard from again.

This page is intentionally left blank.
Teacher content resumes on the next page.

**2.** In context, where would the following sentence best be placed?

*As a result of these successes, Fawcett's status as an explorer and his ability to befriend the local tribes became legendary among local governments.*

Ⓐ After sentence 8
Ⓑ After sentence 9
Ⓒ After sentence 12
Ⓓ After sentence 15

## Application

*In this section, students will eliminate answer choices that create a disconnect in the flow of ideas.*

**Another way to approach organization questions is through an overall test strategy. When we read long passages, we take notes. What kinds of things should we write down?**

A quick summary of each paragraph and the main idea of the whole passage.

**We can apply this to essay revision questions, too. As you read the essay, make a note of the main idea of each paragraph. Let's do that now.**

*Give students 4 minutes to complete this task.*

**What did you write down for the main idea of the first paragraph?**

It gives an introduction to explorers, Percy Fawcett, and how he aced the course he took through the RGS.

**And what about the second paragraph?**

It talks about the conflict between Bolivia and Brazil and how they picked Percy to map the border.

**And the third paragraph?**

All the stuff Percy did throughout his career.

SLIDE 175.1

**Let's come back to question 2 now. What does the detail sentence talk about?**

How his *successes* helped him make connections with local tribes.

**Which paragraph do you think that detail will *best* fit in, based on the main ideas we identified?**

The third paragraph.

**Can you eliminate any choices just using that?**

Choices A and B.

**Choices A and B show up in the second paragraph, so those aren't right. Let's test our remaining two options. Do the ideas still flow if we add the detail after sentence 12?**

No, because sentences 12 and 13 talk about Z, and putting the detail after sentence 12 interrupts that.

**Choice C is no good. What about choice D? Does it work if we add the detail after sentence 15?**

Yes, the ideas flow from his *successes* to the effects of his *successes* in the detail sentence.

**When you come to your first essay revision question, remember to take the time to read the whole essay before moving into the questions. You'll have four whole questions based on that essay, so getting familiar with its content can only help. And, if an organization question pops up, you should be able to eliminate at least two answers based on the main idea of each paragraph. Even if you have to make a guess at that point, you'll have excellent odds of getting it right.**

## Practice

**Instructions**

Complete the practice set. If time remains after you've finished, double-check your work.

**Passage**

**(1)** These days, Barcelona is the only city in Spain where a majority of the residents speak a regional language: Catalan. **(2)** It is taught to every child. **(3)** And to many adults, it is a source of cultural identity. **(4)** Barcelona differs substantially even from other autonomous regions in Spain like Basque Country, which has a majority Basque (rather than Spanish) population. **(5)** In Barcelona, Catalan and Castilian Spanish are both official languages. **(6)** Yet Catalan, alongside Spanish, is considered a primary language, spoken by 70 percent of Barcelonans. **(7)** In Basque Country, which also has two official languages, Basque is secondary to Spanish.

**(8)** Historians and anthropologists argue that the decline of this regional language dates back to the union of the Castile and Aragon crowns in the late 15th century. **(9)** However, as the monarchy sought to replace regional languages with Spanish, the territory that ultimately became Barcelona remained autonomous. **(10)** This helped preserve Catalan.

**(11)** Under General Francisco Franco, who ruled from 1936 to 1975, Catalan suffered. **(12)** General Franco, the son of a naval officer father and Spanish-speaking mother, made it a forbidden language and punished Catalan speakers with imprisonment for their disobedience. **(13)** Democratic government was established in the 1980s. **(14)** Then more actions were taken to preserve Catalan. **(15)** However, not everyone feels confident about Catalan's future, pointing to changes like the growing number of immigrants from Latin America, where Spanish is typically the dominant language, to Barcelona, where Catalan has the upper hand. **(16)** Whether Catalan can continue to grow, or at least hold on, in an increasingly evolving society within an ever-changing world remains an open question.

**1.** In context, where would the following sentence best be placed?

*The 1993 Constitution made Catalan equivalent to Spanish in Catalonia, and superintendents report that they have thoroughly improved Catalan instruction in grade schools.*

Ⓐ After sentence 1
Ⓑ After sentence 6
Ⓒ After sentence 10
Ⓓ After sentence 14

# Practice

SLIDE 176.1

*Give students 10 minutes to complete the practice set.*

SLIDE 176.2

1. **The correct answer is D**. Choices A and B are incorrect because the first paragraph discusses Catalan in Barcelona generally and compares it to Basque, but this sentence is a specific detail about the recent history of Catalan in Barcelona, which is addressed in the third paragraph. Choice C is incorrect because the second paragraph discusses the historical roots of Catalan in Barcelona; the added sentence would be irrelevant to this paragraph. Choice D is correct because sentences 13 and 14 explain that *Democratic government was established in the 1980s. Then more actions were taken to preserve Catalan*. The sentence provides a specific detail that follows chronologically (1993) to back up this claim.

TSIA2 Mastery: ELAR


### Instructions

Complete the practice set. If time remains after you've finished, double-check your work.

### Passage

**(1)** In the course of his life, entrepreneur, navigator, and pilot Wiley Post achieved several aviation feats. **(2)** Among them, he is likely best known for one that he achieved as an airplane pilot. **(3)** In 1933, Post managed an unassisted journey around the globe in a single-engine aircraft. **(4)** He was the first person to accomplish this.

**(5)** On four earlier efforts, Post had piloted a single-engine airplane flight with the goal of traversing the continent. **(6)** These journeys were not completed for a number of reasons. **(7)** The equipment was too damaged for Post to continue the trip safely, and he was compelled to execute a crash landing. **(8)** On another try, a strong headwind forced his plane to land at an Army outpost, where he could refuel.

**(9)** Post's achievement in 1933 was attributed in part to his use of a modified airplane called the *Winnie Mae.* **(10)** The airplane, launched from New York, permitted Post to voyage over the Atlantic Ocean at a speed of more than a hundred miles an hour. **(11)** Throughout this trip, Post also stayed in touch with ground radar, which helped him to avoid the navigational errors that had plagued others. **(12)** Less than eight days after the airplane's takeoff, Post finished his ground-breaking trip and touched down in Brooklyn.

**2.** Where in the passage should the following statement be placed?

*Post's 1933 voyage was not his only shot at breaking a record.*

Ⓐ Immediately before sentence 5
Ⓑ Immediately before sentence 9
Ⓒ Immediately before sentence 11
Ⓓ Immediately before sentence 12

**3.** Where in the passage should the following statement be placed?

*In one attempt, a jealous competitor secretly sabotaged the plane.*

Ⓐ After sentence 3
Ⓑ After sentence 6
Ⓒ After sentence 9
Ⓓ After sentence 11

## Practice

SLIDE 177.1

2. **The correct answer is A.** Choices B, C, and D are incorrect because placing *Post's 1933 voyage was not his only shot at breaking a record* in the third paragraph would be out of place; the passage discusses Post's other flights in the second paragraph, so it would be unnecessary to state that *Post's 1933 voyage was not his only shot at breaking a record* after that paragraph. Choice A is correct because the second paragraph describes Post's earlier efforts to break aviation records, so *Post's 1933 voyage was not his only shot at breaking a record* is a good topic sentence for that paragraph.

SLIDE 177.2

3. **The correct answer is B.** Choice A is incorrect because the first paragraph is about Post's single, successful attempt. Because that trip was successful, it is unlikely that the plane was sabotaged then. Choices C and D are also incorrect because the third paragraph also describes Post's successful flight in 1933 rather than his earlier failures. Choice B is correct because the second paragraph details the setbacks Post encountered during his initial efforts to make aviation history, and it is conceivable that the sabotage might have occurred at this point.

## Wrap-Up

**Instructions**

Complete the wrap-up question. If time remains after you've finished, double-check your work.

**Passage**

**(1)** Before logging into or buying an item from some websites, you may have been asked to identify everyday objects in a series of images. **(2)** Most internet users have encountered this online security measure, but not many are aware that this widget is essential for training artificial intelligence programs for self-driving vehicles.

**(3)** These Turing tests—programs designed to distinguish between humans and computers—work because some images are more easily identified by humans than by computers. **(4)** The primary online Turing test, CAPTCHA, is used to block malware, or "bots," from accessing sensitive parts of websites. **(5)** Initially, CAPTCHAs were made up of smudged text the user had to decipher—a difficult task for a robot.

**(6)** In the new version, users are shown a grid of nine images to identify, instead of a snippet of smudged text. **(7)** Some of the images are known by the program and used for comparison. **(8)** The same image fragment is shown to a number of users, and their identifications are compared by the software. **(9)** Once a consensus is found, the software goes on to the next block of unidentified images.

**(10)** Globally, 200 million image CAPTCHAs are solved daily. **(11)** Each individual fragment is tiny. **(12)** Picture by picture, enormous databases of street views are transformed into driving directions. **(13)** For example, CAPTCHAs have been used to develop algorithms for the first self-driving taxi service and for the Paris Metro's automated trains, which have been in service since 2019. **(14)** So if you find yourself frustrated with a CAPTCHA, try to remember that you are contributing to the technology that may one day change the way we navigate the modern world.

**2.** In context, where would the following sentence best be placed?

*But by 2014, a team of computer programmers at Waymo, a self-driving car company owned by Google, created a new version of the CAPTCHA that put all these identifications to better use.*

Ⓐ Before sentence 3
Ⓑ After sentence 3
Ⓒ After sentence 4
Ⓓ After sentence 5

# Wrap-Up

SLIDE 178.1

*Give students 2 minutes to complete the wrap-up question.*

SLIDE 178.2

2. **The correct answer is D.** The sentence begins with the word *but*, which signals a shift, and it introduces *a new version of the CAPTCHA*. Choices A, B, and C are incorrect because they would place the sentence before CAPTCHA has been fully explained. Choice D is correct because sentence 5 uses *initially* to set up a contrast that the new sentence will address.

CHAPTER 20

# Sentence Revision

In this chapter, students will review and apply a prescribed set of steps that can be used to answer writing-focused questions called Sentence Revision.

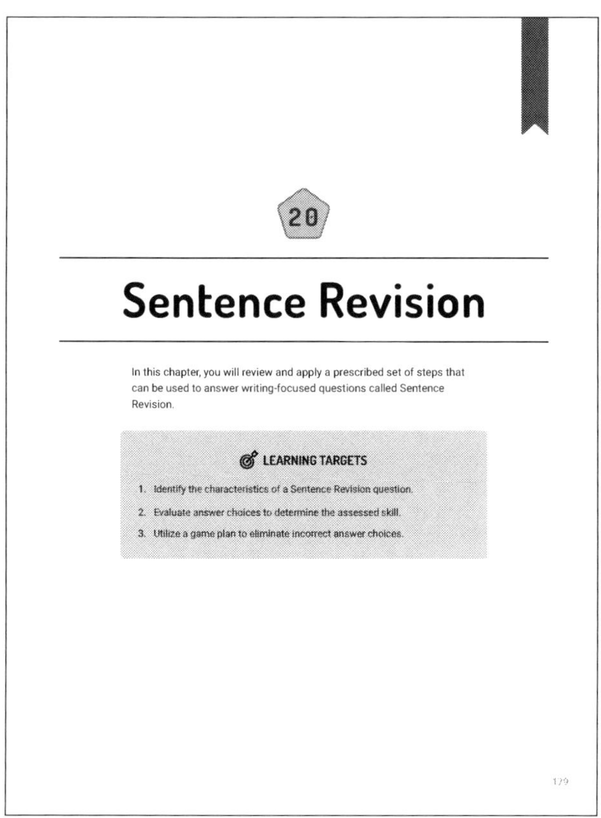

20

Sentence Revision

In this chapter, you will review and apply a prescribed set of steps that can be used to answer writing-focused questions called Sentence Revision.

LEARNING TARGETS

1. Identify the characteristics of a Sentence Revision question.
2. Evaluate answer choices to determine the assessed skill.
3. Utilize a game plan to eliminate incorrect answer choices.

179

## TSIA2 STANDARDS

**Sentence Revision, Editing, and Completion**

The student will edit and complete sentences as necessary to ensure conformity to the conventions of standard written English grammar, usage, punctuation, and (Diagnostic only) spelling and capitalization as well as make effective decisions regarding purpose and organization (Diagnostic only) and sentence combining (Diagnostic only).

## TEKS ALIGNMENT

E1.9 *Composition*: listening, speaking, reading, writing, and thinking using multiple texts—writing process. The student uses the writing process recursively to compose multiple texts that are legible and use appropriate conventions. The student is expected to:

(D) edit drafts using standard English conventions, including:

(i) a variety of complete, controlled sentences and avoidance of unintentional splices, run-ons, and fragments;

(ii) consistent appropriate use of verb tense and active and passive voice;

(iii) pronoun-antecedent agreement;

(v) punctuation, including commas, semicolons, colons, and dashes to set off phrases and clauses as appropriate.

## LEARNING TARGETS

1. Identify the characteristics of a Sentence Revision question.
2. Evaluate answer choices to determine the assessed skill.
3. Utilize a game plan to eliminate incorrect answer choices.

## Groundwork

EXERCISE A

### Instructions

Review the following question as your teacher leads the discussion. Do not answer the question.

*Select the best version of the underlined part of the sentence. If you think the original sentence is best, choose the first answer.*

1. To enter the tournament, the student or <u>teacher have to</u> pay $10, and all of the proceeds go to help build a new greenhouse.

   (A) teacher have to
   (B) teacher has to
   (C) teacher must have to
   (D) teacher had to

# Groundwork

***In this section, students will analyze the structure and style of a sentence revision question.***

EXERCISE A | SLIDE 180.1

**When it comes to the TSIA2, sentence revision questions are puny. The little guys. The small fries. But that doesn't mean they can't pack a big punch on your score. Why do you think that is?**

They make up the biggest portion of the ELAR test.

**Sentence revision questions run from question 20 to question 30, meaning they make up one-third of the ELAR test. In that way, Sentence Revision questions are huge. So, what do I mean when I say they're the little guys?**

They have the smallest amount of text.

**These questions are usually made up of just one single sentence—at most two. Why is that appealing to us as test takers?**

There isn't a lot of reading to bog us down.

**On the flip side, though, we don't have much to work with, so we'll have to pay closer attention to the details.**

SLIDE 180.2

**For instance, let's look at question 1 in your workbook. Don't worry about the answers just yet, though. We only want to focus on the question's structure and style for now. What three things does the test give us?**

Instructions, a sentence with an underlined portion, and four answer choices.

**And how can we tell that this is a sentence revision question?**

It's just one sentence long.

**It's a little guy, so we know we're working with sentence revision. What about the instructions? What does the test say to do?**

*Select the best version of the underlined part of the sentence. If you think the original sentence is best, choose the first answer.*

**What do they mean by the *best version*?**

The correct version.

**How will you be able to tell what's correct, though?**

You'll have to find clues in the question and answer choices.

**Sentence revision questions don't just test you on one skill, though, do they?**

No, they test you on all kinds of writing topics.

**That means just figuring out what the question is testing you on is a challenge all on its own. But don't worry. Despite the range of possibilities, we have a game plan that can help you take on anything.**

TSIA2 Mastery: ELAR 

EXERCISE B

**Instructions**

Review the basic steps for answering a sentence revision question. Put them into the correct sequence by filling in numbers 1–4 in the space provided.

__________ If the sentence sounds wrong, cross off choice A and any choices that repeat the problem.

__________ Use the process of elimination.

__________ Read the sentence.

__________ Compare the remaining answer choices.

## Groundwork

*In this section, students will sequence the steps for a basic strategy that can be used to answer any sentence revision question on the TSIA2.*

EXERCISE B SLIDE 181.1

**Okay, so maybe I could be a super nice teacher and just *tell* you all the details of our game plan, but that takes away the fun. Let's see if you can puzzle it out. Here are the four steps we'll use when we take on every Sentence Revision question the TSIA2 throws at us. What should you do first?**

Read the sentence.

**Why not jump to the answer choices first?**

There's no question, so the clues for what we need to find will be in the sentence.

**Unlike reading questions, Sentence Revision questions won't just come out and ask you for something specific. Instead, it'll be a little like editing an essay. By reading the sentence first, you'll likely notice that something sounds a little off. If that sentence *does* seem like it's got an error, what should you do next?**

*Cross off choice A.*

**How can we use what we learned about choice A and its mistake to help us?**

We can also eliminate any other choices that repeat the problem.

**Think of it like a two-for-one. If you know one answer choice is wrong and there's another one that makes the same error, you can eliminate both choices. What's our next step?**

Compare the remaining answer choices.

**What are you looking for?**

The ways that they're different.

**The differences between answer choices will be the key. A lot of times, answer choices will offer up similar words, punctuation, or other writing elements. If the remaining choices all have the same verb, what does that tell you?**

The verb has to be correct, so there's another kind of mistake happening.

**We can basically stop worrying about verb tense or subject-verb agreement or whatever. Instead, we need to look for the difference between the choices. Something meaningful, like different punctuation or extra words. Why is that a good strategy?**

One of the different elements will be a mistake.

**What you're talking about is the process of elimination, which happens to be our next step in the process. Why do you think it's better to look for answers with mistakes anyway?**

It's easier to find mistakes than to prove something is correct.

**In every set of answer choices, you've got three-to-one odds that an answer is wrong. Plus, wrong answers tend to stick out more. It's easier to spot an error and eliminate it than it is to pick out the perfectly right one. So we've got our game plan. Now, let's put it into action!**

# Application

## THE APPROACH

When answering a sentence revision question on the TSIA2, use these steps ...

1. Read the sentence.
2. If it sounds wrong, cross off choice A and any choices that repeat the problem.
3. Compare the remaining choices.
4. Use the process of elimination.

**1.** To enter the tournament, the student or <u>teacher have to</u> pay $10, and all of the proceeds go to help build a new greenhouse.

Ⓐ teacher have to
Ⓑ teacher has to
Ⓒ teacher must have to
Ⓓ teacher had to

# Application

*In this section, students will practice applying a basic strategy to a sentence revision question.*

SLIDE 182.1

**Let's come back to the question we saw at the beginning of this lesson. Remind me: how can we tell that it's a sentence revision question?**

There's just one sentence.

**What should our first step always be?**

Read the sentence.

**Who'd like to read it for us?**

*To enter the tournament, the student or teacher have to pay $10, and all of the proceeds go to help build a new greenhouse.*

**Okay. The sentence has been read. What now?**

Figure out if it sounds okay.

**Does it?**

Not really.

**Why not?**

*Have* doesn't match the subject, *student or teacher*.

**So, what should we do?**

Cross off the first answer.

**Choice A is out. Do any others make that same mistake?**

Choice C.

**Two-for-one! What's our next step?**

Compare the rest of the answer choices.

**How are choices B and D different?**

Choice B uses *has*, and choice D uses *had*.

**Both of our remaining options match up with the singular subject, so that won't help us make any eliminations. Do we see another mistake happening?**

Choice D is in past tense, but the sentence is in present tense.

**Verbs can match in two different ways: by matching the subject and by matching the tense. In this instance, choices A and C don't match the subject, and choice D doesn't match the tense. We've narrowed our options down to just one. Which answer is correct?**

Choice B.

**This is why using the process of elimination is so helpful. We slowly pick off all the wrong answers until we're left with just one. And, since the TSIA2 is untimed, we know we have plenty of time to do this with each question.**

## THE APPROACH

When answering a sentence revision question on the TSIA2, use these steps ...

1. Read the sentence.
2. If it sounds wrong, cross off choice A and any choices that repeat the problem.
3. Compare the remaining choices.
4. Use the process of elimination.

2. Many people think it to be a myth or a hoax, some truly believe they have seen it.

Ⓐ Many people
Ⓑ Although many people
Ⓒ Groups
Ⓓ Research shows we

## Application

***In this section, students will continue their practice utilizing the steps of the Approach to a sentence revision question.***

SLIDE 183.1

**Let's take on another example. It's just one sentence in the passage, so what kind of question is it?**

Sentence revision.

**What's our first step?**

*Read the sentence.*

**Who'd like to read that for us?**

*Many people think it to be a myth or a hoax, some truly believe they have seen it.*

**Does it seem correct?**

No.

**What's going wrong?**

It's two complete sentences joined by just a comma.

**What should we do then?**

Cross off choice A and any choices that repeat the problem.

**Do you see any more than create a comma splice?**

Choices C and D.

**Choices A, C, and D all create that comma splice error, so we can eliminate them. What are we left with?**

Choice B.

**Only one choice left means we can basically skip the rest of the process. See what I mean when I say it's better to look for wrong answers? That said, let's go ahead and check out choice B, just to make sure we got the right one. What does choice B have that the others don't?**

It has the word *although* to help connect the ideas.

**That connecting word makes all the difference, and it means that choice B is the correct answer. And while you can't guarantee what skill you'll be tested on, you *can* guarantee that the steps to our game plan will help you out every time. Remember to start with the sentence, evaluate the differences between answer choices, and focus on eliminating wrong answers.**

## Practice

**Instructions**

Complete the practice set. If time remains after you've finished, double-check your work.

**1.** With the advancement of identity theft, and some unsuspecting customers being in very real danger.

Ⓐ With the advancement of identity theft, and some unsuspecting customers being
Ⓑ With the advancement of identity theft, some unsuspecting customers are
Ⓒ With identity theft being how it is, some unsuspecting customers being
Ⓓ Identity theft being how it is, thus some unsuspecting customers being

**2.** He can grow his own food, and he knows which kinds of wild berries and plants are safe to eat.

Ⓐ are
Ⓑ is
Ⓒ being
Ⓓ that is

**3.** Seahorses eat with the use of their snouts to suck up plankton or crustaceans, and they use their tails to hook onto seagrass or coral.

Ⓐ with the use of
Ⓑ in using
Ⓒ by using
Ⓓ for use of

# Practice

SLIDE 184.1

*Give students 8 minutes to complete the practice set.*

SLIDE 184.2

1. **The correct answer is B.** The phrase *with the advancement of identity theft* is a prepositional phrase, so it should be joined to an independent clause with a comma only. The independent clause requires the verb *are* to be a complete sentence, making choice B correct. Choice A is incorrect because it uses the participle *being*, which creates a sentence fragment and incorrectly joins a prepositional phrase with a comma and a conjunction. Choices C and D are incorrect because they also use the participle *being* instead of a verb.

SLIDE 184.3

2. **The correct answer is A.** The sentence correctly uses the plural verb *are* to agree with the plural subject *kinds*, so choice A is correct. Choices B and D are incorrect because they use the singular form *is*. Choice C is incorrect because *being* is a participle and therefore does not function as a verb, which is needed to complete the independent clause.

SLIDE 184.4

3. **The correct answer is C.** *With* is somewhat awkward and does not communicate what the author is saying as clearly, so choice A is incorrect. Choice B is incorrect because saying the seahorses eat *in using* their snouts is not idiomatic. Choice D is incorrect because it confuses the intended meaning of the sentence. Choice C is correct because the preposition *by* tells the reader that the following information in the sentence will show how the seahorses eat.

CHAPTER 21

# Subject-Verb Agreement

In this chapter, students will determine whether and where commas are needed to set off or separate adjectives and parenthetical elements in sentences.

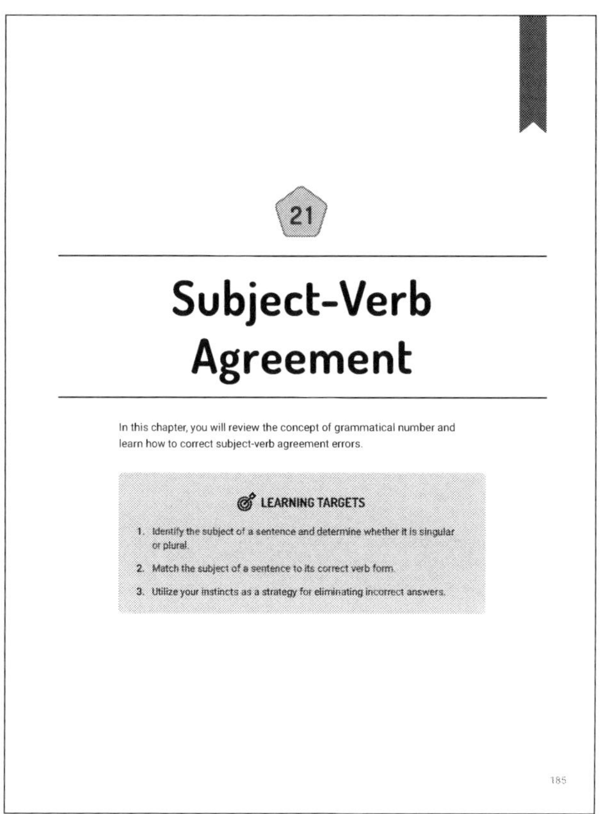

21

Subject-Verb Agreement

In this chapter, you will review the concept of grammatical number and learn how to correct subject-verb agreement errors.

LEARNING TARGETS

1. Identify the subject of a sentence and determine whether it is singular or plural.
2. Match the subject of a sentence to its correct verb form.
3. Utilize your instincts as a strategy for eliminating incorrect answers.

185

## TSIA2 STANDARDS

**Essay Revision and Editing**
Standard English conventions

The student will edit text as necessary to ensure conformity to the conventions of standard written English grammar, usage, and punctuation.

**Sentence Revision, Editing, and Completion**
Conventions of grammar

The student will edit and complete sentences as necessary to ensure conformity to the conventions of standard written English grammar.

## TEKS ALIGNMENT

E1.9 *Composition*: listening, speaking, reading, writing, and thinking using multiple texts—writing process. The student will use the writing process recursively to compose texts that are legible and uses appropriate conventions. The student is expected to:

(D) edit drafts using standard English conventions, including;

(ii) consistent, appropriate use of verb tense and active and passive voice.

## LEARNING TARGETS

1. Identify the subject of a sentence and determine whether it is singular or plural.
2. Match the subject of a sentence to its correct verb form.
3. Utilize your instincts as a strategy for eliminating incorrect answers.

## Warm-Up

**Instructions**

Complete the warm-up question. If time remains after you've finished, double-check your work.

**1.** White Sands, in New Mexico, <u>are</u> the largest dune field in the United States.

Ⓐ are

Ⓑ they are

Ⓒ being

Ⓓ is

## Warm-Up

SLIDE 186.1

*Give students 2 minutes to complete the warm-up question.*

SLIDE 186.2

1. **The correct answer is D.** Choices A and B are incorrect because the plural verb *are* does not agree with the singular subject *White Sands*—it is a place and, therefore, a singular noun. Choice C is incorrect because it fails to provide the sentence with a complete verb, resulting in a sentence fragment. Choice D is correct because the singular verb *is* agrees with the singular subject *White Sands*.

TSIA2 Mastery: ELAR 

## Groundwork

EXERCISE A

### Instructions

Refer to the following phrases as your teacher leads the discussion.

1. _____ The ballerinas

2. _____ The lion

Write an "S" next to the singular nouns. Write a "P" next to the plural nouns.

3. _____ One of the ice cubes
4. _____ The scientists working for NASA
5. _____ The audience at the concert

# Groundwork

*In this section, students will review the process for identifying the subject and main verb of a sentence.*

EXERCISE A | SLIDE 187.1

**According to the big-time grammar laws of English, subjects and verbs should always *agree*. But, that sounds odd, right? It's not like they're picking a place for dinner. When we say subject-verb agreement, we're not talking about them getting along—it's about subjects and verbs matching each other grammatically. Before we get into that, can someone remind me what a subject is?**

It's the main noun in the sentence, or the thing doing the action.

**A subject is a noun—so, a person, a place, or a thing—that's doing the main action in the sentence. Subjects can be either singular or plural. What does it mean if a subject is singular?**

There's only one.

**And what if it's plural?**

There's more than one.

**If we look at the first two phrases—*the ballerinas* and *the lion*—which one is singular?**

*The lion.*

**What about *the ballerinas?* Singular or plural?**

Plural.

**How do you know it's plural? What letter tells you there are multiple people involved?**

The *-s* at the end.

**Most plural nouns in English end in *-s*. It's a quick and easy way to identify them.**

SLIDE 187.2

**Try the rest of the exercise yourself; we'll compare answers in a minute.**

*Give students 90 seconds to complete the activity.*

**What do we think about number 3? Is *one of the ice cubes* singular or plural?**

Note: Students may respond with either.

**Here's where subjects can get tricky. We want to pick out a single word that represents the subject. In this case, is the subject *one* or is the subject *ice cubes*?**

It's *one*.

**Only *one* of the ice cubes is doing something in this sentence, so that's our subject. Which makes it singular or plural?**

Singular.

**The subject for number 4 is *scientists*, right? We see that *-s* at the end. What kind of noun is it?**

Plural.

**How about the last one? What's the subject here?**

*Audience.*

**Singular or plural?**

Singular.

***Audience* is singular, which is kind of tricky. An audience can have thousands of people in it, so we might be tempted to think of it as plural. But in this case, the audience is one big singular group where everybody's cheering in unison.**

EXERCISE B

**Instructions**
Refer to the following sentences as your teacher leads the discussion.

6. The ballerinas ( dances / dance ).
7. The lion ( roars / roar ).

Circle the verb that matches the subject in number.

8. One of the ice cubes ( melts / melt ).
9. The scientists working for NASA ( has / have ) degrees in engineering.
10. The audience at the concert ( cheers / cheer ).

## Groundwork

*In this section, students will review the process for identifying the subject and main verb of a sentence.*

EXERCISE B SLIDE 188.1

**Figuring out what the subject is and whether it's singular or plural is half the battle when it comes to subject-verb agreement. The second half is all about matching it to the verb. We basically need each verb to agree with the subject in *number*—meaning, if a subject is singular, what should the verb be?**

Singular.

**What if the subject is plural?**

The verb should be plural too.

**When it comes down to it, subject-verb agreement is just making sure that the subject and the verb match in *number*. Take a look at number 6. What's your gut instinct here? Does *the ballerinas dances* or *the ballerinas dance* sound better?**

*The ballerinas dance.*

***Dance* is a plural verb. It matches our plural subject, *the ballerinas*. But how do we know it's a plural verb? What letter did we use to identify plural nouns?**

-*s*.

**Verbs also use -*s*, but they follow the opposite pattern. For the most part, <u>singular</u> verbs in the present tense end in -*s*, and plural verbs end in anything else. This balances the sentence, so that only the subject *or* the verb ends in an -*s*. Never both. What about number 7? Is our subject singular or plural?**

Singular.

**There's only one lion, so that's definitely singular. Which verb do we want?**

*Roars.*

***The lion roars* sounds great. The verb ends in an -*s*, which means the subject doesn't need to.**

SLIDE 188.2

**Take a moment to work through the rest of these and see if you can pick out the verb that best agrees with the subject.**

*Give students 90 seconds to complete the activity.*

**Let's start back up with number 8. Which verb is correct?**

*Melts.*

**We don't want to get distracted by other nouns—we don't care about *ice cubes*. We only care about the subject, which is *one*. *One melts*: a singular subject and singular verb. What about number 9? Which verb best fits there?**

*Have.*

**This time, *scientists* has the -*s*, making it plural. The verb doesn't need an -*s*, so *scientists have* is correct. This also works with *is* and *are*. Notice that, even though verbs like that are spelled differently, we still see that -*s* there for singular verbs. Looking at number 10, is *audience* singular or plural?**

*Singular.*

**Which verb is also singular?**

*Cheers.*

***The audience cheers* is our final answer.**

TSIA2 Mastery: ELAR 

EXERCISE C

**Instructions**
Refer to the following sentence as your teacher leads the discussion.

The artists on the bench in the park paints portraits of the people around them.

**11.** Write the subject and verb by themselves: ______________ ______________

**12.** Write the new, corrected subject and verb: ______________ ______________

## Groundwork

*In this section, students will review the process for correcting a subject-verb disagreement.*

EXERCISE C SLIDE 189.1

**Let's see if we can apply this concept to something a little more ... complicated. This sentence in your workbook has a subject-verb disagreement that we need to fix. We'll start simple, though. What's the verb in this sentence?**

*Paints.*

**What's the subject of the sentence? Who's doing the painting?**

*Artists.*

**Let me ask a trickier question: why isn't *the park* the subject? It's a noun, too, right?**

But *the park* isn't doing the painting.

**Even though *the park* is a noun, and it sits near the verb, it's not what's doing the main action. We only care about the subject and verb. If we remove all the other words in the sentence, besides the subject and verb, what are we left with?**

*Artists paints.*

**How does that phrase sound to you?**

Not good.

**Why not?**

There are too many -s sounds, so it doesn't sound natural.

**When you read a subject and verb back-to-back, the extra -*s* sound becomes much more apparent than when they're separated by lots of words. It's almost like they're fighting against each other, which is why it sounds unnatural to us. Is the subject singular or plural?**

Plural.

**The -*s* on *artists* gives it away. What about the verb, *paints*?**

It's singular.

**The subject and verb don't match. To fix this, technically we could change the subject or the verb, but the subject's pretty hard to change. If five artists are sitting in the park, we can't ask four of them to leave just to fix our sentence. Let's lock in our plural subject. What should we do with the verb?**

Make it plural.

**What should we change *paints* to?**

*Paint.*

**We drop that extra -*s* to make it a plural verb. What's our subject and verb pair now?**

*Artists paint.*

**Sounds much better, right? Remember, if the subject and verb of a sentence both end in -*s*, you're probably looking at a subject-verb error.**

# Application

## THE APPROACH

When you are asked to correct a subject-verb agreement error, use the following steps ...

1. Match the underlined verb to its subject.
2. Cross out everything between the subject and verb.
3. Choose the verb that matches the subject in number.

**Instructions**
Refer to the following question as your teacher leads the discussion.

**13.** According to the meteorologist on our local news station, the storm that started east of the mountains represent a threat.

Ⓐ represent
Ⓑ represents
Ⓒ representing
Ⓓ it represented

# Application

*In this section, students will practice applying the steps of the Approach to a subject-verb agreement question.*

SLIDE 190.1

**We have answer choices now—very fancy. But the process of solving the problem remains the same. What do we need to find first?**

The subject.

**Which is?**

*The storm.*

**What's the storm doing? What's our main verb?**

*Represent.*

**Remember that verbs don't always have to be concrete actions, like *kicking* or *shouting*. *Represent* is our verb here. If we cross out all the words in between our subject and verb, what are we left with?**

*The storm represent.*

**And how does that sound?**

Not good. It's missing an -s somewhere.

**To fix this, we need to pick the verb that matches the subject from our answer choices. Is the subject singular or plural?**

Singular.

**Just one *storm*, so it's singular. What's the singular form of our verb?**

*Represents.*

***The storm represents* sounds great, so choice B is looking like the best option. But we have more answer choices than just *represent* and *represents*. What about choice C? *The storm representing the threat*... Why doesn't that work?**

It's not a complete sentence.

***Representing* is something called a verbal. Looks like a verb, but it definitely doesn't act like one. It leaves our sentence without a full verb, and without a full verb there, the sentence becomes a fragment. How about choice D? How is it different from the other answers?**

It's two words long instead of one, and it has an extra noun in it.

**Choice D adds another subject: *it*. But we already have our subject; we don't need another one. We can eliminate choice C and choice D because both of them break the sentence, making choice B correct. Try to eliminate sentence-breaking choices as soon as possible and focus on agreement between the subject and verb.**

## THE APPROACH

When you are asked to correct a subject-verb agreement error, use the following steps ...

1. Match the underlined verb to its subject.
2. Cross out everything between the subject and verb.
3. Choose the verb that matches the subject in number.

**Instructions**
Refer to the following question as your teacher leads the discussion.

**14.** Not one of the adults bustling around the kitchen and shouting orders are the host who actually planned the dinner party.

Ⓐ are
Ⓑ being
Ⓒ is
Ⓓ they are

## Application

*In this section, students will practice identifying common errors that can help them eliminate incorrect answer choices.*

SLIDE 191.1

**This time, guide *me* through the process. What should we find first?**

The subject.

**And what's the subject?**

*Not one of the adults*.

**If you had to pick out a single word to represent the subject, what would it be? Let's take a moment to puzzle it out. Is the sentence talking about all of the adults?**

No.

**Which of the adults is the sentence focused on?**

*Not one* of them.

**Sometimes the test likes to offer up a challenge with long, wordy subjects like *not one of the adults*. Always try to boil the subject down to a single word: in this case, *one*. What should we find next?**

The verb.

**The verb will always be underlined on the test, so that step's done for you. What's the verb?**

*Are*.

**What should we do next?**

Cross out the words in between the subject and verb.

**Which leaves us with what?**

*One are*.

**How does that sound to you?**

Weird.

**It's a pretty awkward phrase. And we can often rely on our "ear" to help us make eliminations. We know that *one are* sounds really wrong, so that means choice A is wrong. Let's check our other options. Is our subject—*one*—singular or plural?**

Singular.

**How should we change the verb so it matches the subject?**

Make it singular.

**So, the correct answer is what?**

Choice C: *is*.

**But tell me, why is choice B wrong?**

It makes the sentence into a fragment.

**Choice B doesn't have a full verb, so we can cross that off our list. What about choice D?**

Choice D is still plural, and it adds an extra subject (*they*), which doesn't match the real subject (*one*).

**The TSIA2 often uses *to be* verbs in these types of questions—small verbs like *are*, *is*, and *am*. You can use the same process on *to be* verbs as you do on regular verbs. The singular verb *is* still ends in an *-s*, and the plural verb *are* doesn't. And when all else fails, use your ear. If something sounds wrong, it probably is. Eliminate it and keep moving.**

## Practice

**Instructions**
Complete the practice set. If time remains after you've finished, double-check your work.

1. Yosemite Falls, in California, are the tallest waterfall in the United States.

   Ⓐ are
   Ⓑ they are
   Ⓒ being
   Ⓓ is

2. The class, in raincoats, were waiting to go outside for recess.

   Ⓐ were
   Ⓑ it was
   Ⓒ being
   Ⓓ was

3. Unlike their cousin the zebra, horses do not have striped coats but instead is taller with long manes and tails, shorter ears, curved backs, and strong, muscular legs.

   Ⓐ is
   Ⓑ they is
   Ⓒ are
   Ⓓ they are

# Practice

SLIDE 192.1

*Give students 5 minutes to complete the practice set.*

SLIDE 192.2

1. **The correct answer is D.** Choices A and B are incorrect because the plural verb *are* does not agree with the singular subject *Yosemite Falls*. Choice C is incorrect because the helping verb *being* creates a sentence fragment. Choice D is correct because the singular verb *is* agrees with the singular subject *Yosemite Falls*, creating a complete sentence.

SLIDE 192.3

2. **The correct answer is D.** Choice A is incorrect because the plural verb *were* does not match the singular subject *class*. Choice B is incorrect because *it* is redundant since there is already a subject: *class*. Choice C is incorrect because *being* is a helping verb and requires a second verb to create a complete sentence. Choice D is correct because the singular verb *was* agrees with the singular subject *class*.

SLIDE 192.4

3. **The correct answer is C.** Choices A and B are incorrect because the singular verb *is* does not agree with the plural subject *horses*. Choice D is incorrect because restating the subject *they* after *instead* creates a run-on sentence that requires punctuation. Choice C is correct because the plural verb *are* agrees with the plural subject *horses*.

TSIA2 Mastery: ELAR 

## Wrap-Up

**Instructions**

Complete the wrap-up question. If time remains after you've finished, double-check your work.

**2.** Unlike their cousin the moose, deer do not have broad antlers but instead is leaner, with narrow antlers and slender bodies, small snouts, light fur, and short, pointed ears.

Ⓐ is
Ⓑ they is
Ⓒ are
Ⓓ they are

## Wrap-Up

SLIDE 193.1

*Give students 2 minutes to complete the wrap-up question.*

SLIDE 193.2

2. **The correct answer is C.** Choices A and B are incorrect because the singular verb *is* does not agree with its plural subject *deer*. Choice D is incorrect because the pronoun *they* adds an unnecessary subject to the sentence. Choice C is correct because the plural verb *are* agrees with its plural subject *deer* (and matches the plural verb *do not have*).

This page is intentionally left blank.
Content resumes on the next page.

This page is intentionally left blank.
Teacher content resumes with the next chapter.

CHAPTER 22

# Verb Tense

In this chapter, students will review verb tenses and determine the appropriate verb tense in the context of sentences. Students will choose the best verb tense to edit sentences.

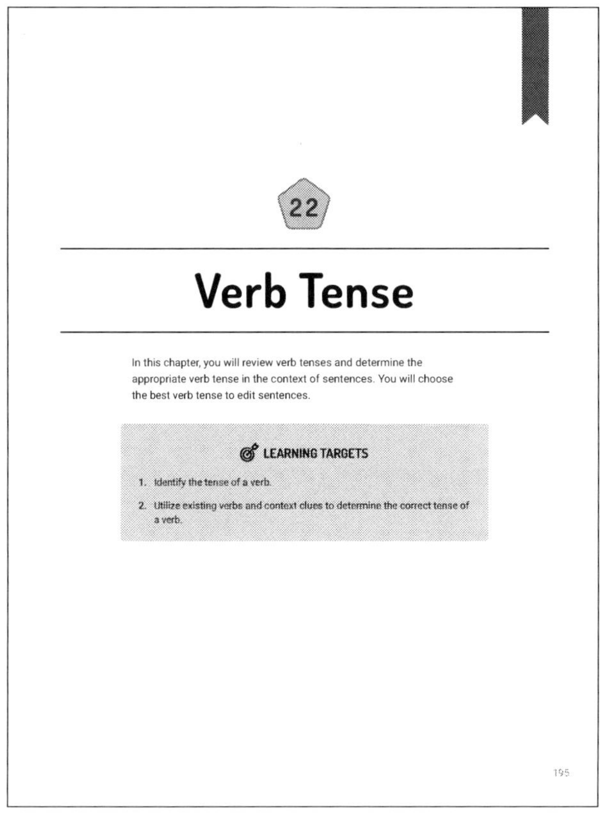

22

Verb Tense

In this chapter, you will review verb tenses and determine the appropriate verb tense in the context of sentences. You will choose the best verb tense to edit sentences.

LEARNING TARGETS

1. Identify the tense of a verb.
2. Utilize existing verbs and context clues to determine the correct tense of a verb.

195

## TSIA2 STANDARDS

**Essay Revision and Editing**
Standard English conventions

The student will edit text as necessary to ensure conformity to the conventions of standard written English grammar, usage, and punctuation.

**Sentence Revision, Editing, and Completion**
Conventions of grammar

The student will edit and complete sentences as necessary to ensure conformity to the conventions of standard English grammar.

## TEKS ALIGNMENT

E1.9 *Composition*: listening, speaking, reading, writing, and thinking using multiple texts—writing process. The student uses the writing process recursively to compose multiple texts that are legible and use appropriate conventions. The student is expected to:

(D) edit drafts using standard English conventions, including:

(ii) consistent, appropriate use of verb tense and active and passive voice.

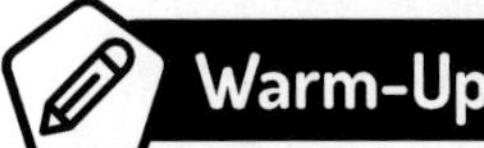

## Warm-Up

**Instructions**
Complete the warm-up question. If time remains after you've finished, double-check your work.

**1.** Most cellphones have short lifespans, becoming unusable once their operating systems or their parts were outdated.

Ⓐ were
Ⓑ will be
Ⓒ are
Ⓓ being

# Warm-Up

SLIDE 196.1

*Give students 2 minutes to complete the warm-up question.*

SLIDE 196.2

1. **The correct answer is C.** Choices A and B are incorrect because the past tense verb *were* and the future tense verb *will be* do not match the present tense verb *have* that appears earlier in the sentence, resulting in awkward shifts of tense. Choice D is incorrect because it fails to provide the dependent clause with a complete verb. Choice C is correct because the plural present verb *are* agrees with its plural subject *systems* and *parts* and matches the present tense verb *have* earlier in the sentence.

## Groundwork

**EXERCISE A**

**Instructions**
Highlight or underline the verb in each sentence. Circle the correct verb tense.

1. You will be on the right path to success.

   past present future

2. You were on the right path to success.

   past present future

3. You are on the right path to success.

   past present future

# Groundwork

*In this section, students will review the basic three verb tenses: past, present, and future.*

EXERCISE A SLIDE 197.1

**Let's talk psychics. While I can't say with absolute certainty that people who claim to be psychic have any actual mystical powers, I *can* say that some people make real money doing it. How do psychics make money?**

They tell people's fortunes.

**When a psychic tells your fortune, it's more than just what they're saying. It's also important to listen to the *verb tenses* they use. For instance, check out sentences 1 through 3. They're all the same fortunes, except for one thing. What's the difference?**

The verb tenses.

**These supposed fortunes are all really similar, with the exception of their verb tenses. But that little shade of difference creates a whole new meaning. For instance, look at sentence 1. What's the verb there?**

*Will be.*

**What does that verb tell us about the tense? Is it happening in the past, right now in the present, or sometime in the future?**

The future.

***Will be* is an example of a future tense verb. If this is our fortune, what does that mean for us?**

We're not on the right track, but we will be in the future.

**What about sentence 2? What's our verb?**

*Were.*

**What does that tell us about our travels on the *path to success?***

We used to be on that path in the past, but we aren't anymore.

***Were* is a past tense verb, meaning the action happened in the past. Go ahead and circle *past* on your page. And what about sentence 3? What verb are we working with?**

*Are.*

**What does *are* tell us about when we're travelling down the right path?**

We're on it right now.

**This is called present tense, meaning it's currently happening. Circle *present* under sentence 3. Now, the important question: if you went to a psychic, which one of these sentences would you want to hear?**

The one in the present, the last one.

**It's good to know that you are on the right path to success, in the present time. And after we complete this lesson today, you definitely *will* be on the right path to success when it comes to answering verb tense questions on the TSIA2.**

EXERCISE B

### Instructions

Fill in the blanks with an ongoing verb that best completes the sentence.

**PRESENT TENSE**

**4.** She **looks** into her crystal ball.

**PRESENT ONGOING TENSE**

**5.** At the moment, she **is looking** into her crystal ball.

**PAST ONGOING TENSE**

**6.** She __________________________ into her crystal ball while I waited patiently.

**FUTURE ONGOING TENSE**

**7.** When I go in for my appointment tomorrow, she __________________________ into her crystal ball.

## Groundwork

*In this section, students will evaluate verbs that have past, present, and future progressive tenses.*

EXERCISE B SLIDE 198.1

**Instead of focusing on the future, let's talk a little more about the past. Tell me: what's something you've spent *hours* doing?**

*Allow 2–3 students to share.*

**When we do something like that over an extended period of time, it's like the action crosses a boundary. It runs from one point in the past to another. It could even go from past, to present, to future. Let's look at some examples to help us better understand, starting with sentence 4. What's our verb there?**

*Looks.*

**What tense is it in?**

Present tense.

**Compare that to sentence 5. What's the verb in that sentence?**

*Is looking.*

**How does the meaning change from sentence 4 to sentence 5?**

In sentence 4, it seems like she looks for just a second, but in sentence 5, she's looking for a long time.

**The verb in sentence 5 is an ongoing, or progressive, verb. The fancy title doesn't matter much on the TSIA2, but you do need to know what the verb form tells you about the meaning of the sentence. Speaking of verbs, something a little weird happened here. How did the structure of the verb change in sentence 5?**

It includes *is* and changed *looks* to *looking.*

**What tense is the verb *is*?**

Present.

SLIDE 198.2

**That makes sense, given that it became a *present* ongoing verb. Those helping verbs are key to creating the tense. Let's practice by filling in sentences 6 and 7 with the right tense of our verb. How might we convert *looks* into a past ongoing verb to fill in sentence 6?**

Add *was* before it and swap -*s* with -*ing*.

**Plug that in. How does the sentence sound?**

*She was looking into her crystal ball while I waited patiently.*

**Notice that it has the effect we want on the sentence's meaning: the action of looking at the crystal ball is now ongoing. It's almost like, just while reading that sentence, you're waiting for all that time along with the narrator. What about future ongoing tense? How can we adjust the verb *looks* to fill in sentence 7?**

Add *will be* before it and swap -*s* with -*ing*.

**By adding *will be looking* to sentence 7, we make it clear that sometime in the future, she'll be looking into her crystal ball for an extended period of time. The TSIA2 won't let you just pick a verb tense, though. It will drop context clues into the sentence that *tell* you what tense you need.**

TSIA2 Mastery: ELAR 

EXERCISE C

**Instructions**
Use context clues to select the verb that best completes the sentence from the options below. Circle your answer.

**8.** My psychic predicted good things in my future, and since no one won the big jackpot yesterday, I now fully ________________ that I will hit the jackpot later this evening.

was expecting am expecting expect

## Groundwork

*In this section, students will practice using context clues to determine the correct verb tense.*

EXERCISE C

**When you run into verb tense questions on the TSIA2, it can be *super* tempting to just match the other verbs in the sentence. Why do you think that's not the best strategy to roll with on test day?**

There might not be any verbs in the sentence.

**A sentence could just have the bare minimum, meaning there aren't any verbs you can match up with. Even worse, the sentence might even change its tense midstream. Then, what? The potential to get stuck in a situation like that is why we go in with a better strategy: context clues. What is a context clue, exactly?**

A hint in the sentence.

**Think about it for a moment. What are some words that might provide context clues that something happened in the past tense?**

Yesterday, earlier, before, last week, a while ago, back then, etc.

**What about some context clues that hint at future tense?**

Tomorrow, later, next, etc.

**And what about context clues that would mean present tense?**

Now, today, currently, at the moment, etc.

**What about something more challenging? What are some context clues that would tell us we had an ongoing tense in the past, for example?**

Someone was doing something before something happened.

SLIDE 199.1

**This is trickier because you usually can't just point to a single word to know it's ongoing. You have to consider the overall meaning of the sentence. Let's try it out with sentence 8. We've got lots of verbs happening in there. What are they?**

*Predicted, won, will hit.*

**What tenses are they in?**

*Predicted* and *won* are past tense, and *will hit* is future tense.

**This mix of tenses is problematic, but it's not a deal breaker. What context clues do we see to help us out?**

*Now.*

**What tense does *now* tell us to use?**

Present.

**Based on that, what verb should we use to fill the blank?**

*Expect.*

**Why not *am expecting*?**

That's an ongoing verb tense, and there's no reason to add it.

**Deciding between our usual simpler tenses and ongoing tenses can get a little muddied sometimes. A good rule of thumb is to stick with the simplest verb tense that still makes sense in the sentence. And since the present tense works, we'll use *expect* to complete sentence 8. So, what do you think? Is it better to use other verbs in the sentence or context clues?**

Context clues.

**If we'd used the tenses of the other verbs in the sentence, we would've picked *anything but* the right answer. All because the context clues led us in the right direction.**

# Application

## THE APPROACH

When deciding which tense of a verb best completes a sentence, follow these steps ...

1. Find the other verbs in the sentence and identify their tense.
2. Test the verb that matches the existing verbs.
3. If there are no other verbs or if the verbs vary in tense, use context clues.

**9.** The psychic on the hotline told me my fortune last week, and I <u>am believing</u> everything she said; that was a big mistake.

(A) am believing
(B) have believed
(C) believed
(D) will believe

# Application

*In this section, students will practice applying the steps of the Approach to a verb tense question.*

SLIDE 200.1

**The TSIA2 offers up all its verb tense questions using same recipe, meaning they'll all look similar to the question 9 on your page here. What are some clues that will tell us it's a verb tense question?**

All the answer choices are verbs.

**Lots of verbs in the answer choices could mean verb tense, *but* it could also mean a subject-verb agreement question. How can we tell the difference? What tells us it's verb tense?**

It's the same verb, but they're all in different tenses.

**Let's dig into question 9. What verbs show up in the answer choices?**

Different tenses of *believe*.

**We know it's a verb tense question, so what's our first step?**

Find the other verbs in the sentence and identify their tense.

**What other verbs show up in this sentence?**

*Told* and *was*.

**What tense are these verbs?**

Past tense.

**Do any of the answer choices match?**

*Believed* in choice C.

**Who would like to read the sentence out loud using the verb *believed*?**

*The psychic on the hotline told me my fortune last week, and I <u>believed</u> everything she said; that was a big mistake.*

**Does this sound right?**

Yes, it makes sense and flows naturally.

**Choice B seems like it could work, too, though. But does it? What's wrong with *have believed*?**

It sounds really awkward when you plug it in.

**Even though *have believed* has a little past tense flavor to it, it breaks the natural flow of the sentence, so we know it's wrong. An answer that *sounds* wrong will always *be* wrong.**

TSIA2 Mastery: ELAR 

## THE APPROACH

When deciding which tense of a verb best completes a sentence, follow these steps ...

1. Find the other verbs in the sentence and identify their tense.
2. Test the verb that matches the existing verbs.
3. If there are no other verbs or if the verbs vary in tense, use context clues.

10. Prior to the 8th century B.C., the *Pythia* was one of the most famous oracles of the time, delivering prophecies from the god Apollo.

Ⓐ was
Ⓑ being
Ⓒ have been
Ⓓ will be

## Application

*In this section, students will work through a more challenging verb tense question using the steps of the Approach.*

SLIDE 201.1

**Let's dig into a question with a little more meat to it. Where do we start?**

By finding the other verbs and figuring out what tense they are.

**Do you see any other verbs besides what's underlined?**

*Delivering.*

**The *-ing* may remind you of something we talked about earlier. Can anyone remember what those verbs were called?**

Ongoing verbs.

***Delivering* has that *-ing* ending, so it feels very present tense. However, it's not actually a verb. It's something called a verbal, which is basically a word that looks like a verb but doesn't act like a verb. It can also really trip us up if we just play the match game. Which other answer choice looks most similar to *delivering*?**

*Being* in choice B.

**Let's take a test run. What does the sentence sound like if we drop *being* into the underlined section?**

*Prior to the 8th century B.C., the Pythia being one of the most famous oracles of the time, delivering prophecies from the god Apollo.*

**Does that sound okay?**

Not at all.

***Being* is another example of a verbal, which is why it sounds so weird in the sentence. What's our next option if we can't match existing verbs?**

Look for context clues.

**What clues from the sentence can help us figure out the tense?**

*Prior to the 8th century.*

**When you think of something happening *prior to the 8th century*, what tense comes to mind?**

Past.

**What past tense verb shows up in our answer choices?**

*Was.*

**Test that verb in the sentence. Does it sound okay?**

Yes.

**That means choice A is the right answer. And while we don't need to be able to predict the future to know that these kinds of questions will definitely show up on the TSIA2, we can't say exactly which option from the Approach you'll use to find the right answer. Start with testing the option that matches the tense of the sentence, and if it sounds wrong, eliminate it and start hunting for context clues. No crystal ball needed.**

## Practice

**Instructions**
Complete the practice set. If time remains after you've finished, double-check your work.

**1.** Most sloths are lazy, becoming active only when their lives or their cubs were threatened.

Ⓐ were
Ⓑ will be
Ⓒ are
Ⓓ being

**2.** By the early 2000s, the World Wide Web had connected once-isolated rural towns with urban city centers.

Ⓐ had connected
Ⓑ had been connecting
Ⓒ is connecting
Ⓓ connected

**3.** By 2007, the world financial crisis had been throwing once-thriving countries into economic turmoil.

Ⓐ had been throwing
Ⓑ is throwing
Ⓒ had thrown
Ⓓ threw

# Practice

SLIDE 202.1

*Give students 8 minutes to complete the practice set.*

SLIDE 202.2

1. **The correct answer is C.** Choice A is incorrect because the past tense verb *were* does not agree with the present tense in the sentence. Choice B is incorrect because the future tense verb *will be* does not agree with the present tense of the sentence. Choice D is incorrect because the helping verb *being* results in an incomplete sentence. Choice C is correct because the present tense verb *are* agrees with the present tense of the sentence.

SLIDE 202.3

2. **The correct answer is A.** Choice B is incorrect because the tense in *had been connecting* suggests an ongoing action in the past, when it should be a completed action in the past. Choice C is incorrect because the present tense verb *is connecting* does not agree with the past tense in the sentence. Choice D is incorrect because the introductory phrase *by the early 2000s* requires a verb tense that points to a particular moment in the past. Choice A is correct because *had connected* agrees with the tense established by the introductory phrase and pinpoints the action to a particular moment in the past.

SLIDE 202.4

3. **The correct answer is C.** Choice A is incorrect because *had been throwing* suggests an ongoing action in the past, whereas the sentence describes a completed action in the past. Choice B is incorrect because the present tense verb *is throwing* does not agree with the past tense in the sentence. Choice D is incorrect because the introductory phrase *by 2007* describes a particular moment in the past, but the past tense verb *threw* describes a general, nonspecific action in the past. Choice C is correct because *had thrown* agrees with the tense established by the introductory phrase and points to a particular moment in the past (*by 2007*).

## Wrap-Up

**Instructions**
Complete the wrap-up question. If time remains after you've finished, double-check your work.

**2.** By the early 1990s, global capital is developing the once-industrial city into an international tech hub.

Ⓐ is developing
Ⓑ had been developing
Ⓒ developed
Ⓓ had developed

# Wrap-Up

SLIDE 203.1

*Give students 2 minutes to complete the wrap-up question.*

SLIDE 203.2

2. **The correct answer is D.** The context *by the early 1990s* suggests an action that happened prior to an event in the past. Choices A and B are incorrect because the tense of *developing* indicates that the action is ongoing in some way. Choice C is incorrect because the verb *developed* is simple past tense, which does not specifically indicate that the action happened prior to the specific point in time *by the early 1990s* mentioned in the sentence. Choice D is correct because *had developed* indicates that the action of global capital developing the city happened prior to a specific point in time from the past—*by the early 1990s*.

This page is intentionally left blank.
Content resumes on the next page.

This page is intentionally left blank.
Teacher content resumes with the next chapter.

CHAPTER 23

# Pronoun-Antecedent Agreement

In this chapter, students will recognize pronouns, identify antecedents, and ensure that they agree in gender, number, and person.

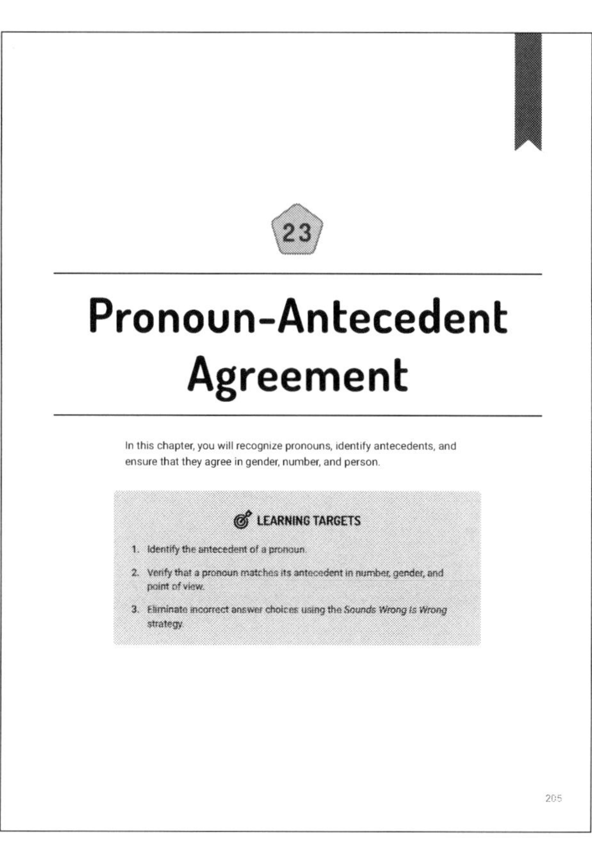

23

## Pronoun-Antecedent Agreement

In this chapter, you will recognize pronouns, identify antecedents, and ensure that they agree in gender, number, and person.

**LEARNING TARGETS**

1. Identify the antecedent of a pronoun.
2. Verify that a pronoun matches its antecedent in number, gender, and point of view.
3. Eliminate incorrect answer choices using the *Sounds Wrong Is Wrong* strategy.

205

## TSIA2 STANDARDS

**Essay Revision and Editing**
Standard English conventions

The student will edit text as necessary to ensure conformity to the conventions of standard written English grammar, usage, and punctuation.

**Sentence Revision, Editing, and Completion**
Conventions of grammar

The student will edit and complete sentences as necessary to ensure conformity to the conventions of standard English grammar.

## TEKS ALIGNMENT

E1.9 *Composition*: listening, speaking, reading, writing, and thinking using multiple texts—writing process. The student uses the writing process recursively to compose multiple texts that are legible and uses appropriate conventions. The student is expected to:

(D) edit drafts using standard English conventions including:

(iii) pronoun-antecedent agreement.

## Warm-Up

### Instructions

Complete the warm-up question. If time remains after you've finished, double-check your work.

### Passage

(1) Historians and anthropologists argue that the decline of the Catalan language dates back to the union of the Castile and Aragon crowns in the late 15th century. (2) However, as the monarchy sought to replace regional languages with Spanish, the territory that ultimately became Barcelona remained autonomous. (3) This helped preserve Catalan.

**1.** In context, which of the following best replaces "This" in sentence 3 (reproduced below)?

*This helped preserve Catalan.*

Ⓐ This independence
Ⓑ This region
Ⓒ This monarchy
Ⓓ This system

# Warm-Up

SLIDE 206.1

*Give students 2 minutes to complete the warm-up question.*

SLIDE 206.2

1. **The correct answer is A.** In the sentence, *this* is a vague pronoun, so it needs to restate the antecedent in order to clarify the information. Choice B is incorrect because it is illogical to state that *this region helped preserve Catalan*. Choice C is incorrect because the passage states that *the monarchy sought to replace regional languages with Spanish*, so it would not preserve Catalan. Choice D is incorrect because *this system* is too vague in context; it's unclear whether it refers to the monarchy, the political situation in general, or Barcelona and Catalan in particular. Choice A is correct because the passage states that *as the monarchy sought to replace regional languages with Spanish, the territory that ultimately became Barcelona remained autonomous*, meaning that *this independence* helped preserve Catalan.

## Groundwork

EXERCISE A

**Instructions**
Refer to the following passage as your teacher leads the discussion.

**Passage**
Years ago, I read a book called *The Giver* by Lois Lowry. The main character of the story, a 12-year-old boy named Jonas, lives in a strictly controlled futuristic society. Jonas lives in a house with Jonas's parents and little sister, Lily. Despite the advanced technology, Jonas rides Jonas's bike everywhere Jonas goes. Jonas is assigned a job which Jonas goes to every day. Jonas learns how Jonas's community works and that the community may not be as perfect as the community seems.

**1.** Draw a line to match each noun to the pronoun it could be replaced with.

| | |
|---|---|
| Jonas | he |
| Jonas's | it |
| The community | his |

**2.** Read the following sentence. Underline the two pronouns and circle their antecedent.

Jonas rides his bike everywhere he goes.

## Groundwork

*In this section, students will review the grammatical purpose of pronouns and practice identifying an antecedent.*

**EXERCISE A**

**Who can tell me what a *dystopian* story is about?**

An imagined future where things have become really awful.

**I can think of a dystopian future I'd hate to be a part of: one without pronouns. Check it out. Take a minute to read this passage about a boy living in one of these dystopian societies.**

**SLIDE 207.1**

*Give students 1 minute to read the passage.*

**What do you notice about the summary? Does anything seem weird about the way it is written?**

It repeats *Jonas* a bunch of times, and near the end, it repeats *the community.*

**In a world without pronouns, our language becomes *so* repetitive to the point where it's almost confusing. Instead, we use pronouns. What is a pronoun exactly?**

A word that replaces a noun.

**What are some examples of pronouns?**

She, he, they, it, we, etc.

**We can't just use any pronoun to replace a noun, though. For instance, could we replace the mentions of *Jonas* with the pronoun *we*?**

No.

**Why not?**

It doesn't match.

**SLIDE 207.2**

**Let's practice matching some nouns to the pronouns we'd use to replace them. Take a look at the activity on your page. What could we use to replace *Jonas*?**

*He.*

**What about *Jonas's*?**

*His.*

**And what about *the community*? What pronoun would we swap it with?**

*It.*

**SLIDE 207.3**

**What if we need to work backwards, though? Look at question 2. What two pronouns appear in that sentence?**

*His* and *he.*

**Underline those on your page. The question, now, is what's the antecedent? What noun do those pronouns replace?**

Jonas.

**Finding the pronoun and matching it to its antecedent is only half the battle. The real challenge comes in when we have to figure out whether or not they match.**

TSIA2 Mastery: ELAR

EXERCISE B

**Instructions**
Circle the pronoun that matches the antecedent in *number*.

3. I love burritos because ___________ never judge(s) me.

 it they

4. I love a good burrito because ___________ never judge(s) me.

 it they

**Instructions**
Circle the pronoun that matches the antecedent in *gender*.

5. A cupcake is a muffin that believes ___________ has witnessed a miracle.

 it he

6. Emilio told me ___________ believes cupcakes are miracle muffins.

 it he

**Instructions**
Circle the pronoun that best matches the antecedent in *point of view*.

7. Before, Eliza would just 'crastinate, but after a while, ___________ went pro.

 she you

8. If you are good at 'crastinating, eventually ___________ can go pro.

 it you

## Groundwork

***In this section, students will identify the best pronoun to match an existing antecedent in the provided example sentences.***

EXERCISE B SLIDE 208.1

**When we say "pronoun-antecedent agreement," what are we really talking about?**

The pronoun and the noun it replaces have to match.

**But match how? There's actually more than one way a pronoun matches its antecedent. For instance, look at question 3. We need to find a pronoun to fill that blank. What are our options?**

*It* and *they*.

**How are those pronouns different?**

*It* would replace just one, but *they* replaces more than one.

**What's our antecedent here? What noun are we trying to replace?**

*Burritos*.

**Is that just one or more than one?**

More than one.

**So which pronoun should we use?**

*They*.

**What about question 4? It's essentially the same information, but something is different about the antecedent. What changed?**

*Burritos* became *a good burrito*.

**We went from more than one burrito to just one. And that's our first way pronouns agree: in number. Which pronoun best fits the singular noun *a good burrito*?**

*It*.

SLIDE 208.2

**Pronouns also need to match based on gender. For instance, the antecedent in question 5 is *a cupcake*. Is that an *it* or a *he*?**

An *it*.

**How do you know?**

*It* means a thing, but *he* is used for male humans.

**What about question 6? What pronoun should we use in that sentence?**

*He*.

**How can you tell?**

The antecedent is a male named *Emilio*.

SLIDE 208.3

**Another way pronouns can match their antecedent is based on point of view. For instance, if the sentence is written from *my* point of view, I would say *I* and *me* and *we*. If the sentence is written from a third person point of view, I would say *they* and *them*. For instance, what point of view is question 7?**

Third person.

**How do you know?**

It talks about *Eliza*, not *me* or *you*.

**So which pronoun will fit that sentence?**

*She*.

**The next one is a little tougher. What pronoun is already being used in question 8?**

*You*.

***You* means we're looking at a second person point of view. Which of our options best fills the blank?**

*You*.

**It's a little like a checklist. You line up the pronoun with its antecedent to see if it matches in all three aspects. If so, you know you have the right choice.**

**TSIA2 Mastery:** ELAR 

# Application

## THE APPROACH

When you are challenged to find the pronoun that best agrees with an antecedent, follow these steps ...

1. Find the antecedent to the underlined pronoun.
2. Eliminate choices that do not match in number, gender, or point of view.

**9.** Watercolor paints, which are often created using a natural pigment, have a translucent appearance when they are painted onto a surface.

Ⓐ they
Ⓑ we
Ⓒ it
Ⓓ she

## Application

***In this section, students will practice applying the steps of the Approach to a pronoun-antecedent agreement question.***

SLIDE 209.1

**We've talked about identifying antecedents quite a bit so far, but how do we even know if that's what we're looking for during the test? What will pronoun-antecedent agreement questions look like on the TSIA2? The key is in the answer choices. Take a look at question 9. What do all the answer choices have in common?**

A pronoun.

**We've got a good variety of pronouns to choose from. How do we figure out which one is the *right* one?**

*Find the antecedent to the underlined pronoun.*

**Take a moment to read the sentence. What's the antecedent in this case?**

*Watercolor paints.*

**Once we've got our antecedent, what's next?**

*Eliminate choices that do not match in number, gender, or point of view.*

**It's usually easiest to start with agreement based on number. Is *watercolor paints* singular or plural?**

Plural.

**We're looking at more than one paint, so that means plural. Can we eliminate any answer choices based on that?**

Choice C.

***It* is a singular pronoun, so we know that can't be right. What about gender? Does *paint* have a gender?**

No.

**Which answer choice should we eliminate next?**

Choice D.

***She* means female, and paint has no gender. We're down to *they* and *we*. Both are plural and gender-neutral. Which one best fits the point of view of the sentence?**

*They.*

**How can you tell?**

The sentence isn't written by *paints*, so it can't be *we*.

## THE APPROACH

When you are challenged to find the pronoun that best agrees with an antecedent, follow these steps ...

1. Find the antecedent to the underlined pronoun.
2. Eliminate choices that do not match in number, gender, or point of view.

**10.** Many people who attend movies find it to be an enjoyable pastime.

- (A) it
- (B) they
- (C) them
- (D) him

## Application

*In this section, students will practice applying the Approach steps to a pronoun-antecedent question.*

SLIDE 210.1

**Come test day, the key will be finding that antecedent to help us figure out which pronoun is the best option. It's even possible for the antecedent to exist outside of the sentence in some kind of phantom reality zone. For example, check out question 10. Read the sentence and then focus in on the underlined section. What does *it* represent?**

Something that's an enjoyable pastime.

**What from the sentence is an enjoyable pastime?**

*Movies.*

**That could work, except *movies* aren't a pastime. *Watching* movies, *reviewing* movies, even *making* movies are all possible pastimes. How does that put a hiccup in our pronoun-antecedent matching game?**

The sentence doesn't say any of those things.

**And guess what? That's okay! We sometimes have to make a bit of an inference, or assumption, about the antecedent from the sentence. Instead of just acting like a robot and plugging random nouns into the sentence, ask yourself, "What's the enjoyable pastime in this sentence?"**

Attending movies.

**Plug that phrase in place of the pronoun. What does the sentence become?**

*Many people who attend movies find attending movies to be an enjoyable pastime.*

**Does that sound right?**

Yes, much better than just plugging in *movies*.

**That means *attending movies* is our antecedent. What pronoun could we use to replace *attending movies*?**

*It.*

**That means the correct answer is?**

Choice A.

**What if we'd gone with *movies* as the antecedent? What wrong answer might we have chosen?**

Choice C.

**You see what I mean about the antecedent being slippery sometimes? The good news is that *most* of the time the antecedent will be a noun in the sentence, but don't take the test on auto-pilot. Always check that you have the right antecedent before moving through the rest of the process, and then focus on finding the pronoun that agrees in number, gender, and point of view. If we're all in *agreement*, I think we're set to work on some practice questions.**

**TSIA2 Mastery:** ELAR 

# Practice

**Instructions**

Complete the practice set. If time remains after you've finished, double-check your work.

**1.** An octopus, which swims with its arms, can expel a jet of water from their body cavity when under threat.

Ⓐ their
Ⓑ his
Ⓒ one's
Ⓓ its

**2.** Damhsa, commonly known as Irish stepdance, is a style of dance in which individuals or groups of dancers, moving any part of your bodies except your arms, perform complicated foot movements and jumps.

Ⓐ any part of your bodies except your
Ⓑ your body, any part except those
Ⓒ their bodies, any part of them except
Ⓓ any part of their bodies except their

**3.** The children in the class showed one's interest in the presentation by asking the park ranger many questions about her job.

Ⓐ one's
Ⓑ their
Ⓒ its
Ⓓ our

# Practice

SLIDE 211.1

*Give students 8 minutes to complete the practice set.*

SLIDE 211.2

1. **The correct answer is D.** Choice A is incorrect because the plural pronoun *their* doesn't agree with the singular antecedent *an octopus*. Choice B is incorrect because it is less appropriate in this instance to assign the gender-specific pronoun *his* to *the octopus* because the sentence is referring to any octopus, male or female. Choice C is incorrect because the pronoun *one's* is meant for human antecedents. Choice D is correct because the singular pronoun *its* agrees with the singular antecedent *an octopus*.

SLIDE 211.3

2. **The correct answer is D.** Choices A and B are incorrect because the second person possessive pronoun *your* does not agree with the antecedent *dancers*. Choice C is incorrect because *their bodies, any part of them except* is confusing and unnecessarily wordy. Choice D is correct because the plural possessive pronoun *their* agrees with the antecedent *dancers* and logically indicates that the *bodies* and *arms* belong to them.

SLIDE 211.4

3. **The correct answer is B.** Choices A and C are incorrect because the singular possessive pronouns *one's* and *its* do not agree with the plural subject *children*. Choice D is incorrect because the first-person pronoun *our* does not match the point of view of the sentence, which is written in third person point of view. Only choice B logically connects the plural possessive pronoun *their* to the plural subject *children*.

## Wrap-Up

**Instructions**
Complete the wrap-up question. If time remains after you've finished, double-check your work.

2. Fan fiction, or "fanfic" for short, is a type of literature in which an admirer of a book, using any aspect of your story besides your exact plot, writes a new story and shares it online for free.

Ⓐ any aspect of your story besides your
Ⓑ your story, any aspect besides your
Ⓒ its story, any aspect besides
Ⓓ any aspect of its story besides its

# Wrap-Up

SLIDE 212.1

*Give students 2 minutes to complete the wrap-up question.*

SLIDE 212.2

2. **The correct answer is D.** Choices A and B are incorrect because the second person possessive pronoun *your* does not agree with the antecedent *book*. Choice C is incorrect because *its story, any aspect besides* is confusing and unnecessarily wordy. Choice D is correct because the singular possessive pronoun *its* agrees with the antecedent *book* and logically indicates that the *story* and *plot* belong to the book.

## CHAPTER 24

# Possessive Nouns

In this chapter, students will distinguish between possessive and non-possessive singular and plural nouns.

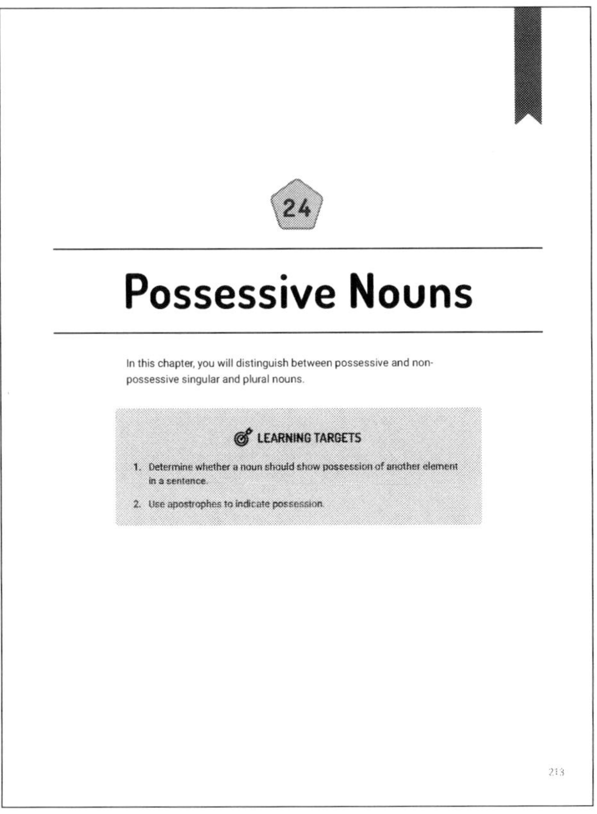

24

## Possessive Nouns

In this chapter, you will distinguish between possessive and non-possessive singular and plural nouns.

**LEARNING TARGETS**

1. Determine whether a noun should show possession of another element in a sentence.
2. Use apostrophes to indicate possession.

213

## TSIA2 STANDARDS

**Sentence Revision, Editing, and Completion**

Conventions of grammar

The student will edit and complete sentences as necessary to ensure conformity to the conventions of standard English grammar.

## TEKS ALIGNMENT

E1.9 *Composition*: listening, speaking, reading, writing, and thinking using multiple texts—writing process. The student uses the writing process recursively to compose multiple texts that are legible and use appropriate conventions. The student is expected to:

(D) edit drafts using standard English conventions, including:

(v) punctuation, including commas, semicolons, colons, and dashes to set off phrases and clauses as appropriate;

(vi) correct spelling.

## Warm-Up

**Instructions**

Complete the warm-up question. If time remains after you've finished, double-check your work.

1. Some such films aim to portray many Americans' ideal's from a specific era.

   Ⓐ Americans' ideal's
   Ⓑ American's ideal's
   Ⓒ Americans ideal's
   Ⓓ Americans' ideals

# Warm-Up

SLIDE 214.1

*Give students 2 minutes to complete the warm-up question.*

SLIDE 214.2

1. **The correct answer is D.** Choices A, B, and C are incorrect because none of them include both the plural possessive noun *Americans'* and the correct plural noun *ideals*. Choice D is correct because it correctly includes the plural possessive form of *Americans'* and the plural noun *ideals*.

TSIA2 Mastery: ELAR 

## Groundwork

EXERCISE A

**Instructions**
Work with your teacher to evaluate the following phrases.

| | Who is owning something? | Is the owner singular or plural? |
|---|---|---|
| **1.** the teacher's pencil | | |
| **2.** the students' pencils | | |
| **3.** the teachers down the hall | | |

# Groundwork

***In this section, students will review the basic rules of singular and plural possession.***

EXERCISE A

*Prepare a random pencil—yours, or a spare one from a supply closet.*

**Hey, whose pencil is this?**

*Allow students to guess about the owner of the pencil.*

**If we wanted to play detective, how could we try to figure out who owns this pencil?**

Ask people from a previous class, see if there's a name on it, ask more people, etc.

**We could ask every single student who stepped foot in my classroom today—but you know what would be a lot faster? If the pencil had its owner's name printed on it. Okay, that might be overkill for a little pencil, but the point is, ownership problems disappear when stuff is labeled clearly. When we're writing, we also want to be very clear about ownership. Based on your workbook, what punctuation mark do you think we use to show ownership?**

Apostrophe.

SLIDE 215.1

**When we talk about ownership in grammatical terms, we call it possession. One noun possesses another. In the first phrase, *the teacher's pencil*, what noun is possessing another?**

*Teacher.*

**What is the *teacher* possessing?**

The *pencil*.

**How many teachers do we have—one or many?**

Just one.

**That means we have a singular possessive noun. Go ahead and write that on your worksheet. What was added to *teacher* to make it show possession?**

An apostrophe and an *s*.

**When we have a singular possessive noun, we need to add an apostrophe and an *s* to show that it's owning something else. What about the second phrase? Does it have a possessive noun?**

Yes.

**Which one?**

*Students'.*

**How can you tell?**

The *students* own the *pencils*, and there is an apostrophe.

**Is this noun singular or plural?**

Plural.

**What was added to *students* to show possession?**

Just an apostrophe after the *s*.

**For possessive nouns, all we need to add is an apostrophe. And where you place that apostrophe will depend on whether the noun is singular or plural. What about the last phrase here?**

There's no possessive noun.

***Teachers* is a plain old plural noun, but it's not showing ownership. No apostrophe needed. But *teachers*, in this sentence, sounds awfully close to *teacher*-apostrophe-*s* in the first sentence, doesn't it? Pretty much identical. Unfortunately, that means we can't count on our ears to help us pick out problems, like we're able to do with so many other grammatical errors. The problem is all on the page.**

EXERCISE B

**Instructions**

Circle the subject of each sentence. Then, label the sentence based on whether the subject of the sentence contains a **possessive (PO)** or **plural (PL)** noun. If it's possessive, add an apostrophe in the appropriate location.

_________ **4.** A snails nap can last up to three years.

_________ **5.** Kangaroos are not able to walk backward.

_________ **6.** A dogs nose print is like a human's fingerprint; each nose print is unique to its owner.

_________ **7.** Zebras stripes act as a natural bug repellent.

_________ **8.** Elephants are one of the few mammalian species that cannot jump.

## Groundwork

*In this section, students will distinguish between possessive and non-possessive nouns.*

EXERCISE B SLIDE 216.1

**When you're testing a sentence's pieces to see if ownership crops up anywhere, the best place to start is the subject. From there, we can figure out if the subject contains a possessive noun or if it's just a plural noun. Can someone read the first sentence out loud?**

*A snails nap can last up to three years.*

**What's the subject here?**

*A snails nap.*

**Circle that phrase. Is one of the nouns possessing the other?**

*Snail* is possessing *nap*.

**And how many snails are we talking about—one or many?**

Just one.

**How can you tell?**

The *A* means just one snail.

**In that case, we have a singular possessive noun. Where should the apostrophe go?**

Before the *s*.

**Next, look at number 5. What's our subject, and is it possessive?**

*Kangaroos*. It's not possessive.

**How do you know?**

The word *kangaroos* is followed by *are*, which is a verb and not something the kangaroo can own.

**The *kangaroos* don't own anything in this sentence. Do we need to add an apostrophe?**

Nope.

**How about number 6? Do we have a possessive noun in the subject?**

Yes—*a dogs*.

**And is it singular or plural?**

Singular.

**If we have a singular possessive noun, where should we place the apostrophe?**

Before the *s*.

**Next, number 7. Do we have a possessive noun?**

Yes—*zebras*.

**What do the zebras own?**

Their *stripes*.

**Next, we need to figure out if it's singular or plural. Are we talking about one or many zebras?**

Many.

**If we have a plural possessive noun, where should the apostrophe go?**

Outside the *s*.

**How about number 8? Is there any possession happening there?**

There's no possessive noun.

**How do you know?**

*Elephants* is followed by a verb, not something that it owns.

**In that case, do we need an apostrophe?**

Nope.

**Do you notice any pattern that can help us figure out whether a noun owns something? What usually comes right after?**

The thing it owns will come right after.

**If the noun is followed by something other than what it owns, it's not possessive, meaning we won't need any apostrophes.**

**TSIA2 Mastery:** ELAR 

## Application

### THE APPROACH

When you are asked to correct a sentence with a possession error, use the following steps ...

1. Find the possessive noun, if there is one.
2. Determine whether the noun is singular or plural.
3. Eliminate choices that don't punctuate the possessive noun correctly.

**9.** Unfortunately for the nursing staff, the doctor and the anesthesiologist frequently disagreed about <u>patients treatments</u>.

Ⓐ patients treatments
Ⓑ patients' treatments
Ⓒ patients treatments'
Ⓓ patients' treatments'

# Application

*In this section, students will practice applying the steps of the Approach to a possessive nouns question.*

SLIDE 217.1

**Take a second to read the sentence to yourself—and the answer choices. What do you see that makes you think, ah, I bet this is a possessive nouns question?**

The answer choices have apostrophes in different places.

**Possessive nouns questions are pretty easy to identify because their answer choices will have *lots* of apostrophes. Once we know it's a possessive nouns question, what's our first step?**

*Find the possessive noun.*

**We have *patients* and *treatments*. Do the *patients* belong to the *treatments*, or the other way around?**

The *treatments* belong to the *patients*.

**Which makes *patients* our possessive noun. Is there just one patient, or more than one?**

More than one.

**Multiple patients, so our noun is plural. If we have a plural possessive noun, where should the apostrophe go?**

After the *s*.

**Which answer choices do NOT have an apostrophe after the *s* in *patients*?**

Choices A and C.

**Choices A and C don't punctuate *patients* correctly, so we know they can't be the right answer. Let's eliminate them. That leaves us with choices B and D. What's the difference between those two?**

Choice D has an apostrophe after *treatments* too.

**Does *treatments* need an apostrophe?**

No.

**Why not?**

It's not possessing anything.

**We can cross out choice D. Which answer is correct?**

Choice B.

**In formal writing, it's rare to see two possessive nouns in a row—never mind three or four. It makes people dizzy to try to listen to a story about "my mom's cousin's hairdresser's daughter's next-door-neighbor's dog," you know? If you see two or more possessive nouns, like in choice D, you should be very skeptical about that being the right answer.**

## THE APPROACH

When you are asked to correct a sentence with a possession error, use the following steps ...

1. Find the possessive noun, if there is one.
2. Determine whether the noun is singular or plural.
3. Eliminate choices that don't punctuate the possessive noun correctly.

**10.** After comparing their class' schedules, Tia and Casey realized that they wouldn't be able to eat lunch together this year.

- (A) class' schedules
- (B) class schedules'
- (C) class's schedules
- (D) class schedules

## Application

*In this section, students will eliminate answer choices that show unnecessary possession.*

SLIDE 218.1

**Can someone read the sentence in question 10 out loud?**

*After comparing their <u>class' schedules</u>, Tia and Casey realized that they wouldn't be able to eat lunch together this year.*

**What should we look for first?**

Which of the words is the possessive noun.

**So, which is it? Does the *class* own anything in this sentence?**

No.

***Class* is working as a description, not a possessive. The students are looking at *class* schedules, meaning they aren't *weekly* schedules or *official* schedules or any other kind of schedule. And what about the *schedules* themselves? Do they own anything?**

No.

**What does that tell us about this underlined section?**

Nothing's possessing anything.

**If that's the case, what kind of punctuation do we need?**

Nothing.

**No apostrophes needed. Which option should we pick?**

Choice D.

**Choice D is the only answer with no apostrophes. That's what we want. But let's double-check our work by looking at the rest of the sentence a little more closely. These *class schedules*, they must belong to somebody. Who do they belong to?**

Tia and Casey.

**What word tells us that the *schedules* belong to Tia and Casey?**

Their.

***Their schedules*, right? Does anybody happen to remember what type of speech *their* is? Or *they*?**

It's a pronoun.

***Their* is a plural pronoun. We've only been talking about possessive nouns so far, but pronouns can be possessive too. You can say that a pencil is his, or hers, or theirs. If *their* is a possessive, would we expect it to be followed by another possessive?**

No.

**Why not?**

The sentence gets confusing.

**The test almost never puts two possessive words in a row—whether they're nouns or pronouns. If you're unsure about your answer, try scouting around the underlined section. If the word before the underlined section is possessive, avoid any answer choices that put another possessive noun right after it.**

TSIA2 Mastery: ELAR 

## Practice

**Instructions**
Complete the practice set. If time remains after you've finished, double-check your work.

1. One of the farm's roosters crows all morning long, and it wakes us up.

Ⓐ One of the farm's roosters crows
Ⓑ One of the farms rooster's crows
Ⓒ One of the farm's rooster's crows
Ⓓ One of the farms roosters crows

2. So many stories begin to reveal many citizen's experience's from that time period.

Ⓐ citizen's experience's
Ⓑ citizens' experiences
Ⓒ citizens experience's
Ⓓ citizen's experiences

3. A howdunit always offers a clear picture of who the guilty party is but keeps the stories character's in the dark about how the killer did it.

Ⓐ stories character's
Ⓑ story's characters
Ⓒ stories' character's
Ⓓ stories' characters

# Practice

SLIDE 219.1

*Give students 8 minutes to complete the practice set.*

SLIDE 219.2

1. **The correct answer is A.** Choices B and C are incorrect because *crows* is the verb of the sentence, so making *rooster's* possessive with an apostrophe is incorrect. Choice D is incorrect because the rooster belongs to *the farm*, so *farm* needs an apostrophe. Choice A is correct because it appropriately places an apostrophe before the *s* to indicate that the rooster belongs to *the farm*.

SLIDE 219.3

2. **The correct answer is B.** Choices A and C are incorrect because the *experiences* are not possessive and, therefore, do not require an apostrophe. Choice D is incorrect because *many* indicates that *citizens* is a plural noun, so the apostrophe should not be placed before the *s*. Choice B is correct because it appropriately adds an apostrophe after the *s* to indicate that more than one citizen possesses the *experiences*.

SLIDE 219.4

3. **The correct answer is B.** Choices A, C, and D are incorrect because the context of the sentence indicates that the *story* is singular, and *stories* is a plural noun. Additionally, choices A and C incorrectly add an apostrophe to *character's*, and that noun does not show ownership over anything in the sentence. Choice B is correct because it appropriately places an apostrophe before the *s* in *story's* to indicate that the *characters* belong to the story.

## Wrap-Up

**Instructions**

Complete the wrap-up question. If time remains after you've finished, double-check your work.

**2.** A biopic often explores a new perspective on a well-known historical figure to keep the <u>films' viewers</u> engaged about a familiar subject.

Ⓐ films' viewers

Ⓑ film's viewers

Ⓒ film's viewers'

Ⓓ films viewers'

# Wrap-Up

SLIDE 220.1

*Give students 2 minutes to complete the wrap-up question.*

SLIDE 220.2

2. **The correct answer is B.** Choice A is incorrect because the plural possessive *films'* does not agree with the singular *biopic*. Choices C and D are incorrect because *viewers* shouldn't be possessive. Choice B is correct because it uses the singular possessive *film's* and does not make *viewers* possessive.

CHAPTER 25

# Transitions

In this chapter, students will learn how to use transition words and phrases to connect ideas within and between sentences.

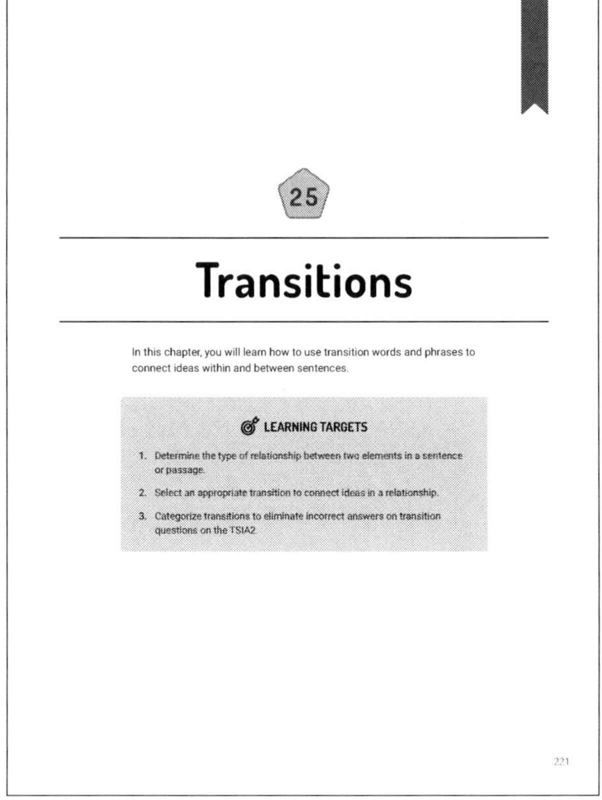

25

Transitions

In this chapter, you will learn how to use transition words and phrases to connect ideas within and between sentences.

LEARNING TARGETS

1. Determine the type of relationship between two elements in a sentence or passage.
2. Select an appropriate transition to connect ideas in a relationship.
3. Categorize transitions to eliminate incorrect answers on transition questions on the TSIA2.

221

## TSIA2 STANDARDS

**Sentence Revision, Editing, and Completion**
Conventions of usage

The student will edit and complete sentences as necessary to ensure conformity to the conventions of standard written English usage.

## TEKS ALIGNMENT

E1.9 *Composition*: listening, speaking, reading, writing, and thinking using multiple texts—writing process. The student uses the writing process recursively to compose multiple texts that are legible and uses appropriate conventions. The student is expected to:

(B) develop drafts into a focused, structured, and coherent piece of writing, in timed and open-ended situations by:

(i) using an organizing structure appropriate to purpose, audience, topic, and context.

## LEARNING TARGETS

1. Determine the type of relationship between two elements in a sentence or passage.
2. Select an appropriate transition to connect ideas in a relationship.
3. Categorize transitions to eliminate incorrect answers on transition questions on the TSIA2.

## Warm-Up

**Instructions**
Complete the warm-up question. If time remains after you've finished, double-check your work.

**1.** Casey had to buy some new footwear <u>with her shoes being</u> eaten by her dog.

Ⓐ with her shoes being
Ⓑ although her shoes were
Ⓒ whereas her shoes were
Ⓓ because her shoes had been

# Warm-Up

SLIDE 222.1

*Give students 2 minutes to complete the warm-up question.*

SLIDE 222.2

1. **The correct answer is D.** Choice A is incorrect because the preposition *with* and the participle *being* do not communicate the cause-effect relationship between Casey's shoes being eaten and her having to buy some new footwear. Choices B and C are incorrect because *although* and *whereas* both suggest that the two ideas presented in the sentence (that Casey needs to buy new footwear and that her shoes were eaten) contradict each other, which they don't. Choice D is correct because the conjunction *because* logically communicates the cause-effect relationship described in the sentence; Casey needs to buy new footwear *because* her shoes were eaten.

TSIA2 Mastery: ELAR 

## Groundwork

EXERCISE A

**Instructions**
Sort the transitions from the word bank into their correct categories.

| | | | | |
|---|---|---|---|---|
| although | specifically | in addition | as a result | to illustrate |
| in conclusion | first | on the other hand | similarly | in the end |
| in fact | however | consequently | for example | in essence |

**Transition Categories**

1. CONTRAST

______________________

______________________

______________________

2. ADDITION or EMPHASIS

______________________

______________________

______________________

3. CAUSE/EFFECT or SEQUENCE

______________________

______________________

______________________

4. ILLUSTRATION or SUPPORT

______________________

______________________

______________________

5. SUMMARY

______________________

______________________

______________________

# Groundwork

*In this section, students will sort transition words and phrases into categories.*

EXERCISE A

**Why did the chicken cross the *freeway*? Well, he used to cross the *road*, but he's going through a tough *transition*. Okay, that was a cheap pun, but it does *transition* to the topic of—transitions! What are they?**

Words or phrases that connect ideas.

**Transitions make connections between ideas to *get to the other side*. Just like the chicken! We have to be careful to pick just the right transition. Otherwise, our ideas will fall apart.**

SLIDE 223.1

**With so many transition options out there, it's easy to feel overwhelmed. How do you pick just the right one? Sorting them into categories makes our task a whole lot easier. What's the first category in your workbook?**

*Contrast.*

**What do you think the role of a contrast transition is?**

To show a difference.

**Looking at the word bank on the top of your page, can you see any transitions that show contrast?**

*Although, on the other hand,* and *however.*

**I was addicted to the hokey pokey. *However*, I was able to turn myself around. The transition word *however* helps signal to the reader that a twist is coming. What's our next transition category?**

*Addition or Emphasis.*

**These are used to add information or to stress a point. Which transitions in the box fit into this category?**

*In addition, similarly,* and *in fact.*

**It's hard to explain puns to a kleptomaniac. *In fact*, they're always taking things literally. When we use addition or emphasis transitions like *in fact*, we're able to build one idea onto the previous. What's the next transition category?**

*Cause/Effect or Sequence.*

**Which transitions belong in this category?**

*As a result, first,* and *consequently.*

**I accidentally handed my friend a glue stick instead of Chapstick. *Consequently*, they still aren't talking to me. We can use words like *consequently* to help show the reader that what follows happened because of what came before. What's the fourth transition category on our page?**

*Illustration or Support.*

**Illustration and support transitions help you zoom in on a specific example to make a point. Which ones fit here?**

*Specifically, to illustrate,* and *for example.*

**There are plenty of ways to keep your dreams alive. *For example*, hit that snooze button! *For example* helps us tell readers that we're about to give them something specific to prove an idea that came before. That leaves us with our last category: Summary. What do you think Summary transitions do?**

They transition into a section where you restate the main points, or wrap up your ideas.

**Which transitions from our word bank fall into the Summary category?**

*In conclusion, in the end,* and *in essence.*

**If someone's injured by an avalanche of books, *in the end*, they only have their shelfs to blame. *In the end* is a great transition to indicate to the reader that things are coming to a close. Now that we've got an idea of *how* these transitions are used to help us connect ideas, let's see some in action.**

EXERCISE B

**Instructions**
Choose the best transition to complete each sentence.

after that alternatively for instance in fact

6. If you find a doll in the toy section of Target, you might think it's cute; ________________, if you find an old, cracked-face doll in the attic, you might want to destroy it in the nearest fire.

7. Benjamin Franklin was pretty surprised when he discovered electricity; ________________, you could say he was shocked.

8. The teacher wrote the solution to the math problem on the window; ________________, everything was clear.

9. They say music is really good for your brain, but I'm not sold on the idea; ________________, if a piano falls on my head, I'm pretty sure my brain won't like it.

## Groundwork

*In this section, students will practice identifying the category of transition needed and choosing the appropriate transition.*

EXERCISE B

**Of course, the transitions we just talked about are not *all* the transitions that fit into these categories. In the word bank at the top of your page, we have four *different* transitions, each from a different category. Let's see if we can fit them in the right sentences to make the right connections.**

SLIDE 224.1

**Take a look at sentence 6. What's going on there?**

It's describing two kinds of dolls.

**What's going on in that sentence?**

It's describing a regular doll from Target and a creepy doll found in the attic.

**Would you have the same reaction to both dolls?**

No, I'd probably want to burn the creepy one in a fire.

**I don't know about you, but if I found some doll up in the attic just living its best life over by the water heater, I'd definitely be fast-tracking a plan to get rid of that thing. What kind of transition do we need to fill the blank in that sentence?**

A contrast transition.

**Is there a contrast transition in the box to fit the bill?**

Yes, *alternatively*.

**Plug that into the sentence, and re-read it. Does it make sense there?**

Yes.

SLIDE 224.2

**What about sentence 7? What kind of transition would bridge the gap between the first part of the joke and the punchline?**

*Addition or Emphasis.*

**The writer wants to *emphasize* the pun. Which transition from the box would help the writer do that?**

*In fact.*

**Read the sentence to yourselves with *in fact* in there. Does it work?**

Yes.

SLIDE 224.3

**What about the next sentence? What's the relationship between the ideas around the blank?**

*Cause/Effect or Sequence.*

**And which of the transitions left in the box will work to show this relationship?**

*After that.*

**Does it work in context?**

Yes.

SLIDE 224.4

**Same drill with sentence 9. What's the connection between the ideas?**

The second part adds on to what the author is saying in the first part.

**What category of connection is that?**

*Illustration or Support.*

**Which transition helps us make this connection?**

*For instance.*

**Does it work when you fill it in the blank?**

Yes.

**On the TSIA2, you'll be using this same kind of process, but instead of a word bank, we'll have answer choices. Let's see how you do with something that better mirrors what you'll see on test day.**

TSIA2 Mastery: ELAR 

# Application

## THE APPROACH

When you are asked to determine the appropriate transition to make a connection between ideas, use the following steps ...

1. Determine the relationship between the ideas before and after the transition.
2. Eliminate answers that don't make the right bridge between the ideas.

**10.** A judge and an English teacher have different responsibilities. Subsequently, they do have one thing in common: lots of sentences.

Ⓐ Subsequently
Ⓑ However
Ⓒ In short
Ⓓ For example

# Application

*In this section, students will practice applying the steps of the Approach to a transitions question.*

**You'll likely see at least one transitions question during the TSIA2, but how will you know what it is? What clues do you see that tell us this is a transitions question?**

A transition is underlined, and all the answer choices are different transitions.

**If all your options are transition words and phrases, you know you'll be building a bridge between the ideas in the sentence or passage. What's the first thing you should do?**

*Determine the relationship between the ideas before and after the transition.*

SLIDE 225.1

**Let's take a look at question 10, starting with what comes *before* the underlined transition. What does the first sentence tell us?**

Judges and English teachers *have different responsibilities.*

**Then, we switch our focus to what comes *after* the transition. What does that portion say?**

They have something in common.

**So, the first part talks about something that's different, and the next part mentions how they're the same. What kind of relationship do we have between these two ideas?**

A contrast.

**Once we've figured out what kind of relationship we're working with, what's our next step?**

Eliminate answers that don't fit the relationship category.

**Start with choice A. What kind of relationship does *subsequently* signify?**

A *Cause/Effect or Sequence* transition.

**That's not right, so we'll eliminate choice A. What about answer choice B? Could *however* be used to make a contrast?**

Yes, it can.

**Hang onto that one for now. If we can eliminate all the other options, we'll know for sure that choice B is the right answer. What about choice C, *in short*? Should we keep it or cross it off?**

Cross it off since it's a *Summary* transition.

**Choice C is out. Finally, what about choice D, *for example*? What should we do with that one?**

Eliminate it since it's an *Illustration/Support* transition.

**That means choice B is the correct answer. But what happens if you get stuck on a question like this? How can we use these transitions categories to make eliminations? Let's go over a game plan we can use on test day.**

### THE APPROACH

When you are asked to determine the appropriate transition to make a connection between ideas, use the following steps ...

1. Determine the relationship between the ideas before and after the transition.
2. Eliminate answers that don't make the right bridge between the ideas.

**11.** Jacob had to move out of his apartment while he couldn't afford the rent anymore.

Ⓐ while he couldn't afford
Ⓑ despite the fact that he couldn't afford
Ⓒ since he couldn't afford
Ⓓ whereas he couldn't afford

## Application

*In this section, students will evaluate transitional words and phrases to determine which one best completes the sentence.*

SLIDE 226.1

**Question 11 looks a little different. What's changed?**

The answer choices are longer and have more words than just the transition.

**So, how can we tell this is a transitions question?**

All the answer choices begin with a transition word.

**How should this affect how we approach this question?**

We should focus on just the transition words, not the whole answer choice.

**Any other changes to our approach?**

No.

**That means our first step should be what?**

Figure out the relationship between the ideas before and after the transition.

**Let's go down a hypothetical path and say we have *no idea* what the relationship is. Should we panic and freeze?**

Definitely not.

**Instead, let's play the odds. The test will sometimes offer up two transitions that fall into the same category. Why is that a red flag for wrong answers?**

We can only have one right answer.

**If you see two transitions that go into the same category, instead of pondering over which one fits best, eliminate them. If anything, you've given yourself a 50/50 chance of guessing the right answer. So, what transitions do we have in question 11?**

*While*, *despite*, *since*, and *whereas*.

**Do any two of them fall into the same category?**

*Despite* and *whereas* are both Contrast transitions.

**That means we can eliminate choices B and D. What are we left with?**

*While* and *since*.

**Let's come out of our hypothetical and back to our sentence. What information do we see between the ideas before and after the transition?**

Jacob had to move and he couldn't afford his rent.

**What kind of relationship does that imply?**

Cause and effect.

**Which of our remaining transitions best matches that category?**

*Since*.

**That means choice C is the right answer. Remember: when faced with a transition question on the TSIA2, look for the relationships between the ideas. You want to pick the transition that best makes a *bridge* between those ideas. And if all else fails, look for two options that fall into the same category. You'll end up with some excellent odds for guessing correctly.**

TSIA2 Mastery: ELAR 

## Practice

**Instructions**
Complete the practice set. If time remains after you've finished, double-check your work.

1. Miranda had to visit the doctor with her shoulder pain increasing for three months.

   Ⓐ with her shoulder pain increasing
   Ⓑ although her shoulder pain increased
   Ⓒ whereas her shoulder pain increased
   Ⓓ because her shoulder pain had increased

2. Michael had to finish his homework with it being due yesterday.

   Ⓐ with it being
   Ⓑ though it was
   Ⓒ while it was
   Ⓓ because it was

3. Alexander only used his microwave until the repairman fixed his oven.

   Ⓐ until the repairman
   Ⓑ thus the repairman
   Ⓒ consequently the repairman
   Ⓓ because the repairman

# Practice

SLIDE 227.1

*Give students 8 minutes to complete the practice set.*

SLIDE 227.2

1. **The correct answer is D.** Choice A is incorrect because the preposition *with* creates confusion about the sequence of events in the sentence. Choices B and C are incorrect because the transition words *although* and *whereas* imply opposition or contradiction, which is not supported by the sentence. Choice D is correct because the transition word *because* correctly establishes a cause-and-effect relationship in the sequence of events.

SLIDE 227.3

2. **The correct answer is D.** Choice A is incorrect because the transition word *with* does not agree with the sequence of events in the sentence. Choices B and C are incorrect because the transition words *though* and *while* imply opposition or contradiction, which is not supported by the sentence. Choice D is correct because the transition word *because* correctly establishes the cause-and-effect relationship in the sequence of events.

SLIDE 227.4

3. **The correct answer is A.** Choices B and C are incorrect because the transitions *thus* and *consequently* mean *as a result*, which does not establish the correct sequence of events. Choice D is incorrect because the transition word *because* creates an incorrect cause-and-effect relationship between Alexander using his microwave and the repairman fixing the oven. Choice A is correct because the preposition *until* clearly establishes the sequence of events: until the oven was fixed, Alexander could only use his microwave.

## Wrap-Up

**Instructions**
Complete the wrap-up question. If time remains after you've finished, double-check your work.

**2.** Cassandra had yet to return her father's call with him having called her over two weeks ago.

Ⓐ with him having called
Ⓑ nevertheless he called
Ⓒ even though he called
Ⓓ because he had called

# Wrap-Up

**SLIDE 228.1**

*Give students 2 minutes to complete the wrap-up question.*

**SLIDE 228.2**

2. **The correct answer is C.** Choice A is incorrect because the preposition *with* does not clearly establish the sequence of events in the sentence. Choice B is incorrect because the transition word *nevertheless* does not correctly establish the timeline of the sentence. Choice D is incorrect because the transition word *because* implies cause and effect, which is not present in this sentence. Choice C is correct because it establishes a contradiction in the sentence: Cassandra still has not called her father back *even though* it's been two weeks since he called her.

CHAPTER 26

# Coordinating Conjunctions

In this chapter, students will review coordinating conjunctions and explore the process of using these connecting words to bridge independent clauses into compound sentences.

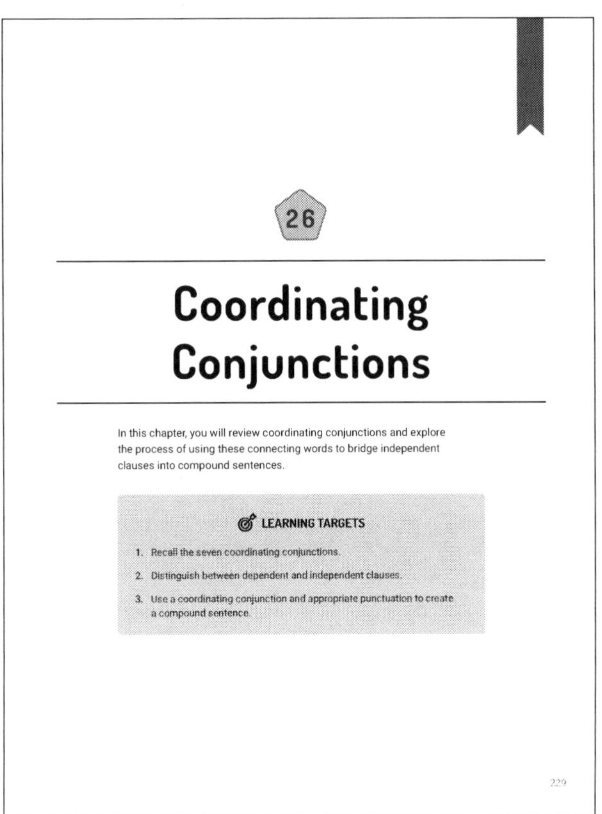

26

Coordinating Conjunctions

In this chapter, you will review coordinating conjunctions and explore the process of using these connecting words to bridge independent clauses into compound sentences.

LEARNING TARGETS

1. Recall the seven coordinating conjunctions.
2. Distinguish between dependent and independent clauses.
3. Use a coordinating conjunction and appropriate punctuation to create a compound sentence.

229

## TSIA2 STANDARDS

**Essay Revision and Editing**
Standard English conventions

The student will edit text as necessary to ensure conformity to the conventions of standard written English grammar, usage, and punctuation.

**Sentence Revision, Editing, and Completion**
Conventions of grammar

The student will edit and complete sentences as necessary to ensure conformity to the conventions of standard English grammar.

## TEKS ALIGNMENT

E1.9 *Composition*: listening, speaking, reading, writing, and thinking using multiple texts—writing process. The student uses the writing process recursively to compose multiple texts that are legible and uses appropriate conventions. The student is expected to:

(D) edit drafts using standard English conventions, including:

(i) a variety of complete, controlled, sentences and avoidance of unintentional splices, run-ons, and fragments;

(v) punctuation, including commas, semicolons, colons, and dashes to set off phrases and clauses as appropriate.

## LEARNING TARGETS

1. Recall the seven coordinating conjunctions.
2. Distinguish between dependent and independent clauses.
3. Use a coordinating conjunction and appropriate punctuation to create a compound sentence.

## Warm-Up

**Instructions**

Complete the warm-up question. If time remains after you've finished, double-check your work.

1. Early audio production was limited to mono recordings, therefore stereo sound arrived with the emergence of "talkie" sound films in the early 1930s.

   Ⓐ therefore
   Ⓑ however
   Ⓒ when
   Ⓓ but

# Warm-Up

SLIDE 230.1

*Give students 2 minutes to complete the warm-up question.*

SLIDE 230.2

1. **The correct answer is D.** Choices A and C are incorrect because *therefore* and *when* imply that there is a similar relationship within the sentence, but the sentence contrasts the features of *mono recordings* and *stereo sound*, so these conjunctions are illogical. Choice B is incorrect because it results in a run-on sentence; *however* and the independent clause that follows require a semicolon or a period to separate them from the rest of the sentence. Choice D is correct because the sentence is made up of two independent clauses, which can be correctly joined with a comma and the coordinating conjunction *but* to create the compound sentence.

## Groundwork

EXERCISE A

### Instructions

Read through the passage and identify the seven coordinating conjunctions that make up FANBOYS.

### Passage

Listen. I'm not saying that I'm the best athlete out there, but I can hold my own in gym class. In fact, I can keep pace with the best of them, <u>for</u> I'm a runner at heart. I don't know if it's my competitive nature that keeps me moving, or maybe there's just nothing quite like the feeling of the mental clarity that comes with a long-distance run.

The other day, I was in said gym class, and we were doing laps around the basketball court. Our gym teacher, Mr. Jordan, was standing on the sidelines with his ever-present stopwatch. I had fallen into a good rhythm and was faster than most of my classmates, so I just maneuvered around them when I'd get close.

I wasn't thinking about anything, nor was I focusing on what was in front of me. As I steered myself around a classmate, BAM! I smacked right into a basketball pole. It didn't hurt too much in the moment, yet when I realized I'd lost about three minutes of time somewhere, I knew I'd hurt my head pretty badly. Sure enough, the ER doctor would tell me a few hours later that I'd given myself a concussion.

F → ____ ____ ____

A → ____ ____ ____

N → ____ ____ ____

B → ____ ____ ____

O → ____ ____

Y → ____ ____ ____

S → ____ ____

# Groundwork

*In this section, students will search a passage to locate the seven coordinating conjunctions used to connect compound sentences.*

EXERCISE A

**Coordination. Not everyone has it. Some people are actually the complete opposite of coordinated, so they clumsily make their way through life. But if someone is coordinated, what kinds of things are they good at?**

Sports, dance, or other physical activities.

**We can also talk about things like a *coordinated effort*. What happens if that effort isn't so coordinated, though?**

Things fall apart.

SLIDE 231.1

**Coordination is all about things working together, whether it be hand-eye coordination or people joining forces to accomplish something. We also have coordination in writing. We use coordinating conjunctions, which is a really big term to describe a group of just seven tiny words. Let's see if we can find all seven hiding in this passage. The first one—*for*—is given to you. Write the remaining ones in the spaces provided. The conjunctions won't show up in order, so be sure to look through the entire passage for them.**

SLIDE 231.2

*Give students 2 minutes to complete this task.*

**We use the acronym FANBOYS to remember all of our coordinating conjunctions. What does FANBOYS stand for?**

*For, and, nor, but, or, yet, so.*

**Based on how they're used in the sentence, what do these words do?**

They make connections in a sentence.

**Notice the placement of these coordinating conjunctions. Where do they appear in the sentence?**

In the middle.

**They show up smack dab in the middle of our sentences. Do you notice anything about the punctuation near those words?**

They always follow a comma.

**Coordinating conjunctions, or FANBOYS, are words used to create what's called a compound sentence. Essentially, a compound sentence is two independent clauses connected with a comma and a coordinating conjunction. But how can you tell if a clause is independent? The secret is in the name and what it means to be independent. I'll show you in the next exercise.**

EXERCISE B

**Instructions**
Label each clause as either independent (I) or dependent (D).

1. Even though it was raining cats and dogs. ______
2. I really missed the boat on that one. ______
3. Because she was the one calling the shots. ______
4. It's the opposite of having a green thumb. ______
5. He went out on a limb for me. ______

## Groundwork

*In this section, students will differentiate between independent and dependent clauses.*

EXERCISE B

**Show of hands: who's excited about getting a job and making your own money?**

*Pause for a show of hands.*

**You'll be free to make your own decisions! Independent! But what does that mean, exactly? What makes someone independent?**

They can take care of themselves.

**In the same way, independent clauses take care of themselves. In fact, they can stand alone as a complete sentence—no help needed. Based on that, what do you think a *dependent* clause is?**

One that can't be its own sentence.

SLIDE 232.1

**Dependent clauses are *dependent* on something else to be a complete sentence. When we see one on its own, it's really just a fragment. For instance, take a look at number 1. Is that clause independent or dependent?**

Dependent.

**Why?**

It's an incomplete sentence.

**What words make it feel incomplete?**

*Even though.*

***Even though* gives the clause an incomplete feeling, like someone left off in the middle of a thought. We'd need to attach it to an independent clause to complete the sentence. Take some time now to work through the rest of these, and label them as either independent or dependent.**

*Give students 1 minute to complete this task.*

**What do you think about number 2? Is it independent or dependent?**

Independent.

**How can you tell?**

It can stand on its own as a complete sentence.

**What about number 3? How did you label it?**

Dependent.

**What word made it feel incomplete?**

*Because.*

**Starting a clause with *because* makes the thought feel incomplete, so we know it's dependent. What did you get for number 4?**

Independent.

**That one is a complete sentence, so we know it's independent. And number 5?**

Independent.

**Another complete sentence. But these sentences are short and kind of plain. To spice them up, we can join clauses together—we can coordinate them using our FANBOYS and a comma. But we can only do this with independent clauses. A dependent clause would definitely throw a wrench into our plan.**

EXERCISE C

### Instructions

Identify whether the clauses in the sentence are independent (I) or dependent (D). Then, add a coordinating conjunction to the appropriate sentence.

6. It doesn't challenge you, ________ it's not going to change you.

7. If it doesn't challenge you, ________ it's not going to change you.

## Groundwork

*In this section, students will evaluate the characteristics of a compound sentence and a complex sentence and determine which structure requires a coordinating conjunction.*

EXERCISE C SLIDE 233.1

**A dependent clause is a weakling, unable to stand on its own. It needs a big, strong independent clause to make it complete. All we need to connect dependent clauses is something small like a comma, a colon, or maybe even nothing at all. But when two independent clauses get connected, we need a heavy lifter to make that connection. For instance, check out sentence 6. How should we start?**

Figure out if the clauses are independent or dependent.

**Start with the first clause. Is that independent or dependent?**

Independent.

**How can you tell?**

It could stand on its own as a complete sentence.

**What about the second clause? How should we label that one?**

Independent, since it could be its own complete sentence.

**Two independent clauses mean using a stronger connection. What should we add?**

One of the FANBOYS.

**We've got seven options: *for*, *and*, *nor*, *but*, *or*, *yet*, or *so*. How do we decide which one will work best?**

Look at the details of the sentence.

**If we can figure out how one clause relates to the other, we'll be able to pick the best coordinating conjunction for the job. What kind of relationship do we see here?**

Cause and effect.

**Which of our FANBOYS would work well in that space?**

*So.*

**Let's read it back to ourselves, just to make sure it works.**

*It doesn't challenge you, so it's not going to change you.*

**Does that sound okay?**

Yes.

SLIDE 233.2

**Using *so* to connect the ideas works well, and we've given our two independent clauses the strong connection they need. Let's look at sentence 7 next. Is the first clause dependent or independent?**

Dependent.

**How do you know?**

It can't be its own complete sentence.

**What about the second clause? Independent or dependent?**

Independent.

**So, we've got a dependent clause connected to an independent clause. Do we need to add a coordinating conjunction?**

No.

**Since the sentence begins with a dependent clause, we don't need anything besides that little comma to make the connection.**

## Application

### THE APPROACH

When a question contains a sentence with two clauses and the answer choices contain connecting words, use these steps ...

1. Determine whether the clauses are dependent or independent.
2. Eliminate inappropriate connecting words.
3. Compare the remaining choices and select the one that best fits the sentence.

**8.** Money can't buy happiness, <u>for</u> it's hard to be sad on a jet ski.

Ⓐ for
Ⓑ however
Ⓒ but
Ⓓ or

## Application

*In this section, students will practice applying the steps of the Approach to a coordinating conjunctions question.*

SLIDE 234.1

**On the TSIA2, you'll run into coordinating conjunctions questions that challenge you in two ways: first, they'll want you to figure out if the sentence needs a coordinating conjunction, and then they'll want to know which one fits best. But how can you tell if it's testing you on coordinating conjunctions? What clues will appear in the question?**

The answer choices will be connecting words, including at least one of the FANBOYS.

**Once you've figured out what they're testing you on, what should be your first step?**

*Determine whether the clauses are dependent or independent.*

**Let's do that. Is the first clause dependent or independent?**

Independent.

**How do you know?**

It's a complete sentence on its own.

**What about the second clause?**

It's independent because it could be its own complete sentence.

**So, what kind of connection do we need?**

A comma and a coordinating conjunction.

**Step 2 tells us to *eliminate inappropriate connecting words*. What might make a connecting word *inappropriate*?**

It's the wrong kind of conjunction.

**We know we need a coordinating conjunction, so we can eliminate choices that *aren't* what we need. Which of these options aren't included in FANBOYS?**

*However* in choice B.

**This is why memorizing the FANBOYS is so important. If we didn't know that *however* isn't a coordinating conjunction, it might be pretty tempting to pick it since it seems like it bridges the ideas in the sentence accurately. But, since we know that it breaks our sentence structure, we can eliminate choice B. What else might make a conjunction inappropriate?**

It doesn't logically connect the ideas.

**Let's look at our sentence. What kind of relationship do we see between these clauses?**

Compare and contrast.

**This sentence talks about how money can't buy happiness and then contrasts this with the fact that they've never seen someone looking sad on a jet ski. It's describing a difference. Can we eliminate any of the answer choices because they create inappropriate connections?**

Choices A and D.

***For* is usually used to show cause and effect, while *or* is used to offer up alternatives. What does that leave us with?**

Choice C.

**Using *but* to connect the contrasting ideas works, and since it's a coordinating conjunction, we're not breaking the grammar of the sentence. Choice C is definitely the best option.**

## THE APPROACH

When a question contains a sentence with two clauses and the answer choices contain connecting words, use these steps ...

1. Determine whether the clauses are dependent or independent.
2. Eliminate inappropriate connecting words.
3. Compare the remaining choices and select the one that best fits the sentence.

**9.** Although this may kill me, <u>and it</u> could make me stronger.

- (A) and it
- (B) otherwise it
- (C) or it
- (D) it

## Application

*In this section, students will answer a TSIA2-style question that does not require the use of a coordinating conjunction to connect the clauses.*

SLIDE 235.1

**Let's do it again. Where should we start?**

By figuring out whether the clauses are dependent or independent.

**What kind of clauses do we have?**

The first clause is dependent because it's not a complete sentence on its own, but the second clause is, so it's independent.

**If we have a dependent clause, what do we know we *can't* use? And what does that mean about our answer choices?**

We can't use a coordinating conjunction, so choices A and C are out.

**Sometimes knowing grammar rules means knowing what *doesn't* work in a sentence. Now, what's the difference between the last two choices?**

One uses *otherwise* before *it*, and the other one just uses *it*.

**Let's think for a second. What's one way we know to connect a dependent clause to an independent clause?**

With a comma.

**Many dependent clauses already have their own connecting word, which is why they feel incomplete by themselves. What connecting word shows up in our sentence at the start of the dependent clause?**

*Although.*

***Although* is a great connecting word to help us show contrast. So, do we need another connecting word to bridge these clauses?**

No, it would be repetitive.

**If we don't want to add any more connecting words, which of our remaining choices is out?**

Choice B.

**Leaving us with what as the correct answer?**

Choice D.

**Since we eliminated three wrong answers, we can be pretty sure that our remaining option is correct. But always double-check your answer. What does the sentence sound like if we use choice D in the underlined portion?**

*Although this may kill me, it could make me stronger.*

**Does that sound correct?**

Yes.

**A lot of times, your natural instincts will be a good gauge for figuring out if you've got an error in your answer. Essentially, if it sounds wrong, it is wrong. If choice D had sounded awkward here, what would we do?**

Go back to step 1 and start again.

**During the test, if you find that you've gotten down to one answer, and it just doesn't sound good, don't be afraid to retrace your steps. Start at step 1 and make sure that the clauses actually are independent or dependent. Move on to make eliminations, and see if you end up in the same place. The test can't hear your thoughts, so there's no shame in starting over. The system will have no idea that you're waffling over an answer choice. The only thing that matters is what you've picked when you hit that "continue" button. Take your time, and be sure before you submit your answer.**

## Practice

**Instructions**
Complete the practice set. If time remains after you've finished, double-check your work.

**1.** Early automobiles only had side-door mirrors, since larger reflectors were installed after the introduction of the gasoline engine in the early 1900s.

Ⓐ since
Ⓑ however
Ⓒ as
Ⓓ but

**2.** The postal railway system delivered mail across the United States for decades, therefore mail trucks replaced mail trains in the late 1970s.

Ⓐ therefore
Ⓑ however
Ⓒ when
Ⓓ but

**3.** Even though Miguel played baseball last season, but he tried out for the tennis team this year.

Ⓐ but he
Ⓑ but
Ⓒ he had
Ⓓ he

# Practice

SLIDE 236.1

*Give students 8 minutes to complete the practice set.*

SLIDE 236.2

1. **The correct answer is D.** Choice A is incorrect because *since* implies that *side-door mirrors* were used in *early automobiles* because *larger reflectors* were later installed, which is illogical. Choice B is incorrect because *however* results in a comma splice. Choice C is incorrect because *as* implies that *larger reflectors were installed* as a result of *side-door mirrors*, which is illogical. Choice D is correct because *but* suggests a contrast between the mirrors in *early automobiles* and those made *after the introduction of the gasoline engine in the early 1900s*, and *but* is a conjunction that can be used with a comma to join two independent clauses.

SLIDE 236.3

2. **The correct answer is D.** Choices A and B are incorrect because *therefore* and *however* are adverbs, and they cannot join two independent clauses without a period or semicolon. Choice C is incorrect because *when* doesn't make sense with *for decades*—trucks replacing trains did not happen at the same time that trains were delivering mail for decades. Choice D is correct because the comma followed by *but* correctly separates the two independent clauses, and the conjunction establishes the contrast between the two clauses.

SLIDE 236.4

3. **The correct answer is D.** Choices A and B are incorrect because *even though* and *but* have similar meanings, so using them together makes the sentence redundant and confusing. Choice C is incorrect because *had tried out* is not the correct verb tense since chronologically, *last season* took place before *this year*. Choice D is correct because it correctly separates the dependent and independent clauses with a comma.

TSIA2 Mastery: ELAR 

## Wrap-Up

**Instructions**
Complete the wrap-up question. If time remains after you've finished, double-check your work.

**2.** While Hector loved cheeseburgers as a teenager, but he decided to become a vegetarian as an adult.

Ⓐ but he
Ⓑ but
Ⓒ he had
Ⓓ he

# Wrap-Up

SLIDE 237.1

*Give students 2 minutes to complete the wrap-up question.*

SLIDE 237.2

2. **The correct answer is D.** Choices A and B are incorrect because this sentence has a dependent clause followed by an independent clause, so a comma without a conjunction is sufficient to separate them. Choice C is incorrect because the helping verb *had* would unnecessarily indicate an action that was completed before a specific time. Choice D is correct because it uses a comma to properly join the dependent clause to the independent clause without any unnecessary conjunctions or illogical verb tense changes.

This page is intentionally left blank.
Content resumes on the next page.

This page is intentionally left blank.
Teacher content resumes with the next chapter.

## CHAPTER 27

# Sentence Formation

In this chapter, students will review and practice dependent and independent clauses with a focus on subordinating conjunctions and how they indicate the beginning of a dependent clause.

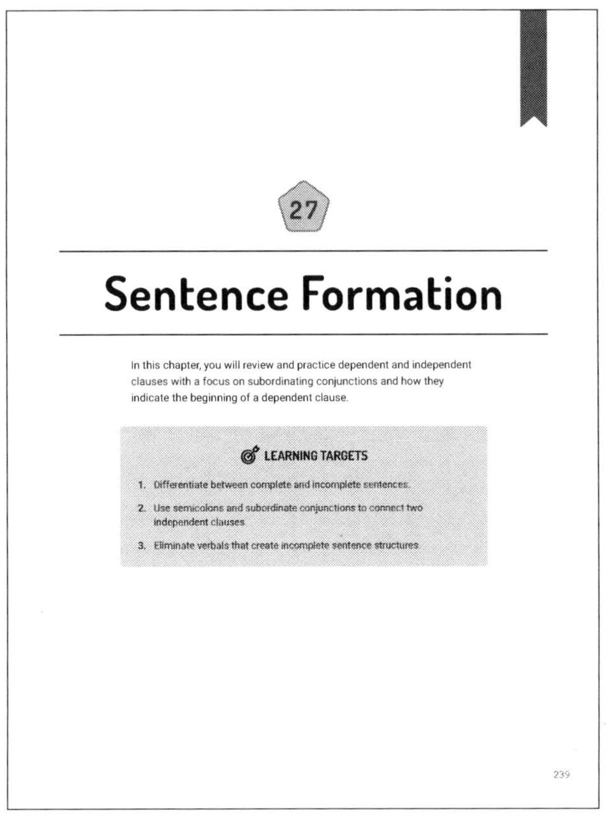

27

Sentence Formation

In this chapter, you will review and practice dependent and independent clauses with a focus on subordinating conjunctions and how they indicate the beginning of a dependent clause.

LEARNING TARGETS

1. Differentiate between complete and incomplete sentences.
2. Use semicolons and subordinate conjunctions to connect two independent clauses.
3. Eliminate verbals that create incomplete sentence structures.

239

## TSIA2 STANDARDS

**Essay Revision and Editing**
Standard English conventions

The student will edit text as necessary to ensure conformity to the conventions of standard written English grammar, usage, and punctuation.

**Sentence Revision, Editing, and Completion**
Conventions of grammar

The student will edit and complete sentences as necessary to ensure conformity to the conventions of standard English grammar.

## TEKS ALIGNMENT

E1.9 *Composition*: listening, speaking, reading, writing, and thinking using multiple texts—writing process. The student uses the writing process recursively to compose multiple texts that are legible and uses appropriate conventions. The student is expected to:

(C) revise drafts to improve clarity, development, organization, style, diction, and sentence effectiveness including use of parallel constructions and placement of phrases and dependent clauses.

## LEARNING TARGETS

1. Differentiate between complete and incomplete sentences.
2. Use semicolons and subordinate conjunctions to connect two independent clauses.
3. Eliminate verbals that create incomplete sentence structures.

## Warm-Up

**Instructions**
Complete the warm-up question. If time remains after you've finished, double-check your work.

**1.** The Bergen Dice, which became notorious for its ability to help its user obtain an unfair advantage, discovered by archeologists exploring villages of Norway dating back to the Middle Ages.

Ⓐ advantage, discovered by
Ⓑ advantage, to be discovered by
Ⓒ advantage, having been discovered by
Ⓓ advantage, was discovered by

# Warm-Up

SLIDE 240.1

*Give students 2 minutes to complete the warm-up question.*

SLIDE 240.2

1. **The correct answer is D.** The sentence contains a parenthetical element that separates the subject of the sentence, *the Bergen Dice*, from its verb. Choices A and C are incorrect because *discovered by* and *having been discovered by* turn the last clause of the sentence into a participial phrase. Choice B is incorrect because *to be discovered* is a verbal and therefore cannot act as the verb of the sentence. Choice D is correct because *the Bergen Dice was discovered* provides a subject and verb that create a complete sentence structure.

TSIA2 Mastery: ELAR 

## Groundwork

EXERCISE A

**Instructions**

Determine whether the following sentences are complete or incomplete. Circle your answer.

1. Komodo dragons, which were once thought to be venomous, have so much bacteria in their mouths that their prey dies from infection rather than damage from the attack.

   complete    incomplete

2. A certain species of snail, found in parts of eastern Russia as well as Japan, known for throwing their shells at predators as a means of protection.

   complete    incomplete

# Groundwork

*In this section, students will practice identifying complete and incomplete sentences when a parenthetical element is included.*

EXERCISE A

**There's this trope in all kinds of TV shows, books, and movies where the characters talk about how something "completes" them. A baseball player feels incomplete without their glove. An artist feels like something is missing until they pick up a paintbrush. A villain finds his trusty old laser blaster and proclaims, "At last! My arm is complete again!" Think about things that you're good at. What "completes" you?**

*Allow 2–3 students to share.*

**Even though this trope of "completion" is overused and even a little corny, it's got to be relatable because it shows up *everywhere*. Even in writing! For instance, what do we need to create a complete sentence?**

A subject and verb that create a complete thought.

SLIDE 241.1

**Complete sentences are the building blocks of just about any kind of writing. The TSIA2, especially, loves to see if you can create complete sentences. But they won't make it easy. They've got a few tricks up their sleeve to up the difficulty level. For instance, let's look at sentence 1. What's the subject of that sentence?**

*Komodo dragons.*

**And what's the verb?**

*Have.*

**Why isn't the verb *were* or *thought*? Those are closer to the subject.**

Those are inside a descriptive phrase.

**The TSIA2 loves to separate the subject and verb of a clause with descriptive phrases like that. What clues help us see that the description is separate from the rest of the sentence?**

There are commas on both sides.

**Does the description contribute to the completeness of the sentence?**

No.

**So what should we do with it as we check to see if the whole sentence is complete?**

Ignore it.

**Let's go ahead and cross it out. Without that extra detail in the way, what does our sentence look like?**

*Komodo dragons have so much bacteria in their mouths that their prey dies from infection rather than damage from the attack.*

**Is that sentence complete?**

Yes.

**It's got a matching subject and verb, and it expresses a complete thought, so we know it's a complete sentence.**

**What about sentence 2? What's our subject?**

*A certain species of snail.*

**And what's our verb?**

*Known.*

**Why isn't the verb *found*?**

It's a part of an added detail, not a part of the main sentence.

**So, if we take that out, what does the sentence become?**

*A certain species of snail known for throwing their shells at predators as a means of protection.*

**Is that a complete sentence?**

No.

**In this instance, our verb doesn't seem to be pulling its weight. In fact, it's not even really used as a verb. That makes the sentence feel like an incomplete thought. How could we fix it to make the sentence complete?**

Change *known* to *is known*.

**Remember to watch out for those added descriptions during the TSIA2. The test-makers will drop them right between the subject and the verb to make the question more challenging. By ignoring them completely, we can better see if the sentence is or isn't complete.**

EXERCISE B

**Instructions**

Determine which of the following sentences is complete. Circle the complete sentence.

3. Sloths often mistaking their arms for branches and falling out of trees.

4. Sloths often to mistake their arms for branches and to fall out of trees.

5. Sloths often mistake their arms for branches and fall out of trees.

## Groundwork

*In this section, students will evaluate the effects of verbals on the structure of a sentence.*

EXERCISE B SLIDE 242.1

**These sentences seem straightforward enough, don't they? Not even a single comma in the lot, which means no pesky parenthetical elements to deal with. Does that mean we can assume the sentences are correct as is and move on?**

No, there's probably some other kind of error in the sentences.

**There are thousands of ways to build a complete sentence. And with all that opportunity for creativity comes a whole lot of other ways the TSIA2 can mess up a sentence. Take a moment to read sentence 3. In fact, read it aloud. Everyone together:**

*Sloths often mistaking their arms for branches and falling out of trees.*

**Without evaluating anything grammatical, just listen to your instincts. Does that sentence seem complete?**

No.

**Where does the sentence feel like something's off?**

Somewhere around *mistaking*.

**Let's step back and check to see if this sentence has everything it needs to be complete. What's the subject?**

*Sloths.*

**What's the verb? What are the sloths doing?**

*Mistaking.*

***Mistaking* looks like a verb, but it doesn't seem to be acting like a verb. That *-ing* changed it into something called a verbal. And the reality is, verbals can't be the main verb of a sentence. They steal the verb and turn it into something else, like a descriptive phrase. What about sentence 4? Does that one seem complete?**

No.

**Why not?**

*To mistake* doesn't really work as the verb.

**Verbals come in a few flavors. On the TSIA2, the most popular verbals you'll see are the ones that end in *-ing* and the ones that start with *to*. Again, these verbals can't act as the main verb of the sentence. What about sentence 5? Does that seem complete?**

Yes.

**What are the subject and verb?**

*Sloths mistake.*

**When you run into sentence formation questions like this, focus on pulling out just the subject and verb. If they connect well and can create the essence of a complete sentence, you know you've got the right choice.**

**TSIA2 Mastery:** ELAR 

EXERCISE C

**Instructions**

Determine whether the clauses of each sentence should be separated by a comma or a semicolon.

6. Hummingbirds are able to flap their wings at 200 times per second they need to eat up to eight times their own body weight every day to compensate.

7. Because turkeys are so mesmerized by rain they will often spend upwards of 30 minutes staring at the sky turkey farmers must take caution because turkeys often drown by doing this.

## Groundwork

*In this section, students will learn how semicolons can be used to connect two independent clauses.*

EXERCISE C

**When verbals enter the mix, it's like there isn't enough sentence to make it complete. But sometimes, the TSIA2 will give you *too much* sentence, which can be equally as grammatically destructive.**

> Note: if you have not yet reviewed the Conjunctions chapter, you may need to adjust the following dialogue.

**What's one way we know to connect two complete sentences into one?**

With a comma and one of the FANBOYS.

**Sometimes the test won't give you that option, though, and you'll need to use something not as common but with just as much connecting power: the semicolon. The same basic rules apply, though. What kinds of clauses do we separate with a comma and coordinating conjunction?**

Independent clauses.

**Can we put an incomplete thought before a semicolon? Or after one?**

No, semicolons can only separate two complete thoughts.

SLIDE 243.1

**Let's test this out on number 6. There isn't any punctuation in this sentence, but we still have an error. What is it?**

It's a run-on sentence.

**We need to find a place to separate these two clauses. Where should we put our punctuation?**

After *second*.

**Does the clause before that create a complete sentence on its own?**

Yes.

**What about the clause after, starting with *they*?**

It's a complete sentence on its own, too.

**So, should we separate these clauses with a semicolon or a comma?**

A semicolon.

**A semicolon would definitely work.**

**Number 7 is also a run-on. And this time, we've got three clauses to work with. But don't worry. If we break it into pieces and evaluate each clause one at a time, it will simplify the process for us. What's the first clause in that sentence?**

*Because turkeys are so mesmerized by rain.*

**That clause feels like it leaves off in the middle of a thought, so we know it's not complete. What about the second clause? Who can read that part for us?**

*They will often spend upwards of 30 minutes staring at the sky.*

**Is that a complete sentence on its own?**

Yes.

**That one is independent. Check out the rest of that sentence, starting with *turkey farmers*. Is that a complete sentence on its own?**

Yes.

**So we've got a dependent clause followed by an independent clause. What kind of punctuation should go there?**

A comma.

**We don't need that super strong connection to connect a dependent clause to an independent one, so a comma works perfectly in that spot. What about between the second and third clause? What kind of punctuation could we use?**

A semicolon, since they are both independent clauses.

**We need a strong piece of punctuation to connect those independent clauses, so we'll add a semicolon after *sky*. That will do the trick.**

## Application

### THE APPROACH

When you encounter a writing question that contains a mix of verbals and verbs in the answer choices, use these steps ...

1. Determine whether the clause is missing a complete verb.
2. If it is, select a verb that appropriately completes the sentence.
3. If it isn't, select a verbal that appropriately completes the sentence.

**8.** The young explorer, aware of the many obstacles that lay in her path, embarked on her adventure with a determination to succeed.

Ⓐ path, embarked
Ⓑ path, she embarked
Ⓒ path, embarking
Ⓓ path, to embark

# Application

***In this section, students will be introduced to a set of steps that can be used to answer sentence formation questions on the TSIA2.***

**When it comes to sentence formation, the TSIA2 has a lot they can work with to create their questions. In fact, it's one of the most diverse question types on the entire ELAR test. So how will we be able to tell if it's testing us on sentence formation? Who has some ideas?**

The sentence will be a run-on. The answers will have verbs in them.

SLIDE 244.1

**Sentence formation questions can be a little hard to spot. The key is to look for those verbals. If the answer choices offer up different verb forms, and at least one of them is a verbal, there's a really good chance you're being asked about sentence formation. Does question 8 have a verbal?**

Yes, *embarking* in choice C and *to embark* in choice D.

**When we run across questions like this, what should we always do first?**

*Determine whether the clause is missing a complete verb.*

**Why do you think this step is important to sentence formation in particular?**

Because every complete sentence needs a verb.

**This is actually the number one way the TSIA2 will try to break the sentence: either by offering an extra verb when what we really need is a verbal or by including a verbal where a complete verb is needed. Let's check our sentence. What's the verb here?**

Different versions of *embark*.

**Who's doing the embarking?**

*The young explorer.*

**What do you notice about the placement of the subject and verb of this sentence?**

They're separated by a parenthetical element.

**And what should we do when we see one of those?**

Ignore it.

**Let's take out the parenthetical element. What does the sentence become?**

*The young explorer embarked on her adventure with a determination to succeed.*

**How does the verb look now? Does it help complete the sentence, or is it just adding extra clutter?**

We need it.

**What should we do?**

Eliminate choices that don't have a complete verb.

**Which choices should we get rid of?**

Choices C and D, since they have verbals.

**Compare what's left. What's the difference between choices A and B?**

Choice B has the extra subject *she*.

**Do we need that extra subject?**

No.

**Why not?**

The sentence already has a subject.

**That means our correct answer is choice A. Take a moment to check, though. Ignore the parenthetical element and re-read the sentence using choice A. Does that sound like a complete sentence?**

Yes.

**If we've eliminated all the other choices and confirmed that the answer we like sounds good in the sentence, we can be confident when we make our selection and continue to the next question.**

### THE APPROACH

When you encounter a writing question that contains a mix of verbals and verbs in the answer choices, use these steps ...

1. Determine whether the clause is missing a complete verb.
2. If it is, select a verb that appropriately completes the sentence.
3. If it isn't, select a verbal that appropriately completes the sentence.

**9.** Because they had been working for hours, the students decided to take a break the group knew that pushing themselves to a mental breaking point wouldn't be helpful anyway.

Ⓐ break the group knew
Ⓑ break and the group knowing
Ⓒ break; the group knew
Ⓓ break, the group had known

## Application

*In this section, students will practice applying the steps of the approach to a sentence formation question.*

SLIDE 245.1

**Question 9 looks a little longer, right? How many clauses does it have?**

Three.

**With so many clauses flying around, what do you think is the most common problem we'll have to worry about?**

Run-ons.

**We have to be careful with all these clauses. It can be hard to look at them separately and make sure their verbs connect to their subjects. Let's take it slow. What verbs do you see in the underlined bit?**

*Break* and *knew*.

**Double-check that they're actually being used as verbs in the sentence. Are either of them verbs?**

*Break* is being used as a noun, but *knew* is being used as a verb.

**What's the subject of *knew*?**

*Group*.

**Pick out the clause using that subject and verb combo. What's the clause?**

*The group knew that pushing themselves to a mental breaking point wouldn't be helpful anyway.*

**Is that complete?**

Yes.

**What does that tell us? And can it help us make any eliminations?**

We need a verb in that clause, so we can eliminate choice B since it's a verbal.

**We still have three answer choices, though. Essentially, what's the main difference between them?**

One has a comma, one has a semicolon, and one has nothing.

**Where should we look to figure out which one is correct?**

The clause that comes before.

**What is that clause?**

*The students decided to take a break.*

**The answer choices give us three options to separate two complete clauses: a comma, a semicolon, or no punctuation at all. Which one works best?**

A semicolon.

**How do you know?**

The clauses are both complete sentences on their own, so they need a stronger connection than a comma.

**Let's read it through with choice C plugged in. What do you think? Does it work?**

Yes.

**With the break created by the semicolon, the sentence still flows nicely and feels complete. Choice C is definitely correct. This is a good strategy to remember: if all the grammar and punctuation rules fail you, and you can't tell which answer choice would be best, take each one for a test run. A lot of times, your natural instinct can at least help you eliminate a few of the options and give you a better chance at getting the question right.**

## Practice

**Instructions**
Complete the practice set. If time remains after you've finished, double-check your work.

**1.** Now that computers are becoming more popular in classrooms, teachers are taking advantage of the opportunity, students were insisting that the update has improved their daily experiences.

Ⓐ opportunity, students were insisting
Ⓑ opportunity and students insist
Ⓒ opportunity students insist
Ⓓ opportunity; students insist

**2.** The Hope Diamond, which became part of the English crown jewels before being shipped to France, purchased by Pierre Cartier for an American heiress in 1910.

Ⓐ France, purchased by
Ⓑ France, having been purchased by
Ⓒ France, was purchased by
Ⓓ France, to be purchased by

**3.** Ryan loves video games so much that he will not play anything else when video games are an option.

Ⓐ that he will not play
Ⓑ that not playing
Ⓒ to not play
Ⓓ not to play

# Practice

SLIDE 246.1

*Give students 8 minutes to complete the practice set.*

SLIDE 246.2

1. **The correct answer is D.** Choice A is incorrect because it separates two independent clauses with only a comma, creating a comma splice. Choice B is incorrect because it attempts to join two independent clauses with a coordinating conjunction, but it is missing a necessary comma. Choice C is incorrect because without punctuation or a conjunction, the independent clauses form a run-on sentence. Choice D is correct because it appropriately connects two independent clauses with a semicolon.

SLIDE 246.3

2. **The correct answer is C.** This sentence contains the parenthetical phrase *which became part of the English crown jewels before being shipped to France* offset with commas. Choices A, B, and D are incorrect because they form incomplete sentences. Choice C is correct because *The Hope Diamond ... was purchased by Pierre Cartier for an American heiress in 1910* is a complete and logical sentence.

SLIDE 246.4

3. **The correct answer is A.** Choice B is incorrect because while it provides the conjunction *that* to connect the two clauses, the second clause is incomplete because it does not contain a complete verb or a subject. Choices C and D are incorrect because the use of the verbal *to play* makes the sentence illogical, and the sentences lack a conjunction to join the two clauses. Choice A is correct because *that* logically connects the two independent clauses.

TSIA2 Mastery: ELAR 

## Wrap-Up

**Instructions**
Complete the wrap-up question. If time remains after you've finished, double-check your work.

**2.** Despite its dilapidated condition, the sculpture was widely beloved by the community; everyone agreed that it was a wonderful example of late-modernist art.

Ⓐ community; everyone agreed
Ⓑ community everyone agreed
Ⓒ community and everyone agreeing
Ⓓ community, everyone was agreed

# Wrap-Up

SLIDE 247.1

*Give students 2 minutes to complete the wrap-up question.*

SLIDE 247.2

2. **The correct answer is A.** Choice B is incorrect because it is a run-on sentence. Choice C is incorrect because it illogically makes the clause *everyone agreeing that it was a wonderful example of late-modernist art* function as a noun phrase. Choice D is incorrect because it results in a comma splice. Choice A is correct because the semicolon properly separates two related independent clauses.

This page is intentionally left blank.
Content resumes on the next page.

This page is intentionally left blank.
Teacher content resumes with the next chapter.

CHAPTER 28

# The 4 C's

In this chapter, students will learn how to strategically eliminate incorrect answers based on the 4 C's: Correct, Consistent, Clear, and Concise.

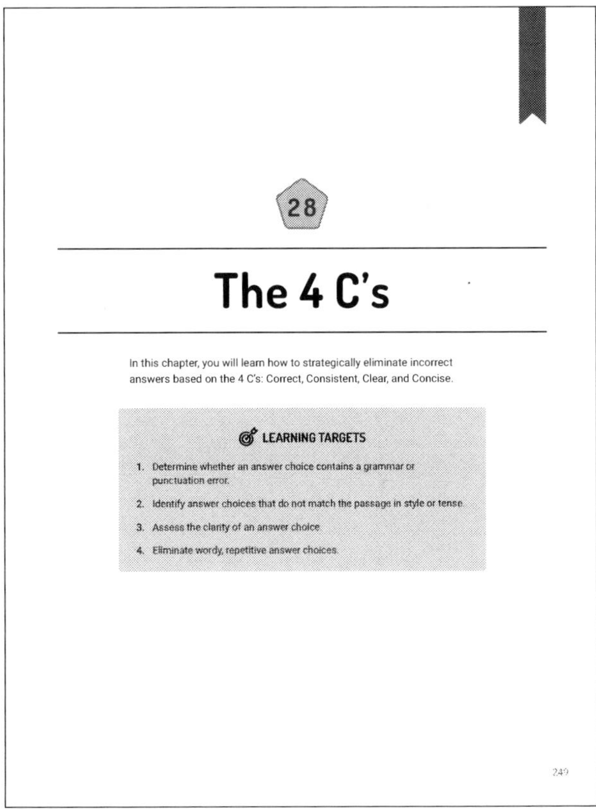

28

The 4 C's

In this chapter, you will learn how to strategically eliminate incorrect answers based on the 4 C's: Correct, Consistent, Clear, and Concise.

LEARNING TARGETS

1. Determine whether an answer choice contains a grammar or punctuation error.
2. Identify answer choices that do not match the passage in style or tense.
3. Assess the clarity of an answer choice.
4. Eliminate wordy, repetitive answer choices.

249

## TSIA2 STANDARDS

**Essay Revision and Editing**
Standard English conventions

The student will edit text as necessary to ensure conformity to the conventions of standard written English grammar, usage, and punctuation.

**Sentence Revision, Editing, and Completion**
The student will edit and complete sentences as necessary to ensure conformity to the conventions of standard written English grammar, usage, punctuation, and spelling and capitalization as well as make effective decisions regarding purpose and organization and sentence combining.

## TEKS ALIGNMENT

E1.9 *Composition*: listening, speaking, reading, writing, and thinking using multiple texts—writing process. The student uses the writing process recursively to compose multiple texts that are legible and use appropriate conventions. The student is expected to:

(C) revise drafts to improve clarity, development, organization, style, diction, and sentence effectiveness, including use of parallel constructions and placement of phrases and dependent clauses;

(D) edit drafts using standard English conventions.

## LEARNING TARGETS

1. Determine whether an answer choice contains a grammar or punctuation error.
2. Identify answer choices that do not match the passage in style or tense.
3. Assess the clarity of an answer choice.
4. Eliminate wordy, repetitive answer choices.

## Groundwork

**EXERCISE A**

### Instructions

Review the following question as your teacher leads the discussion. Do not answer the question.

*Select the best version of the underlined part of the sentence. If you think the original sentence is best, choose the first answer.*

1. The children thought that their father was being serious when he told them that the word "gullible" is not in the dictionary.

   (A) serious when he told
   (B) serious he told
   (C) serious, he telling
   (D) serious, him telling

# Groundwork

*In this section, students will be introduced to the structure of typical writing-style questions as seen on the TSIA2.*

**Writing questions make up 50% of the ELAR multiple-choice section, running from question 16 to question 30.**

*Pause for dramatic effect and look increasingly exasperated.*

**Does anyone know the answer?**

*Pause until someone points out that you haven't asked a question.*

EXERCISE A | SLIDE 250.1

***Exactly*. And neither will the TSIA2 when it comes to *a lot* of the writing questions. For instance, let's look at question 1 in your workbook. Don't worry. This isn't a pop quiz. It's just for looks, so no need to start hunting for the right answer. Do you notice anything weird about it, though? What's missing from the question?**

An actual question.

**The test won't come out and say, "Hey! What's the best verb for this sentence?" or "Sheesh, this sentence is so wordy; how do we make it better?" What *do* they give us?**

Instructions that say to pick *the best version of the underlined part of the sentence.*

**But what is *best*? The best verb? The best punctuation? A version of the sentence that somehow solves world hunger? We can't tell what *best* might be just yet. Where might we find some clues to help us?**

In the underlined portion of the sentence and the answer choices.

**How is the underlined portion related to the answer choices?**

The answer choices are alternatives for the underlined portion.

**This question structure is seen across all kinds of standardized tests. You're given a sentence with a piece that's underlined, along with some answer choices that offer up options for completing the sentence. It'll be your job to figure out which one effectively and correctly completes that sentence. Will all these kinds of questions test you on the same topic, or is any writing topic fair game?**

All writing topics are fair game.

**These kinds of questions offer up tons of variety in the skills they test, from transitions and concision to comma usage and verb tense. Luckily, we have a strategy that can help you out, no matter the subject being tested. It's called *The 4 C's*.**

TSIA2 Mastery: ELAR 

EXERCISE B

**Instructions**
Write the letter of each definition next to its matching term.

**1.** ____ Correct

**2.** ____ Consistent

**3.** ____ Clear

**4.** ____ Concise

A. The answer presents ideas in a logical manner.

B. The answer is brief but comprehensive.

C. The answer maintains correct verb tense, parallel structure, and point of view.

D. The answer does not contain or create any grammar or punctuation errors.

## Groundwork

*In this section, students will be introduced to the building blocks of the 4 C's strategy.*

EXERCISE B | SLIDE 251.1

**Four C's. Easy enough to remember, right? But what are they exactly? Think of it like a checklist to help you eliminate bad answers on the TSIA2. If they're not *correct, consistent, clear,* and *concise*, then you know you can toss them out. Take a moment now and see if you can match each of the 4 C's to its definition.**

*Give students 60 seconds to complete this task.*

**Let's start with number 1. Which definition did you match with *correct*?**

Letter D.

**What does the definition tell us?**

Correct answers won't have any problems with punctuation or grammar.

**What should you do if you find an answer choice that creates a punctuation or grammar error?**

Eliminate it.

**What about number 2? Which definition matches up with *consistent*?**

Letter C.

**What does *consistent* mean?**

It *maintains correct verb tense, parallel structure, and point of view.*

**So, for instance, if a sentence is written in past tense, what kinds of answers would we eliminate to make sure it's *consistent*?**

Ones that are in future or present tense.

**What's our third C?**

*Clear.*

**And which definition matches up?**

Letter A.

**What characteristics does a *clear* answer have?**

The information is logical and easy to understand.

**And our last C: *concise*. Which definition matches up with number 4?**

Letter B.

**What does it mean for an answer choice to be *concise*?**

The answer says the information in the fewest words possible.

**Again, we use these 4 C's like a checklist. Start with the first C, and work through your options. The best answer choice will always be correct, consistent, clear, and concise. Every. Time. Let's see this strategy in action.**

EXERCISE C

**Instructions**
Use the first C (Correct) to eliminate incorrect answers.

5. A pair of runners whip by me, assaulting the quiet with short steps that splash through the water, I love to run, but today it is time to appreciate the serenity of this world.

   (A) water,
   (B) water and
   (C) water
   (D) water;

## Groundwork

*In this section, students will practice using the first C (Correct) to help them eliminate incorrect answer choices.*

EXERCISE C SLIDE 252.1

**The 4 C's offer up a solid arsenal to help you take on the writing questions of the TSIA2. Which one should we always start with?**

*Correct.*

**The best answer choice will always have perfect grammar and punctuation, so this is a good place to start. For example, let's look at question 5. There are three answer choices there that create a run-on sentence. Who knows what a run-on sentence is?**

Two complete sentences that have been connected incorrectly.

**What are the two complete sentences we're working with?**

*A pair of runners whip by me, assaulting the quiet with short steps that splash through the* water and *I love to run, but today it is time to appreciate the serenity of this world.*

**Let's check each of our answer choices and eliminate anything that's not correct, starting with choice A. Does that answer connect the complete sentences correctly?**

No.

**Why not?**

It only has a comma to separate them.

**When we have two complete sentences like this, we can't just drop a comma between them. It creates an error called a comma splice. If we wanted to keep that comma, we'd need a connecting word, too, like *and*. That means we can eliminate choice A. What about choice B? Does that one connect the sentences appropriately?**

No.

**What went wrong there?**

It has *and* but no comma.

**Just adding *and* to the sentence, without a comma for support, breaks the sentence structure. To connect two complete sentences, you need both the comma and the coordinating conjunction to be correct, so choice B is definitely out. Does choice C connect the sentences without breaking any rules?**

No.

**What's wrong with that choice?**

It just runs the first sentence into the second with nothing in between.

**Choice C creates the textbook definition of a run-on: two complete sentences connected without any punctuation. That leaves us with choice D. How does it connect the sentences?**

With a semicolon.

**Can we use semicolons to connect two complete sentences?**

Yes.

**In fact, that's the only time the TSIA2 will let you use semicolons. They work the same way as periods, though you don't need to capitalize the first letter of the word that follows it. That means choice D is the most correct and the right answer to this question.**

TSIA2 Mastery: ELAR 

# Application

## THE APPROACH

When answering a writing question that does not actually contain a question, use these steps ...

1. Eliminate answers that are not correct, consistent, clear, and concise.
2. If more than one option remains, select the answer that sounds the most natural.

**Instructions**

Use the second C (Consistent) to eliminate incorrect answers.

**6.** I walk at a decrepit pace; the soft sand squeaks peacefully beneath my feet. I hear the calls of the seagulls above and the crashing of waves in the background. I feel the silky breeze slip quietly across the coast.

Ⓐ I hear
Ⓑ You can hear
Ⓒ One can hear
Ⓓ While hearing

# Application

*In this section, students will practice using the second C (*Consistent*) to help them eliminate incorrect answers.*

**What comes to mind when you think of the term *consistent*?**

Matching or compatible.

**And how does being *consistent* help us eliminate answer choices?**

If the answer doesn't match the sentence, we know it's wrong.

**There are actually a few ways we can test for consistency. For instance, we can match in tone, whether it's formal or informal. Another way, which you'll commonly see on the TSIA2, is consistency of person. What do I mean by person?**

1st person, 2nd person, or 3rd person.

**All writing comes from one of three perspectives, or persons. How can we tell if something is in 1st person?**

It uses words like *I*, *me*, or *we*.

**What word tells us a passage is in 2nd person?**

*You*.

**What about 3rd person? What are some words we might see?**

*They*, *them*, *she*, *he*, etc.

SLIDE 253.1

**Take a close look at question 6 in your workbook. What tells you that we're working with consistency of person?**

All the answer choices are in different person.

**What do we need our answer choice to be *consistent* with again?**

The sentence or sentences that make up the question.

**So where will we find what we need to pick the right answer?**

In those sentences.

**Let's dig in. Do you see any words or phrases that help you figure out what person the passage is in?**

*I walk*, *my feet*, *I feel*.

**What person is that?**

1st.

**Let's check our answer choices. Which ones can we eliminate and why?**

Choice B is in 2nd person, and choice C is in 3rd.

**We're left with two options. Can we eliminate any others using another C we already learned about?**

Choice D.

**What's wrong with that one?**

It's not correct.

**Starting that sentence with *while* creates an incomplete sentence, so we know it's wrong. That leaves us with choice A. Does that one match up with our C's?**

Yes, it's *correct* and *consistent*.

**That means we can confidently say that choice A is the right answer.**

### THE APPROACH

When answering a writing question that does not actually contain a question, use these steps ...

1. Eliminate answers that are not correct, consistent, clear, and concise.
2. If more than one option remains, select the answer that sounds the most natural.

**Instructions**

Use the third C (Clear) and fourth C (Concise) to eliminate answer choices.

**7.** Throughout human history, people of various cultures and religions around the world have developed their own stories regarding rivers.

Ⓐ stories regarding

Ⓑ stories to

Ⓒ stories which they connected to

Ⓓ stories, related to

## Application

*In this section, students will practice using* Clear *and* Concise *to help them eliminate incorrect answers.*

SLIDE 254.1

**Once we've checked to make sure that the answer choices are *correct* and *consistent*, what's left?**

*Clear* and *concise*.

**What do you think would make an answer seem *clear*?**

It makes sense.

**Sometimes, as you're evaluating an answer choice, you might find yourself thinking, "Huh? What?" If you find yourself experiencing that confusion, it's a good sign that the answer choice isn't *clear*, and it can be eliminated. Let's practice using question 7. Do any of those answer choices seem unclear?**

Choice B.

**Why does that one seem unclear?**

It seems like they're turning stories *into* rivers.

**Saying their stories turn into rivers doesn't make sense, so we know it's wrong. Can we eliminate any other answer choices using the C's we've learned about so far?**

Choice D.

**Which of the 4 C's does that one break?**

It's not *correct*.

**Choice D has an extra comma thrown in there, which isn't necessary. It's bad punctuation, so the answer is wrong. Which of the 4 C's haven't we covered yet?**

*Concise*.

**What does it mean to be concise?**

To say things in the fewest words possible.

**As a general rule of thumb, good writing is concise. It gets to the heart of the matter without adding any extra fluff, like wordiness or repetition. Between choices A and C, which one is *more* concise?**

Choice A.

**Writing questions are challenging because of the simple fact that they aren't really questions. But the 4 C's will never let you down. The best answer will always be correct, with no grammar or punctuation errors, consistent with the passage, clear and logical, and concise. Use these C's to eliminate bad choices and narrow your options to just one answer: the right one.**

## Practice

**Instructions**
Complete the practice set. If time remains after you've finished, double-check your work.

1. According to researchers, many of the vast deserts of the world, in ancient times, lush forests full of plants and animals.

   Ⓐ the world, in ancient times
   Ⓑ the world, being in ancient times
   Ⓒ the world were, in ancient times
   Ⓓ the world was, in ancient times

2. The land that is now Alaska, which was inhabited by the Tlingit tribe before being colonized by Russia, sold by Tsar Alexander II to the United States in 1867.

   Ⓐ Russia, sold by
   Ⓑ Russia, having been sold by
   Ⓒ Russia, was sold by
   Ⓓ Russia, to be sold by

3. Though the polecat looks like a weasel in appearance, but has more developed scent glands than a weasel.

   Ⓐ but has
   Ⓑ but it's having
   Ⓒ it is having
   Ⓓ it has

# Practice

SLIDE 255.1

*Give students 6 minutes to complete the practice set.*

SLIDE 255.2

1. **The correct answer is C.** Choices A, B, and D can be eliminated because they are not Correct. Choice A is incorrect because it does not provide a necessary verb to complete the sentence. Choice B is incorrect because it lacks a verb to complete the sentence and *being in ancient times* is wordy and confusing. Choice D is incorrect because the singular verb *was* does not match the plural subject *many*. Only choice C provides the appropriate plural verb *were* to complete the sentence while remaining concise.

SLIDE 255.3

2. **The correct answer is C.** Choices A and D can be eliminated because they are not Correct. Choice A is incorrect because *sold by* creates a parenthetical element, which means that the sentence does not contain the verb it needs to be grammatically correct. Choice D is incorrect because *to be sold* is a verbal and doesn't provide the sentence with the verb it needs to complete the sentence. Choice B can be eliminated because it is neither Correct nor Concise. Choice B is incorrect because it also turns the last clause into a parenthetical element, and *having been sold by* is unnecessarily wordy. Choice C is correct because *was sold by* provides the necessary verb that completes the sentence.

SLIDE 255.4

3. **The correct answer is D.** Choices A and B are incorrect because they are not Concise; the sentence already contains the contrasting conjunction *though* to connect the ideas in the sentence, so adding *but* is repetitive. Choice C is incorrect because *it is having* is unnecessarily wordy which means the sentence is neither Clear not Concise. Choice D is correct because *it has* appropriately completes the independent clause of the sentence, making it grammatically correct.

This page is intentionally left blank.
Content resumes on the next page.

This page is intentionally left blank.
Teacher content resumes with the next chapter.

CHAPTER 29

# Punctuation

In this chapter, students will determine whether and where commas are needed to set off or separate adjectives and parenthetical elements in sentences.

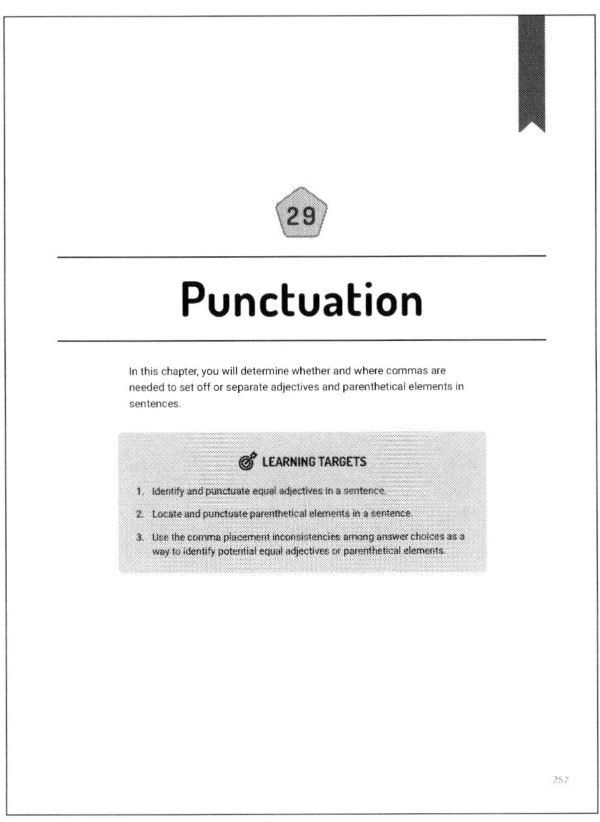
29

Punctuation

In this chapter, you will determine whether and where commas are needed to set off or separate adjectives and parenthetical elements in sentences.

LEARNING TARGETS

1. Identify and punctuate equal adjectives in a sentence.
2. Locate and punctuate parenthetical elements in a sentence.
3. Use the comma placement inconsistencies among answer choices as a way to identify potential equal adjectives or parenthetical elements.

257

## TSIA2 STANDARD

**Essay Revision and Editing**
Standard English conventions

The student will edit text as necessary to ensure conformity to the conventions of standard written English grammar, usage, and punctuation.

**Sentence Revision, Editing, and Completion**
Conventions of punctuation

The student will edit and complete sentences as needed to ensure conformity to the conventions of standard written English punctuation.

## TEKS ALIGNMENT

E1.9 *Composition*: listening, speaking, reading, writing, and thinking using multiple texts—writing process. The student uses the writing process recursively to compose multiple texts that are legible and use appropriate conventions. The student is expected to:

(D) edit drafts using standard English conventions, including:

(v) punctuation, including commas, semicolons, colons, and dashes to set off phrases and clauses as appropriate.

## LEARNING TARGETS

1. Identify and punctuate equal adjectives in a sentence.
2. Locate and punctuate parenthetical elements in a sentence.
3. Use the comma placement inconsistencies among answer choices as a way to identify potential equal adjectives or parenthetical elements.

## Warm-Up

**Instructions**

Complete the warm-up question. If time remains after you've finished, double-check your work.

**Passage**

**(1)** When schools of fish gather again after time apart, they will swim around each other while waving their fins and performing elaborate dances. **(2)** Stingrays have been seen, frolicking over fields of coral, twirling and flapping their wings, even when ample open ocean is readily available. **(3)** Some have argued that these kinds of behaviors show that fish can feel emotions like joy and delight.

**(4)** Even advocates for the argument that fish have feelings acknowledge that scientists can easily misidentify what they are seeing. **(5)** The shape of a fish's mouth makes it look like it is surprised; it looks that way even when it is excited or in danger. **(6)** Fish are social, communicating underwater using clicks and bubbles. **(7)** Feelings are challenging to understand even in humans, who have the ability to talk about their emotions.

**(8)** Many oceanographers who devote their time to studying fish behavior have argued that at least some fish, such as triggerfishes and eels, have strong feelings like the ones we experience as humans. **(9)** Other researchers are doubtful. **(10)** They argue that it has not yet been proven that fish feel emotion in any reliable, reproducible scientific experiments.

**(11)** Regardless, scientific consensus on the question of fish emotion is beginning to shift. **(12)** Many biologists have accepted that fish most likely have "primary" emotions such as fear or anger. **(13)** These responses seem to be found in most fish. **(14)** For instance, a zebrafish will avoid a part of the tank where it was once shocked even if the shock has been removed. **(15)** Additionally, scientists believe that feelings can be inferred from fishes' changes in activity and eye movement, or even from involuntary responses like scale shedding.

**1.** Which of the following is the best version of the underlined portion of sentence 2 (reproduced below)?

*Stingrays have been <u>seen, frolicking over fields of coral, twirling and flapping their wings,</u> even when ample open ocean is readily available.*

- Ⓐ (as it is now)
- Ⓑ seen frolicking over fields of coral, twirling and flapping their wings,
- Ⓒ seen, frolicking over fields of coral, twirling and flapping their wings
- Ⓓ seen frolicking, over fields of coral, twirling and flapping their wings,

# Warm-Up

SLIDE 258.1

*Give students 5 minutes to complete the warm-up question.*

SLIDE 258.2

1. **The correct answer is B.** Choice A is incorrect because the phrase *frolicking over fields of coral* describes what the *stingrays have been seen* doing and is the object of the verb, so it should not be separated with a comma. Choice C is incorrect because it does not include a comma after *wings* to correctly separate the parenthetical element from the rest of the sentence. Choice D is incorrect because the adverbial phrase *over fields of coral* should not be separated from the verb *frolicking*. Choice B is correct because it correctly separates the parenthetical element *twirling and flapping their wings* from the rest of the sentence using commas.

TSIA2 Mastery: ELAR 

## Groundwork

EXERCISE A

**Instructions**
Test each phrase to determine if a comma is needed to separate the adjectives. If a comma is needed, add it to the phrase.

> **Test #1:** Swap the adjectives. Adjectives that can be swapped easily need a comma between them.

1. the adorable grumpy-looking viscacha
2. the ferocious hungry tiger
3. the graceful adult giraffe
4. the rare African parrot

# Groundwork

*In this section, students will review uses of commas as separators of "equal" adjectives.*

**Wild animals, adorable animals, furry animals. Animals that have thick fur, animals that are endangered or extinct, animals who are massive and sharp-clawed. The words *wild, adorable, furry, thick, endangered, extinct, massive,* and *sharp-clawed* are all used to describe animals. We have a specific name for these. Does anyone know the term used to identify describing words?**

Adjectives.

**Adjectives are describing words. They answer questions like, what color is it? What size? What kind? Is it expensive? Old? Famous? They also answer the question of *how* something appears—is it tired? Cheerful? Aggressive? Those are all adjectives. Who else can give me an example of an adjective?**

*Allow 2–3 students to share.*

**The English language is weird because a single description can be tweaked and shuffled around and even separated from the sentence altogether. Some of those descriptions need punctuation to keep them separated—and some don't. What kind of punctuation do you think we'll use to separate adjectives in a sentence?**

A comma.

**Commas are our best option for separating those description words, but they aren't needed in every instance where two adjectives appear next to each other. The key is to figure out if the adjectives are *equal*, meaning they equally describe the same noun as a team. Equal adjectives always need that separating comma.**

EXERCISE A SLIDE 259.1

**Let's practice with number 1. What two adjectives are we working with?**

*Adorable* and *grumpy-looking*.

**To figure out whether these adjectives are equal, let's try our first test: swapping the order. How does *the grumpy-looking, adorable viscacha* sound?**

Good.

**If we can switch the adjectives without things sounding awkward, we know they're equal, and they need a comma.**

SLIDE 259.2

**Take a moment to practice on your own. See if those phrases need a comma to separate the adjectives.**

*Give students 90 seconds to complete the activity.*

**What do we think about number 2? Does that phrase need a comma?**

Yes.

**How do you know?**

When we switch the adjectives, *hungry, ferocious tiger* doesn't sound weird.

**What about number 3? Does that need a comma?**

No.

**Why not?**

*Adult graceful giraffe* sounds weird.

**And finally, number 4. Do we need a comma there?**

No.

**If we switch *rare* and *African*, the phrase sounds really awkward, so we know we don't need the comma.**

EXERCISE B

### Instructions

Test each phrase to determine if a comma is needed to separate the adjectives. If a comma is needed, add it to the phrase.

> **Test #2:** Add an "and." If the phrase still sounds correct with "and" between the adjectives, they should be separated by a comma.

**5.** the four large rattlesnakes

**6.** the falcon's lightweight aerodynamic body

**7.** the friendly Dalmatian puppies

**8.** the loud annoying frogs outside

## Groundwork

*In this section, students will practice using a second "test" to determine whether two adjectives are equal.*

EXERCISE B

**What's our second test to help us figure out if we need a comma between equal adjectives?**

Add an "and" between the adjectives.

SLIDE 260.1

**Let's try it together first. What adjectives are we working with in number 5?**

*Four* and *large*.

**How does the phrase sound if we add "and" between those words?**

*The four and large rattlesnakes.*

**Do we like the way that sounds?**

No.

**It sounds pretty weird, so we know those adjectives aren't equal. No comma needed.**

SLIDE 260.2

**Take a minute now and apply this test to the next three phrases. See if the adjectives are equal and need a comma to separate them.**

*Give students 90 seconds to complete this task.*

**What adjectives are we testing in number 6?**

*Lightweight* and *aerodynamic*.

**What happens if we put "and" between those adjectives?**

Nothing really. *Lightweight and aerodynamic body* sounds fine.

**Do we need the comma?**

Yes.

**What about number 7? Are *friendly* and *Dalmatian* equal adjectives?**

No.

**How do you know?**

*Friendly and Dalmatian puppies* sounds weird.

**Do we need a comma there?**

No.

**And what about number 8? Do we need a comma?**

Yes.

**How can you tell?**

*Loud and annoying frogs* still sounds good, so they're equal adjectives.

**Being able to tell when to separate single adjectives is a good skill, but what if the description is more than that? What if the describing words are long phrases or even clauses? Let's turn to the next page.**

EXERCISE C

### Instructions

Refer to the following sentence as your teacher leads the discussion.

9. The common ostrich, the world's largest species of bird, can sprint at speeds of over 40 mph.

---

### Instructions

Determine whether the underlined portions in the passage contain a parenthetical element. If so, add commas to separate them from the rest of the sentence.

### Passage

**(1)** You may have heard that the pufferfish a creature containing enough toxin to kill several dozen people at once is considered a delicacy in Japan. **(2)** Chefs wishing to serve this fish known in Japanese as *fugu* must undergo years of study and pass a final examination that involves the live preparation and consumption of *fugu*. **(3)** *Fugu* is most commonly served raw often with thin slices of meat arranged into the shape of a flower, but it can also be fried, stewed, and grilled like any other fish. **(4)** Those brave enough to ingest it report a delicate, savory, and surprisingly non-fishy taste.

## Groundwork

*In this section, students will learn how to identify and punctuate a parenthetical element.*

EXERCISE C SLIDE 261.1

**This lesson is all about descriptive phrases and how to punctuate them. Just based on that, what do you think a parenthetical element *is*?**

A description of some kind.

**A parenthetical element is like an adjective on steroids. It's a phrase or a clause that adds more detail or information to a sentence. And it has a unique feature: it's removable. Check it out in sentence 9. Which phrase makes up the parenthetical element here?**

*The world's largest species of bird.*

**That phrase adds a little more info about ostriches. Let's take that phrase out and see what happens. Who'd like to read the sentence without the parenthetical element?**

*The common ostrich can sprint at speeds of over 40 mph.*

**Notice that we still have a grammatically complete sentence, *and* the information still makes sense. How does this sentence punctuate the parenthetical element?**

It has commas around it.

**A parenthetical element will always have some kind of punctuation surrounding it to separate it from the rest of the sentence, and on the TSIA2, you'll be using commas.**

SLIDE 261.2

**Next, let's turn our attention to the paragraph, starting with sentence 1. We need to figure out if the sentence contains a parenthetical element and, if so, where to place the commas. Do you see a parenthetical element in sentence 1?**

*A creature containing enough toxin to kill several dozen people at once.*

**How do you know it's a parenthetical element?**

You can take it out of the sentence, and what's left is still grammatically correct and didn't lose any essential information.

**Where should we put the commas?**

Before *a creature* and after *at once*.

SLIDE 261.3

**Take a moment now to review sentences 2 through 4. See if the underlined portion contains a parenthetical element, and if so, where to add commas.**

*Give students 2 minutes to complete this task.*

**Let's start with sentence 2. Does the underlined portion contain a parenthetical element?**

Yes.

**What is it?**

*Known in Japanese as fugu.*

**Where should we add our commas?**

Before *known* and after *fugu*.

**What about sentence 3? Who can walk me through that one?**

The parenthetical element is *often with thin slices of meat arranged into the shape of a flower*, but there is already a comma after *flower*, so we just need a comma before *often*.

**And what about sentence 4? Do we need to add commas there?**

There's no parenthetical element, so we don't need to add any commas.

**And just like that, we've got all our commas in place.**

## Application

### THE APPROACH

When you are challenged to correctly punctuate descriptive words and phrases on the test, use the following steps ...

1. Locate equal adjectives or parenthetical elements, if any appear.
2. Eliminate answer choices that contain incorrect comma placement.

**10.** Which version of the sentence below is punctuated correctly?

*Cephalopods, a class of animals that includes octopuses and squids possess three separate hearts that pump oxygen-rich, blue-colored blood throughout their bodies.*

Ⓐ (as it is now)

Ⓑ Cephalopods, a class of animals that includes octopuses and squids, possess three separate hearts that pump oxygen-rich, blue-colored blood throughout their bodies.

Ⓒ Cephalopods, a class of animals that includes octopuses and squids possess three separate hearts that pump oxygen-rich blue-colored blood throughout their bodies.

Ⓓ Cephalopods a class of animals that includes octopuses and squids possess three separate hearts that pump oxygen-rich, blue-colored blood throughout their bodies.

# Application

***In this section, students will review how to answer these types of punctuation questions on the TSIA2.***

**On the test, you won't be given a question that asks you specifically about equal adjectives or parenthetical elements. Instead, you'll see a question like this one in your workbook.**

SLIDE 262.1

**Take a close look at the answer choices. How are they the same?**

They all have the exact same words.

**What's different about them?**

They have different comma placements.

**So what do you think this question is testing you on?**

Comma rules.

**Let's work through an example together. What should we do first?**

Find any equal adjectives and parenthetical elements.

**Do you see any equal adjectives?**

Yes. *Oxygen-rich* and *blue-colored* equally describe *blood*.

**Take a quick pass through your answer choices. Can we eliminate any that don't have a comma between those two adjectives?**

Choice C.

**We still have three possible answer choices, so we know there's something else happening in the sentence. Are there any parenthetical elements?**

*A class of animals that includes octopuses and squids.*

**Let's test it. If we take it out of the sentence, does it still make sense? And is it still a complete sentence?**

Yes.

**What does that phrase need, then?**

Commas around it.

**Can we eliminate any answer choices because they're missing commas around the parenthetical element?**

Choice A doesn't have one at the end of the phrase, and choice D is missing both commas.

**That leaves us with our correct answer: choice B.**

TSIA2 Mastery: ELAR 

## THE APPROACH

When you are challenged to correctly punctuate descriptive words and phrases on the test, use the following steps ...

1. Locate equal adjectives or parenthetical elements, if any appear.
2. Eliminate answer choices that contain incorrect comma placement.

**Passage**

**(1)** Flamingos can survive in remarkably harsh climates. **(2)** Some flamingo species make their home in the barren frigid peaks of the Andes Mountains, while others reside in boiling hot springs. **(3)** Because flamingos can eat the toxic algae that grows in these remote and lifeless places, they have no trouble living there.

**11.** Which of the following is the best version of the underlined portion of sentence 2 (reproduced below)?

*Some flamingo species make their home in the barren frigid peaks of the Andes Mountains, while others reside in boiling hot springs.*

Ⓐ (as it is now)

Ⓑ in the barren frigid peaks of the Andes Mountains, while others reside in boiling, hot springs

Ⓒ in the barren, frigid peaks of the Andes Mountains, while others reside in boiling hot springs

Ⓓ in the barren, frigid peaks of the Andes Mountains, while others reside in boiling, hot springs

## Application

*In this section, students will answer one more practice problem that requires identifying correct use of commas.*

SLIDE 263.1

**Let's try another one. How is this one different from the first one we looked at?**

Only part of the sentence is underlined.

**Why might this be trickier than the previous question?**

It can be tempting to just look at the underlined portion.

**What kind of trouble could we run into if we only focused on what's underlined?**

If we only focus on the underlined part, we might miss a piece of punctuation or a portion of a parenthetical element.

**That's why it's a good idea to always read the *entire* sentence. Let's start our process again with this question. What should we look for?**

Equal adjectives and parenthetical elements.

**A good way to find those is to focus on the differences between the answer choices. Is there a comma that appears in one answer choice but not the other? That's a good clue that you're getting close to either a pair of equal adjectives or a parenthetical element.**

**Looking through our answer choices, where do we see the first comma that may or may not be needed?**

There's a comma between *barren* and *frigid* in choice C and D, but it's not in choice A or B.

**Are there any equal adjectives or parenthetical elements near that comma placement?**

*Barren* and *frigid* are equal adjectives.

**Do we need a comma to separate them?**

Yes.

**How can you tell?**

We can swap them or put "and" between them, which means they're equal adjectives.

**Which answers are missing the necessary comma between those two words?**

Choices A and B.

**Let's cross those off. What's the difference between the two remaining choices?**

Only one has a comma between *boiling* and *hot.*

**Are those equal adjectives?**

No.

**How can you tell?**

You can't swap them, and you can't put "and" between them.

**So, do we need that comma?**

No.

**Which answer should we eliminate?**

Choice D.

**That leaves us with choice C as the correct answer.**

## Practice

**Instructions**

Complete the practice set. If time remains after you've finished, double-check your work.

**1.** Which of the following is the best version of the underlined portion of the sentence below?

*Crocodiles have been spotted, hovering near empty river banks, waiting and biding their time, until some unsuspecting prey comes along for a drink of water.*

Ⓐ (as it is now)
Ⓑ spotted hovering near empty river banks, waiting and biding their time,
Ⓒ spotted, hovering near empty river banks, waiting and biding their time
Ⓓ spotted hovering, near empty river banks, waiting and biding their time,

**2.** Which of the following is the best version of the underlined portion of the sentence below?

*Admiral Lavigne, the child of a Belizean, immigrant mother and a Garifuna-speaking father, made it an official language, and offered native Garifuna speakers an agreement to create peace.*

Ⓐ (as it is now)
Ⓑ Belizean immigrant mother and a Garifuna-speaking father, made it an official language and offered native Garifuna speakers an agreement
Ⓒ Belizean immigrant mother, and a Garifuna-speaking father, made it an official language and offered native Garifuna speakers an agreement,
Ⓓ Belizean, immigrant mother and a Garifuna-speaking father, made it an official language, and offered native Garifuna speakers an agreement,

**3.** Which of the following is the best version of the underlined portion of the sentence below?

*Despite its dilapidated condition, the sculpture was a widely, beloved feature of the community.*

Ⓐ (as it is now)
Ⓑ widely beloved,
Ⓒ widely beloved
Ⓓ widely, beloved

# Practice

SLIDE 264.1

*Give students 8 minutes to complete the practice set.*

SLIDE 264.2

1. **The correct answer is B.** Choices A and C are incorrect because *spotted* and *hovering* are not equal adjectives, nor is *hovering near empty river banks* a parenthetical element, so adding a comma is unnecessary. Choice D is incorrect because *near empty river banks* is not a parenthetical element, so it does not need to be separated from the sentence with commas. Choice B is correct because it correctly separates the parenthetical element *waiting and biding their time* from the rest of the sentence.

SLIDE 264.3

2. **The correct answer is B.** Choices A and D are incorrect because *Belizean* and *immigrant* are not equal adjectives, so they do not need a comma between them. Choice C is incorrect because no comma is needed to separate *a Belizean immigrant mother* and *a Garifuna-speaking father* within the parenthetical element. Choice B is correct because it includes the comma needed at the end of the parenthetical element without adding any unnecessary punctuation.

SLIDE 264.4

3. **The correct answer is C.** Choices A and D are incorrect because *widely* and *beloved* are not equal adjectives, so they do not need a comma to separate them. Choice B is incorrect because a comma should not be used to separate an adjective from the noun it describes. Choice C is correct because it does not add any unnecessary commas.

TSIA2 Mastery: ELAR 

## Wrap-Up

### Instructions

Complete the wrap-up question. If time remains after you've finished, double-check your work.

### Passage

**(1)** These days, Barcelona is the only city in Spain where a majority of the residents speak a regional language: Catalan. **(2)** It is taught to every child. **(3)** And to many adults, it is a source of cultural identity. **(4)** Barcelona differs substantially even from other autonomous regions in Spain like Basque Country, which has a majority Basque (rather than Spanish) population. **(5)** In Barcelona, Catalan and Castilian Spanish are both official languages. **(6)** Yet Catalan, alongside Spanish, is considered a primary language, spoken by 70 percent of Barcelonans. **(7)** In Basque Country, which also has two official languages, Basque is secondary to Spanish.

**(8)** Historians and anthropologists argue that the decline of this regional language dates back to the union of the Castile and Aragon crowns in the late 15th century. **(9)** However, as the monarchy sought to replace regional languages with Spanish, the territory that ultimately became Barcelona remained autonomous. **(10)** This helped preserve Catalan.

**(11)** Under General Francisco Franco, who ruled from 1936 to 1975, Catalan suffered. **(12)** General Franco, the son of a naval officer father and Spanish-speaking mother, made it a forbidden language and punished Catalan speakers with imprisonment for their disobedience. **(13)** Democratic government was established in the 1980s. **(14)** Then more actions were taken to preserve Catalan. **(15)** However, not everyone feels confident about Catalan's future, pointing to changes like the growing number of immigrants from Latin America, where Spanish is typically the dominant language, to Barcelona, where Catalan has the upper hand. **(16)** Whether Catalan can continue to grow, or at least hold on, in an increasingly migratory society within an ever-changing world remains an open question.

**2.** In context, which of the following is the best version of the underlined portion of sentence 12 (reproduced below)?

*General Franco, the son of a <u>naval officer father and Spanish-speaking mother, made it a forbidden language and punished Catalan speakers with imprisonment</u> for their disobedience.*

- Ⓐ (as it is now)
- Ⓑ naval, officer father, and Spanish-speaking mother, made it a forbidden language, and punished Catalan speakers with imprisonment
- Ⓒ naval officer father, and Spanish-speaking mother, made it a forbidden language, and punished Catalan speakers with imprisonment,
- Ⓓ naval, officer father, and Spanish-speaking mother, made it a forbidden language, and punished Catalan speakers with imprisonment,

# Wrap-Up

SLIDE 265.1

*Give students 5 minutes to complete the wrap-up question.*

SLIDE 265.2

2. **The correct answer is A.** Choices B and D are incorrect because *naval officer* is an adjectival phrase that should not be separated with a comma. Choice C is incorrect because the phrase *the son of a naval officer father and Spanish-speaking mother* should not be separated with a comma because it describes Franco as the son of a father and ... mother. Choice A is correct because it correctly offsets the parenthetical element *the son of a naval officer father and Spanish-speaking mother* from the sentence using commas.

This page is intentionally left blank.
Content resumes on the next page.

This page is intentionally left blank.
Teacher content resumes with the next chapter.

CHAPTER 30

# Additional Phrases and Clauses

In this chapter, students will learn how to utilize participial phrases and relative clauses to avoid sentence structure errors, such as fragments and comma splices.

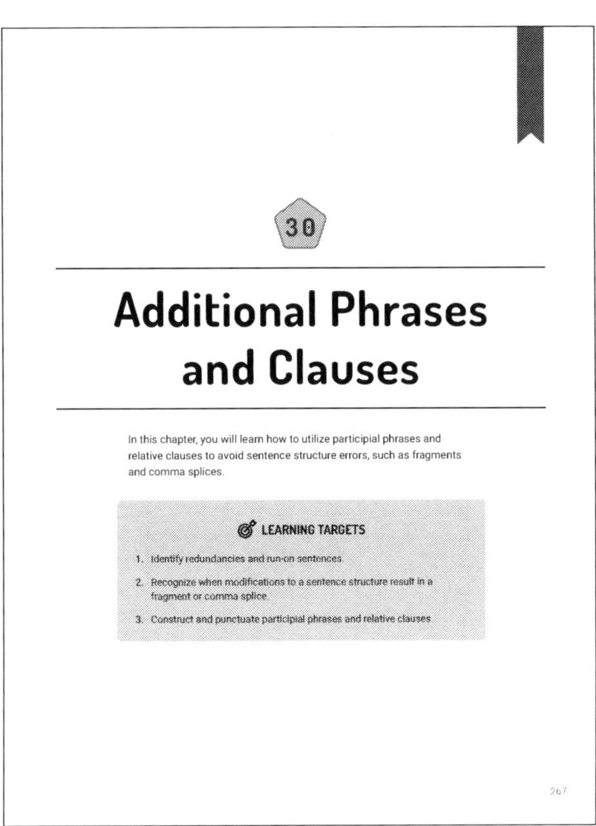

30

Additional Phrases and Clauses

In this chapter, you will learn how to utilize participial phrases and relative clauses to avoid sentence structure errors, such as fragments and comma splices.

LEARNING TARGETS

1. Identify redundancies and run-on sentences.
2. Recognize when modifications to a sentence structure result in a fragment or comma splice.
3. Construct and punctuate participial phrases and relative clauses.

267

## TSIA2 STANDARDS

**Sentence Revision, Editing, and Completion**
**Conventions of grammar**

The student will edit and complete sentences as necessary to ensure conformity to the conventions of standard English grammar.

## TEKS ALIGNMENT

E1.9 *Composition*: listening, speaking, reading, writing, and thinking using multiple texts—writing process. The student uses the writing process recursively to compose multiple texts that are legible and use appropriate conventions. The student is expected to:

(D) edit drafts using standard English conventions, including:

(i) a variety of complete, controlled sentences and avoidance of unintentional splices, run-ons, and fragments.

## LEARNING TARGETS

1. Identify redundancies and run-on sentences.
2. Recognize when modifications to a sentence structure result in a fragment or comma splice.
3. Construct and punctuate participial phrases and relative clauses.

## Warm-Up

**Instructions**
Complete the warm-up question. If time remains after you've finished, double-check your work.

**1.** By 1990, Nabisco's Oreos had become the most popular cookie in the United States, they sold millions of units.

Ⓐ they sold
Ⓑ they had sold
Ⓒ with selling
Ⓓ selling

# Warm-Up

SLIDE 268.1

*Give students 2 minutes to complete the warm-up question.*

SLIDE 268.2

1. **The correct answer is D.** Choices A and B are incorrect because they result in comma splices. Choice C is incorrect because *with selling millions of units* uses the unnecessary preposition *with*. Choice D is correct because it correctly uses the participle *selling* to describe how Oreos had become so popular.

TSIA2 Mastery: ELAR 

## Groundwork

EXERCISE A

### Instructions
Locate two grammatically incorrect sentences in the following passage. Underline your answers.

### Passage
**(1)** Did you know that the original drive-through window was invented for a very specific group of Americans? **(2)** Drive-throughs were designed to make life a little more convenient for U.S. military members, they were prohibited from wearing their uniforms in public. **(3)** That meant they'd have to go home and change clothes before heading out for a burger. **(4)** But in 1975, one McDonald's owner decided to do something that created a kind of loophole. **(5)** He cut a hole in the side of his building, he had allowing soldiers to drive up in their cars and order food without breaking any rules.

## Groundwork

*In this section, students will practice recognizing errors in sentence structure.*

EXERCISE A

**Has anyone ever heard of Murphy's Law?**

*Pause for a show of hands.*

**Does anyone know what it means?**

If anything can go wrong, it *will* go wrong.

**I may be wrong, but I'm pretty sure that the TSIA2 intentionally fell prey to Murphy's Law when they made most of their questions for the writing section of the test. They found any and every way a sentence structure could go wrong and ran with it. Off the top of your head, what are some ways you know of that a sentence structure could be broken?**

An incomplete sentence, a run-on, a comma splice, a missing subject or verb, etc.

SLIDE 269.1

**Believe it or not, additional phrases and clauses questions on the TSIA2 cover just about every single one of those issues. But let's not get too far ahead. Before we dive into correcting broken sentences, let's just practice finding them. There are two broken sentences hiding in the passage in your workbook. Let's see if we can find them, starting with sentence 1. Does that sentence seem complete?**

Yes.

**How can you tell?**

It has a subject and a verb, and it expresses a complete thought.

**There's nothing off about sentence 1, so it's solid. What about sentence 2? Anything strange going on there?**

Yes.

**What seems off?**

There are two sentences in one.

**Sentence 2 is made up of two complete sentences connected with just a comma. This error is called a *comma splice*. When that happens, we need to change things up in one way or another. Usually we fix the issue by replacing the comma with a period. Other less conventional options include swapping the comma for a semicolon or adding a connecting word like *and*. Take a moment now to pass through the rest of the sentences. Of the three that remain, which one is broken?**

Sentence 5.

**What's wrong with it?**

*He had allowing* in the middle of the sentence sounds weird.

**Murphy's Law struck again, and this time, it took out the verb structure in sentence 5. That sentence needs a bit of restructuring to make it correct.**

EXERCISE B

**Instructions**
Determine which solution best completes the sentence. Circle your answer.

**(2)** Drive-throughs were designed to make life a little more convenient for U.S. military members, they were prohibited from wearing their uniforms in public.

To correct the error in this sentence ...

... remove the comma.

... change "they were prohibited" to "prohibiting."

... change "they" to "who."

## Groundwork

*In this section, students will decide how to complete the broken sentences using limited options.*

EXERCISE B   SLIDE 270.1

**So, let's fix these broken sentences. After all, that'll be the goal when we're taking the TSIA2. But we won't get to fix these sentences just any way we want. We're limited by something. What limits our options?**

We only have four answer choices.

**You'll need to practice choosing a solution instead of crafting your own. Let's start with sentence 2. What error did we find there again?**

A comma splice.

**Who remembers the ways I mentioned that we could fix that error?**

With a period, a semicolon, or a connecting word like *and*.

**Let's check our options. Does this exercise give us any of those options?**

No.

**The TSIA2 not only goes wrong in their sentence construction, but they also love to let things go haywire in their answer choices. And that means the most common ways to fix errors don't always show up. How can we decide which option works best?**

Test each one.

**Let's start with our first option. Sentence 2 is a comma splice, so what if we just take out that problematic comma? Does that fix the issue?**

No, because it's still two full sentences with nothing to break them up.

**We need to do something more. What if we make a big change and swap *they were prohibited* with just *prohibiting*? What would the sentence become?**

*Drive-throughs were designed to make life a little more convenient for U.S. military members, <u>prohibiting</u> from wearing their uniforms in public.*

**Does that sentence structure seem better?**

No, it needs something else between *prohibiting* and *from*.

**Let's try the last option. Replace *they* with *who*. How does the sentence sound?**

*Drive-throughs were designed to make life a little more convenient for U.S. military members, <u>who</u> were prohibited from wearing their uniforms in public.*

**Is the problem resolved?**

Yes, it's much better.

**By switching *they* with *who*, we created something called a *relative clause*. Don't worry. You don't need to remember that term for test day. But recognize that it may be one of the correct options for fixing a sentence structure gone wrong. What do you notice about the punctuation before that relative clause?**

It has a comma before it.

**Relative clauses start with pronouns like *who* or *which*, and they should always have a comma right before them to separate them from the rest of the sentence. That's one thing the TSIA2 will always get right, though. If a relative clause is the solution to a problem, they'll always have that comma in place for you.**

**TSIA2 Mastery:** ELAR 

EXERCISE C

**Instructions**
Determine which solution best completes the sentence. Circle your answer.

**(5)** He cut a hole in the side of his building, he had allowing soldiers to drive up in their cars and order food without breaking any rules.

To correct the error in this sentence ...

... change "he" to "who."

... change "he" to "him."

... remove "he had" from the sentence.

## Groundwork

*In this section, students will decide on an alternative solution to correct a sentence structure error.*

EXERCISE C | SLIDE 271.1

**What about sentence 5? What issue did we find here?**

The verb in *he had allowing* sounds wrong.

**What if we just fix it the same way we fixed sentence 2? That seemed to work out really well for us last time. What would the sentence become if we replaced *he* with *who*?**

*He cut a hole in the side of his building, <u>who</u> had allowing soldiers to drive up in their cars and order food without breaking any rules.*

**Better, right?**

Not at all.

**Okay, so maybe these fixes aren't one-size-fits-all. What's our next option?**

Change *he* to *him*.

**What does that make the sentence look like?**

*He cut a hole in the side of his building, <u>him</u> had allowing soldiers to drive up in their cars and order food without breaking any rules.*

**Does that sound better?**

No, if anything it sounds worse.

**Changing up the pronoun clearly isn't working. How come?**

The issue is with the verb.

**How does the last option fix the verb?**

It takes off the helping verb.

**Let's test it. What does the sentence become when we take out *he had*?**

*He cut a hole in the side of his building, <u>allowing</u> soldiers to drive up in their cars and order food without breaking any rules.*

**Does that sentence sound okay?**

Yes.

**When we have this kind of structure, where there's a phrase starting with an *-ing* verb, we create what's called a *participial phrase*. These phrases start with *-ing* or *-ed* verbs, depending on what's in the sentence. How do we keep these phrases separated from the rest of the sentence?**

With a comma.

**These kinds of phrases won't always show up at the end of the sentence, though. Sometimes, they're at the beginning. If that happens, where do you think the comma goes?**

At the end of the phrase.

**For instance, we could revise this sentence to say *cutting a hole in the side of his building, he allowed soldiers to drive up in their cars and order food without breaking any rules*. The comma would follow the phrase *cutting a hole in the side of his building*.**

## Application

### THE APPROACH

When you are asked to find the appropriate phrase and clause, use these steps ...

1. Determine if the underlined portion contains the main verb of the sentence.
2. If it does, eliminate answer choices that contain inappropriate verbs.
3. If it doesn't, eliminate answers that create run-ons, comma splices, or fragments.
4. If more than one answer remains, eliminate answers that *sound* wrong.

1. The crew of astronauts, they were studying the effects of weightlessness on the human heart.

   (A) astronauts, they were studying
   (B) astronauts studied
   (C) astronauts to have studied
   (D) astronauts, who were studying

# Application

***In this section, students will practice applying the steps of the Approach to an additional phrases and clauses question.***

SLIDE 272.1

**These questions can be really challenging to identify on the TSIA2. Why do you think that might be?**

Because there are a lot of ways the sentences can be broken.

**With so many options, it's hard to figure out which writing questions will challenge you to create additional phrases and clauses to complete the sentence. In fact, you might not even realize you have one of these questions until you find your answer. For this reason, step 1 is a fail-safe and will work with almost any sentence revision question. What should we do?**

*Determine if the underlined portion contains the main verb of the sentence.*

**Additional phrases and clauses take a solid chunk of the sentence and turn it into a description. If that underlined part has the main verb of the sentence and we turn it into a description, what happens to the sentence?**

It breaks again.

**Check out question 1. What's the subject of this sentence?**

*The crew of astronauts.*

**And what's the crew doing?**

*Studying.*

**So, is the sentence's main verb included in that underlined section?**

Yes.

**What should we do then?**

*Eliminate answer choices that contain inappropriate verbs.*

**Do any of the answer choices make those errors?**

Yes, choices C and D make the sentence incomplete.

**Let's eliminate both of those. Compare what's left. What's the difference between choices A and B?**

Choice A has *they were studying,* and choice B just has *studied.*

**Read the sentence using choice A. Does it sound weird at all?**

Yes, it's repetitive to say *the crew of astronauts, they.*

**Choice A throws in an extra pronoun that gives the sentence *two* subjects. Again, Murphy's Law. The TSIA2 is going to mess up these sentences any and every way they can. That means we should eliminate choice A. Let's test choice B just in case something went wrong there, too. What does the sentence look like?**

*The crew of astronauts studied the effects of weightlessness on the human heart.*

**How does that sound?**

Good and complete.

**A lot of times, your natural instincts will be your most valuable asset for these kinds of questions. Anything that sounds wrong *is* wrong. Use your instincts to help you make eliminations and narrow your options to the one that sounds best.**

## THE APPROACH

When you are asked to find the appropriate phrase and clause, use these steps ...

1. Determine if the underlined portion contains the main verb of the sentence.
2. If it does, eliminate answer choices that contain inappropriate verbs.
3. If it doesn't, eliminate answers that create run-ons, comma splices, or fragments.
4. If more than one answer remains, eliminate answers that *sound* wrong.

**2.** By 1969, Union Pacific had become the most successful rail company in the United States, they laid 800 miles of rail line.

Ⓐ they laid
Ⓑ with laid
Ⓒ they had laid
Ⓓ laying

## Application

*In this section, students will practice applying the steps of the Approach to a question that does not include the sentence's main verb in the underlined portion.*

SLIDE 273.1

**Let's run through things one more time with a new question. Take a moment to read number 2. What are we checking for first?**

To see if the underlined portion has the main verb of the sentence.

**We do have the verb *laid* in the underlined portion, but it's not really the main verb in the sentence. How can you tell?**

The subject is the *Union Pacific* and the main verb is *had become*, so what's underlined must be an extra verb.

**If the underlined portion doesn't have our main verb, what kinds of errors are we looking for?**

*Run-ons, comma splices, or fragments.*

**Start with choice A. Does that one have any sentence structure errors?**

Yes, it has a comma splice.

**How can you tell?**

It connects two complete sentences with just a comma.

**Do a quick pass. Does that same error show up in any of the other answer choices?**

Yes, in choice C.

**We can eliminate choices A and C since the extra *they* in the underlined portion creates a comma splice. What if, at this point on the test, I panic? I can't figure out which of the two options is technically more correct and all my grammar skills fall out of my brain? I mean, anything that can go wrong will go wrong, right? Should I just guess and hope it's right?**

No.

**What else, besides my grammar skills, can I use to help me figure out if an answer isn't right?**

Instincts.

**While we may not always be able to pick out perfect grammar every time, we can *definitely* pinpoint stuff that sounds wrong. Try it with choice B. What does the sentence become?**

*By 1969, Union Pacific had become the most successful rail company in the United States, with laid 800 miles of rail line.*

**What do you think? Does your instinct like that construction?**

No.

**It sounds awkward, so we know it's wrong. But let's check the last option just in case. Maybe we missed something. What does the sentence sound like using choice D?**

*By 1969, Union Pacific had become the most successful rail company in the United States, laying 800 miles of rail line.*

**Do you like the way that sounds?**

Yes.

**That *-ing* verb *laying* creates a perfectly constructed participial phrase. But we didn't need to know that term or even how to construct those kinds of phrases. All we needed was our ears and instincts to figure out which option worked best.**

## Practice

**Instructions**

Complete the practice set. If time remains after you've finished, double-check your work.

1. The children thought that their father was being serious when he told them that the word "gullible" is not in the dictionary.

   Ⓐ serious when he told
   Ⓑ serious he told
   Ⓒ serious, he telling
   Ⓓ serious him telling

2. The opera singer utterly amazed the audience they cheered for an encore and threw flowers for an entire minute after the last song.

   Ⓐ audience they cheered
   Ⓑ audience to cheer
   Ⓒ audience, cheering
   Ⓓ audience, who cheered

3. It had just been removed from the freezer the casserole was nearly frozen solid.

   Ⓐ It had just been removed from the freezer
   Ⓑ Just been removed from the freezer and
   Ⓒ Having just been removed from the freezer,
   Ⓓ Had just been removed from the freezer,

# Practice

SLIDE 274.1

*Give students 8 minutes to complete the practice set.*

SLIDE 274.2

1. **The correct answer is A.** Choice B is incorrect because it creates a run-on sentence: two independent clauses joined together without proper punctuation or a conjunction. Choice C is incorrect because the comma followed by the pronoun *he* and the participle *telling* produces an incorrectly formed sentence with an illogical second clause. Choice D is incorrect because it adds an unnecessary pronoun to the participle phrase *telling them that the word "gullible" is not in the dictionary* and does not separate the phrase with a comma. Choice A is correct because the conjunction *when* introduces a relative clause, logically indicating that the first clause happened at the time of the second clause.

SLIDE 274.3

2. **The correct answer is D.** Choice A is incorrect because it is a run-on sentence. Choice B is incorrect because *utterly amazed the audience to cheer* is an awkward construction that doesn't express the idea clearly. Choice C is incorrect because the construction of the sentence makes it unclear who is cheering. Choice D is correct because the comma followed by the relative pronoun *who* logically indicates that the audience is the subject of the following clause, and the verb *cheered* agrees in tense with the verb *threw*.

SLIDE 274.4

3. **The correct answer is C.** Choice A is incorrect because it creates a run-on sentence. Choice B is incorrect because it attempts to connect *just been removed from the freezer* to the independent clause of the sentence with the conjunction *and*, which is an illogical sentence construction. Choice D is incorrect because the phrase *had just been removed from the freezer* uses the past perfect tense to create a participial phrase, which is grammatically incorrect. Choice C is correct because it accurately uses the participle *having just been removed from the freezer* offset with a comma to describe the casserole.

TSIA2 Mastery: ELAR 

## Wrap-Up

**Instructions**
Complete the wrap-up question. If time remains after you've finished, double-check your work.

**2.** The party of <u>Dwarves, they were determined</u> to reclaim the right to their homeland, fought bravely to defend the Lonely Mountain from the Orcs and the Wargs.

Ⓐ Dwarves, they were determined
Ⓑ Dwarves determining
Ⓒ Dwarves to have determined
Ⓓ Dwarves, who were determined

## Wrap-Up

SLIDE 275.1

*Give students 2 minutes to complete the wrap-up question.*

SLIDE 275.2

2. **The correct answer is D.** Choice A is incorrect because it adds the unnecessary subject *they* to the sentence and forms a grammatically incorrect sentence structure. Choice B is incorrect because it creates an incomplete sentence. Choice C is incorrect because *to have determined* creates an unclear sentence structure. Choice D is correct because it converts the phrase between the commas into a participial phrase with the pronoun *who* and separates the phrase from the rest of the sentence with commas.

This page is intentionally left blank.
Content resumes on the next page.

This page is intentionally left blank.
Teacher content resumes with the next chapter.

CHAPTER 31

# Essay Orientation

In this chapter, students will become familiar with the characteristics and grading standards of the TSIA2 Essay section.

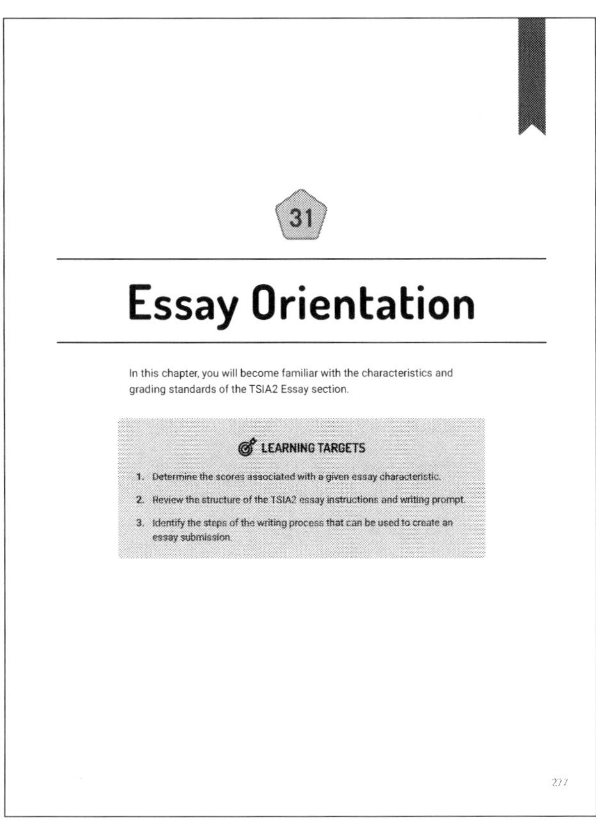

31

Essay Orientation

In this chapter, you will become familiar with the characteristics and grading standards of the TSIA2 Essay section.

LEARNING TARGETS

1. Determine the scores associated with a given essay characteristic.
2. Review the structure of the TSIA2 essay instructions and writing prompt.
3. Identify the steps of the writing process that can be used to create an essay submission.

277

## LEARNING TARGETS

1. Determine the scores associated with a given essay characteristic.
2. Review the structure of the TSIA2 essay instructions and writing prompt.
3. Identify the steps of the writing process that can be used to create an essay submission.

## Groundwork

### Instructions

Refer to the following table as your teacher leads the discussion.

| Subject | Passing Score |
|---|---|
| **English Language Arts and Reading** | |
| Multiple Choice | 945+ |
| Essay* | 5+ |
| **Mathematics** | |
| Multiple Choice | 950+ |

### How Is the Essay Scored?

The essay is scored according to your performance in the following areas:

- **Purpose and Focus:** the essay remains on topic and has a clear main idea.
- **Organization and Structure:** the essay's ideas are well-organized, typically through paragraphs.
- **Development and Support:** evidence is provided to support the main idea of the essay.
- **Sentence Variety and Style:** the essay contains correct and varied sentence structures, along with a formal tone and appropriate vocabulary use.
- **Mechanical Conventions:** the essay is written using correct grammar and punctuation.
- **Critical Thinking:** there is a logical progression of ideas through the essay.

## Groundwork

*In this section, students will learn what scores are required to pass the Essay section of the TSIA2, along with what elements of the essay contribute to the overall score.*

SLIDE 278.1

**Half of the multiple-choice section of the ELAR test is made up of questions on grammar and punctuation. The TSIA2 includes those questions because they want you to prove that you can write, and write well, based on conventional English grammar and punctuation rules. They even call them "writing-based" questions. Think about it, though: do those questions really prove that you're a good writer?**

No.

**What better way to figure out if someone can write than to have them actually write something? Enter the TSIA2 Essay section. Before you can show off those mad essay skills, though, you first have to pass the multiple-choice section. Take a look at the chart in your workbook. What do you need to score on the multiple-choice section to pass?**

945 or higher.

**If you don't hit that 945 benchmark, the test will drop you into something called the Diagnostic. That part of the test gives you more opportunity to prove what you know, and if you do well on that, you'll still get the opportunity to come back to the essay. But, in this course, we aim high, so let's assume you hit that 945 score. What will you need to score on the essay to pass?**

5

SLIDE 278.2

**On the essay, you can score anywhere from a 1 to an 8, but a 5 is all you need. So, how do they grade your essay? Well, I'll let you in on a secret: the graders aren't people. It's a grading *system* that analyzes your writing and grades it based on six performance areas. What are those areas?**

*Purpose and focus, organization and structure, development and support, sentence variety and style, mechanical conventions, critical thinking.*

**Essentially, the grading system looks for an essay that zeroes in on one main idea, presents the ideas in an organized way, and offers plenty of support to prove that the main idea is true. It also checks to make sure that you're writing well and with accuracy, and that your ideas follow a logical progression. Which area do you think will be the most challenging for you?**

*Allow 2–3 students to share.*

**Knowing where you might struggle is an important step in preparing for the TSIA2 Essay. If you know what you need to work on, you can practice. And practice we will! But before we talk about writing the actual essay, let's get into more detail on these performance areas. What *exactly* is the test looking for?**

TSIA2 Mastery: ELAR 

EXERCISE A

**Instructions**
Review the TSIA2 Essay grading standard and circle the score an essay with that characteristic would earn on the test.

**1.** Presents a vague or limited point of view on the issue

2 or 6

**2.** May stray from the audience and purpose but is able to refocus

5 or 8

**3.** Exhibits skillful use of language, using a varied, accurate, and apt vocabulary

5 or 8

**4.** Demonstrates adequate variety in sentence structure

3 or 6

**5.** Provides inappropriate or insufficient examples, reasons, or other evidence to support its position

3 or 5

**6.** Organizes ideas ineffectively, demonstrating a problematic progression of ideas

2 or 6

## Groundwork

*In this section, students will review several grading standards and determine which score an essay with that characteristic would earn.*

EXERCISE A

**Think of the essay's grading system like scoring in the Olympics, except instead of scoring you out of 10, your max score is an 8. Each of the performance areas act like a judge, and the final score is an average of how each judge scored you. How can that work to our advantage?**

If we don't score well in one performance area, we can make up for it with a strong score in another area.

SLIDE 279.1

**Check out these statements in your workbook. These are descriptions based on performance areas that directly relate to a specific score. For instance, look at number 1. What performance area do you think it relates to?**

Purpose and Focus.

**When it comes to your point of view on the essay prompt, you want to have a strong stance. If you present a *vague or limited point of view* on the topic, what score do you think you'll get?**

2

**Why did you pick that score?**

*Vague or limited point of view* means that the argument isn't very strong, which means a low score.

**If you're not offering up a strong, specific stance on the essay prompt, chances are that you won't get a good score in the Purpose and Focus performance area. What about number 2? What kind of score will you get if you *stray from the audience and purpose* but pull it back together at the end?**

5

**Remember that a 5 is all you need to pass, so this statement is really reassuring. It goes to show that we can have some errors in our essay but still earn a passing score. What about number 3? What score do you think you'll get if the test thinks your use of vocabulary is *skillful*?**

8

**How do you know?**

If an essay is so well-written that the test calls it *skillful*, it's getting a top score.

SLIDE 279.2

**What about number 4? What score would that essay earn?**

6

***Adequate* isn't a rave, but it's definitely not going to leave you with a low score. Using just enough sentence variety to prove you can do it is perfectly acceptable. And number 5? What score should we give it?**

3

**Why did you pick that score?**

If it's *inappropriate* or *insufficient*, it's not enough to pass.

**Finally, let's look at number 6. What score would an essay with poor organization earn?**

2

**The TSIA2 has these kinds of statements for every score in all six performance areas. But the thing to remember is that the test isn't looking for something amazing. You're not taking huge hits to your score for a few mistakes here and there. You should try your best but don't let your anxiety take over. If this was just the TSI-Essay with no other parts on the test, I'd tell you to go for broke. With that math section still ahead, though, we don't want you to burn up that precious mental energy aiming for an 8 on the essay only to run out of steam on the math section.**

## Instructions

Refer to the following instructions as your teacher leads the discussion.

---

The essay gives you an opportunity to show how effectively you can develop and express your ideas in writing.

You will first read a short passage and an assignment question that are focused on an important issue. You will then write an essay in which you develop your own point of view on the issue. You should support your position with appropriate reasoning and examples. The position you take will not influence your score.

Your essay will be given a holistic score that represents how clearly and effectively you expressed your position. The following six characteristics of writing will be considered.

- **Purpose and Focus** - The extent to which you present information in a unified and coherent manner, clearly addressing the issue.
- **Organization and Structure** - The extent to which you order and connect ideas.
- **Development and Support** - The extent to which you develop and support ideas.
- **Sentence Variety and Style** - The extent to which you craft sentences and paragraphs demonstrating control of vocabulary, voice, and structure.
- **Mechanical Conventions** - The extent to which you express ideas using standard written English.
- **Critical Thinking** - The extent to which you communicate a point of view and demonstrate reasoned relationships among ideas.

Scores on WritePlacer range from 1 to 8. An essay will be given a score of zero if it is too short to be evaluated, written on a topic other than the one presented, or written in a language other than English.

**PLEASE NOTE: The WritePlacer essay must be completed in one sitting. You will not be allowed to stop and finish your essay later. Please see your Proctor if you have questions regarding timing.**

## Groundwork

*In this section, students will evaluate the style and structure of the TSIA2 essay prompt.*

SLIDE 280.1

**So far, we've talked about the Essay section in the hypothetical. But what about the concrete? What *actually* shows up on the test? While I can't guarantee exactly what the essay will ask you to write about, I *can* give you a good idea of what to expect. Let's take a step back, though. If you reach the screen where the test shows you the essay instructions, what does that mean about the multiple-choice section?**

You earned a passing score.

**Just seeing the essay instructions should be a mini-celebration moment. It means you've conquered one of the three pieces of the TSIA2, which means you've started out strong. But, that doesn't mean you can let down your guard. The essay is no joke. Just take a look at how *massive* the instructions are. Why might it be a good idea for us to review the instructions now, rather than on test day?**

It will save some mental energy.

**We won't be running short on time, but we may be feeling a little brain numbness after the multiple-choice section. And we want to be fresh when we roll into the actual writing. By knowing what we need to do before we even get there, we save ourselves some energy. Do you notice anything familiar in these instructions?**

The performance areas.

**All six performance areas show up here, and there are even descriptions that go along with each of them. For instance, what does it say for Development and Support?**

*The extent to which you develop and support ideas.*

**Is that a helpful description?**

Not really.

**The description just kind of restates the performance area title, so it's not giving us any secret recipe for writing our essay. Take a moment now and read the rest of these instructions.**

*Give students 60 seconds to complete this task.*

**What do the instructions say you'll do first?**

Read a passage and assignment question.

**We'll look over an actual example in just a moment, but for now, let's keep digging into the details of the instructions. What does it tell you *won't* affect your score?**

Our position on the topic.

**It doesn't matter which side of the argument you take. The only important thing is that you provide ... what? What does the previous sentence tell us?**

*Appropriate reasoning and examples.*

**The TSIA2 is also pretty specific about what qualifies for a zero on the test. What earns a zero?**

Essays that are too short, talk about the wrong topic, or that aren't in English.

**There's also a really important note at the bottom. What does it say?**

That we have to do the essay in one sitting.

**That means no bathroom breaks and no leaving the test room. Does that mean no breaks *at all*?**

No, you can sit at the computer and take a moment to rest.

**Once you're done reading the instructions, it's time to hit that "continue" button. What do you expect to see on the next screen?**

The writing prompt.

**Let's check out an example of one on the next page.**

TSIA2 Mastery: ELAR 

EXERCISE B

**Instructions**

Review the following as your teacher leads the discussion.

**Passage**

"I learned that courage was not the absence of fear, but the triumph over it. The brave man is not he who does not feel afraid, but he who conquers that fear."

Adapted from Nelson Mandela, *Long Walk to Freedom*

---

**Assignment**

Are we in control of our fears?

Plan and write a multiparagraph essay (300–600 words) in which you develop your point of view on the above question. Support your position with reasoning and examples taken from your reading, studies, experience, or observations.

## Groundwork

*In this section, students will evaluate the elements of a TSIA2 essay prompt.*

EXERCISE B SLIDE 281.1

**How many elements make up this writing prompt?**

Two.

**What's the first piece called?**

The passage.

**The passage will always be a quote of some kind, usually by someone famous. What else do we have to work with?**

The assignment.

**Take a closer look at the text of the assignment. What's the first sentence?**

A question.

**That question is the *key* to this essay. Why do you think it's so important?**

It gives the topic that you need to write about.

**You'll use that question in every step of writing your essay, from figuring out what your opinion is all the way to reviewing your essay to make sure you've created an effective argument. How does the assignment question relate to the passage?**

The passage's quote is a possible answer to the question.

**Does that mean you have to take the same side as the passage did?**

No.

**Why not?**

Your stance doesn't affect your score, so you can decide for yourself.

**The passage is more like inspiration. It gives a little extra context and color to the assignment question. You don't need to agree with it, and you *shouldn't* include it in your essay. What else do we learn in the assignment?**

The essay needs to be between 300 and 600 words.

**The average page of text is usually about 250 words, so really, they want about two pages worth of essay. But you won't have to keep track. There will be a word counter on the bottom left of your text entry box that keeps count as you type. The instructions also remind us of something from the previous screen: that we should support our ideas with reasoning and examples. But it gives a little more. What kinds of examples should we use?**

Ones *taken from your reading, studies, experience, or observations*.

**This is just an example of what a TSIA2 essay prompt looks like. The passage and assignment question will change, but you can count on the instructions to stay the same. Take a moment to fold down the corner of this page or to add a bookmark here. The day before the test, come back and review these instructions so that you go into the test knowing *exactly* what you need to do.**

## Application

**Instructions**
Sequence the steps for writing your TSIA2 essay by placing the numbers 1–6 in the space provided.

### THE APPROACH

When you reach the Essay section of the TSIA2, follow these steps ...

_____ Write the introduction.

_____ Write the conclusion.

_____ Decide your opinion.

_____ Brainstorm and outline.

_____ Write two body paragraphs.

_____ Review your essay.

## Application

***In this section, students will sequence the steps they should take when working on the Essay section of the TSIA2.***

SLIDE 282.1

**After reading the instructions, we know what we're going to do. The question now is "how will we do it?" Should we start typing away and hope all our ideas make sense?**

Definitely not.

**A mad dash approach isn't an effective strategy for this kind of essay. Remember: we have a whole performance area that focuses on organization. Instead, we need a game plan. In fact, we've got the steps for our game plan right here in your workbook. But they're not in the right order. Let's fix that. Once you've read the assignment prompt, what's the first step you should take before you do anything else?**

*Decide your opinion.*

**You can't make any writing decisions until you've made up your mind about what side of the argument you plan to take. Usually, it's as simple as saying "yes" or "no" to the question. What should we do after that?**

*Brainstorm and outline.*

**What kinds of things do you think we'll be brainstorming?**

The details we'll use in the essay.

**It's a good idea to have at least *two* specific examples to support your main idea. What's the outline for?**

To organize what we brainstormed.

**You'll actually be given a piece of scratch paper during the test, which means you'll have space to brainstorm *and* create a rough outline. Once your ideas are in place, is it time to start writing yet?**

Yes.

**Where do you start?**

By writing the introduction.

**What follows the introduction?**

The two body paragraphs.

**We'll pick two examples during brainstorming, and we'll write two body paragraphs. What's the connection there?**

Each paragraph will be about one example.

**How do we end our essay?**

*Write the conclusion.*

**That's it, right? We've got the whole thing written, so we can submit our essay?**

Not yet.

**What's left to do?**

*Review your essay.*

**What kinds of things are we looking for?**

Everything makes sense. No grammar or punctuation errors.

**The essay might feel daunting, but remember that it's a moment of achievement. Reaching the essay means you nailed the multiple-choice section. And our game plan? We'll spend plenty of time in this course going over each of these 6 steps in detail so you know *exactly* what to do come test day.**

CHAPTER 32

# Brainstorming and Pre-Writing

In this chapter, students will learn a variety of techniques for gathering and selecting relevant ideas that will support their argument. In addition, students will learn how to organize ideas into a standard essay outline.

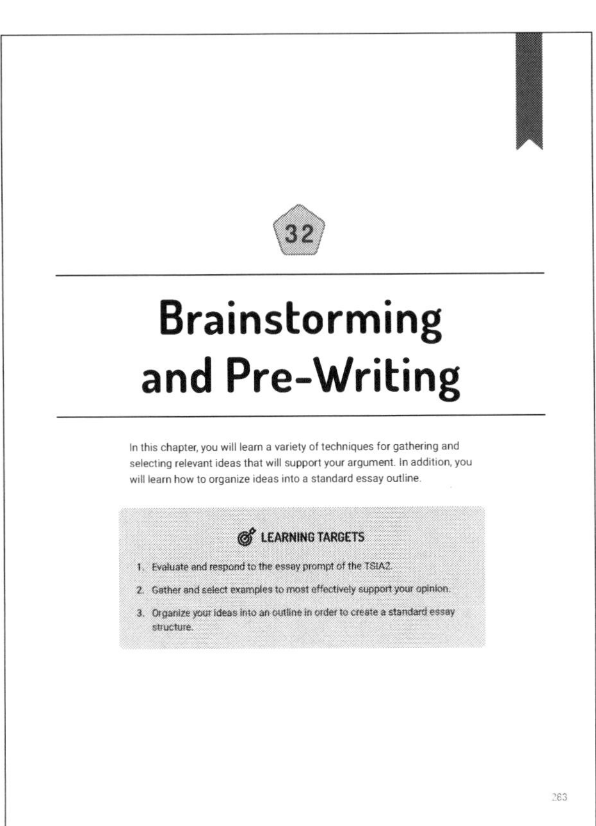

32

Brainstorming and Pre-Writing

In this chapter, you will learn a variety of techniques for gathering and selecting relevant ideas that will support your argument. In addition, you will learn how to organize ideas into a standard essay outline.

LEARNING TARGETS

1. Evaluate and respond to the essay prompt of the TSIA2.
2. Gather and select examples to most effectively support your opinion.
3. Organize your ideas into an outline in order to create a standard essay structure.

283

## TEKS ALIGNMENT

E1.9 *Composition*: listening, speaking, reading, writing, and thinking using multiple texts—writing process. The student uses the writing process recursively to compose multiple texts that are legible and uses appropriate conventions. The student is expected to:

(A) plan a piece of writing appropriate for various purposes and audiences by generating ideas through a range of strategies such as brainstorming, journaling, reading, or discussing.

## LEARNING TARGETS

1. Evaluate and respond to the essay prompt of the TSIA2.
2. Gather and select examples to most effectively support your opinion.
3. Organize your ideas into an outline in order to create a standard essay structure.

## Groundwork

EXERCISE A

**Instructions**
Fill in the following diagram using word association.

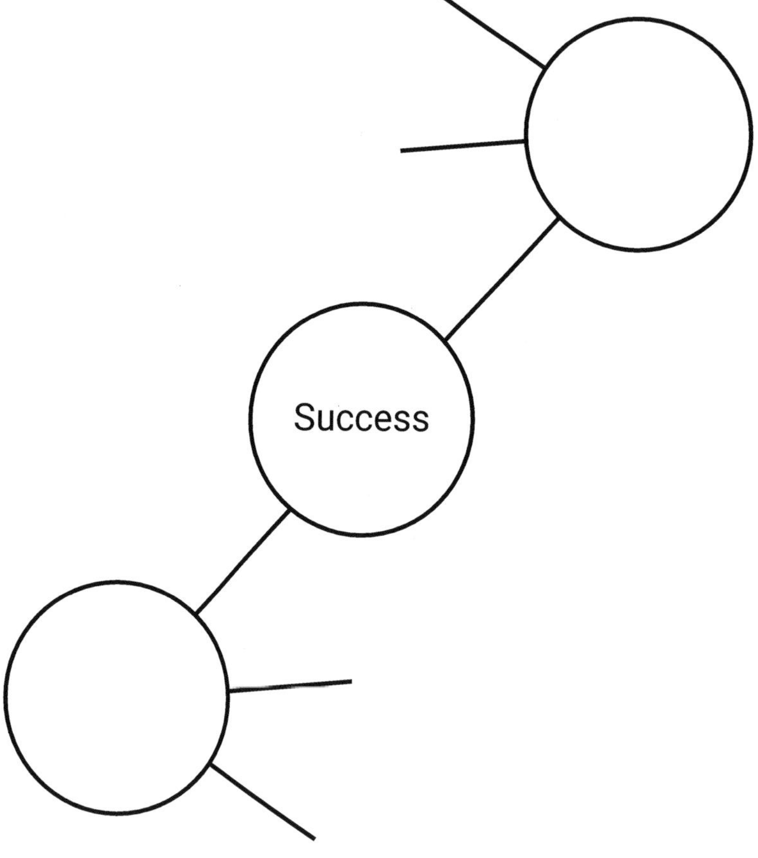

# Groundwork

***In this section, students will be introduced to the process of brainstorming using word association.***

EXERCISE A

**When I say the word "essay," what's the first word that pops into your brain?**

Writing, paper, pencil, homework, etc.

**What about if I say "test"? What comes to mind?**

Questions, studying, answers, etc.

**Our brains are funny, aren't they? All they need is one little word to spark a new idea. This exercise, in particular, is what the thinking experts like to call *word association*. When we hear a word, our brain automatically starts thinking of other words that relate to the original word. They're *associated*.**

SLIDE 284.1

**For instance, what does your brain associate with the word *success*?**

*Call on students until one says "money."*

**The American culture often associates money with success, which makes sense. Let's add that into one of the blank circles. Let's keep going with it. What comes to mind when you think of *money*?**

*Allow 2–3 students to share.*

**Write your ideas next to the branches coming off of our circle that says *money*. Notice that it's almost creating a chain. We could keep going, associating one word to the next, on and on forever. Our brains are just that powerful.**

**Let's come back, though. Take a moment to fill in the rest of the diagram. Come up with a word you associate with *success*, along with two more words that are connected.**

*Give students 90 seconds to complete this task.*

**Who'd like to share what they came up with?**

Example response: *Success* is related to *happiness*, which I connected to *dogs* and *vacation*.

**This process of using a suggestion to come up with more ideas has another name, and we actually use it a lot when it comes to essays. Does anyone know what it is? Here's another hint: it's in the title of this chapter.**

Brainstorming.

**Show of hands: who here *always* brainstorms before they write an essay? Be honest.**

*Pause for a show of hands.*

**Why do you think it might be worth it to take the time to brainstorm?**

So that we have lots of ideas to fill our essay.

**And on the flip side, what happens if we skip brainstorming?**

We go into writing without a clear idea of what we'll actually talk about.

**The TSIA2 is also unique from other tests in that it's not timed. How does this help you on the essay?**

We'll be able to brainstorm and plan the essay before actually writing it without risking running out of time.

**The question, now, is: what will you be brainstorming? Let's take some time to look at what you'll see on the actual test.**

EXERCISE B

**Instructions**
Refer to the following as the teacher leads the discussion.

**Passage**
"I learned that courage was not the absence of fear, but the triumph over it. The brave man is not he who does not feel afraid, but he who conquers that fear."

Adapted from Nelson Mandela, *Long Walk to Freedom*

---

**Assignment**
Are we in control of our fears?

Plan and write a multiparagraph essay (300–600 words) in which you develop your point of view on the above question. Support your position with reasoning and examples taken from your reading, studies, experience, or observations.

1. Circle your response to the question posed in the Assignment: *Are we in control of our fears?*

Yes No

## Groundwork

*In this section, students will evaluate the characteristics of a typical TSIA2-style essay prompt.*

EXERCISE B SLIDE 285.1

**Let's talk prompts. The TSIA2 has a rather unique set-up. How many sections make up the prompt?**

Two.

**What are they?**

The passage and the assignment.

**What's in the passage?**

A quote.

**In this case, it's a quote from Nelson Mandela, who was the first Black president of South Africa. This guy even won a Nobel Peace Prize. Do you think you'll need to be able to recognize the person who wrote whatever quote shows up in the passage?**

No.

**The quote is like a cake mix box. We need it for the instructions, the context, the inspiration. But, we won't actually put it in our cake. So, if you don't recognize the name, don't panic. You won't put the quote in your essay. As long as you can understand what the author's getting at, that's all you need.**

**What part of the prompt *will* we use to create our essay?**

The assignment.

**And what does the assignment want us to do?**

Write an essay responding to a specific question.

**In this example, what question do we need to answer?**

*Are we in control of our fears?*

**Take a moment to pick your side in the debate. Notice that there are only two options: yes or no. Why do we want to avoid *maybe*-type answers?**

Because our essay would lose focus.

**Show of hands: who thinks we *can* control our fears? Who thinks it's not so easy to keep strong emotions like that in check?**

*Pause for a show of hands.*

**Should we ever try to answer with *maybe*?**

No.

**Why not?**

Then the essay won't have a strong focus.

**Remember to be confident in your opinion. Even if you don't feel super strongly in one direction or another, act like you do. A strong argument comes from a strong opinion. How many words does our answer need to be?**

Between 300 and 600.

**With just a yes or no, we've technically answered the question. But, that's not enough to meet the word count minimum. The trick is that there's a secret question here: *why* do you think that? This is where our brainstorming skills will come in handy. Let's see if we can come up with a few ideas to support our opinion.**

EXERCISE C

### Instructions

Use your response to the question posed in the Assignment to practice brainstorming.

2. Brainstorm some ideas in the space below. Write down at least 3 examples you could use in your essay to support your opinion.

## Groundwork

*In this section, students will practice brainstorming ideas that support their response to the question posed in the Assignment section of the essay prompt.*

EXERCISE C SLIDE 286.1

**Once we know our initial response to the question, what's next?**

Brainstorming ideas.

**What are we brainstorming for, though, if we already have our answer?**

The stuff we plan to use to fill the rest of the essay.

**Specifically, we need examples: two of them. That's the "baby bear's porridge was just right" kind of recipe for these essays. With only one example, it's just not enough. And any more than two examples? You'll run into issues keeping your essay under the 600-word max. What should our examples prove?**

That our opinion is right.

**The goal is to pick two examples that prove to our reader that our response to the question is 100% correct. What are some good sources for our examples?**

Books, movies, current events, history, stuff we learned in other classes, personal experiences.

**It's just like word association, but this time, instead of using a word to inspire our ideas, we use our answer. For example, if you think that yes, we can control our fears, what should your examples include?**

People controlling their fears.

**Take a moment now to brainstorm. See if you can come up with at least 3 examples that support your opinion. Remember: you don't need to write full sentences. Just jot down what comes to mind.**

*Give students 90 seconds to complete this task.*

**Who would like to share an example they came up with?**

*Allow 2–3 students to share.*

**So, we've got all these ideas, but we really only need two of them. What should we do next?**

Pick the two we want to use.

**There are a few different ways to narrow your ideas to the best ones. Start by thinking about how much you know about each example. Why isn't it a good idea to pick something you don't know much about?**

It'll be harder to add specific details.

**Another way to narrow your options is to look at *where* the example came from. For instance, would it be better to pick an example from history or something from your personal experience?**

An example from history.

**Personal experiences are okay if you have a *really good* story to tell, but in general, you should leave those as a last resort. Focus on the examples that are clearly related to your opinion, that are specific, and that you have a good working knowledge of. That way, when it comes time to write, you have plenty to work with.**

# Application

## THE APPROACH

When you begin working on your essay during the TSIA2, you should ...

1. Review the Passage and respond to the question in the Assignment.
2. Brainstorm and select two examples to support your response.
3. Construct an outline to organize your ideas.

**Instructions**
Fill in the blanks as the teacher leads the discussion.

### CREATE AN OUTLINE

Introduction Paragraph

1. ______________________________
2. ______________________________
3. ______________________________

Body Paragraph 1

1. ______________________________
2. ______________________________

Body Paragraph 2

1. ______________________________
2. ______________________________

Conclusion Paragraph

1. ______________________________
2. ______________________________

# Application

*In this section, students will practice creating an outline of their essay using a provided format.*

SLIDE 287.1

**Once you've picked your ideas, it's time to start writing, right?**

No.

**Why not?**

Nothing is organized.

**Before you dive into that draft, it's important to take time to create an outline. We've got the bones of one here, on this page. How many paragraphs do you need to plan for?**

Four.

**Where do you think your examples will go?**

In the body paragraphs.

**The two paragraphs in the middle will each focus on an example. Example 1 goes into body paragraph 1, and Example 2 goes into body paragraph 2. Take a moment to add your ideas to the outline.**

*Give students 30 seconds to write down their first and second examples in the correct locations.*

**Notice that there's still one more thing that goes into each body paragraph. What do you think you'll need to include, along with each example?**

Some kind of explanation.

**Why should we always include the word "explanation" for each body paragraph?**

So that when we're writing, we don't forget.

**It's easy to get carried away when we start describing our example, and we might end up forgetting a key piece: a connection to the main idea of our essay. We have a specific sentence that shows up in our introduction paragraph that explains this main idea. Who remembers what that's called?**

A thesis.

**The thesis should always be the last sentence of our introduction. What else goes into that paragraph? How do we always want to open our essay?**

With something that catches the reader's attention.

**We need a hook to pull the reader in and make them *want* to know what we have to say. Between the hook and thesis, you'll also add something called a preview. What do you think a preview does?**

It mentions what's going to show up in the essay.

**The preview is like a movie trailer. It gives the reader some quick info about what's to come in the body paragraphs of the essay, without giving away any spoilers. Hmm ... looks like we're pretty close to wrapping up this outline. What's left?**

The conclusion paragraph.

**How many elements go into the conclusion?**

Two.

**What should we always start the conclusion with?**

A quick summary.

**Summarizing your ideas in a single sentence is a good way to transition into the conclusion. Following that, we want to end our essay with that mic drop moment, something that reaches out and *connects* to the reader. Why do we want to create that connection?**

So they are more likely to remember or agree with what we wrote.

**Will we need anything else in our essay?**

No.

**This stuff in your outline? They're the building blocks, the essential pieces of any strong essay. Be sure to save your notes from brainstorming and your outline because we're going to use them again and again over the next few chapters. We'll build each piece of your essay, one at a time, and hopefully, by the end of it all, you'll feel ready to tackle any old prompt the TSIA2 throws at you.**

This page is intentionally left blank.
Content resumes on the next page.

This page is intentionally left blank.
Teacher content resumes with the next chapter.

## CHAPTER 33

# Writing the Introduction

In this chapter, students will be introduced to the three main elements of an introduction paragraph. Additionally, they will evaluate and use strategies to draft an opening hook, preview, and thesis statement.

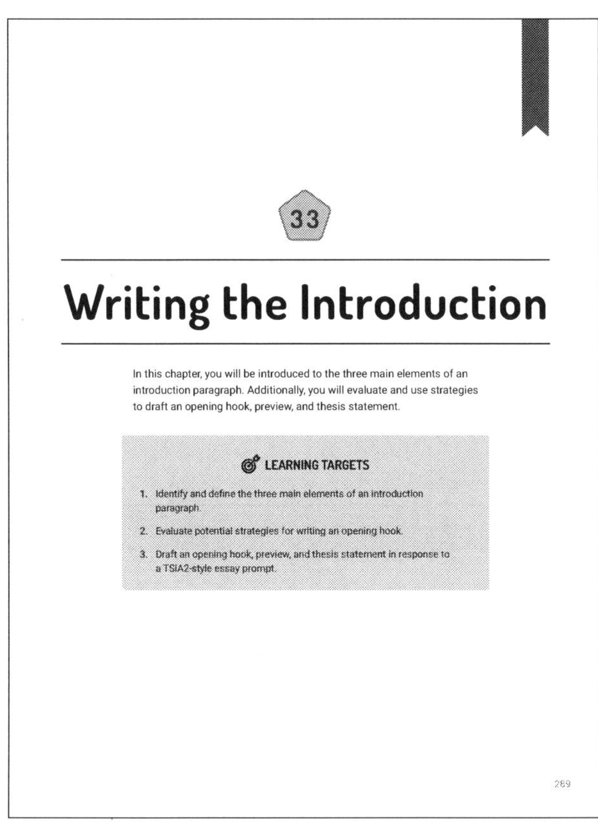

33

Writing the Introduction

In this chapter, you will be introduced to the three main elements of an introduction paragraph. Additionally, you will evaluate and use strategies to draft an opening hook, preview, and thesis statement.

LEARNING TARGETS

1. Identify and define the three main elements of an introduction paragraph.
2. Evaluate potential strategies for writing an opening hook.
3. Draft an opening hook, preview, and thesis statement in response to a TSIA2-style essay prompt.

289

## TEKS ALIGNMENT

E1.9 *Composition*: listening, speaking, reading, writing, and thinking using multiple texts—writing process. The student uses the writing process recursively to compose multiple texts that are legible and uses appropriate conventions. The student is expected to:

(B) develop drafts into a focused, structured, and coherent piece of writing, in timed and open-ended situations by:

(i) using an organizing structure appropriate to purpose, audience, topic, and context.

## LEARNING TARGETS

1. Identify and define the three main elements of an introduction paragraph.
2. Evaluate potential strategies for writing an opening hook.
3. Draft an opening hook, preview, and thesis statement in response to a TSIA2-style essay prompt.

## Groundwork

EXERCISE A

**Instructions**
Fill in the following definitions as your teacher leads the discussion.

1. Hook: ______________________________

2. Preview: ______________________________

3. Thesis: ______________________________

## Groundwork

***In this section, students will review the importance and characteristics of an introduction paragraph.***

EXERCISE A

**Has anyone ever been to a party or event where they didn't know anyone? We've all been there. What's your go-to strategy in those cases?**

*Answers will vary.*

Examples: Say "hey" to the person next to me. Stick close to the food. Scope out the room for people I think I could chat with. Devote all attention to the household pet.

**Introducing yourself can be tricky because you have to put yourself out there and hope to make a connection. What's your favorite opening line to get that conversation started?**

*Answers will vary.*

Examples: "Hey." "Hi, how are you?" "Do I know you?" "The weather's been great/awful!"

SLIDE 290.1

**That opening is definitely a make-or-break moment for the conversation. We don't want to nosedive into a full-blown description of something we enjoy, but we do want to offer up enough of ourselves that they get a chance to learn something about us, little by little. And we do the same thing with essays. What does a typical introduction paragraph do for the reader?**

Gives them a sneak peek at what the essay will be about.

**An introduction has three main pieces. The first is a hook. What's the goal of a hook?**

To grab the reader's attention.

**Let's write that down. *Hook 'em* isn't just a phrase for ranchers and fishermen. We use it for essay writing too. It's how we get people to be interested in what we have to say, just like when we meet a new person—we want them to find us interesting. Our essay should begin by engaging our audience. What's the next piece of our intro?**

The preview.

**What does *preview* make you think of?**

The trailer to a movie. Or a sneak peek at something.

**A preview has to walk a thin line between giving the reader enough information that they know what to expect in the essay, but not so much that we give away all the details. Make sure to note this on your page. Why do we want to avoid offering up too much in the preview?**

It would be too much information for one paragraph.

**If we give away everything up front, we'll have nothing to add to our body paragraphs later on. And, it can make the essay feel a bit repetitive. What's the last piece in our introduction?**

The thesis.

**The thesis will pack the biggest punch in your intro. What do you think we should include in this statement?**

Our opinion.

**Your thesis should *always* respond to the question in the assignment as well as specifically identify your opinion. Make sure to write that down in your notes. And now that we have the *what* of introductions, let's talk about the *how*.**

TSIA2 Mastery: ELAR 

EXERCISE B

**Instructions**

Evaluate each of the following strategies for writing a hook. Place a check mark next to the ones you think are effective options.

_______ Ask a relevant question.

_______ Use at least three exclamation points at the end of your sentence.

_______ Make an interesting or strong statement about the topic.

_______ Write a confusing sentence so that the reader has to continue reading to figure out what you meant.

_______ Describe a relevant image or scene.

## Groundwork

*In this section, students will evaluate potential strategies that could be used to write an opening hook that grabs the reader's attention.*

EXERCISE B  SLIDE 291.1

**Check out this list. We've got a few strategies we might use to create the opening of our essay. There's a problem, though: not all of them are good choices. Take a moment now to see if you can pick out which ones are good strategies and which ones aren't so great.**

*Give students 90 seconds to complete this task.*

**Show of hands: who thinks asking a relevant question is effective?**

*Pause for a show of hands.*

**Notice that even our lessons sometimes start with a warm-up question. Depending on the topic, you're challenged to answer a math, grammar, or reading question before you even learn any of the rules or strategies. You're asked to come up with an answer related to whatever the topic is. Why do you think that's an effective way to start?**

We immediately figure out what the lesson will be about and what we need to learn to find the right answer.

**The same thing works for our essay. When you ask a question, the reader automatically starts thinking about your topic. Or, they want to find out if their answer is the same as yours. That's why questions work so well as an opening hook strategy. What about exclamation points? Is more always better?**

No.

**Why might exclamation points be not-so-great for an academic-style essay?**

It feels too casual and seems out of place.

**When we write something for any school-related purpose, we always want to keep a formal tone. And exclamations don't really vibe with that tone. Plus, it might even make the reader feel like you're yelling at them. Not a good strategy. On the other hand, is making a strong statement a good way to open?**

Yes.

**A strong statement could be something as simple as, "Tacos are gross." What's your first thought when I say that?**

*Students will either agree or disagree with the statement.*

**Whether or not you agree, it doesn't matter. As a writer, I've already won the hook battle because you're thinking about the topic. And you'll be more interested in reading my argument explaining exactly why I wrote that. What about writing a confusing statement? Is that a good strategy?**

No.

**Why not?**

More likely, the reader will be confused and stop reading.

**Chances are the reader won't stick it out. If that first sentence is hard to get through, they're going to bail rather than try to sift through the confusion to figure out what you're trying to say. What about the last strategy? What do you think of opening with a description?**

It could work.

**Descriptions are tricky. You want to make sure to stay on-topic and lead into something that relates well to your thesis. But if you can nail a really good description of an image or a scene, you'll definitely hook the reader.**

EXERCISE C

**Instructions**
Refer to the following as the teacher leads the discussion.

**Passage**
"I learned that courage was not the absence of fear, but the triumph over it. The brave man is not he who does not feel afraid, but he who conquers that fear."

Adapted from Nelson Mandela, *Long Walk to Freedom*

---

**Assignment**
Are we in control of our fears?

Plan and write a multiparagraph essay (300–600 words) in which you develop your point of view on the above question. Support your position with reasoning and examples taken from your reading, studies, experience, or observations.

**4.** Which of the following is the *most* effective preview? Circle your answer.

A. Can we ever be without fear? No. Fear is a part of our lives.

B. There are many examples from history, literature, and film that show characters who are put in difficult situations in which they have to face their fears.

C. Nour and Mulan, strong fictional characters, both face challenging moments that make them fearful, but they overcome their fears and save those they love.

## Groundwork

***In this section, students will practice evaluating preview statements to determine whether or not the structure and content are effective.***

EXERCISE C | SLIDE 292.1

**Once you've got the reader hooked, what comes next?**

The preview.

**And what does a preview need to have?**

A sneak peek at the examples that will appear in the essay.

**How many examples will you have in your essay?**

> Note: The outline created in the Brainstorming and Pre-Writing chapter contains two examples, which is where students will have learned this concept. If you skipped that lesson, please provide students with the following answer:

Two.

**This is all good in theory, but what does this really look like? Let's review a few examples to get a clearer picture. Start with choice A. What do you think? Does that one work as a preview?**

No.

**What's wrong with it?**

It's a question, so it's more of a hook than a preview.

**The question there leads into an answer, but it doesn't really mention any specific examples, so it's not a good preview. What about choice B? That one seems a bit better. What does it do well?**

It talks about examples of characters who have to face their fears.

**Choice B is a good example of not being *quite* specific enough. Though it says the word *examples*, that's not our goal. We want to actually provide the reader with a hint of those examples. What about choice C? Is that a good preview?**

Yes.

**What does it do well?**

It specifically mentions both examples.

**Notice that the sentence doesn't end there. It also leads into the discussion about overcoming fear. Why do you think it's important to connect the examples to the topic of the essay?**

It'll connect to the thesis better.

**We want every paragraph in our essay to have a train of thought, so that each idea, each sentence, moves easily into the next.**

TSIA2 Mastery: ELAR 

EXERCISE D

**Instructions**

Determine whether each statement is a fact or an opinion. Circle your answers.

5. The summer heat in southern states like Texas and Arizona can cause severe dehydration if a person does not take the necessary precautions.

   **Fact** **Opinion**

6. The most worthwhile part of any NFL Super Bowl is the commercials because they are the most entertaining.

   **Fact** **Opinion**

## Groundwork

*In this section, students will evaluate the characteristics of an effective thesis statement.*

EXERCISE D SLIDE 293.1

**What's the last sentence we'll write in every introduction paragraph?**

The thesis.

**And what does the thesis contain?**

Our opinion.

**Think about the definition of a fact. What is it, exactly?**

A true statement.

**Facts can definitely be true statements, but did you know that even *false* statements can be facts? The real secret to identifying a fact is whether you can prove that statement is true or false. What about an opinion? How would you define that?**

A statement you *can't* prove right or wrong.

**Another way to think about it is that you can't use science, math, history, or any other evidence to prove an opinion is "wrong." For instance, let's look at number 5. Who can read that out loud for us?**

*The summer heat in southern states like Texas and Arizona can cause severe dehydration if a person does not take the necessary precautions.*

**What can we ask ourselves to figure out whether it's fact or opinion?**

Can we prove it's right or wrong?

**And can we?**

Yes.

**Summer heat in desert states is no joke. It can definitely lead to dehydration if someone isn't careful. Don't believe me? You could look up hospital records to prove me wrong. And that makes it a fact. What about statement 6? Can we prove that's right or wrong?**

No.

**Why not?**

Some people might like other parts of the Super Bowl better than the commercials. There's no evidence to prove it right or wrong.

**Since we can't use evidence to prove it one way or the other, it's an opinion. Which of these statements would make a better thesis?**

Sentence 6.

**Sentence 6 is definitely the better choice since it states an opinion.**

EXERCISE E

**Instructions**

Circle the key words in the question as your teacher leads the discussion.

7. Are we in control of our fears?

8. Does wealth make us happy?

9. Is adversity a potentially good motivator?

## Groundwork

*In this section, students will discuss how to develop a thesis statement in response to a prompt.*

EXERCISE E SLIDE 294.1

**Another key feature of a good thesis statement is that it responds directly to the question in the prompt. We *could* just offer up a "yes" or "no" answer. But is that a good plan?**

No, it's not enough.

**Offering a direct answer like "yes" or "no" is considered bad form for a thesis, but we still want to make sure that the grading system of the TSIA2 *knows* we're responding to the prompt. And we can do that by channeling our inner parrot. Essentially, that means repeating key words from the question back to them in our thesis. Take a look at question 7. What do you think are some key words we could use?**

*Control* and *fears*.

**We can use those to create our thesis without having to say "yes" or "no." For instance, if we agree and think controlling our fears is something we're definitely capable of, what might our thesis statement look like?**

*Answers will vary.*

Example: We are always in control of our fears.

**What if we didn't agree? What could our thesis say?**

*Answers will vary.*

Example: People are not capable of controlling strong emotions like fear.

**In both cases, we didn't have to resort to answering the question in a super direct way. Try it again with question 8. First, what are some key words there?**

*Wealth* and *happy*.

**Do we have to use *happy* exactly as it is?**

Probably not.

**You could also use different forms of the word, like "happiness" or "happier." What about question 9? What key words do we want to parrot back?**

*Adversity* and *good motivator*.

**Why not use *potentially*?**

It will make our opinion sound weaker.

**Words like *potentially, probably, sometimes*, or anything else in that realm will take what could be an excellent thesis and coat it in weak sauce. Instead, stay strong in your opinion, even if you don't necessarily feel that passionate about the subject.**

## Application

### THE APPROACH

When writing the introduction paragraph for your essay during the TSIA2 ...

1. Craft an attention-grabbing hook.
2. Mention the subject of your two examples as a preview.
3. Draft a thesis that flows from the preview, responds to the assignment's question, and states your opinion clearly.

**Passage**

"I learned that courage was not the absence of fear, but the triumph over it. The brave man is not he who does not feel afraid, but he who conquers that fear."

Adapted from Nelson Mandela, *Long Walk to Freedom*

---

**Assignment**

Are we in control of our fears?

Plan and write a multiparagraph essay (300–600 words) in which you develop your point of view on the above question. Support your position with reasoning and examples taken from your reading, studies, experience, or observations.

**Instructions**

Refer to the following example as your teacher leads the discussion.

We have two choices when we are afraid: we can run and hide or we can stand and face our fears. Nour and Mulan, strong fictional characters, both face challenging moments that make them fearful, but they overcome their fears and save those they love. These characters prove that even though we may be afraid, we are in control of our fears.

## Application

*In this section, students will evaluate an example introduction paragraph.*

SLIDE 295.1

**Three sentences. That's it! You *could* use more, but in reality, just three sentences stand between you and an excellent introduction paragraph. Take a moment now to read this example.**

*Give students 30 seconds to read the passage.*

**Let's see how well this writer did checklist-style. Do they have an opening hook?**

Yes.

**What strategy did they use?**

They made a strong statement.

**Remind me again: what other strategies might we use?**

Ask a question, describe an image or scene.

**Opening hook, check. Next, do they have a preview?**

Yes.

**What are we looking for in the preview?**

A hint about which examples are in the essay.

**Which examples does this writer mention?**

Nour and Mulan.

**Preview, check. What about the thesis? Is it the last sentence of the paragraph?**

Yes.

**Does it state an opinion? And if so, how can you tell?**

Yes, because we can't use evidence to prove it's right or wrong.

**And does it parrot words from the prompt's question?**

Yes.

**Thesis, check. Now, it's your turn! What two examples do you plan to use?**

Note: If students have completed the Brainstorming and Pre-Writing chapter, remind them to utilize the outline they created.

*Allow 2–3 students to share.*

**Let's get drafting.**

**Chapter 33:** Writing the Introduction **TSIA2 Mastery:** ELAR

 **THE APPROACH**

When writing the introduction paragraph for your essay during the TSIA2 ...

1. Craft an attention-grabbing hook.
2. Mention the subject of your two examples as a preview.
3. Draft a thesis that flows from the preview, responds to the assignment's question, and states your opinion clearly.

**Passage**

"I learned that courage was not the absence of fear, but the triumph over it. The brave man is not he who does not feel afraid, but he who conquers that fear."

Adapted from Nelson Mandela, *Long Walk to Freedom*

---

**Assignment**

Are we in control of our fears?

Plan and write a multiparagraph essay (300–600 words) in which you develop your point of view on the above question. Support your position with reasoning and examples taken from your reading, studies, experience, or observations.

**Instructions**

Draft your introduction paragraph here:

______________________________

______________________________

______________________________

______________________________

______________________________

______________________________

## Application

***In this section, students will construct their own version of an introduction paragraph.***

SLIDE 296.1

**Take some time now to create a first draft of your introduction paragraph. Remind me: what three things do you need?**

A hook, a preview, and a thesis.

**Let's see what you can do!**

*Give students 8 minutes to write their introduction paragraph.*

TSIA2 Mastery: ELAR 

### Instructions

Review your partner's introduction paragraph on the previous page. Then, provide feedback in the space below.

Positive: ____________________

Constructive: ____________________

## Application

*In this section, students will provide a peer with feedback on their introduction paragraph.*

**Now that we've got our intros ready, let's do a little writing workshop. First, we need to pair up.**

*Take a moment to group students into pairs.*

SLIDE 297.1

**Before we start, trade workbooks with your partner. When we start, you'll flip to the previous page and read their introduction. Then, turn to this page and write down your feedback. Offer up at least 1 positive comment and 1 constructive comment. Feedback style is important, too. Should we be vague or specific?**

Specific.

**Specific feedback is going to be the most helpful. Don't just write "good job" or "it was okay" on their paper. Point to specific elements or phrases in their writing. Give the kind of feedback *you* want to receive! Once you're done writing your comments on this page, you can trade back. Let's get started!**

*Allow students 4 minutes to complete the exercise.*

**A lot of times, we struggle with the same elements of an essay again and again, so if you had trouble with any element of your introduction, focus on it. Dig into where you go wrong or why it's so hard for you to come up with something that works. The more you practice, the easier these introductions will get. You got this.**

This page is intentionally left blank.
Content resumes on the next page.

This page is intentionally left blank.
Teacher content resumes with the next chapter.

CHAPTER 34

# Developing Body Paragraphs

In this chapter, students will learn how to expand their introductory paragraph into two well-formed body paragraphs. Students will also develop skills to transition between body paragraphs.

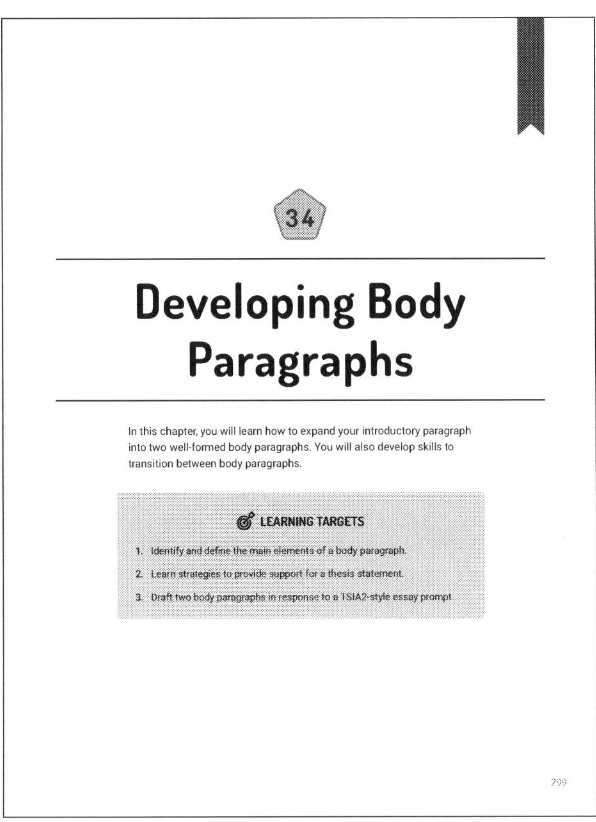

34

## Developing Body Paragraphs

In this chapter, you will learn how to expand your introductory paragraph into two well-formed body paragraphs. You will also develop skills to transition between body paragraphs.

LEARNING TARGETS

1. Identify and define the main elements of a body paragraph.
2. Learn strategies to provide support for a thesis statement.
3. Draft two body paragraphs in response to a TSIA2-style essay prompt

299

## TEKS ALIGNMENT

E1.9 *Composition*: listening, speaking, reading, writing, and thinking using multiple texts—writing process. The student uses the writing process recursively to compose multiple texts that are legible and use appropriate conventions. The student is expected to:

(B) develop drafts into a focused, structured, and coherent piece of writing in timed and open-ended situations by:

(ii) developing an engaging idea reflecting depth of thought with specific details, examples, and commentary.

## LEARNING TARGETS

1. Identify and define the main elements of a body paragraph.
2. Learn strategies to provide support for a thesis statement.
3. Draft two body paragraphs in response to a TSIA2-style essay prompt.

## Groundwork

EXERCISE A

**Instructions**
Review the following topic sentence as your teacher leads the discussion.

*The love we have for our family can give us the courage to face our fear and overcome it.*

**Topic Sentence for Body Paragraph #1:**

# Groundwork

*In this section, students will develop a topic sentence for their first body paragraph.*

EXERCISE A

**Think about your favorite band or music artist. If you could see anyone in concert, who would it be?**

*Allow 2–3 students to share.*

**Let's say you won free tickets on the radio, and now you get to see them in concert. You get there, and the opening act is *amazing*! But then the band appears. They have no energy as they perform, and they only play two songs before disappearing behind the stage. How do you think you'd feel after the show?**

Disappointed.

**But the opening act was awesome! How come that doesn't make up for the not-so-great stuff?**

It's not the reason we were excited to go to the concert in the first place.

**Even if the opening act puts on the best performance ever, if the reason we came to see the show isn't great, we're going to call the whole night a bust. And the same thing happens with your essay during the TSIA2. Let's say you write an exceptional introduction paragraph but leave your body paragraphs a little lacking. How do you think that will affect your score?**

It's going to lower it.

**The body of an essay is the main attraction. It's where all your details will combine to form the meat and potatoes of your argument. Without giving those paragraphs the time and energy they deserve, you'll leave readers feeling disappointed. Remind me: how many body paragraphs will we write for our essay during the TSIA2?**

Two.

**And what should every paragraph open with?**

A topic sentence.

**Think of the topic sentence as a sort of mini thesis for each paragraph. What do you think I mean by this?**

Use the topic sentence to introduce the ideas that will show up in that paragraph.

**Take a moment to flip back to your outline. Which example will you talk about in your first body paragraph?**

*Allow 2–3 students to share.*

SLIDE 300.1

**For example, take a look at the topic sentence for body paragraph #1. What do you think this paragraph will be about?**

A way that family love helps us conquer our fears.

SLIDE 300.2

**Notice that it connects directly to the topic of our essay: overcoming fears. Your topic sentence should do the same. Take a moment now to draft the topic sentence of your *first* body paragraph.**

*Give students 2 minutes to complete this task.*

TSIA2 Mastery: ELAR 

EXERCISE B

**Instructions**
Refer to the following example summaries as your teacher leads the discussion. Then, write your own summary for your first body paragraph.

**Option 1**

The main character, a girl who is in a country in the Middle East, dives in the water at some point during the story to save her sister from a terrible fate.

**Option 2**

Nour, an 11-year-old girl in the novel *The Map of Salt and Stars*, has long been afraid of the water because of a traumatic incident when she was little and has not learned how to swim since. She also has a little sister, Zahra. They haven't always had the best relationship. In fact, it's often been really turbulent at times. After her father dies of cancer, Nour's mother decides to make a change. She moves them from their home in New York back to Syria, which isn't what it used to be. One day, Nour sees her sister, Zahra, struggling in the dark and churning sea. She doesn't hesitate and dives in, overcoming her fear of the water and saving her sister all in one fell swoop.

**Option 3**

Nour, the main character in the novel *The Map of Salt and Stars*, not only doesn't know how to swim but has always feared the water. However, when she sees her sister, Zahra, struggling in the sea, Nour dives in without hesitation and pulls her to safety.

**Example Summary for Body Paragraph #1:**

______________________________

______________________________

______________________________

______________________________

______________________________

______________________________

*In this section, students will learn how to write a strong example summary for each body paragraph.*

EXERCISE B

**Once you've got your topic sentence in place, it's time to introduce the first example. Why do you think we should take the time to summarize the example?**

To give the reader some background information.

**We can't guarantee that our reader is familiar with whichever example we chose, so we need to give some context. How long do you think a summary should be?**

A couple of sentences.

**You only need a few sentences for your summary, but be careful that you don't offer something too sparse. What happens when you see a huge chunk of text in the middle of a page?**

Our eyes glaze over, or we skim it quickly without really reading it.

SLIDE 301.1

**When a writer throws too much information at a reader, it's hard for them to take it all in. Take a look at the example summaries in your workbook. Which one do you think overwhelms the reader with information?**

Option 2.

**That one is huge. And if we try to include something that big in our essay, we run the risk of losing focus. Summaries definitely don't need to be that long. Option 1 doesn't seem to have that problem, though. But there's still something wrong there. Why doesn't that one work?**

It tries to give the whole summary in just one sentence.

**What's wrong with using just one sentence?**

It won't be enough information.

**One sentence just isn't enough to give your example the support that it needs. You'll either give too little information, or you'll create a massive sentence that's overflowing and jumbled with too much detail.**

**Where do you think the sweet spot is then? How many sentences make a good summary?**

Two or three.

**Which example in Exercise B section best supports the topic sentence and why?**

Option 3, because it gives a good amount of detail without going overboard.

**Does option 3 include the entire story?**

No.

**What part of the story does it summarize?**

Only the part that relates to proving the thesis.

SLIDE 301.2

**Let's take some time to write your own summary for your first body paragraph. In two or three sentences, tell me about your example. Focus on the details that help you prove your point.**

*Give students 4 minutes to complete this task.*

EXERCISE C

### Instructions

Review the following body paragraph as your teacher leads the discussion.

**(1)** The love we have for our family can give us the courage to face our fear and overcome it. **(2)** Nour, the main character in the novel *The Map of Salt and Stars*, not only doesn't know how to swim but has always feared the water. **(3)** However, when she sees her sister, Zahra, struggling in the sea, Nour dives in without hesitation and pulls her to safety. **(4)** This shows that Nour's love for her sister is stronger than her fear of water. **(5)** Because of her love for Zahra, Nour conquers her fear of the water and is able to save her sister. **(6)** Without that compelling force, Nour may not have been able to gather the courage to dive into the sea.

### Commentary for Body Paragraph #1:

______________________________________________

______________________________________________

______________________________________________

______________________________________________

______________________________________________

______________________________________________

*In this section, students will learn how to provide reasoning that connects an example to its thesis.*

EXERCISE C  SLIDE 302.1

**Say we write a paragraph, including our topic sentence and a summary of our example. Why can't we stop there?**

We have to explain why it proves the argument.

**We don't want to just give a summary of our example and leave the reader to connect the dots on their own. We have to convince the reader that the example proves the thesis. For instance, take a look at the example in your workbook. Every good body paragraph needs to start with a topic sentence. Who can read that for us?**

*The love we have for our family can give us the courage to face our fear and overcome it.*

**Following that, we have the summary. Which sentences from the paragraph make up the summary?**

Sentences 2 and 3.

**Let's add a little hash mark at the end of sentence 3 to cut the paragraph into two pieces. Just focus on the first half, for now. Put yourself in the author's shoes. Why do you think they picked this example? Why is it a good example to support the idea of overcoming fear?**

It shows a character who overcame a fear.

**How does the author show us that Nour had a fear that needs to be overcome?**

The author says that Nour *doesn't know how to swim but has always feared the water.*

**The author didn't just stop at the summary, right? We've got a whole half of the paragraph left. Look at what comes after the hash mark we added. Why is the story of Nour a good example of overcoming fear?**

Because love for her sister helped her overcome her fear of water.

**We call this part of a body paragraph the *commentary*. This commentary gives the reader more insight into why exactly our example supports the thesis. What do you notice about the fourth sentence?**

It brings up the main idea of the essay: overcoming fear.

**The commentary is the perfect moment to explain to your reader why you chose to include the example in your essay. What does the next sentence of the commentary accomplish?**

It shows this example does exactly what the thesis claims is possible.

**A sentence that says *exactly* how your example proves the thesis is a great way to really hammer down your point. Think about those cliché courtroom scenes that always show up in movies. Do the lawyers just present the evidence and then sit down?**

No.

SLIDE 302.2

**Instead, they talk to the jury about *why* that evidence is important. It makes for a much more convincing argument. Take a few minutes now to channel your inner lawyer and write the commentary that explains why your example proves your thesis is true.**

*Give students 4 minutes to complete this task.*

**TSIA2 Mastery:** ELAR 

# Application

## THE APPROACH

When writing a body paragraph for your essay during the TSIA2 ...

1. Develop a clear topic sentence.
2. Write 2–3 sentences that summarize your example.
3. Write 2–3 sentences of supporting commentary to explain how your example proves your thesis.

**Passage**

"I learned that courage was not the absence of fear, but the triumph over it. The brave man is not he who does not feel afraid, but he who conquers that fear."

Adapted from Nelson Mandela, *Long Walk to Freedom*

**Assignment**

Are we in control of our fears?

Plan and write a multiparagraph essay (300–600 words) in which you develop your point of view on the above question. Support your position with reasoning and examples taken from your reading, studies, experiences, or observations.

Draft your second paragraph here. Be sure to include a transition at the start of your topic sentence.

# Application

*In this section, students will review the importance of using a transition at the start of the second body paragraph.*

SLIDE 303.1

**With the first body paragraph drafted, we're halfway through the body of our essay. Writing the second paragraph will follow a similar process, with one specific difference: it adds on to the example from the first paragraph. How does that impact the way we write the first sentence of the second paragraph?**

We have to write the sentence in a way that flows together.

**If you've ever been to a concert, you'll know that the artists don't just play one song after another, with nothing between them. What do they usually do between songs?**

Talk to the audience, introduce the next song, play transition music, etc.

**It's like they create little bridges that make the whole show more seamless. How do we do the same thing in our writing? What should we add to the beginning of that second body paragraph?**

We add a transition.

**To bridge our body paragraphs, we can add a transition word or phrase. The question is: what kind should you use? We're using one example on top of another, so what category of transition do you think will help?**

Transitions that show addition.

**Give me some examples. What are some good addition transitions we could use?**

In addition, likewise, similarly, etc.

**For instance, when transitioning from talking about Nour to discussing a different subject, Mulan for example, I might say *similar to the way Nour uses love to gain courage* ... and then continue on with my topic sentence to introduce the next paragraph's main idea. Remind me one more time. What four things do we need to build this paragraph?**

A transition, a topic sentence, a summary of the example, and commentary to explain why it proves the thesis is true.

**Let's see what you can do!**

*Give students 10 minutes to write their second body paragraph.*

### THE APPROACH

When writing a body paragraph for your essay during the TSIA2 ...

1. Develop a clear topic sentence.
2. Write 2–3 sentences that summarize your example.
3. Write 2–3 sentences of supporting commentary to explain how your example proves your thesis.

**Instructions**
Review your partner's second body paragraph on the previous page. Then, provide feedback in the space provided.

Positive:

______________________________

______________________________

______________________________

______________________________

______________________________

Constructive:

______________________________

______________________________

______________________________

______________________________

______________________________

## Application

*In this section, students will provide a peer with feedback on their second body paragraph.*

SLIDE 304.1

**Now that we've got our second body paragraph drafted, we're going to do some peer workshopping again. Everyone needs a partner.**

*Group students into pairs.*

**Go ahead and trade workbooks with your partner and read through each other's work. As you read, look for things that your partner did really well and for places in their paragraph they can improve. Write down at least one positive comment and one constructive comment in the space provided on this page. How can you make sure your feedback is useful for your partner?**

Be really specific about what they did in their writing.

**Specific feedback is very important. Without it, your partner won't be able to make the changes necessary to improve their writing. Try your best to come up with solid examples for your feedback, rather than just writing "Good job!" The more specific you can be, the better.**

*Give students 5 minutes to complete the exercise.*

**Let's swap back and read what our partners wrote. Who would like to share a specific comment their partner gave that's really helpful?**

*Allow 2–3 students to share.*

**If you ask any professional writer out there, they'll tell you that no first draft is perfect. This is why reviewing and editing are so important, even for standardized tests like the TSIA2. We'll talk about revising and editing more in a later chapter, but for now, just remember that the first draft doesn't have to be perfect, as long as you take the time to come back around and polish things up. Once your essay is all bright and shiny, that's when you can hit the submit button.**

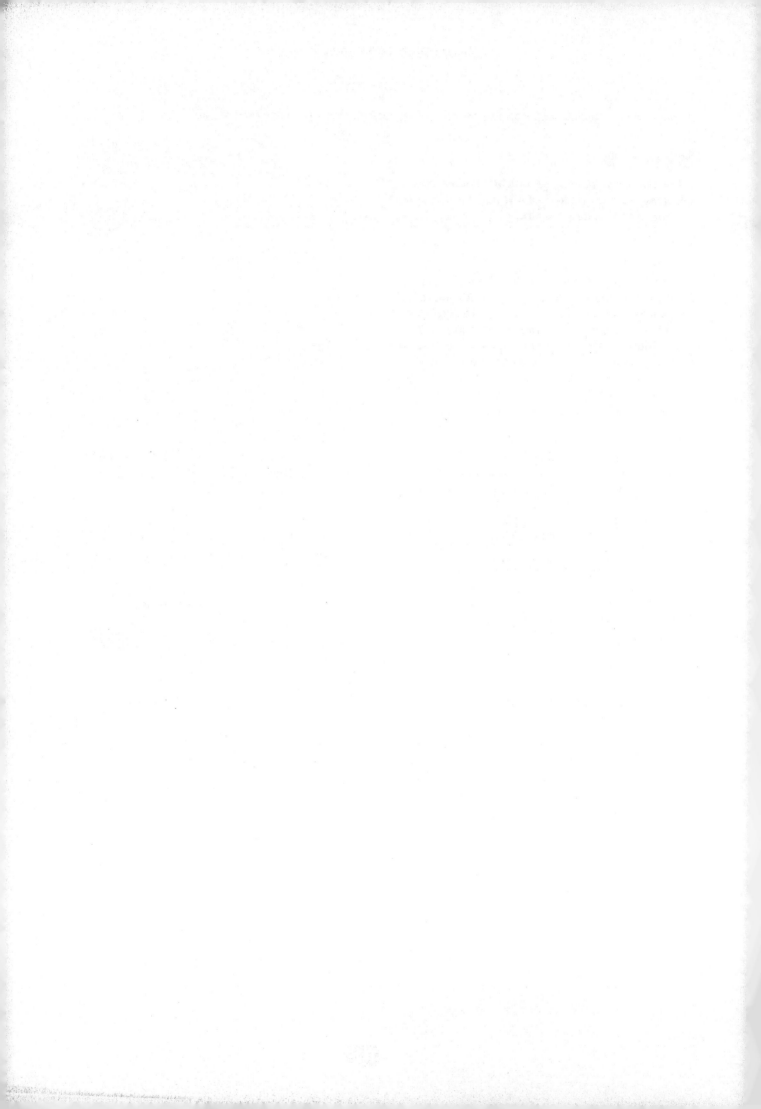

## CHAPTER 35

# Writing the Conclusion

In this chapter, students will learn how to craft a concluding paragraph that will recap the main point of their essay and create a connection with the reader.

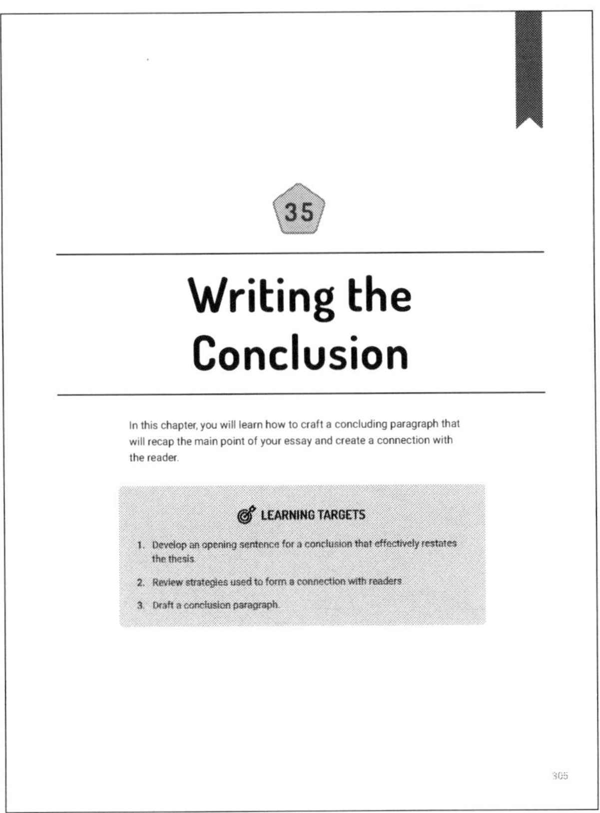

35

Writing the Conclusion

In this chapter, you will learn how to craft a concluding paragraph that will recap the main point of your essay and create a connection with the reader.

LEARNING TARGETS

1. Develop an opening sentence for a conclusion that effectively restates the thesis.
2. Review strategies used to form a connection with readers.
3. Draft a conclusion paragraph.

305

## TEKS ALIGNMENT

E1.9 *Composition*: listening, speaking, reading, writing, and thinking using multiple texts—writing process. The student uses the writing process recursively to compose multiple texts that are legible and uses appropriate conventions. The student is expected to:

(B) develop drafts into a focused, structured, and coherent piece of writing in timed and open-ended situations by:

(i) using an organizing structure appropriate to purpose, audience, topic, and context.

## LEARNING TARGETS

1. Develop an opening sentence for a conclusion that effectively restates the thesis.
2. Review strategies used to form a connection with readers.
3. Draft a conclusion paragraph.

## Groundwork

EXERCISE A

### Instructions

Underline the thesis statement in the example introduction paragraph. Then, place a check mark next to the options that would make an effective opening sentence for the conclusion paragraph.

### Introduction Paragraph

*We have two choices when we are afraid: we can run and hide or we can stand and face our fear. Nour and Mulan, strong fictional characters, both face challenging moments that make them fearful, but they overcome their fears and save those they love. These characters prove that even though we may be afraid, we are in control of our fears.*

1. ______ These characters prove that even though we may be afraid, we are in control of our fears.

2. ______ There is much to fear in this world, but at the end of the day, we must face it or perish.

3. ______ Nour and Mulan were able to conquer their fear because of special circumstances, but most of us are not able to do that because we are riddled with uncertainty.

4. ______ Although they encountered dangerous situations, Nour and Mulan put the lives of others before themselves and show that we are in control of our fear.

## Groundwork

*In this section, students will evaluate possible opening sentences for a conclusion paragraph.*

**Believe it or not, telling a joke is a skill. You've got the setup, where you give the details that pull the reader in and set up their expectations. But that's not really the funny part. Which part of a joke is what actually makes people laugh?**

The punchline.

**The end of the joke is where you use everything you've just set up to pack a humor punch and draw out the laugh. But sometimes, that punchline doesn't hit quite right, and you end up with that proverbial "womp womp" moment. Just like the ending of a joke, the ending of an essay is super important. Why do you think that is?**

Because a bad conclusion ruins the whole essay.

**Even if we nailed the introduction, built amazing body paragraphs, and transitioned between ideas like a professional, dropping the ball on the conclusion paragraph means the reader walks away thinking the essay wasn't so great. Luckily, we have a recipe for a super sweet conclusion paragraph that'll work with any essay you write for the TSIA2. Who remembers what the conclusion paragraph should open with? Flip back to your outline if you need to.**

A thesis restatement.

**Why do you think we restate our thesis?**

To remind the reader of our main argument.

EXERCISE A | SLIDE 306.1

**It's a little like a quick recap before you dive into the final element of your essay. You've just spent two paragraphs digging into the details of your examples, so it's good to take a step back and remind your reader exactly what you're trying to prove as you head into the thesis. But restating is a delicate process. For instance, take a look at the example intro in your workbook. Who can read the thesis aloud for us?**

*These characters prove that even though we may be afraid, we are in control of our fears.*

**When we restate our thesis as an opening to our conclusion, do you think we should just rewrite that sentence word-for-word, like in option number 1?**

No.

**Why not?**

It's repetitive.

**You don't want to tell the reader *exactly* what you've already said. That would be repeating, and it would make things pretty boring. We really just want to recap the thesis, which means we "hit the highlights" of the essay to remind our reader of our main argument. What about number 2? Do you think it's a good way to open up our conclusion?**

It's okay.

**It's on-topic and gives the general idea of our essay, but it's a little vague. We could definitely use something stronger. What do you think about number 3?**

It mentions the examples but says the opposite of the main argument.

**Number 3 starts with a good recap, but then it gets confused and undermines its own argument. Not good. What about number 4?**

Number 4 is really solid.

**Option 4 highlights our thesis by reminding the reader how Nour and Mulan were afraid but still able to overcome that fear. That's a pretty solid recap. This is ultimately the goal with the first sentence of your conclusion paragraph: focus on reminding the reader of what you want to say, not repeating the thesis.**

TSIA2 Mastery: ELAR 

EXERCISE B

### Instructions

Use the space provided to develop the first sentence of your conclusion paragraph.

1. Rewrite your thesis:

2. Write the first sentence of your conclusion paragraph:

*In this section, students will write their own opening sentences for their conclusion paragraphs.*

**EXERCISE B** SLIDE 307.1

**Let's start building our own concluding paragraphs, starting with that first sentence recap. If we want to avoid repeating our thesis, we should probably take a look back at what we have in our intro. Take a moment now to go back and copy your thesis to this page so you have it as a reference.**

*Give students 2 minutes to complete this task.*

**A good way to construct this sentence is to answer the question, "What did my examples prove?" Take some time now to draft your recap. What did your examples prove to your reader?**

*Give students 3 minutes to complete this task.*

**Let's get some volunteers. Read your thesis statement and follow it up with the first sentence of your conclusion paragraph.**

*Allow 2–3 students to share their writing.*

EXERCISE C

## Instructions

Match each strategy to its definition by writing the corresponding letter in the space provided.

1. ______ So What?
2. ______ Anticipating the Objection
3. ______ Powerful Words

A. Provide an opposing argument and explain why it's incorrect.
B. Use strong, descriptive words that evoke an emotional response from the reader.
C. Explain why the topic should be important to the reader.

## Groundwork

*In this section, students will define strategies that can be used to create the final sentences of their conclusion paragraphs.*

EXERCISE C SLIDE 308.1

**Once you've got your recap to open your conclusion, it's time for that mic drop moment. It's the last thing our reader will see from us, so we want to end on a high note. What do you think our goal might be for those last few sentences?**

To convince the reader to agree with us.

**We don't necessarily have to convince the reader that we're right—although that's always nice—but we want to write something that makes them personally connect to our essays. Of course, we usually don't know who our reader might be, so how do we do that?**

Write something most people would agree with.

**Connecting your argument to universal values like truth, family, and loyalty helps your readers *feel* something, which makes them more likely to at least give your argument some consideration. And we have a few strategies we can use to help us make that connection. The first is called *So What?* Think of it like a question from your reader. If you write that "Many people experience fear in the face of danger," imagine your reader thinking, "So what?" What could your answer to them be?**

Note: This is a sample answer. There are many possible suggestions that could also work.

Even though people experience fear, they should know that they can overcome it.

**The goal of this strategy is to anticipate the reader's lack of interest. The way you would respond to their "So what?" is the perfect filler for the end of your conclusion paragraph because you give them a reason to care before they get a chance to ignore your ideas. What are you really trying to get them to do?**

To pay attention to what we say, to give us a good score, or even to agree with what we said.

**Another strategy is called *Anticipating the Objection*. What's an objection to an argument?**

A reason why they disagree with you.

**When we anticipate the objection, we step into the opposing side's shoes and think about a reason why they might not agree with what we have to say. For example, what are some objections you think people might raise in response to your thesis?**

Note: This is a sample answer. There are many possible suggestions that could also work.

That even though the characters in the examples overcame their fear, some people can't.

**When you include an objection in your essay, you don't just want to leave it at that. What should you follow it with?**

A reason why their objection is wrong.

**And how does that strengthen your essay?**

It makes it harder for them to disagree.

**When we offer up reasons why an opposing view is wrong, we're taking an opportunity to say, "I know what you're thinking, and here's why you're mistaken." Addressing that opposing viewpoint adds a whole other dimension that proves your argument is right. But how do you begin? A good way to start a sentence with this strategy is with, "Although you might think..." What are some other ways you could offer up an objection?**

Something like "I know it sounds crazy but ..." or "Those who disagree might say ..."

**Another way you can connect with the reader is through *Powerful Words*. Think back to the example essay we've been working with. What are some strong words you could use to describe Nour and Mulan?**

Heroic, brave, loyal, fierce, decisive, etc.

**Using words like *heroic* and *fierce* triggers strong emotions in your reader and makes them more likely to agree with your argument.**

TSIA2 Mastery: ELAR

## Application

### THE APPROACH

When you draft the conclusion paragraph for your essay during the TSIA2, use these steps ...

1. Open the paragraph with a restatement of your thesis.
2. Close the paragraph with a connection with the reader.

Conclusion Paragraph Draft:

# Application

***In this section, students will draft their conclusion paragraphs.***

SLIDE 309.1

**Time to put those strategies to good use. Which strategy do you plan to use to create that connection with the reader?**

*Allow 2–3 students to share.*

**Take a moment to rewrite your opening sentence in the space provided. Then, follow it up with your connection to the reader. Use one of the strategies from the previous page and really aim for that mic-drop moment.**

*Give students 10 minutes to complete this task.*

**How did everyone feel about their paragraphs?**

*Answers will vary.*

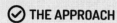

## THE APPROACH

When you draft the conclusion paragraph for your essay during the TSIA2, use these steps ...

1. Open the paragraph with a restatement of your thesis.
2. Close the paragraph with a connection with the reader.

**Instructions**
In the space provided, give your peer feedback on their conclusion paragraph.

Positive:

______________________________________________

______________________________________________

______________________________________________

______________________________________________

______________________________________________

Constructive:

______________________________________________

______________________________________________

______________________________________________

______________________________________________

______________________________________________

## Application

*In this section, students will review a peer's conclusion paragraph and provide constructive feedback.*

SLIDE 310.1

**Let's swap workbooks and do some peer evaluation. Y'all know the drill by now. Make sure you're giving the type of specific, helpful feedback that you'd like to receive. Something good and something to improve on.**

*Give students 10 minutes to complete this task.*

**Go ahead and look over the notes your peer gave you. Who got a really good piece of positive feedback? What does it say?**

*Allow 2–3 students to share.*

**Constructive feedback can be a little more challenging, but it's a necessary element of writing. All writers get feedback, even the most popular authors who've written tons of books. Who'd like to share a piece of constructive feedback they received?**

*Allow 2–3 students to share.*

**Remember: not all constructive feedback has to be taken. If you feel strongly enough about something, you can definitely keep it the way it is. But remember that your peer has the reader's perspective, so if something seems unclear or awkward for one reader, it's likely going to come up for others, too. Along with all this constructive feedback, I don't want to miss out on acknowledging that we've hit a really important milestone in our writing process. What do you think that might be?**

Our whole essay is written now.

**Once you write that final sentence, you've officially got a first draft on your hands. When you're taking the TSIA2, is this the point when we go ahead and hit that submit button?**

No.

**What do we still need to do?**

Revise and edit.

**Don't worry. We've got a whole chapter on it with some special tips and tricks we can use during the test to help us polish our essay to a passing-score shine.**

CHAPTER 36

# Revising and Editing

In this chapter, students will learn strategies for revising and editing their essay submission for the TSIA2.

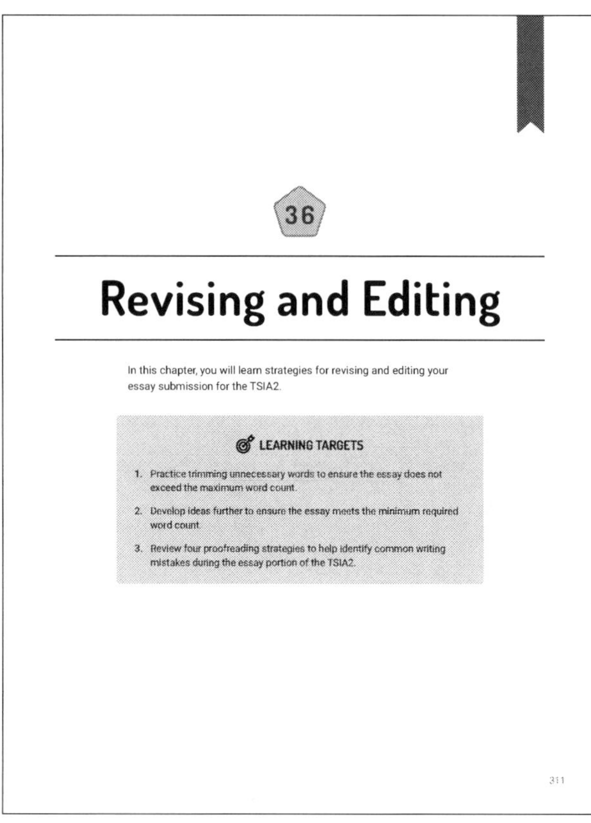

36

Revising and Editing

In this chapter, you will learn strategies for revising and editing your essay submission for the TSIA2.

LEARNING TARGETS

1. Practice trimming unnecessary words to ensure the essay does not exceed the maximum word count.
2. Develop ideas further to ensure the essay meets the minimum required word count.
3. Review four proofreading strategies to help identify common writing mistakes during the essay portion of the TSIA2.

311

## TEKS ALIGNMENT

E1.9 *Composition*: listening, speaking, reading, writing, and thinking using multiple texts—writing process. The student uses the writing process recursively to compose multiple texts that are legible and use appropriate conventions. The student is expected to:

(C) revise drafts to improve clarity, development, organization, style, diction, and sentence effectiveness, including use of parallel constructions and placement of phrases and dependent clauses;

(D) edit drafts using standard English conventions.

## LEARNING TARGETS

1. Practice trimming unnecessary words to ensure the essay does not exceed the maximum word count.
2. Develop ideas further to ensure the essay meets the minimum required word count.
3. Review four proofreading strategies to help identify common writing mistakes during the essay portion of the TSIA2.

## Groundwork

EXERCISE A

**Instructions**
Refer to the following as the teacher leads the discussion.

**Passage**
"I learned that courage was not the absence of fear, but the triumph over it. The brave man is not he who does not feel afraid, but he who conquers that fear."

Adapted from Nelson Mandela, *Long Walk to Freedom*

---

**Assignment**
Are we in control of our fears?

Plan and write a multiparagraph essay (300–600 words) in which you develop your point of view on the above question. Support your position with reasoning and examples taken from your reading, studies, experience, or observations.

We have two choices when we are afraid: we can run and hide or we can stand and face our fear. Nour and Mulan, strong fictional characters, both face challenging moments that make them fearful, but they overcome their fears and save those they love. These characters prove that even though we may be afraid, we are in control of our fears.

The love we have for our family can give us the courage to face our fear and overcome it. Nour, the main character in *The Map of Salt and Stars*, not only doesn't know how to swim but has always feared the water. However, when she sees her sister, Zahra, struggling in the sea, Nour dives in without hesitation and pulls her to safety. This shows that Nour's love for her sister is stronger than her fear of water. Because of her love for Zahra, Nour conquers her fear of the water and is able to save her sister. Without that compelling force, Nour may not have been able to gather the courage to dive into the sea.

Word Count: 487

# Groundwork

*In this section, students will discuss the importance of taking a mental break between writing and revisions, as well as identify their first priority when they decide to begin reviewing their work.*

**Imagine it's test day, and in true TSIA2 fashion, you've just typed out an entire essay in one sitting. It's gut check time: what's the first thing you're probably going to want to do after you finish typing those last words?**

To submit it and be done.

**Writing an entire essay in one sitting is challenging, and it can be so tempting to just hit that "Continue" button and keep moving to the next portion of the test. Why should we avoid that temptation, though?**

We need to check our essay for errors.

**Taking a pass—or a few—through your writing in search of mistakes is definitely something we need to get to before submitting our essays. But there's something even more important you should start with. Something related to taking care of your brain. What do you think that might be?**

Taking a break.

**You technically can't take a real break mid-essay, like heading to the bathroom or for a quick walk to get your blood flowing again. The essay is a marathon. You've got to do it all in one sitting. But there's nothing stopping you from closing your eyes and taking a few minutes to clear your mind. Why do you think that's helpful before you start revising and editing?**

So we can come back to our writing with fresh eyes.

**By taking a break to clear your mind, you can come back to your writing with a fresher perspective on the writing on your screen, meaning you've got a better chance of actually spotting those mistakes. How else might this break help you, especially in terms of your mental energy?**

It keeps us from feeling burned out.

**If you stayed on-task while you were writing, that means you just spent a good amount of time thinking about nothing but your essay. That break is almost a necessity when it comes to avoiding running out of steam before the test ends.**

EXERCISE A | SLIDE 312.1

**Check out your workbook now. What do you see?**

The passage, assignment, and the box where you type.

**While a book and a computer have some pretty significant visual differences, this is *super* close to what you'll see on your screen on test day. What do you notice just under the text box?**

The word count.

**Why is it important to use this tool?**

Because our essay has to be between 300 and 600 words.

**The TSIA2 has a minimum word count they'll accept and a maximum cutoff they don't want you to go over. In fact, it's so important to them that it shows up at the beginning of your instructions, right after the question of the assignment. After you've taken your mental break and feel ready to take on revising and editing, start the process with a quick check to see just how many words you've written and whether or not you've fallen within the word count limits.**

EXERCISE B

### Instructions

Review the following passage. Cross out or replace any unnecessary words to reduce the word count.

### Passage

**(1)** I really and truly love fostering animals for the shelter. **(2)** It is very satisfying to know that I am helping animals build incredibly strong bonds with humans again. **(3)** On the other hand, though, I find it difficult to let go of some fosters and sometimes end up adopting them! **(4)** My dog, Summer, is one of those. **(5)** Her sweet, delightful, charming, friendly nature won me over.

## Groundwork

*In this section, students will practice identifying words and phrases that can either be removed or replaced in order to reduce word count.*

**Let's say you check your word count and *gasp*! You've gone over and have 650 words written. What should you do?**

Go through and cut words we don't need.

**What kinds of words do you think are unnecessary?**

Filler words, words that add extra description, or repetitive words.

**Cutting things from an essay is a little like taking scissors to a piece of art we've created. It almost hurts to take away from it, especially after we put in all that effort. But if it doesn't fit the word count max, we have to make some hard decisions. Start with words that seem repetitive and then move on to extra things like descriptions or even elaboration. Anything that can be cut without ruining the essential meaning or creating an incomplete sentence is fair game.**

EXERCISE B | SLIDE 313.1

**For instance, check out the passage in your workbook. Who'd like to read sentence 1 for us?**

*I really and truly love fostering animals for the shelter.*

**Is there anything in there that could be cut out?**

*Really and truly.*

**Perhaps this writer wants to emphasize just how much they enjoy fostering animals. And these words help them do so. However, it's not really necessary. Saying they *love fostering animals* gives us the same message, just in fewer words. We can cross those out. What about sentence 2? Is there anything we can cut there?**

*Very* or *incredibly*.

**Adverbs are the archnemesis of concision. They add extra details to the sentence, but they aren't really important to the sentence. If we take *incredibly* out of the sentence, we don't lose the fact that the *bonds* made are *strong*. Let's jump to sentence 3. Anything we can cut there? Or is there something we can replace with a more concise version?**

*On the other hand, though.*

**This sentence has a really wordy transition. In fact, it's almost two transitions to show contrast. What could we use to replace all those words?**

*But* or *however*.

**By swapping five words for one, we get a much more concise transition. Moving forward, can we trim sentence 4?**

No.

**If we trim anything there, we'd lose essential meaning. We can leave that one alone. What about sentence 5? What needs to go?**

*Sweet, delightful, charming, friendly.*

**All of those words mean basically the same thing, so it's repetitive. Sometimes you may want to be repetitive on purpose, which is totally okay. If you have words that make your writing voice unique or that add to the style of your essay, go for it. Pick your favorite details and cut the extras.**

### Instructions

Review the following essay and identify three places where more information could be added.

### Passage

Perhaps humankind's greatest mystery is the purpose of life. Why do humans exist? And what are they meant to do with their time on this planet? While many might argue that every human should spend their life in pursuit of some goal or level of greatness, it is equally possible that the purpose of life is to live in a manner that leads to a feeling of contentment. This is evident in the story of Ove, an elderly gentleman, along with Mrs. Dalloway and her attempts to throw the perfect dinner party. It is in the ordinary and mundane that humans will find the most happiness and greatest meaning in life.

In the story of *A Man Called Ove*, a young couple and their two daughters move into a home next to a curmudgeon of a man named Ove. He is everything you'd expect in a cranky old neighbor. He hollers, scoffs, and absolutely never smiles. As his neighbors' antics irritate him, he reacts with annoyance and guidance. By helping the new couple in many ways, Ove and his new neighbors experience great joy.

*Mrs. Dalloway* is another prime example of finding happiness in living a life doing things that one loves. She spends her time preparing for and ultimately succeeding at planning an exceptional dinner party. Her story is average, potentially boring even. Despite being the story of a housewife planning and preparing for a party, the story has become a classic.

Word Count: 243

## Groundwork

*In this section, students will locate areas of an essay that could be further developed by adding more description or explanation.*

**Perhaps the more common issue students run into during the TSIA2 is actually the opposite of what we looked at on the previous page: their essay is too short. If this happens to you, should you panic?**

No.

**You have plenty of time, so there's no rush to get all the words into the text box. But we still *do* need to get those words out. And the question is, what will those words be? The best place to start is to look at where you began. What's the first thing we wrote for our essay?**

The outline.

EXERCISE C · SLIDE 314.1

**Go back to your outline—which should be on your scratch paper—and see if you're missing anything. For instance, check out this example on your page. Take a moment to read through it and see if it's missing any essential elements.**

*Give students 2 minutes to complete this task.*

**Start with what the essay *does* have. What elements of the essay did this writer include?**

An introduction with the hook, preview, and thesis. Two body paragraphs with one specific example each.

**What really obvious piece is missing from this essay?**

The conclusion paragraph.

**There's no conclusion! The essay describes the second example and then just stops. It's like leaving off in the middle of a story. We want to know what happens at the end. What else do you notice is missing, specifically from the body paragraphs?**

There's no explanation. It doesn't connect the examples to the thesis.

**If you don't take the time to connect the dots for your reader, your essay will feel a little disjointed. Remember to tell your reader how your example specifically proves your thesis is true. What if your essay has all the elements, though? Maybe you followed the outline perfectly and don't have anything missing. What could you add to make your essay a little longer?**

More details.

**Should we just throw them in at the end?**

No, they need to go into the essay where they make sense.

**Focus on those body paragraphs, especially. See if there's a place where you can add a little more to the summary of your example or if there's something else you can add to better explain how the example proves your thesis is right. You might also consider adding a whole new example, too. Where do you think that should go?**

As the third body paragraph.

**And what else should you make sure to change to reflect that addition?**

The introduction and conclusion.

**If you do decide to add a third example, make sure you check your introduction and conclusion for any references to the specific examples. You'll want to add something to make sure you're covering all your bases in those opening and closing paragraphs.**

EXERCISE D

**Instructions**
Identify and correct the four grammar, punctuation, and spelling errors that appear in the following essay.

We have two choices when we are afraid: we can run nad hide or we can stand and face our fear. Nour and Mulan, strong fictional characters, both face challenging moments that make them fearful, but they overcome their fears and save those they love.
The love we have, for our family can give us courage to face our fear and overcome it. Nour, the the main character in the novel The Map of Salt and Stars not only doesn't know how to swim but has always feared the water. However, when she sees her sister Zahra struggling in the sea, Nour dives in without hesitation and pulls her to safety. This shows that Nour's love for her sister is stronger than her fear of water. Because of her love for Zahra. Nour conquers her fear of the water and is able to save her sister. Without that compelling force, Nour may not have been able to gather the courage needed to dive into the sea.

## Groundwork

*In this section, students will review and practice using strategies for proofreading an essay during the TSIA2.*

**Grammar errors? Spelling mistakes? You might think it's not possible to miss those kinds of things on a computer-based test. What usually happens when you make a spelling or grammar mistake on the computer?**

It underlines it in red.

**Won't those little red squiggle lines show up during the TSIA2? The short answer? No. The long answer? They shut off all those helpful tools before you take the test so there's no safety net if you make a typo. You've got to rely on your own writing know-how to proofread your essay. Take a closer look at the example in your workbook. What else might make it challenging to proofread?**

The text is really small and close together.

**As you type your essay, the text box fills in with really small, cramped text. This makes searching for small mistakes really hard. Take a moment now to see if you can find the four errors in this essay.**

*Give students 3 minutes to complete this task.*

EXERCISE D | SLIDE 315.1

**Let's start with the first paragraph. Did you find any errors there?**

*And* was misspelled as *nad*.

**Oh, the good ol' *nad* error. This happens to the best of us, especially when we're typing really quickly. It's easy to mix up some of the letters in words that we tend to use a lot. Be sure to watch for that simple kind of typo. What about the second paragraph? I see a punctuation error in the first sentence. What is it?**

There's a comma after *have*.

**Who remembers our general rule about commas?**

*Commas cause pauses.*

**While commas cause pauses, the reverse is not true. Just because you might have a natural pause somewhere in a sentence doesn't mean that it needs a comma. Err on the side of caution. If the pause sounds even a little awkward, skip the comma. The next sentence has an error, too. What's wrong there?**

There's an extra *the*.

**Sometimes, when we're mid-sentence, we pause for a moment to figure out what we want to say. And sometimes, we accidentally add an extra word we don't need. The double *the* is usually the result. Watch for that error, especially across line breaks. That's when we're most likely to skim over that repetition. Any other errors?**

*Because of her love for Zahra* is an incomplete sentence.

**Incomplete sentences should be a top priority when it comes to writing your essay because it's something the grading system will *definitely* flag. What should we have in place of that period?**

A comma.

**We can use a comma to connect that incomplete sentence to the next one, and our ideas flow nicely. That won't always be the case, though. What if you can't connect an incomplete sentence to a neighboring sentence?**

Add more words to make it complete.

**Be careful that adding those extra words doesn't bump you over the word limit, but definitely make sure that sentence is complete when you're done with it.**

# Application

## THE APPROACH

When you are finished drafting your essay during the TSIA2, use these steps ...

1. Take a mental break.
2. Add or cut words to ensure the essay is between 300 and 600 words.
3. Review the essay to check for common grammar, punctuation, and spelling errors.

**Instructions**

Collect your writing from the previous essay chapters into a single written piece. You should either rewrite the essay in your workbook or type your essay into a text document on the computer. As you collect the pieces of your essay, check the word count to ensure your work fits within the 300–600 limit of the TSIA2.

**Essay:**

# Application

*In this section, students will either rewrite or type the essay they've created during the previous lessons, ensuring that their essay fits within the word count limit.*

SLIDE 316.1

**Remember when I said that the essay section of the TSIA2 is a marathon? Well, revising and editing is a little like the cool-down period. If you skip it, you could end up injuring a muscle—or your essay score. But before we start that, let's go back through our previous chapters and collect the pieces of our essay. Start with the introduction, and move through the body paragraphs and conclusion. As you combine those elements into one essay, check your word count to make sure you've got between 300 and 600 words written.**

*Give students 15 minutes to rewrite or type their essay into one piece of text.*

**The essay is complete! What should we do now?**

*Take a mental break.*

**Depending on your preference, focus on either clearing your mind completely or take a little mental vacation. What kinds of things could you imagine to relax and refocus your brain?**

*Allow 2–3 students to share.*

**Game time. Let's start working on revising. First, check your word count. If you don't want to count out every word in your essay, just count the total words in 2 to 3 lines and use that to help you estimate your total. If your essay is below the 300-word minimum, add details. Use the margins of the page and draw arrows to show where a new detail would plug into the essay. If you've got too much essay, make some cuts by crossing off anything unnecessary.**

*Give students 5–10 minutes to complete this task.*

TSIA2 Mastery: ELAR 

**Essay (Continued):**

This page is intentionally left blank.
Teacher content resumes on the next page.

## THE APPROACH

When you are finished drafting your essay during the TSIA2, use these steps ...

1. Take a mental break.
2. Add or cut words to ensure the essay is between 300 and 600 words.
3. Review the essay to check for common grammar, punctuation, and spelling errors.

### Proofreading Strategies

- ✓ Start at the bottom and work your way up.
- ✓ Focus on one error type at a time.
- ✓ Read the sentence under your breath to listen for mistakes.
- ✓ Highlight one line at a time with your cursor to improve focus.

## Application

*In this section, students will review proofreading strategies that are specifically applicable to the essay section of the TSIA2.*

**We already mentioned that proofreading on the TSIA2 is challenging. Why was that again?**

The text is small and close together.

**To top it all off, there's no way to format the text. For instance, it doesn't let you bold or italicize anything. It won't even let you indent your paragraphs. Why does that create a challenge for proofreading?**

All the lines will look like they run together.

SLIDE 318.1

**If it's hard to even separate the words visually, it's even harder to check for mistakes in that tiny text. Luckily, though, we have some specific strategies that can help you overcome this visual obstacle. What's our first suggestion?**

*Start at the bottom and work your way up.*

**There's actually a scroll bar on the text box, and depending on the screen's resolution, you'll likely only be able to see between 8 and 12 lines of text at a time. Scroll all the way to the bottom and start with your last sentence. Check it for mistakes and then back up another sentence to do the same. Why do you think this is helpful?**

By moving backward, you can't skim.

**When you read from bottom to top, it takes a little more mental focus, meaning you're paying closer attention to what you're reading. That gives you a much better chance of catching a simple typo or other kind of error. We also suggest focusing on one error type at a time. Why do you think that's helpful?**

It makes your search more focused.

**For instance, you can check to make sure you've got all your capital letters in the right places. Then, you can check for incomplete sentences. Spend another pass looking at just the commas. By targeting your search, you'll find errors more effectively. What's our third strategy?**

*Read the sentence under your breath to listen for mistakes.*

**So much of what we know about English is instinctual. And if something *sounds* off, it probably has some kind of mistake. Use your ears to find things like incomplete sentences, unnecessary commas, or verb errors. Finally, a good strategy for focusing your eyes is to highlight each line one at a time. Why do you think that's helpful?**

It makes your eyes focus on a smaller section of the text.

**When you highlight a line, it creates a visual barrier, which can help keep your eyes focused on smaller sections of the text at once. This is especially helpful for catching typos, like *nad* and the double *the*.**

TSIA2 Mastery: ELAR 

### THE APPROACH

When you are finished drafting your essay during the TSIA2, use these steps ...

1. Take a mental break.
2. Add or cut words to ensure the essay is between 300 and 600 words.
3. Review the essay to check for common grammar, punctuation, and spelling errors.

**Instructions**

Proofread your essay. Note any mistakes you correct in the space provided.

1. ______________________________

2. ______________________________

3. ______________________________

4. ______________________________

5. ______________________________

6. ______________________________

7. ______________________________

8. ______________________________

9. ______________________________

10. ______________________________

## Application

*In this section, students will proofread their essay and collect a list of errors they found.*

SLIDE 319.1

**Time to dig into your own essays. Take some time now to review what you've written. Use some of the strategies from the previous page and see if you can find some mistakes. And keep a log as you write! As you proofread, write down the errors you find and correct.**

*Give students 5 minutes to complete this task.*

**What kinds of errors did you find?**

*Allow 4–5 students to share.*

**Why do you think we kept a list of the mistakes we made?**

So we know where we went wrong.

**We're all creatures of habit. And that goes for writing mistakes, too. We often make the same kinds of errors each time we write a new essay. By writing them down and taking the time to review them, we get insight into our habits. How should we use this list to help us during the TSIA2?**

We should check for these same errors on the test.

**Your list is a great place to start when it comes to proofing your essay on test day. These mistakes are also good study opportunities. For instance, if you tend to put commas in weird places, you can take a little extra time to review comma rules. Focus on your weaknesses so that come test day, you feel confident when you press that button to submit your essay.**

This page is intentionally left blank.
Content resumes on the next page.

This page is intentionally left blank.
Teacher content resumes with the next chapter.

CHAPTER 37

# Practice Prompts

In this chapter, students will practice constructing standardized essays using prompts similar to what they will see on the TSIA2.

37

Practice Prompts

In this chapter, you will practice constructing standardized essays using prompts similar to what they will see on the TSIA2.

LEARNING TARGETS

1. Utilize effective pre-writing strategies.
2. Draft 4-paragraph essays that adhere to a standardized structure.
3. Revise an essay to ensure it falls within the word limit.
4. Identify errors in an essay using standard English conventions.

321

## TEKS ALIGNMENT

E1.9 *Composition*: listening, speaking, reading, writing, and thinking using multiple texts—writing process. The student uses the writing process recursively to compose multiple texts that are legible and uses appropriate conventions. The student is expected to:

(A) plan a piece of writing appropriate for various purposes and audiences by generating ideas through a range of strategies such as brainstorming, journaling, reading, or discussing;

(B) develop drafts into a focused, structured, and coherent piece of writing in timed and open-ended situations;

(C) revise drafts to improve clarity, development, organization, style, diction, and sentence effectiveness, including use of parallel constructions and placement of phrases and dependent clauses;

(D) edit drafts using standard English conventions.

## LEARNING TARGETS

1. Utilize effective pre-writing strategies.
2. Draft 4-paragraph essays that adhere to a standardized structure.
3. Revise an essay to ensure it falls within the word limit.
4. Identify errors in an essay using standard English conventions.

## Groundwork

EXERCISE A

### Instructions

Review the writing prompt. Then, decide which side of the argument you want to support. Place a check mark next to your selection.

### Passage

All of the great social justice advances that we ever had in this country have come not from people with big titles and not from people at the top, but just from everyday people getting together saying, "Enough is enough. I'm going to change this, and I'm going to get involved, and I am going to be engaged."

Adapted from Nina Turner, "Nina Turner at the Women's Convention"

### Assignment

Who has the greatest potential to set social change into motion: someone with a high social status or an individual who lacks power but has a great amount of determination?

Plan and write a multiparagraph essay (between 300 and 600 words) in which you explain your opinion about the above question. Support your ideas with a clear argument and examples from media, books, current events, or personal experiences.

1. Which side of the argument do you plan to take?

    _____ Someone with a high social status has the most potential to inspire social change.

    _____ An individual with no power but a lot of determination has the most potential to inspire social change.

## Groundwork

***In this section, students will review a writing prompt and select their stance.***

Note: This chapter is not intended to be completed all at once. Throughout the lesson, students will write a total of three 4-paragraph essays. The Groundwork of this chapter walks students through the first essay, and the Application provides students the opportunity to write two more essays independently. It is recommended that students write each essay during a separate learning period.

**Think about something you're *really* good at. Maybe you're really great at knocking baseballs out of the park, you might have amazing anime-drawing skills, or perhaps you can microwave the world's tastiest bowl of ramen. It can be anything. What's your talent?**

*Allow 2–3 students to share.*

**Now, think about the first time you tried to do whatever it is that you're good at. How did that go?**

Not good.

**Chances are, your first time doing just about anything didn't go so great. And that's just how it goes. Learning is a process. How do we get better at things?**

Practice.

**Just like anything else you want to get better at, writing standardized essays is a skill. And that means improving takes practice. Don't worry. You're not jumping into the deep end just yet. We'll take things a little slowly at first, starting with the prompt. What two pieces make up every TSIA2 essay prompt?**

The Passage and the Assignment.

**Where will you find the question you need to answer in your essay?**

At the beginning of the Assignment.

EXERCISE A SLIDE 322.1

**Take a moment now to read the essay prompt in your workbook.**

*Give students 1 minute to complete this task.*

SLIDE 322.2

**What's the question asking?**

Who has the most power to create social change?

**Check out your options just below the prompt. What do you think? Does someone with a lot of social status have more power? Or will the more determined person have more influence?**

*Allow 2–3 students to share.*

**Put a check mark next to your choice, and let's get into the pre-writing process. What will we do first?**

Brainstorm ideas.

**TSIA2 Mastery:** ELAR 

EXERCISE B

**Instructions**

Brainstorm examples you can use to support your essay's central argument.

*In this section, students will brainstorm ideas they can use as examples to support their central argument.*

EXERCISE B

**Brainstorming isn't a one-size-fits-all process. Remember that we have options. You can list your ideas or create a mind map of sorts. You can use word association, jot down short phrases, or even write in full sentences. It's up to you how you want to get the ideas out of your brain and onto the page. What kinds of ideas do we need?**

Examples to fill our body paragraphs.

**The types of examples you'll pick will depend on which stance you took when you answered the question in the prompt. Where might we pull these examples from?**

Books, movies, history, current events, or our personal experiences.

**Which kinds of examples should you pick for your essay only as a last resort?**

Personal experiences.

**You can brainstorm as many ideas as you'd like, but in the end, how many will you end up using in your essay?**

Two.

SLIDE 323.1

**We need one example for each body paragraph, so that means two solid examples that support the central argument of the essay. Take some time now to write down a few ideas.**

*Give students 5 minutes to complete this task.*

**You'll have scratch paper or a white board when you take the TSIA2, so you should definitely use it as a place to capture your brainstormed ideas. Once you feel like you've come up with enough options, go back through what you wrote down. Pick the two you want to use for your essay. Let's do that now. What examples will you use in your essay?**

*Allow 2–3 students to share.*

**Once you know what you'll write about, will you dive into the first draft?**

No.

**We still have one more step before we start actually writing. What is it?**

Creating an outline.

EXERCISE C

### Instructions

Use the provided structure to create an outline for your essay. You do not need to use complete sentences.

### Introduction

Hook: ______________________________

Preview: ______________________________

Preview: ______________________________

### Body Paragraph 1

Example: ______________________________

Significance: ______________________________

### Body Paragraph 2

Example: ______________________________

Significance: ______________________________

### Conclusion

Thesis Restatement: ______________________________

Connection to the Reader: ______________________________

***In this section, students will organize their ideas into an outline.***

**EXERCISE C** SLIDE 324.1

**Why is it so important to write an outline? How come we don't just jump into drafting?**

Because the outline will help us stay organized.

**Organization is a major element the essay grading system will look for. If you don't have four distinct paragraphs that make up your essay, your score will take a hit. What should go into your first paragraph?**

A hook, a preview, and a thesis.

**And what does the thesis tell your reader?**

What you plan to talk about in your essay.

**After that comes two body paragraphs. What should fill each of those?**

One example for each paragraph, with a summary and an explanation about how it proves the thesis is true.

**Finally, we dive into the conclusion. What are the two elements of that last paragraph?**

A thesis restatement and a connection to the reader.

**What do we want to avoid doing as we write that thesis restatement?**

Rewriting the thesis word-for-word.

**Let's take some time now to outline. Use the examples you brainstormed on the previous page and fill in this outline.**

*Give students 10 minutes to complete this task.*

**TSIA2 Mastery:** ELAR 

EXERCISE D

**Instructions**

Use the space provided to draft your essay.

**Introduction** Word Count ____________

____________

**First Body Paragraph** Word Count ____________

____________

**Second Body Paragraph** Word Count: ____________

____________

**Conclusion** Word Count: ____________

____________

Total Word Count: ____________

***In this section, students will draft their essays, as well as apply revising and editing strategies.***

**EXERCISE D** **SLIDE 325.1**

Note: It is recommended that students draft their essay on a computer so that their practice is more authentic. Utilize a program that includes a word count tool, and if possible, turn off any assistive editing tools, such as Spellcheck. However, if they are unable to use a computer, they can write their drafts in their workbook. Have students keep track of the word count of each paragraph to ensure they are within the word limit.

**Finally, we're ready to draft our essay. Use your outline as a guide and keep track of your word count as you write. That way, if you do end up outside of the word limit, you won't stray too far. Remind me: what's the TSIA2's word limit for the essay?**

300–600 words.

**Let's get writing!**

*Give students 30 minutes to draft their essay.*

**Take a moment to go through your essay one more time, this time focusing on the positives. Who has a really awesome hook?**

*Allow 2–3 students to share.*

**What about examples? Let's have some volunteers read their thesis and give us the examples they used to support their central argument.**

*Allow 2–3 students to share.*

**Zone in on that closing paragraph. What strategy did you use to connect to the reader? And how did it turn out?**

*Allow 2–3 students to share.*

**A lot of times, we get bogged down by searching for errors and forget to celebrate the successes. By taking time to recognize where you went right, you'll become more confident in your essay-writing skills.**

EXERCISE E

### Instructions

Review your essay on the previous page and note three errors you discovered while revising and editing.

### Errors Discovered

1. ______________________________

2. ______________________________

3. ______________________________

*In this section, students will identify errors discovered while revising and editing their work.*

EXERCISE E

**So, we're done, right? Should we submit our work?**

No, we still need to revise and edit.

**When you're revising, focus on the word count first. What should you do if you went over the 600-word maximum?**

Cut stuff out.

**What if you're under the 300-word minimum?**

Add more details.

**What if you went *way* under the minimum and only have 200 words? Is there another strategy you could use to bulk up your essay?**

Add another example.

**If you find that, no matter how hard you try, you can't hit that 300-word minimum with just two body paragraphs, go back to your brainstorming ideas. You likely have a third example there that you can use to create another body paragraph. What else should you edit if you add a third example?**

The introduction and conclusion.

**Your preview in the introduction and the opening to your conclusion may have mentioned your specific examples. Go back to those sections to make sure you add in your third example to those areas. That way, you maintain good organization throughout the essay. What about editing? What kinds of things will you look for?**

Typos, misspelled words, incorrect punctuation, incomplete sentences, etc.

SLIDE 326.1

**Let's do this now. Go back through your essay and see if you can find at least three things to correct. There's no such thing as perfect writing, so everyone will have something.**

*Give students 8 minutes to complete this task.*

**Let's stop and do a little reflection. What kinds of errors did you find?**

*Allow 2–3 students to share.*

**Taking note of the errors we make is a good practice when we're working on our essay skills. Why do you think that is?**

It helps us figure out which errors to watch out for.

**Being a good writer often means knowing your weak spots. If you know you misspell a word all the time or if you notice that you forget a lot of commas, you know what you can work on to improve. And, with a little more practice, pretty soon that error will disappear from your writing completely.**

# Application

## THE APPROACH

When writing your essay for the TSIA2, follow these steps ...

1. Read the prompt and decide your stance.
2. Brainstorm ideas and organize them into an outline.
3. Draft your introduction, two body paragraphs, and conclusion.
4. Revise and edit.

**Passage**

1. Competition brings out the best in products and industry, and yet, it seems to draw out the absolute worst in people.

Adapted from David Sarnoff

2. Competition is one of the most important drivers of innovation because you have to stay in the race. You have to think of something new, and if you don't, well, of course you bow out.

Adapted from Margrethe Vestager

### Assignment

In today's world, is competition a healthy motivation or a driving force that encourages pride, selfishness, and greed?

Plan and write a multiparagraph essay (between 300 and 600 words) in which you explain your opinion about the above question. Support your ideas with a clear argument and examples from media, books, current events, or personal experiences.

# Application

***In this section, students will draft, revise, and edit an essay.***

Note: This chapter is not intended to be completed all at once. Throughout the lesson, students will write a total of three 4-paragraph essays. It is recommended that students write each essay during a separate learning period. If your class period is much less than 1 hour, we suggest writing one paragraph per session. Provide feedback only after the entire essay has been written so students can work on building a coherent essay without coaching.

**Time to rip off the band-aid. Let's get rid of those training wheels. We're about to take the bull by its horns. It's time to ... hmm. I'm out of idioms. But what I'm trying to say is that it's time to create an essay all on your own. Start by reading the prompt. Once you decide how you want to answer the question in the assignment, take time for brainstorming and pre-writing, and then turn the page and use the space there to draft, revise, and edit your essay. You got this.**

SLIDE 327.1

*Allow students 1 hour to complete this task. If students are writing in their workbooks, indicate that they should keep track of the word count of each paragraph to help them stay within the word limit.*

**Instructions**
Use the space provided to draft your essay.

**Introduction** Word Count ____________________

________________________________________

________________________________________

________________________________________

________________________________________

**First Body Paragraph** Word Count ____________________

________________________________________

________________________________________

________________________________________

________________________________________

**Second Body Paragraph** Word Count ____________________

________________________________________

________________________________________

________________________________________

________________________________________

**Conclusion** Word Count ____________________

________________________________________

________________________________________

________________________________________

________________________________________

Total Word Count: ________________________________

## Application

*In this section, students will review their work and identify the types of errors they made.*

SLIDE 328.1

**Well? How was your experience?**

*Allow 2–3 students to share.*

**It's a bit of a marathon to work through one of those essays, isn't it? But with practice, we can build up your stamina. Who feels a little more confident in their ability to write an essay on test day?**

*Pause for a show of hands.*

**And even if you're not 100% confident, there is still plenty of opportunity to practice. In fact, let's go back over what you just did. Was anyone below or above the word limit? What did you do to remedy it?**

*Allow 2–3 students to share.*

**As you edited your essay, what kinds of errors did you find?**

*Allow 2–3 students to share.*

**This kind of self-reflection on our writing is going to pay off when you take the TSIA2. When you take on the next prompt, try to anticipate the errors you made during this go-around and see if you can avoid making those same mistakes. Even fixing just one small error between this essay and the next means you've improved. After all, every long journey starts with that one small step forward.**

TSIA2 Mastery: ELAR 

## THE APPROACH

When writing your essay for the TSIA2, follow these steps ...

1. Read the prompt and decide your stance.
2. Brainstorm ideas and organize them into an outline.
3. Draft your introduction, two body paragraphs, and conclusion.
4. Revise and edit.

**Passage**

To be hopeful in bad times is not just foolishly romantic. It is based on the fact that human history is a history not only of cruelty, but also of compassion, sacrifice, courage, kindness. What we choose to emphasize in this complex history will determine our lives. If we see only the worst, it destroys our capacity to do something. If we remember those times and places—and there are so many—where people have behaved magnificently, this gives us the energy to act, and at least the possibility of sending this spinning top of a world in a different direction.

Adapted from Howard Zinn, *A Marvelous Victory*

### Assignment

Is it better to look at the world from an optimistic viewpoint, or is it more advantageous to expect things to go wrong?

Plan and write a multiparagraph essay (between 300 and 600 words) in which you explain your opinion about the above question. Support your ideas with a clear argument and examples from media, books, current events, or personal experiences.

## Application

***In this section, students will draft, revise, and edit a 4-paragraph essay.***

**Let's take on one last essay prompt. Third time's a charm, right? Who can walk me through the process one more time before we get started?**

Read the prompt, decide on our stance, brainstorm, outline, draft, revise, and edit.

SLIDE 329.1

**And we want to learn from our experiences, right? Who can tell me one mistake they made last time that they will try to avoid making this time around?**

*Allow 2–3 students to share.*

**Remember those mistakes as you work through the writing process. I'll see you on the other side!**

*Give students 1 hour to complete their essay.*

**Instructions**
Use the space provided to draft your essay.

**Introduction** Word Count ____________

______________________________________________

______________________________________________

______________________________________________

______________________________________________

**First Body Paragraph** Word Count ____________

______________________________________________

______________________________________________

______________________________________________

______________________________________________

**Second Body Paragraph** Word Count ____________

______________________________________________

______________________________________________

______________________________________________

______________________________________________

**Conclusion** Word Count ____________

______________________________________________

______________________________________________

______________________________________________

______________________________________________

Total Word Count: ____________________

## Application

***In this section, students will draft and review their essays.***

Note: Review students' essays once they've completed their drafts. Include time for revising and editing. Once complete, have students share excerpts from their writing that they feel they crafted particularly well and encourage students to share the types of errors they discovered when reviewing their writing.

TSIA2 Mastery: ELAR


**Instructions**

In this section, review your writing and take notes on your strengths and weaknesses.

I do these things really well:

1. ________________________________

2. ________________________________

3. ________________________________

I should double-check these things on test day:

1. ________________________________

2. ________________________________

3. ________________________________

## Application

*In this section, students will review their strengths and identify common problems they should double-check when they take the TSIA2.*

SLIDE 331.1

**Let's take a look back at all the essays we've written throughout this course. What are some things you feel you're really good at?**

*Allow 2–3 students to share.*

**Whether you've got some amazing hooks up your sleeve or a keen eye for incorrect comma usage, it's always good to take time to focus on your strengths. Write down at least three things you've done well as we've worked on these essays.**

*Give students 1 minute to complete this task.*

**Time to game plan. We know what we're good at. But what missteps are we taking? Are there errors you make consistently? What are they?**

*Allow 2–3 students to share.*

**Write down three things you plan to watch out for, whether it's something you can plan for during pre-writing or little errors to look for during editing.**

*Give students 1 minute to complete this task.*

**And that's it. Essay complete. At this point, you're free to hit that submit button. And when you do, take a moment to check in with yourself. What are you usually feeling when you finish an essay like this?**

*Allow 2–3 students to share.*

**During the TSIA2, you'll go from the essay straight into the math section. If you ended the essay and feel pumped about how well you did, let that momentum carry you into the first math problem. On the flip side of things, what if you feel drained? What should you do?**

Take a break.

**There's nothing in the TSIA2 rulebook that says you have to immediately start working on that first math problem. In fact, there's no rush at all. Why is that?**

There's no time limit.

**If your brain is feeling a little woozy after the essay, take a break. If your testing site allows it, get up and walk around to get your blood flowing again. And if you're stuck in your seat, there's nothing that says you can't take a little mental vacation. Give yourself the best chance at doing well and let your brain rest. Your test score will thank you.**

## Chapter Name, Alphabetized

## Chapters by Chapter Type

### Test and Question-Type Strategy Chapters

**These chapters are focused on the structure, rules, or unique qualities of the question types that appear on the test.*



### Test-Taking Skills Strategy Chapters



### Essay-Writing Chapters



### Content Mastery Chapters (Writing Topics)



### Content Mastery Chapters (Reading Topics)

# Chapters by TSIA2 Standard

# CHAPTERS BY COMMONLY-ASSOCIATED PASSAGE TYPE

# Chapters by TEKS

E1.2 *Developing and sustaining foundational language skills:* listening, speaking, reading, writing, and thinking—vocabulary. The student uses newly acquired vocabulary expressively. The student is expected to:

(B) analyze context to distinguish between the denotative and connotative meanings of words.

**Vocabulary, 27**

E1.4 *Comprehension skills:* listening, speaking, reading, writing, and thinking using multiple texts. The student uses metacognitive skills to both develop and deepen comprehension of increasingly complex texts. The student is expected to:

(F) make inferences and use evidence to support understanding.

**Supporting Details, 81**

**Inferences, 91**

(G) evaluate details read to determine key ideas.

**Main Idea, 37**

(H) synthesize information from two texts to create a new understanding.

**Synthesis: Central Arguments, 57**

**Synthesis: Evaluating Claims, 65**

E1.5 *Response skills*: listening, speaking, reading, writing, and thinking using multiple texts. The student responds to an increasingly challenging variety of sources that are read, heard, or viewed. The student is expected to:

(B) write responses that demonstrate understanding of texts, including comparing texts within and across genres.

**Synthesis: Central Arguments, 57**

**Synthesis, Evaluating Claims, 65**

E1.8 *Author's purpose and craft*: listening, speaking, reading, writing, and thinking using multiple texts. The student uses critical inquiry to analyze the author's choices and how they influence and communicate meaning within a variety of texts. The student analyzes and applies author's craft purposefully in order to develop his or her own products and performances. The student is expected to:

(B) analyze use of text structure to achieve the author's purpose;

(D) analyze how the author's use of language achieves specific purposes.

**Author's Craft, 47**

# Chapters by TEKS

E1.9 *Composition*: listening, speaking, reading, writing, and thinking using multiple texts—writing process. The student uses the writing process recursively to compose multiple texts that are legible and uses appropriate conventions. The student is expected to:

(A) plan a piece of writing appropriate for various purposes and audiences by generating ideas through a range of strategies such as brainstorming, journaling, reading, or discussing.



(B) Develop drafts into a focused, structured, and coherent piece of writing, in timed and open-ended situations by:

(i) using an organizing structure appropriate to purpose, audience, topic, and context.



(ii) developing an engaging idea reflecting depth of thought with specific details, examples, and commentary.



(C) revise drafts to improve clarity, development, organization, style, diction, and sentence effectiveness, including use of parallel constructions and placement of phrases and dependent clauses;



(D) edit drafts using standard English conventions



(i) a variety of complete, controlled sentences and avoidance of unintentional splices, run-ons, and fragments;



(ii) consistent, appropriate use of verb tense and active and passive voice;



(iii) pronoun-antecedent agreement;



(v) punctuation including commas, semicolons, colons, dashes, and parentheses to set off phrases and clauses as appropriate; and



(vi) correct spelling.

## Chapters by Difficulty

**Reading**



**Writing**

# Contributors

**Director of Curriculum**
Stephanie Constantino

**Publisher**
Craig Gehring

**Layout and Design Lead**
Jeff Garrett

**Item Lead**
Peter Franco

**Cover Design**
Nicole St. Pierre

**Chief Academic Officer**
Oliver Pope

**Quality Control Team Lead**
Allison Eskind

**Senior Proofreader**
AndreAnna McLean

**Content Creation**
Anne Delatte
Amelia Emery
Sandy Fahringer
Lee Hair
Lana Johnson
Nick Pilewski
Lauren Pope
Daniel Romero
Michelle Wolf

**Item Creation**
Eric Manuel
Megan Reynolds
Daniel Romero
Zora Rush
Theresa Schlafly
Minrose Strausman
Luke Switzer

**Proofreaders**
Juan Aponte
Lauren Brecht
Andrea Broussard
Andrea Cole
Ainsley Davis
Cassandra Galentine
Ginny Gillikin
Alison Hertz
May Lane
Lauren Miklovic
Llaina Rash
Luke Switzer
Maghie Zeigler

**Layout and Graphics**
Kayla Manuel
Hope Oswald
Amanda Pfeil
Jaye Pratt

**Subject Matter Experts**
Destiny Blue
Lauren Brecht
Colin Brinkerhoff
Kerri Denholm
Amelia Emery
Lee Hair
Eric Manuel
Rebecca Pickens
Nick Pilewski
Daniel Romero
Theresa Schlafly
Stephanie Stewart
Luke Switzer
Mark Teel

**Slide Designers**
Lisa Halem
Karen Kilpatrick
June Manuel
Hope Oswald
Luke Switzer